MAKING SPACE

France Overseas: Studies in Empire and Decolonization

SERIES EDITORS: A. J. B. JOHNSTON, JAMES D. LE SUEUR

FOUNDING EDITOR: TYLER STOVALL (1954–2021)

Making Space

*Neighbors, Officials, and
North African Migrants in the
Suburbs of Paris and Lyon*

MELISSA K. BYRNES

University of Nebraska Press

LINCOLN

Parts of the introduction and chapters 1, 2, and 4 appeared within
"Liberating the Land or Absorbing a Community: Managing North
African Migration and the Bidonvilles in Paris's Banlieues," *French Politics,
Culture & Society* 31, no. 3 (Winter 2013): 1–20. Parts of chapters 2, 3,
and 6 appeared within "Ramadan in the Republic: Imperial Necessity
and Religious Assistance in the Rhône Department," *French Cultural
Studies* 28, no. 1 (February 2017): 5–16.

The University of Nebraska Press is part of a land-grant institution with
campuses and programs on the past, present, and future homelands of the
Pawnee, Ponca, Otoe-Missouria, Omaha, Dakota, Lakota, Kaw, Cheyenne,
and Arapaho Peoples, as well as those of the relocated Ho-Chunk,
Sac and Fox, and Iowa Peoples.

Publication of this volume was assisted by Southwestern University.

Library of Congress Cataloging-in-Publication Data

Names: Byrnes, Melissa K., author.
Title: Making space: neighbors, officials, and North African
migrants in the suburbs of Paris and Lyon / Melissa K. Byrnes.
Description: Lincoln: University of Nebraska Press, [2023] | Series:
France overseas: studies in empire and decolonization | Includes
bibliographical references and index. | Summary: "Melissa Byrnes
explores the ways local communities in the French suburbs reacted
to the growing presence of North African migrants in the decades after
World War II and the decolonization of Algeria"—Provided by publisher.
Identifiers: LCCN 2023012227
ISBN 9780803290730 (hardback)
ISBN 9781496237583 (paperback)
ISBN 9781496238269 (epub)
ISBN 9781496238276 (pdf)
Subjects: LCSH: Suburbs—France. | Suburban life—France. | North
Africans—France—Public opinion. | France—Ethnic relations. | France—
Race relations. | France—Emigration and immigration. | Africa, North—
Emigration and immigration. | BISAC: HISTORY / Europe / France | SOCIAL
SCIENCE / Emigration & Immigration Classification: LCC HN440.S62 B97
2023 | DDC 305.800944—dc23/eng/20230831
LC record available at https://lccn.loc.gov/2023012227

Set in Minion Pro by Scribe Inc.

To Thérèse Keoseian,
who gave me the gift of the French language

CONTENTS

ILLUSTRATIONS

Photographs

Tables

ACKNOWLEDGMENTS

A book like this requires so much unseen support and labor—even more when parenting a toddler far from friends and family during a global pandemic. First, then, I need to acknowledge the invaluable work done by the staffs of the Stepping Stone School at Hyde Park, the University of Texas Child Development Center at Comal, and the Budapest Fővárosi Önkormányzat Óvodája. These remarkable professionals kept our child safe and healthy while helping teach him to be kind, generous, and independent.

This project began as a doctoral dissertation under the patient, insightful, and pun-filled guidance of Aviel Roshwald, with tremendous support from Richard Kuisel. I learned many things from both of them, not least that you should always work with good humans. I had arrived at Georgetown University to get a graduate degree in foreign policy, but Jim Collins talked me into applying for the history PhD in my first year and set a new trajectory for my professional life. When I moved to Paris for my research year, Nancy Green welcomed me into her seminar at the École des hautes études en sciences sociales and became a vital mentor for the thesis and after.

Countless scholars have given me their time and shared their thoughts on my work. I had the great pleasure of meeting Mary Lewis and Amelia Lyons in that initial research year and am deeply grateful for all the advice and support they have offered since. Patrick Weil made important suggestions early in my archival digging and supported my grant and *carte de séjour* applications.

Jeannette Miller was a wealth of information, advice, and true friendship.

Others who have shared their work, commented on mine, and otherwise contributed to this project include Marc André, Jean Beaman, Elise Franklin, Gillian Glaes, Elizabeth Heath, Burleigh Hendricksen, Ethan Katz, Carrie Landfried, Itay Lotem, Emily Marker, Jim Mokhiber, Michael Mulvey, Minayo Nasiali, Ed Naylor, Clifford Rosenberg, Spencer Segalla, Jennifer Sessions, Yann Scioldo-Zürcher, Marlou Schrover, Alexis Spire, Janoé Vulbeau, and Gary Wilder. Special thanks to Nicole Bauer, Jennifer Davis-Cline, Sarah Griswold, Jess Pearson, and Pete Soppelsa for our monthly "I-35 meetings" and the sanity and sound advice they provided.

I have so much admiration and gratitude for the professionals who staff the French archives, without whom I could never have undertaken this project. I spent a great deal of time in the excellent municipal archives of Asnières-sur-Seine and Saint-Denis. The archives for Vénissieux and Villeurbanne were smaller but no less welcoming. The personnel at the Paris police archives and the departmental archives for Hauts-de-Seine and Seine-Saint-Denis found me many useful files and connected me with other scholars. I received much help at the Archives de Paris, the Centre Historique des Archives Nationales in Paris, and the Centre des Archives Contemporaines in Fontainebleau. I benefited from the staff knowledge and rich collections of the Rhône department archives in Lyon. I also spent many profitable hours at the Bibliothèque Administrative de la Ville de Paris, enjoying the beautiful reading room at the top of the Hôtel de Ville. I also want to acknowledge the Central European University (CEU) library, in whose Budapest reading rooms I found scholarly refuge for many summers—until CEU relocated to Vienna to take refuge from a hostile Hungarian government.

My colleagues at Southwestern University (SU) have been another amazing source of support. Thom McClendon and Eric Selbin each read multiple parts and iterations of this work, offering constructive feedback and lots of cheerleading. Steve Davidson, Shana Bernstein, Elizabeth Green, Jess Hower, Jethro Hernández Berrones,

Joe Hower, and Sooji Han have been phenomenal department colleagues. su's history department also connected me with Melissa Kravetz and Erik Loomis, who continue to be great supporters and good friends. Erik deserves special thanks (and some blame) for bringing me onto the Lawyers, Guns & Money blog team. Allison Marr, Emily Sydnor, and especially Katy Ross have been a source of friendship and accountability through many semesters of writing together. Katherine Hooker from the su library made sure my images were publication quality. Down the road at the University of Texas–Austin, Julie Hardwick brought me into the Institute for Historical Studies (ihs) as a space for additional scholarly engagement and met me for a number of delightful meals when we happened to be in Lyon together. Ben Brower and other ihs members gave me fantastic comments on what became two of the following chapters.

My undergraduate students constantly push me to ask new questions, find better explanations, and make the case for why what we study matters. I was especially honored to work closely with Meili Criezis and Sarah Woods. Meili traveled to the Paris archives to help me think through how French activists and local leaders engaged with various Algerian nationalist parties (and to conduct her own research on Algerian women in the independence struggle). Sarah shared her language and data analysis skills for a remote semester of research assistance digging into police actions and strategies around Lyon. Both are well on their way to becoming fantastic scholars in their own rights.

I have been fortunate to receive considerable financial support for my archival adventures over the years. My dissertation research in and around Paris was funded by a Jeanne Marandon Fellowship from the Société des Professeurs Français et Francophones d'Amérique, a Forris Jewett Moore and Henry P. Field Fellowship from Amherst College, graduate student funding from Georgetown University, and an inaugural American Council of Learned Societies (acls) / Mellon Dissertation Completion Fellowship. Expanding the project to include the Lyon region was possible thanks to an acls / Mellon Recent Doctoral Recipient

Fellowship and multiple years of competitive development funding from Southwestern University, as well as su funding for faculty-student research and an undergraduate research assistant.

Bridget Barry at the University of Nebraska Press (unp) has been a wellspring of patience, support, enthusiasm, and constructive feedback. I am grateful to all the unp staff who made publication possible. I extend special thanks to the anonymous reviewers whose valuable advice benefited my writing greatly. Any remaining faults are entirely my own.

None of this would have been possible without the love and encouragement of my family. My mom made me love history, my dad made me love writing, and my brother has been a rock of support and understanding. The Epstein family offered me a home away from home in the Paris region.

Lőrinc Rédei has been at my side through the entire process, dragged throughout France and to central Texas of all places. He is my first reader, my joy and comfort, my heart's companion. I'm sorry you had to learn what sonacotral meant. Félix Rédei brings both of us so much light and laughter—and reminds me what is truly important (sleep—and making a more just world).

A View from the Field

The first official goal scored at the Stade de France in Saint-Denis was kicked by a Frenchman of North African descent in January 1998. Zinedine Zidane is, of course, less known for this particular football match (a friendly game against Spain) than for captaining the French national team to a spectacular World Cup victory against Brazil in the same stadium later that year. Zidane was born in France—in the Castellane neighborhood of Marseille. His father had migrated from Algeria in 1953 and actually worked for a number of years in Saint-Denis, long before the stadium was built in that city.[1] The 1998 FIFA trophy was widely hailed as a testament to France's diversity, to its strengths as a multiracial republic, to its dedication to making Frenchmen out of migrants like Zidane's father.[2] Images of Zidane and his teammates were projected onto immense screens throughout France in a celebration of brown, Black, and white unity. French fans likewise projected a multitude of meanings onto these men's bodies and accomplishments. Lilian Thuram—the other star footballer of the moment—was one of the first to worry that of all the potential messages to emerge from the victory, the story to gain traction was one of republican integration.[3] Raising up the supposed success of the French system to mold its citizens recalled long-standing imperial doctrines that elevated white Frenchness over the myriad contributions and cultures of its global subjects. To claim the 1998 World Cup as a national victory, the actual voices, experiences, and accomplishments of its Black and brown participants were often occluded or ignored.

National glory is not, however, what interests me about this moment—nor is this book a national history. My fascination with this stadium and these victories is rooted in their location on Saint-Denis's soil. The Stade was built in the Parisian *banlieues* (suburbs) as part of an urbanization plan closely overseen by Saint-Denis's communist municipality. The "France" in the stadium's name refers not to the country but rather to the geological plain around Paris.[4] This slippage between the local and the national, between inhabited space and imagined identities, is central to the story I tell. Saint-Denis, like its stadium, might be seen as a testament to inclusion: a workers' city that embraced its migrant communities, embodying over many decades the euphoric belonging of the fabled "*black-blanc-beur*" ("Black-white-Arab") World Cup win. Yet even the Stade's experience of community interaction is more complex than those two games in 1998. Take, for example, the friendly match between the French and Algerian national teams in 2001, during which spectators hissed through the French anthem and later spilled onto the field, causing the game to be canceled. Or consider, more chillingly, the bombings that were part of the constellation of attacks in November 2015. Diversity may often be showcased in the Stade de France, but it is also critiqued, challenged, and even attacked. Examining Saint-Denis's municipal activism on behalf of the city's North African population over the decades after the Second World War offers a closer look at the stakes of supporting—and failing to support—local migrants. This local story gains still deeper meaning when compared with those of other suburban cities around Paris and Lyon.

Making Space: Neighbors, Officials, and North African Migrants in the Suburbs of Paris and Lyon examines the ways that predominantly white French administrators, actors, and activists got involved with their North African neighbors by detailing daily, on-the-ground experiences in four French suburbs: Saint-Denis and Asnières-sur-Seine in the Paris region and Vénissieux and Villeurbanne around Lyon. Chronologically, this research emphasizes the development of support for North African migrants from the inception of the Fourth Republic (in 1945), through the decolonization process, and

up to the moment, in 1974, when the global economic crisis triggered a moratorium on migration to France. The historical willingness of autochthonous members of these local communities to
engage with North African migrants proves that there are work-
able models of inclusive republican citizenship that do not require
newcomers to negate all other personal identities—whether cultural or religious.

This book answers the question of why particular local actors
in France advocated for North African migrant rights and welfare in the decades following the Second World War. It details the
experiences of municipal officials, regional authorities, employers,
and others to establish the wide variety of strategies that French
community leaders developed in the face of rapidly growing North
African (especially Algerian) populations. I pay close attention to
how these actors explained and justified their positions regarding
North African migrants, to the claims they made on broader social
and political ideals, and to the connections they drew between
their actions and their worldviews.[5] I explore the ways that local
attitudes and policies, whether inclusive or exclusionary, formed
and re-formed communities. This view from below offers a deeper
understanding of the decisions that led to the current tensions surrounding race, migration, identity, and belonging in French society.

It is important to clarify that North African migrants are not
themselves the subject of my research. Their lives and experiences
are certainly at the heart of the debates and policies that this book
does address. I have, wherever possible, included their perspectives and considered how they could influence, support, or oppose
state and community actions.[6] Migrant voices are absent from the
bulk of the sources that this study rests upon, and so I have often
relied on the ethnographic work of other scholars to provide context.[7] This scrutiny of white French actors who thought of themselves as North African allies seeks to reveal underlying race-based
assumptions and critique the racialized structures that they created
and supported. The object is not to recenter these white experiences or craft another "vanilla history" of North African migration to France but rather to problematize local French assertions

of expertise and authority, especially their claims to be acting in the name of North Africans.[8] Likewise, the goal is not to further silence North African voices in this history but rather to call attention to the variety of ways that even those local actors most dedicated to migrant rights and welfare regularly ignored or erased actual North Africans in their discussions and decisions. Instead of developing programs with sustained North African input, these French actors regularly made use of migrant policy to project and further their own goals and interests. These local activists thus mirrored, in a way, the attitudes of the French football fans who invested heavily in the images of North African and other non-white star players without meaningfully engaging those individuals or the communities they came from.

Making Space contributes to three main currents in the history of migration. First, it deepens the understanding we gain from Amelia Lyons's examination of the social welfare system built to address the needs of Algerian families by diving into specific local debates and developments.[9] It broadens the base of scholarship on colonial migrants within particular French communities by adding suburban examples to the substantial literature on Paris as well as to Minayo Nasiali and Ed Naylor's studies of Marseille, Marc André and Fatiha Belmessous's work on Lyon, and Janoé Vulbeau's examination of Roubaix.[10] It extends Mary Lewis's local comparative approach into the post-1945 era, focusing on the experiences of imperial migrants and the effects of decolonization on migration policy.[11] This intersects with the second main avenue of discussion: the study of decolonization. I draw in particular on Todd Shepard's analysis of French decolonization as a process—an often contested one—to explore how imperial and anti-imperial ideas functioned and evolved even within municipalities and local businesses.[12] I likewise follow Françoise de Barros's close attention to the postcolonial afterlives of imperial officials and ideas within local settings.[13] Third, this book builds on scholarship by Danielle Beaujon, Emmanuel Blanchard, Jim House, Neil MacMaster, Amit Prakash, and Clifford Rosenberg that connects colonialism to community policing.[14] Taken together, these strands support a vision of locally lived migration policies that connected North African welfare to imperial control in ways that continue to structure French systems and neighborhood interactions alike.

Why a Local History of Migration?

Immigration, nationality, and citizenship are defined and controlled by the nation-state. France is well known for its highly centralized system and a republican ideology in which the primary political relationship is between the individual and the state. Many great histories of immigration to France have established the evolution of ideals, procedures, and policies at the national level. More recent scholarship has begun to look at particular migrant groups and localities.[15] Even with a high level of state involvement and state funding, local authorities were hardly without influence. Residential construction was carried out by mixed public-private ventures, often run through local administrations. Before any work could be done, these entities needed to acquire land and building permits, most often from city officials. Many regulatory and welfare services were provided through regional governments, city halls, and local organizations. Local officials implemented national policies, often mediating them or shifting their definition. They also brought local concerns into regional and national fora, directly linking individual migrant experiences with national debates and state practices.[16] These local actors therefore served as the main interface between the state and migrants.

Smaller geographic limits also reveal the intersection of migration with other issues whose influence could be direct (health, lodging, employment, education, welfare benefits, economic growth or decline) or indirect (war, visions for urbanization, ideas about community). Many migration scholars use housing and urbanization as their main lens. The housing crisis was certainly a major concern for officials at all levels and received the most systematic attention. Finding or constructing residences was the most concrete way that cities made space for North African migrants.[17] Yet housing and urban development plans were intertwined with a variety of other social issues. Examining a wider array of policy approaches offers a more complex view of the relationship between French communities and North African workers. Saint-Denis's municipality, for example, regularly connected support for housing to opposition to the Algerian War, while officials in Villeurbanne resorted to educational statutes as a means to disperse concentrated migrant populations. In the chapters that follow, I will show how local officials regularly sought to affect migration patterns using a variety of tools and drawing on different areas of local autonomy in hopes of creating the change they wished to see.

Selecting multiple cities makes for a comparative approach that highlights the differences that existed within a French system too often accepted as monolithic and uniform.[18] Migration histories have tended to assume a singular French identity, enforced by a universal mechanism for integration that entailed one ideal path to success. The theory (and practice) behind this integration has often been called into question; rarer are studies that explore the multiplicity thriving beneath the veneer of the indivisible republic. Instead of assuming a singular national identity (to which migrants must try to conform), this comparative local analysis provides a window into alternative notions of nationhood, community, and belonging. To do this requires an approach that doesn't take French-ness for granted. Rather, following scholars like Beth Epstein, this study asks how individuals and groups made their local communities meaningful and how they understood themselves and their experiences in relation to each other.[19]

The histories in this book highlight the multiplicity and pluralism that thrive beneath the veneer of a republican universalism that is, at its core, both imperial and racialized. Emmanuelle Saada has explored the role of race in defining French citizenship and subjecthood within the colonies, while Gary Wilder has demonstrated how imperial ideology and its racialized assumptions were constitutive of French republicanism, not in tension with it.[20] Mayanthi Fernando calls attention to the "privileged particular" that hides beneath universal claims and has made it possible to exclude ethnic, racial, and religious minorities on the basis of their nonnormative particularities.[21] Sarah Mazouz likewise argues that French universalism and its claims to colorblindness have masked the assumption that only white experiences can be abstracted, while nonwhites are always assigned to particular—and racialized—categories.[22] Yet in the face of exclusionary definitions of what it means to be French, local communities and nonwhite citizens regularly asserted their own definitions of belonging. If some of the historical cases in this book reveal prejudices and persisting modes of exclusion, others offer models for inclusion, tolerance, and even solidarity. Andrew Newman emphasizes the importance of everyday practices like gardening in creating new ways for republicanism to be "lived" on the ground. Newman further explains how activism by nonwhite French citizens "harness[es] the local to reimagine the national, and at times even the global."[23]

Thus, even as local migration histories offer further insight into the contours of French citizenship and belonging, they also allow us to connect large global processes and ideologies to community and individual experiences.[24] Though states and scholars alike define migration as the crossing of international borders, migration is *lived* as movement from one community to another. Decisions by municipal and regional actors that implemented national immigration policies or intervened in debates on North African rights and welfare were informed by particular experiences and officials' ideas about the populations they represented. This book is less concerned with Frenchness than with local belonging or with broader transnational identities and is particularly interested in identity as a basis for collective action.[25]

Ultimately, the existence of local identities that did not conform to the dominant national French identity indicates that there were valid alternatives to commonly espoused national understandings of belonging and underscores the flexibility and permeability of national categories. Even within a system as centralized as the French state, local case studies offer scholars a laboratory of sorts—where multiple attempts to tackle the same issue can be weighed against each other. In other words, the answers to the current French identity crisis could well lie within the past experiences of the very suburbs that so worry the country.

North African Empire and Migration

North Africans arrived in France as both migrants and colonial subjects. Algerians in particular had a complicated relationship to the French state.[26] Since 1848, Algeria had been claimed as part of France itself, its three regions designated as French departments and not imperial territories. European settlers were part of the initial military pacification campaign, displacing local populations and forging a stratified society.[27] The Senatus-Consulte of July 1865 attributed French nationality to Algerians, though not the rights of citizenship. The 1870 Crémieux decree granted French citizenship to all European settlers and Algerian Jews but still not to the majority Arab and Kabyle Muslim population. In the wake of revolts against this policy, the French sequestered more land, triggering the first wave of Algerian migration to the French mainland.[28]

French cities hosted a variety of migrants in the nineteenth and twentieth centuries. Industrialization had brought Bretons and others from rural provinces, soon followed by Belgians, Swiss, Italians, and Poles, then Spaniards and Portuguese. Colonial migrants arrived in large numbers during the First World War, both as soldiers and as a labor force. By the end of the war, 240,000 Algerians were in France (two-thirds of them soldiers). Though most of these men were sent back across the Mediterranean, French employers had learned that colonial migrants could work effectively in their factories, while the North Africans had come to appreciate the potential advantages of working in the metropole.[29] To support reconstruction and the postwar boom, France solicited migrant workers through the 1920s.[30] Roughly 100,000 Algerians arrived during this period, mostly to the Paris region.[31] The economic crisis in the 1930s sparked an unfavorable public view of immigration, while high unemployment caused many migrants to head back home.[32] After World War II, the French government again encouraged a tremendous influx of foreign workers.[33] While many foreigners continued to come from the southern European states (Italy, Portugal, Spain), workers from French colonies, especially those in North Africa, poured across the Mediterranean.

From 1946, Algerians benefited from the free-circulation rules between Algeria and France. The law of September 20, 1947, granted Algerians full citizenship rights in France (though maintaining their separate and not-quite-equal status in Algeria).[34] By 1954, one in seven Algerian men of working age and ability was living and working in the metropole: a total of 212,000 individuals, or one-twentieth of the entire Algerian population.[35] That year, the Algerian Front de libération nationale (National Liberation Front, or FLN) launched their War of Independence and fundamentally altered the French imperial system. By the time the peace agreement was signed at Evian in March 1962, hundreds of thousands of soldiers and civilians had died,[36] ten thousand Algerians had been interned by the French police in the metropole,[37] the French army and police were revealed to have used torture against Algerian militants (and even French supporters),[38] a French paramilitary terrorist organization had formed and launched attacks in Algeria and on the mainland (the Organisation de l'armée secrète [OAS] sought to keep Algeria French at any cost), the empire was dismantled,[39] and the Fourth Republic itself had tumbled. Algerian migration to France continued, however; the pace increased as workers, and unprecedented numbers of families, fled the violence and instability brought by the conflict. While these migrants were viewed with growing suspicion, government authorities also recognized that they constituted a possible avenue to the hearts and minds of all Algerians.

The Algerian War was thus a watershed for new social and security policies targeting Algerian migrants—and this system was later expanded to the rest of France's migrant populations. The Labor and Interior Ministries launched a wide array of social services, with housing being a top priority.[40] Migrants' occupation of overcrowded slums, dilapidated hotels, and mushrooming *bidonvilles* (shantytowns) led to a flurry of demolition, reconstruction, and rehousing programs. At the war's end, with the birth of an independent Algerian state, Algerian migrants lost their automatic claim to French citizenship. In contrast to earlier efforts to promote Algerian welfare, the state now proclaimed that "Algerians are foreigners in France and this status compels an objective attitude toward them."[41] Individuals were welcome to apply to retain their French citizenship, though they were asked to prove that they did not figure on Algerian voting lists.[42] This process, while administratively straightforward, was complicated by Algerians' sense of attachment to their new, hard-won national independence as well as by the difficulties posed by bureaucratic paperwork. Still, the Algerian population in France grew significantly over the 1960s: from 350,000 in 1961, to 530,000 in 1967, to 800,000 in 1972.[43]

Faced with 480,000 "foreigners" in 1963, compared with the 320,000 "rightful French citizens" of 1958, the state system required restructuring, or at least renaming.[44] The national construction program for housing Algerians, SONACOTRAL, lost its *L* to become SONACOTRA (*travailleurs* in general, not just *travailleurs algériens*), while the SAT-FMA police forces dropped their association with "French Muslims from Algeria" (FMA) and expanded their jurisdiction to include Moroccans, Tunisians, and migrants from France's former sub-Saharan territories. At the same time, positions in national government offices for immigration were filled with personnel from the colonial administrations, essentially repatriating the colonial system to regulate postcolonial migrants.[45] Officials continued to be preoccupied with the bidonvilles, whose residents were as likely to be Portuguese as Algerian and included Spaniards, Yugoslavs, some Italians, and even French natives. North Africans thus found themselves folded into the more general category of immigrant (even as popular opinion began to correlate "immigrants" more closely with "Arabs" or "Algerians"). The 1960s also saw a shift in French ideas about migrant assimilation. Postcolonial migrants (as opposed to earlier European migrants) were expected to work in France temporarily, with the intention of returning home, not of assimilating into French society. This reflected concerns about economic downturn as well as perceptions that these migrants were too culturally, socially, civilizationally, religiously, or ethnically distinct to be successfully integrated.

The early 1970s brought a global oil crisis and high rates of unemployment. As the bidonvilles disappeared, the general population grew susceptible to the notion that migrants were reaping extra benefits from state agencies and occupying newly valued jobs. Yves Gastault has named the period from 1969 to 1973 "the apogee of anti-Arab racism" in France.[46] The flame was fanned when Algeria nationalized its hydrocarbon production, seizing many French interests.[47] Algerian migrants became the victims of violent attacks and murders all across France, particularly in and around Lyon.[48] Concerned that virulent racism proliferated in various state offices as well as among the population and seeing reflections of the violence of the Algerian War, Algerian president Houari Boumédiène suspended emigration to France on September 19, 1973.[49] In turn, France, under the center-right presidency of Valéry Giscard d'Estaing, halted all immigration on July 5, 1974 (family reunifications were also banned until this ruling was judged illegal and repealed in May 1975).[50]

The major immigration issues facing France in the latter half of the 1970s—and through today—had less to do with arriving migrants and more to do with the second and third generations who called France their home. At the same time as the French Right began to garner support for increasingly anti-immigrant rhetoric and proposals, migrants and their French children and grandchildren experienced their own political and cultural awakening. Calling themselves "Beurs" (*verlan*, or inverted slang, for "Arab") and invoking both their French citizenship and the daily discrimination they suffered in French society, they led a march from Marseille to Paris in 1983.[51] Despite the development of numerous organizations and the lip service paid by successive government officials, racial discrimination (now linked to Islamophobia) has persisted, and youths from immigrant backgrounds overwhelmingly still live in poor neighborhoods with substandard schools and suffer prohibitive levels of unemployment. Meanwhile, the debate in France continues today to center on "immigration," affirming and perpetuating the idea that those who arrived from France's former colonies were neither welcomed into French society nor believed capable of making themselves at home there.

All of these later developments stand in stark contrast to the earlier imperial imperative to include colonial migrants. Algerians faced a particularly acute change in official status from subjects to citizens to foreigners. This book will show that these formal changes were not always reflected precisely at the local level; rather, they were refracted through a variety of interests, experiences, and ideals. Local actors employed their own logics when engaging North Africans within their communities.

A Tale of Four Cities

I first walked into Saint-Denis's municipal archives in the fall of 2005 (just weeks before riots broke out in the suburbs over the deaths of two boys hiding from the police). I had arrived in France to launch the research for my doctoral dissertation and was curious about how Saint-Denis, as a small city just north of Paris, in the fabled banlieues, connected to important moments and major developments in the history of France.[52] Named for the patron saint of France (credited with converting the Franks and transforming France into the Catholic Church's first daughter),[53] the basilica around which the city grew housed the necropolis for all French royalty (until it was sacked during the Revolution of 1789).[54] From the nineteenth century onward, Saint-Denis claimed the more rebellious side of French politics, identifying with workers' parties from the early days of the Third Republic. The French Communist Party (PCF) acceded to city hall in 1925 (socialists had been in power since 1892). In the mid-1930s, Auguste Gillot emerged as a major political force, tasked by the party with reestablishing its position on the city council and combating Jacques Doriot's influence.[55] Trained as a blacksmith, Gillot had joined the Jeunesses communistes (Young Communists) in 1925 and even spent a year (1931–32) at the International Lenin School in Moscow. Gillot distinguished himself as a hero in the French Resistance and was nominated in 1944 to be the new mayor of Saint-Denis.[56] This selection was confirmed by popular vote in 1945, and Gillot remained mayor through 1971. The PCF held the municipality through 2020 (when it returned to socialist leadership).

Beyond this long, varied, and wholly French heritage, and the

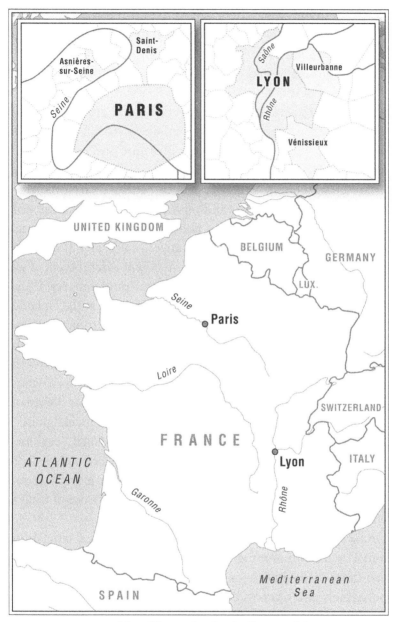

FIG. 1.1. Map of France showing Asnières-sur-Seine,
Saint-Denis, Vénissieux, and Villeurbanne. Map by Erin Greb.

transition to outspoken criticism of the central state, came the charm of a people who identify as "Dionysien" (Denis being a derivative of Dionysius). More importantly, I knew that the area's booming industries had ensured that the city experienced each of the major waves of migration into France, including that of North Africans. And still, I was shocked at the material I found in those first few boxes. The Dionysien files were full of surprises for a scholar steeped in the existing literature on French migration and relations with North Africans. The first difference was the extraordinary amount of municipal documentation on North African affairs. Internal memos and reports aside, officials cataloged hundreds of press clippings and bulletins from the departmental and police prefectures, the national government, private associations, and individuals. The mayoral staff kept careful track of all actions taken on behalf of North African or immigrant residents, compiling long and detailed lists of interventions at the General Council for the Seine or directly with other government offices and ministries. Gillot and his colleagues were heavily involved with the cause of North African workers (both in Saint-Denis and in Algeria). This wealth of information on engaging North Africans was all the more surprising when compared to the near silence of municipal records in other cities. Saint-Denis's municipal policy, and especially the rhetoric and energy of Mayor Gillot, was simply not what I expected to find. While there are certainly trends in Saint-Denis that map onto the usual story, there is much about this project that developed as a means of making sense of what I found there.

As some of the following chapters make clear, local officials in Saint-Denis took a much greater interest in North African migrants than those in neighboring cities. Mayor Gillot and his colleagues spoke loudly and often on behalf of North African workers' rights. They castigated a national and imperial system for its treatment of these fellow workers and their families. Perhaps most surprising is the way these city officials connected migrant welfare to the question of Algerian independence, which they supported outright even before the Algerian War of Independence was launched. Many local case studies of migration that examine left-ist municipalities in the Paris region view the French Left, and the PCF in particular, in terms of failure: a failure to address migration issues, programs of purposeful inaction, deep hypocrisy in their supposed support for all workers, and explicit policies of exclu-sion.[57] While Saint-Denis aligned more closely with this trend by the 1970s, the first two decades after World War II looked quite different.[58]

My curiosity about Saint-Denis led me to look for a Paris sub-urb with another political color. I soon arrived in Asnières-sur-Seine, which is conveniently located on the other northern fork of Metro line 13. Asnières, which gained its epithet only in 1968, was a twelfth-century village that took its name from the don-keys (*ânes*) that grazed in its fields and carried building materials to the Abbey of Saint-Denis.[59] Asnières was not without its own royal connections (mostly living and breathing): Anne of Cleves set up a residence in 1653, and the Marquis de Voyer d'Argenson arrived a century later to build the castle for which the city is now known.[60] Industrialization took a milder form; where Saint-Denis sprouted massive forges, Asnières developed printers, woodwork-ers, locksmiths, and clothiers; in 1859, Louis Vuitton opened his atelier in town.[61] The banks of the Seine grew popular for pic-nics and other leisure activities; Monet, Pissarro, Renoir, Seurat, and Van Gogh all painted scenes from Asnières. After the First World War, heavy industry became more prominent, with metal works (mostly in the auto industry) and chemical plants (spe-cializing in perfumes and cosmetics) setting up shop.[62] In 1952, the city received the Croix de Guerre for its service during the Second World War.[63] Its long-serving mayor, Michel Maurice-Bokanowski (1959–94), had served in the Free French forces, gain-ing a different set of Resistance credentials than Gillot. Politically, Asnières became a Gaullist anchor in the sea of red banlieues. The municipality's alignment with national policies was strengthened by Bokanowski's roles in various Fifth Republic governments: in addition to his terms as deputy (1955–59 and 1962–63) and then senator (1968–94), he served as secretary of state for the Interior

(1959–60), minister for posts and telecommunications (1960–62), and minister of industry (1962–66).

Asnières ranked with Saint-Denis among the most populous cities in the Seine department in the 1950s:[64] Saint-Denis had a total population of sixty-nine thousand in 1945 and surpassed one hundred thousand by 1967;[65] Asnières numbered over seventy-two thousand in 1946 and over eighty thousand by 1968.[66] Each city received a share of the migrants who flocked to the Paris region to work in its factories, usually within the chemical or metallurgical industries. Saint-Denis, being both more heavily industrialized and known for a warmer reception of migrant workers, hosted a larger proportion of migrants than Asnières. In the early 1950s, Asnières held around one thousand North Africans, while Saint-Denis counted more than five thousand.[67] For my purposes, Asnières was especially intriguing given its ambitious and early project to get rid of the city's bidonvilles and their predominantly North African residents. Once I delved into those archives, it was clear that Asnières followed national policies more than it challenged or reshaped them. This initial comparison thus centered on the similarities and contrasts along political lines—in place of leftist hypocrisy, Asnières's story offered an open and unapologetic rejection of local North Africans. Saint-Denis, in turn, faltered in its commitment to inclusion in the early 1970s, in part due to the success of projects in places like Asnières.[68]

I decided, as a postdoctoral fellow, to add another layer of comparison by journeying south to Lyon. Heading outside of the capital region helped further decenter the role of Paris, particularly given my interest in how migration policy functioned at a variety of levels from city to nation. There were a few major French cities with large North African populations that I could have chosen. Marseille, though, has a very different urban fabric, which would have added some tricky variables to my suburban comparisons.[69] Lille in the north was a promising option, but Lyon was sunnier and had a set of intriguing characteristics; it is also France's second largest urban agglomeration.[70] Mary Lewis's work on the interwar era meant I had a foundation to build on—with a number of allusions to a wide set of local actors.[71] Moreover, I knew that by the early 1970s, race relations in Lyon were perhaps the most strained in France—in 1971, the national press referred to the city as the "capital of racism."[72] Having found some models of tolerance and inclusion in Saint-Denis, I was especially curious to know how a PCF banlieue in the Lyon region would compare.

Once in the Rhône, I settled on the cities of Vénissieux and Villeurbanne, which had become the two largest cities in the department by population—and had the two largest North African populations (after Lyon, of course) during the postwar decades. Vénissieux, named for a Roman legionnaire, was once known for its wine and is still known for its roses.[73] It became a major industrial site during the First World War, especially after Marius Berliet built his massive automaking plant on the east side of the city (by 1918, Berliet employed three thousand workers in Vénissieux, including a number of colonial recruits).[74] World War I brought a regimen of *tirailleurs sénégalais* (colonial infantry from Senegal and other African colonies) to town; between the soldiers, their civilian support staff, and industrial workers, colonial migrants briefly constituted 40 percent of the city's population.[75] The city can claim its own history of political opposition: it was the gathering site for the 1744 taffeta-makers' revolt; was run by a "red," Commune-aligned municipality in 1870–71; and kicked off massive strikes in 1936 both leading to and after the election of the Popular Front.[76] Vénissieux has been a PCF stronghold since 1935, with mayors serving in national and regional roles. Louis Dupic (mayor, 1944–62) was also a senator (1946–59), while his successor, Marcel Houël (1962–85), was in the National Assembly (1962–81). Though the city was involved in regional antibidonville projects, the HLM block that took their place was even more significant. Its Minguettes neighborhood was the site of riots in the summer of 1981; in 1983, Toumi Djaïda was shot by police while leading a hunger strike against racism and police violence. These experiences inspired the 1983 Marche pour l'egalité et contre le racisme (March for Equality and against Racism).[77] The year 1983 also saw the first demolition of Minguettes housing blocks.[78]

Villeurbanne also retained its Roman moniker, its designation as "villa urbanna," or the agricultural center for the city, already suggesting an exceptionally close relationship with Lyon itself.[79] By the late nineteenth century, Villeurbanne's economy was more industrial than agricultural, heavily marked by the regional textile industry with factories for lace, tulle, dyeing, and leather.[80] These factories employed large numbers of Italian and, later, Spanish migrants.[81] Through the early twentieth century, the textile sector waned, while offshoot industries in chemical, machine, and electrical production came to dominate.[82] Socially and politically, Villeurbanne developed as a workers' city, promoting (and funding), for example, the right to strike as early as 1899.[83] The 1890s also saw the first *cités ouvrières* (workers' housing complexes) built by (and near) local factories.[84] The municipality has been dominated by socialists since 1892, with a few short stints by PCF mayors in the early 1920s and late 1940s. Despite this left-leaning tradition, Mayor Étienne Gagnaire (1953–77) was quite centrist and staunchly anticommunist. Gagnaire began his political career as a union activist and member of the socialist SFIO (Section française de l'Internationale ouvrière). He was taken as a prisoner of war in 1940 and became, with François Mitterrand, one of the founders of the Rassemblement national des prisonniers de guerre Resistance movement.[85] His municipal tenure began as an explicit SFIO bid to unseat the PCF from Villeurbanne's city government; he was briefly elected to the National Assembly (1956–58), then thrown out of the SFIO in 1967.[86] Villeurbanne's bidonvilles were made famous by Azouz Begag in his autobiographical novel *Le gone du Chaâba*.[87] The city also held the infamous Olivier de Serres housing complex, which figured heavily in the racial unrest of the 1970s.

While these two Lyon suburbs worked as good focal points, I quickly discovered that many of the dynamics in the Rhône were so different as to make for a different set of players. So many of my stories about Saint-Denis and Asnières were driven by the cities' mayors and municipal officials. Yet in the Rhône, departmental authorities played a relatively larger role—or at least, the municipalities were less involved in daily interactions with local

North Africans. This tracks with the region's history and the multiple attempts by the city of Lyon to annex Vénissieux and, especially, Villeurbanne.[88] I also discovered a larger role for employers,
landowners, and charitable associations. Departmental and non-
governmental actors did enormous amounts of work in the Paris
region too, of course, and I would be remiss not to acknowledge
that workers' unions were involved with migrant issues throughout France. These actors figure less in my research because of
how much else I found about others, though there is ample room
for further study on these fronts. This book comprises a particular set of stories about the people who claimed to work on behalf
of North African migrants—and who left traces in the archives I
could access.

As I thought through the implications of these different roles
and players, I realized that this shift away from a purely municipal
analysis opened up new questions about who was getting involved
with local North Africans—and why. What moved these varying
casts of local leaders to spend time, energy, and often funds to
support the rights and welfare of migrants in their communities?
This new set of questions about motivations connected with my
long-standing interests in the history of rights and activism and
provided the organizing structure for this book. Moving past the
question of what happened in these four cities, I identify a set of
rationales and broader worldviews that encouraged local white
French actors' engagement with North African migrants. Elected
city officials, prefectural bureaucrats, police officers, social workers, business owners, and priests certainly held vastly different
positions and capabilities. Yet the particular individuals I examine
here were all concerned with North Africans' rights and welfare.
Ultimately, I hope to show not only how local officials interacted
with migrants in the decades before and after decolonization but
also the ways that migrants and their allies more generally can
continue to identify and use the interests of local powers to their
own benefit.

Making Space

When newcomers arrive in an established community, one of the most pressing questions is where they will fit—how groups and individuals make space for themselves and for others. This book thus considers the ways that local French actors, predominantly white ones, did what they did to promote North African rights and welfare as strategies for "making space." My narrative starts with the literal interpretation of how space was made for North African migrants within the urban fabric of these four cities. From there, I move into the metaphorical spaces of politics, ideology, identity, and belonging. As will quickly become clear, the vast majority of the reasons underlying engagement with North African migrants proved to be self-serving.[89] Over and over again, the wants, needs, and lived experiences of actual North Africans were subsumed, even erased, by both the underlying assumptions and the overt goals of white French officials. Like the World Cup celebrations that cast famous athletes' success as a triumph for republican values, local actors continued to project onto North African migrants whatever purpose, role, or identity best fit their own objectives.

I begin with the stories that most closely track with the existing scholarship on migrant welfare, examining housing questions with special attention to how local officials articulated their priorities and goals. For many local actors, programs that claimed to support North African welfare often cloaked initiatives to force out populations deemed undesirable in these cities. Chapter 1, "The Mission to Modernize," examines three major urban renovation projects that aimed to remove and disperse North African migrants. Asnières launched one of France's earliest (and most efficient) antibidonville projects in 1954, targeting the "northern zone" of the city and the majority migrant population that resided there. North African migrants, labeled as obstacles to modernization, were shuffled into departmental housing programs and sent to neighboring cities. In the 1950s, Lyon began a similar process with the Centre de la Part-Dieu, while Villeurbanne initiated the lengthy process of dissolving the Olivier de Serres "ghetto" in the 1960s. All three of these projects followed a similar racist logic: large concentrations of North Africans were believed to be uncivilized, unhealthy, even dangerous. Cities sought to clean up these areas in terms of both infrastructure and demography, making "modern" urban spaces for their ideal residents and relying on others to make space elsewhere for the migrants who were unwanted and therefore displaced.

Not all North African welfare programs were built on implicit xenophobia. Saint-Denis's municipality, as mentioned previously, seemed to operate with a very different set of assumptions and objectives. The second chapter, "Politics," looks at how city officials in Saint-Denis made space for North Africans within their political calculus and considers some of their projects to make new living spaces. Algerian migrants (who had full French citizenship from 1947 to 1962) were cultivated by municipal officials as potential voters. Mayor Gillot and his colleagues decided as early as 1946 to create housing for North African workers, whom they declared to be welcome in the city. The Dionysien example also underscores the importance of looking beyond housing to other migrant concerns. Gillot and his colleagues positioned themselves as unique advocates for migrants and as the local purveyors of a wide variety of social benefits. Elected communists in Saint-Denis also agitated for North African rights as part of their opposition to the French national government—and, by extension, capitalist and imperialist systems. This contrasts with Vénissieux, whose PCF officials saw North Africans as less significant (in numbers and in overall importance) and therefore did not devote themselves to support or advocacy. Saint-Denis's municipal officials also routinely connected their engagement with local North Africans to their opposition to French imperialism, which serves as the backbone of the next two chapters.

"In Defense of Empire," the third chapter, more explicitly addresses the question of how global and imperial events affected local treatment of North African migrants, with a focus on the Algerian War (1954–62). Departmental officials in the Rhône, most of whom were appointed through the Interior Ministry, were deeply invested in the French Empire and France's position on the global stage. These ideas, in turn, had a direct impact on the policies and recommendations made by these officials. In particular, North African migrants in the suburbs of Lyon were subjected to powerful and discriminatory policing practices. Yet for the prefects and their allies, both in the administration and in local associations, ascribing to the notion of a French Algeria meant that the region had to make space for Algerians. This led to efforts to promote better housing, employment, and education—which furthered the connections between welfare and surveillance. In their own way, rife with problems and paradoxes, these defenders of empire found themselves advocating for closer integration and deeper acceptance of North African migrants even as they subjected them to violent controls and discrimination.[90] Paying attention to how these actors enmeshed their local activities within the logic of empire furthers our understanding of how French imperialism operated in concrete, everyday domestic terms on the mainland.

Chapter 4, "Anti-imperialism," returns to Saint-Denis to look at how municipal leaders there mobilized their anti-imperial and antiwar stances as part of their campaign for greater North African rights. Gillot in particular was a strong proponent of Algerian nationalism, even before the armed struggle broke out. The municipality perceived the police as a local extension of the imperial state from whom the mayor and his colleagues were obliged to protect their North African residents. Officials vociferously opposed police tactics, including racial profiling, mass detainment, and the presence of auxiliary forces. Gillot continuously drew connections between the treatment of migrant workers and the evils of the empire: not only did imperial ideology affect the lives of local migrants, but the presence of North Africans within Saint-Denis made imperialism and war city concerns. Just as the municipality sought to make safe spaces for local Algerians, the existence of those Algerians on city soil carved out space for Algeria itself within Saint-Denis's jurisdiction. Here we can see the ways that anti-imperialism also functioned within daily local contexts and trace the development of specific tactics to shield North Africans from the imperial state.

In chapter 5, "Profit," I consider the economic and financial motivations for encouraging migration from North Africa. Most migrants were workers, after all, and employers regularly intervened on their behalf. This is particularly true for housing; many North African residences were built, funded, or operated by employers who wanted their laborers to be healthy, close, and—in some cases—monitored. Many employers, such as the Berliet factories in Vénissieux, wrote to city and departmental officials to request or promote better housing, education, and employment initiatives. Property owners and builders were also involved in constructing and managing housing options. Overall, this chapter suggests that making space for North Africans within the labor market entailed a series of further obligations to ensure that these workers were supported well enough to continue to contribute to local and national economies.

The final chapter, "Solidarity," considers more humanitarian motivations. From the Foyer Notre-Dame des Sans-Abris in the Rhône and the PCF leadership in Saint-Denis to a set of new leftist groups emerging in the late 1960s and early '70s, we find activists who reached out to North African migrants simply as fellow humans. While these groups differed significantly from each other (and often opposed one another), they shared a dedication to broader worldviews not bounded by national identities. These local leaders made space for North Africans in their communities through their understandings of human connection. These final examples provide alternative ideas of belonging that supersede or elide the nation-state logic that defines migrants as outsiders. While there is a bit of this negation of the insider-outsider divide at the core of the imperialist motives discussed in chapter 3, these Christians, communists, and leftists did not require allegiance to a French system as part of their acceptance, nor did they leverage state force to ensure compliance. Indeed, for communists and leftists, and even some more progressive religious groups, North Africans were valued precisely because of their connection to protest, opposition, and global liberation struggles.

Back to the Field

Let us return for a moment to the Stade de France. Stories about the national football team show us a wide set of interacting identities. There are, of course, many claims to Frenchness, and to French greatness, through the creation of racially diverse national teams and the celebration of their victories. That racial diversity, emblematic as it is of France's national and imperial histories, has also been a subject of critique and derision (particularly when the team loses). The very same space has also hosted invocations of North African (or mixed) identities, such as when fans cheer for the Algerian team over the French one or—to further complicate the notion of national identities—wave Algerian flags to celebrate the achievements of players of North African origin on the French national team. These games are played on an international stage, set up as an encounter between two nations (typically involving many more), watched by fans around the globe, and promoted by multinational organizations. Yet they are also played on a piece of land in Saint-Denis, in a stadium built to support the local economy even as it showcases these national and international talents.[91] Within the Stade de France, the view from the field can reveal more about the spectators in the stands than it does about the players. It can pique our curiosity about the everyday spaces where people live and work and play. It raises questions about the city that pushed both for the construction of this modern-day national cathedral and for the rights of the young fans who boo the Marseillaise and occasionally invade the field. From this bit of well-groomed grass in Saint-Denis, we start to see that not only are all politics local, but even the most local of politics may also be global in scope and in motivation.

ABBREVIATIONS AND FRENCH TERMS

Asniérois	resident of Asnières-sur-Seine
banlieue	suburb
beur	person of North African descent
bidonville	shantytown
bidonvillier	resident of a shantytown
cité	housing complex
cité de transit	transitional housing center
Dionysien	resident of Saint-Denis
foyer	workers' dormitory or hostel
garni	furnished room for rent
harkis	Algerians who served in the French military
hôtel de ville	city hall
mal-logés	poorly housed
pieds-noirs	European settlers in Algeria
seuil de tolérance	housing quota for migrants
taudi	slum
Vénissian	resident of Vénissieux
Villeurbannais	resident of Villeurbanne
AFNA	Association des foyers nord-africains de la région parisienne (Association for North African Dormitories in the Paris Region)
ALHNA	Association lyonnaise pour l'hébergement des Nord-Africains (Lyon Association for North African Housing)

CFDT	Confédération française démocratique du travail (French Democratic Confederation of Labor)
CFTC	Confédération française des travailleurs chrétiens (French Confederation of Christian Workers)
CGT	Confédération générale du travail (General Confederation of Labor)
CTAM	Conseiller technique pour les affaires musulmanes (Technical Consultant for Muslim Affairs)
FAS	Fonds d'action sociale pour les travailleurs algériens en métropole et leurs familles (Social Action Fund for Algerian workers in the metropole and their families)
FIFA	Fédération internationale de football association (International Soccer Federation Association)
FLN	Front de libération nationale (Algerian National Liberation Front)
FMA	Français musulman d'Algérie (Muslim French citizen from Algeria)
FN	Front national (French National Front)
FPA	Force de police auxiliaire (Auxiliary Police Force)
HLM	Habitation à loyer modéré (Low-Rent Housing)
IGAME	Inspecteur général de l'administration en mission extraordinaire (Inspector General for the Administration on Special Mission)
LOGIREL	Logement et gestion immobilière pour la région lyonnaise (Housing and Real Estate Management for the Lyon Region)
LOGIREP	Logement et gestion immobilière pour la région parisienne (Housing and Real Estate Management for the Paris Region)

MAN	Maison de l'Afrique du Nord (North Africa House)
MNA	Mouvement national algérien (Algerian National Movement)
MTE	Maison du travailleur étranger (Foreign Workers' House)
MTLD	Mouvement pour le triomphe des libertés démocratiques (Movement for the Triumph of Democratic Liberties)
NDSA	Notre-Dame des Sans-Abris (Our Lady of the Homeless)
OAS	Organisation de l'armée secrète (Secret Army Organization)
PCA	Parti communiste algérien (Algerian Communist Party)
PCF	Parti communiste français (French Communist Party)
SAMAS	Service des affaires musulmanes et de l'action sociale (Muslim Affairs and Social Action Service)
SAT-FMA	Service d'assistance technique aux Français musulmans d'Algérie (Technical Assistance Service for French Muslim Citizens from Algeria)
SEMARA	Société d'économie mixte d'équipement et de rénovation d'Asnières (Asnières Public-Private Society for Facilities and Renovation)
SFIO	Section française de l'Internationale ouvrière (French Socialist Party)
SLPM	Service de liaison et promotion des migrants (Migrant Liaison and Promotion Service)
SONACOTRA	Société nationale de construction de logements pour les travailleurs (National Society for the Construction of Workers' Housing)

SONACOTRAL   Société nationale de construction pour les
                travailleurs algériens (National Society for the
                Construction of Algerian Workers' Housing)
ZUP   Zone à urbaniser en priorité (Prioritized
                Urban Zone)

MAKING SPACE

ONE

The Mission to Modernize

In June 1970, Asnières-sur-Seine celebrated the inauguration of the city's newly renovated northern zone. The Asniérois were invited to enjoy a weekend of speeches and sporting events, including a bike race and a *boules* competition.[1] Five thousand people turned out to welcome Prime Minister Jacques Chaban-Delmas despite local communists' attempts to protest (twenty people did shout the "Internationale" when the gathering sang the "Marseillaise").[2] While the city reveled in this achievement for urban planning and construction, there was little attention paid to what—or whom—the new northern zone had replaced. A municipal brochure neatly framed a series of before and after pictures: the new towers in orderly rows, named for various flowers, stood atop scenes of run-down, empty streets and dilapidated buildings and shanties, hovered over by construction cranes.[3] Only the last picture invoked the term *bidonville*, and none referred to the people portrayed, many of whom were North African migrants.

That same month, the Rhône prefecture announced its own policy to replace concentrated North African communities with renovated neighborhoods and more desirable populations. Racialized fears about North African "ghettos" in and around Lyon had reached a fever pitch. Local officials cannily channeled anxieties about education to curb North African settlement in certain neighborhoods in the Lyon region. In particular, they hoped to rid themselves of Villeurbanne's Cité Olivier de Serres, which housed hundreds of North African families in a single complex.

This followed a similar program to dissolve Lyon's original North African housing center at Part-Dieu, which had finally closed in 1965. Both processes sought to disperse North Africans across the region and, like the renovation of Asnières's northern zone, were motivated by the problematic, race-based notion that it was undesirable—even dangerous—to house so many North Africans in one place.

This chapter examines how some local officials who got involved in North African housing projects did so with ulterior motives: to displace or disperse the migrant population or, failing that, to find ways to make migrants "adapt" to French norms. Urban planners in Asnières, Lyon, and Villeurbanne were as focused on demographic evolution, and particularly the dispersal of North African migrants, as they were on construction.[4] Diluting migrants' presence was supposed to make their existence within the community more tolerable, more easily digestible, for white residents. Breaking up concentrated centers of North African residence was thought to serve both the health and welfare of those migrants and the further evolution of French cities and citizens. Migrants would move into new and better housing, would continue to receive paternalistic instruction from French social services, and would so evolve into "proper" members of their communities (or be sent away). Cities would escape the dreaded process of "ghettoization"—or "casbah"-ization—and benefit from a reduced overall presence of North Africans on their soil. City land would be liberated from a foreign presence, while migrants would be liberated from the traditions, habits, and practices that marked them as backward and undesirable. Making modern urban spaces thus extended well beyond construction projects to include efforts both to spur North Africans' assimilation into French norms and to remove them from renewed cityscapes.

These are the stories that hew most closely to traditional narratives about French migrant policy, particularly with respect to housing North Africans, where local projects clearly mirrored the national trajectory. Beneath the building and urban renewal projects that targeted the slums and bidonvilles around France's major cities lay deeply racialized assumptions about assimilation and modernity. Historians have traced the transition of French imperial rhetoric after the Second World War from a discourse of "civilizing" to one of "modernizing."[5] Scholars of French housing and urban development more broadly have examined both the claims made on behalf of modernizing and residents' responses to these.[6] The following cases demonstrate how these ideas were applied to North African welfare programs on the mainland. Constructing the "right" sorts of buildings was expected to attract the "right" sorts of people into these spaces. Others, especially North African workers and their families, would be encouraged into spaces deemed more appropriate for their needs and, conveniently, farther away. These spaces were carefully constructed to induce social and cultural evolution, whether in *cités de transit* (temporary housing designed for families "transitioning" to a modern French lifestyle) or in workers' *foyers* (dormitories), with strict codes of conduct. The ultimate goal was to create modern metropolitan spaces that erased all traces of slums and bidonvilles—and their North African residents—from these cities and replaced them with a particular vision of urban life, and with white French residents.

A National Housing Crisis

The first foyers for single male North African workers in France were built between the World Wars, beginning in Marseille.[7] In 1927, the Paris police prefecture's North African Brigade opened a small foyer of eighty beds at their rue Lecomte office. By 1931, more private foyers had opened in the Paris suburbs, and a private association (the Régie des foyers ouvriers nord-africains) was recruited to manage existing facilities and construct more (including one in Asnières).[8] A few more foyers opened in the Seine in the 1930s, but these efforts fell far short of offering enough beds for the North African workers in France.[9] World War II brought an enormous housing shortage, and the resulting Courant Plan set common standards for public housing, offered incentives for companies to build Habitations à loyer modéré (HLMs, or subsidized low-rent housing), and raised funds through a new tax on employers.[10] Into the late 1940s, most initiatives for housing North Africans came not from the national government but rather from private individuals, associations, and occasionally employers.[11] The Association des foyers nord-africains de la région parisienne (AFNA) operated twenty-nine foyers by 1956, housing roughly one thousand North Africans—a minority of those living in the Paris region.[12] The vast majority found shelter in hotels, basements, run-down apartment buildings, and the mushrooming bidonvilles. Even as local officials, like Asnières's municipality, believed the problems associated with North African migration fell within the purview of national, not local, authority, the state sought to shift the burden of action and organization to associations that received funds for the work they accomplished on behalf of—but also instead of—the French government. The outbreak of war in Algeria in 1954 further politicized housing debates, raised the profile of North African migrants, and increased the racialization measures within urban development policies.

The watershed for North African housing policies came in 1956 with the creation of SONACOTRAL (the Société nationale de construction pour les travailleurs algériens) under the auspices of the Interior Ministry. The joint public-private venture served as an intermediary among the various private associations and government ministries, even as it developed its own projects. Eugène Claudius-Petit, former minister of housing, was selected to head the new organization (he served as its president until 1977). Another former member of the French Resistance, Claudius-Petit's oversight of North African housing questions was heavily influenced by both social Catholicism and urban modernism.[13]

Soon, public and official attention alike was captured by the bidonvilles. "Bidonville" derived from *bidon*, a metal oil drum, which could be flattened to serve as the walls and roofs of makeshift dwellings. Residents also used bidons to collect, transport, and store water, one of the most valuable resources in the bidonvilles.[14] The first urban slums to be called "bidonvilles" were in colonial Morocco, where Marshal Louis Hubert Lyautey's urbanization projects failed to account for demographic or geographic change and thus resulted in the proliferation of shantytowns around Moroccan cities (in 1950, the population of Casablanca's bidonvilles topped forty-five thousand).[15] Similar constructions appeared on the mainland in the interwar years when older slums, characterized by dilapidated hotels and apartments in working neighborhoods, filled to bursting. The newest arrivals—mostly migrants—built ramshackle residences on vacant lots. These areas were frequently called "zones" or referred to as *baraques* (shacks).[16] Around Lyon, authorities tolerated these makeshift constructions despite their illegality, since to condemn them would have forced the inhabitants into the city's streets, where they would have become even more problematic for local officials.[17] After 1945, these "zones" grew and multiplied. By the mid-1950s, local and national officials had started to refer to "bidonvilles."[18]

This shift to a term that had itself migrated from the Maghreb marked an intensified racialization of these urban spaces. In part, state authorities were concerned with the political dimensions of bidonville life, especially the ability of Algerian nationalists to use bidonvilles as recruiting grounds for their struggle against French imperial control.[19] The idea of the bidonville, however, also helped enforce boundaries of whiteness and Frenchness. Marie-Claude Blanc-Chaléard and Françoise de Barros both emphasize the ways that the term *bidonville* helped differentiate predominantly North African settlements from other white migrant slums.[20] Hugh McDonnell likewise details the association of the bidonvilles with non-, or even anti-, European spaces.[21] This differentiation increasingly allowed colonial experts on "Muslim" populations to take control of urbanization policies in the metropole.[22] Local officials and construction companies meanwhile began to invoke antibidonville efforts as a way of accessing new funding, which further extended racial and imperial logics into French construction efforts.[23]

Yet metropolitan bidonvilles were neither generated nor populated by North Africans alone; indeed, North Africans made up fewer than half of all bidonville inhabitants in 1965.[24] North African migrants in the bidonvilles lived with working-class families of varied origins, including metropolitan French and, by the mid-1960s, a great many Portuguese. Though the bidonvilles became emblematic of the broader migrant housing problem, fewer than 10 percent of all migrants lived in the bidonvilles (this figure rose to 20 percent for the Portuguese).[25] Still, the identification of bidonvilles with a specifically nonwhite population meant that it would take time before the major Portuguese settlements in cities like Champigny and Saint-Denis would be classed as bidonvilles.[26] In the words of one *bidonvillier*: "They always say, 'those from the bidonville' . . . , [but] in reality, they are thinking 'the Arabs,' because only Arabs live in bidonvilles. There are plenty of others, Spaniards, Yugoslavs, gypsies . . . and even French . . . from France, but those they don't see, they don't exist. The bidonville is the Arab bidonville."[27] The attention paid to North African migrants during the Algerian War, the visible growth of the bidonvilles, and the noticeable increase in North African migration in the late 1950s all reinforced the public idea that the bidonvilles were a North African phenomenon and an unwelcome incursion into white French urban environments.

Algerian bidonville residents expressed nuanced understandings of their position within their urban settings in the rich testimonies collected by Abdelmalek Sayad and Éliane Dupuy in Nanterre. Settling in the bidonvilles was not necessarily a last resort; early builders saw their makeshift dwellings as a step up from the slum hotels to which they had previously been consigned.[28] In addition to offering more living space, bidonvilles were subject to less control—fewer rules and reduced oversight—and allowed migrants to gather their families.[29] For some, the bidonvilles were also a place "*comme chez nous*," with familiar traditions and families willing to host overnight visitors.[30] Bidonvilliers created a suite of services for themselves and their neighbors: cafés, small groceries, mobile food sellers, a burgeoning industry of halal butchers, and even hairdressers.[31]

At the same time, they faced immense structural difficulties: a lack of clean water, an abundance of mud, no access to municipal garbage collection, and bureaucratic obstacles to making infrastructure improvements.[32] Residents were acutely aware of how others, including—especially—local authorities, conflated these environmental challenges with personal shortcomings: "It seemed like we wanted to live in the mud and that we refused to open ourselves to progress."[33] Such attitudes, which slid easily into racial prejudice, guided policy discussions and decisions that blamed bidonville residents for their situations, set up paternalistic systems to "educate" North African migrants, and cast the bidonvilles and the people within them as uncivilized and antimodern. For their part, however, bidonville residents continued to push for change, petitioning elected officials, appealing to social services, and finding any open door through which they might make their case.[34] In the face of the campaign to color the bidonvilles as foreign, residents emphasized that this was a French phenomenon, foreign to the migrants before they arrived in the metropole: "After all, the bidonville is French; it exists in Paris, it's something from here."[35]

In 1955, the police claimed that many bidonvilles containing three thousand or more North Africans each could be found throughout the Parisian banlieues.[36] With a growing sense that these marginal communities posed dangers to public health, hygiene, and security, the government launched a plan to rid France entirely of its bidonvilles by 1961. This timeline proved optimistic. Local authorities received substantial legislative support in 1964 with the passage of the Debré law to "facilitate, for the goals of reconstruction or settlement, the expropriation of land on which insalubrious and irrecoverable dwellings, commonly called 'bidonvilles,' have been erected."[37] The law gave cities—or other public actors—the right to claim any and all bidonville land so long as they intended to build upon it or otherwise use it for urbanization projects. The goal was "to make the 'bidonvilles' disappear."[38] This ordinance set the tone for many antibidonville operations. SONACOTRAL, born out of concerns for safety and security, quickly developed its own prerogatives in the destruction of the bidonvilles. Building foyers and HLMs required more land than authorities were willing to grant.[39] Bidonville resorption freed territory that SONACOTRAL

could claim for its construction projects. Moreover, the displacement of inhabitants provided the association with more rent-paying
clientele for their various housing complexes. Municipalities and
departmental prefectures had similar aims; the destruction of
the Nanterre bidonville was supported in part to provide space
for the new prefecture for the nascent department of Hauts-de-
Seine.[40] This logic of land acquisition, in the spirit of the Debré
law and further legislation that allowed authorities to declare and
take possession of "prioritized urban zones" (ZUPS), was a defining factor in Asnières's renovation of its northern zone.

Renovating Asnières's Northern Zone

Asnières's municipality showed little interest in its North African
population until the end of the 1950s, when city officials enthusiastically embraced the antibidonville spirit. The renovation of
the "northern zone" was not only one of the earliest bidonville
clearance endeavors in France but also one of the most efficient.
Rapid population growth through the twentieth century had made
Asnières one of Paris's most heavily populated suburbs (with Bou-
logne and Saint-Denis). City officials believed that the northern
neighborhoods should be "remodeled" to provide better infrastructure, more commercial and public facilities, and more greenery.[41]
They aimed to convert an area they described as "an intolerable
disorder, where the reigning masters are the slums, the bidonvilles,
filth, and all of their calamitous consequences for the inhabitants,"
into a neighborhood worthy of Asnières, the "coquette," admired
by the surrounding towns and a leading example of the orderly
"transformation of the banlieues."[42]

Hand in hand with these construction plans came the project of
rehousing North African bidonville dwellers, who did not conform
to the municipality's image of a modernized banlieue. Few were
deemed worthy of the new apartments built in their wake. Single
workers were shuffled out of the municipal system and into foyers
around the Paris region under the auspices of SONACOTRA/L and
the Seine prefecture. Most families were believed to require additional education and socialization; they were ushered through the

FIG. 1.1. Demolition and construction in Asnières's northern zone (1963). From *Asnières, Votre Nouveau Quartier*, June 1963 (AMASS, Brochures diverses).

paternalistic cocoon of the Cité du Stade to prepare them for their full transition into metropolitan life (symbolized by their eventual accession to HLM housing). This major displacement of North Africans served white municipal and regional officials' desire to alter the city's demographic makeup as well as its urban aesthetic.[43]

The Asniérois municipal council voted in 1959, just after the election of Michel Maurice-Bokanowski (1959–94) as mayor, to launch a massive urban planning project to "renovate" the northern zone.[44] To this end, they created the Société d'économie mixte d'équipement et de rénovation d'Asnières (SEMERA), a public-private venture along the lines of SONACOTRAL, which took charge of the majority of the city's construction projects in December 1961. Asnières's northern zone covered roughly seventy hectares (173 acres, or about a third of a square mile).[45] The 1954 census found 6,300 inhabitants, distributed among 2,031 lodgings in 1,004 buildings of a "horizontal" nature.[46] The future, in the eyes of architects, city planners, and national leaders, was vertical, and plans for northern Asnières included towers of up to twenty floors.[47] The city's first HLM, les Courtilles, was built in 1958 along the western edge of the zone.[48] By 1970, the entire area had undergone reconstruction, including the introduction of more than 2,500 HLM units as well as parks, gymnasiums, schools, and a cultural center.[49]

Certainly, many of the city's North African residents desired better housing for themselves. Though municipal archives in Asnières record fewer demands than other cities (whose officials were known to be more responsive to migrant requests), local North Africans did try to use city services for their own ends.[50] In March 1959, one Algerian man wrote directly to Mayor Bokanowski after receiving no help from other services or the previous municipality (Bokanowski had been elected mayor that same month). His main concern was the "total lack of hygiene or comfort" in the tiny room he inhabited with his wife and three children. They had no running water, no gas, barely any electricity, no kitchen, and no space for a bed for their youngest. The petitioner was adamant about his place within French society: "I have been in France for 40 years and have worked at Usines Chausson for 33. Just as General de Gaulle has said, I consider myself as fully French—I desire only a roof and to raise my children with dignity."[51] Contrary to the bulk of official rhetoric, which ignored North African concerns or blamed the individuals themselves for their poor living conditions, this writer expressed a clear sense of both his and his family's rights to basic health and comfort and his right to belong as a Frenchman.[52] His frustration with the lack of response revealed a conviction that French welfare services were supposed to guard his rights and well-being, particularly given his years of productive labor. He was, alas, to be disappointed yet again: Bokanowski reached out to the Asnières HLM office, but while all parties agreed this case was "worthy of interest," there were no units available.[53]

To begin the massive renovation, the municipality conducted a census of the bidonville "le Curé," which partially transgressed the border with neighboring Gennevilliers (see table 1.1). The population was predominantly North African, with all but one metropolitan man gainfully employed. The survey noted that many of the Algerians were ill, that a majority of the resident Tunisians worked for the city of Paris, and that some occupants had their

Table 1.1. Census of bidonville le Curé, December 1959

Category	Single	Married (legitimate)	Married (irregular)	Persons living with head of household	Total
Metropolitans		4	2	16	22
Algerians					
without work	14	6	1	32	53
with work	95	44	6	172	317
Tunisians					
without work					
with work	222	1	1	11	235
Moroccans					
without work					
with work	174				174
Total	505	55	10	231	801

Notes: Created by author from "Recensement au 25 décembre 1959" (AMASS, 2 I 63). Compiled from results of all three groups.

own small businesses (one café owner, two butchers, and six grocers).[54] Given this large North African presence and the overall rhetoric that racialized the bidonvilles, the municipality regularly referred to the "islands of Muslims" throughout the northern neighborhoods.[55]

City officials clearly signaled their neglect—even contempt—of these North Africans by repeatedly alluding to them as obstacles to be overcome on the way to creating the modern Asnières to which they aspired. In the early planning stages, municipal councillors "fear[ed] that the strong presence of French Muslims in the neighborhood [would] hinder its expansion considerably."[56] Construction took precedence over the people it relocated. A later report insisted that a group of North African families needed to be "expelled" because they "impede[d the chief engineer] in the execution of his storm drain" and emphasized that the "displacement" of the families should in no way "hinder future constructions."[57] The seemingly incidental nature of North Africans' presence revealed officials' preoccupation with recovering land from the bidonvilles in order to proceed with their urban renovation projects. Many reports on their progress, even a lengthy inquiry into the social impact of the project for resident families, dropped all allusions to the presence of North Africans in the area.[58] The disregard for these residents underscored their forced removal from this space and revealed officials' beliefs that North African occupants were at least as problematic as dilapidated buildings.

Displaced migrants were not entirely without recourse during and after clearance operations. Some simply refused to leave or returned to the area soon after being forced out; others attempted more formal disputes. One North African landowner spent the better part of a decade demanding compensation for his destroyed property. This proprietor of a small café, attached to the five-room house where he lived with his wife and three children, had sold property in Algeria to settle in Asnières in 1955. He received an eviction notice in late 1959 and immediately wrote to the mayor asking for aid. Like other petitioners, he emphasized that he had lived in France since 1933 and was "French like everyone else"; moreover, he asserted, "There is nothing left for me in Algeria."[59] City services invited him to meetings, but the municipality's response was largely indifferent. A municipal councillor writing on behalf of Bokanowski first explained that the eviction was in service of a project to make the neighborhood "more rational" and rid it of "mediocre" constructions. He then insisted that this particular building was not actually part of municipal renovations, and thus the city could not be held responsible for compensating this man and his family—a line city officials held through the last recorded request in 1967.[60] Meanwhile, the demolition crew showed up in July 1960. SEMERA offered the family a new residence in La Courneuve, but the rent was too high.[61] Unhappy with the city's response, the café owner wrote directly to Charles de Gaulle in 1961—that request circled back to the city through the Seine prefecture, which followed up again years later.[62] This Algerian's demands made clear his sense of belonging and his conviction that he had rights that French officials—both local and national—were obliged to enforce.

The municipality's position was equally revealing. Even while city officials denied any involvement with the specific destruction of his property, they still classed it within an urban modernization project whose goals they believed to supersede the rights of the neighborhood's North African residents.

Throughout France, discussion of the bidonvilles developed a fairly standard vocabulary. Authorities worked to "eliminate" bidonvilles, to "liquidate" them, and often to "resorb" them. One word employed frequently in Asnières—and around Lyon—was "liberate": the liberation, that is, of land. For example, a municipal council meeting in 1963 opened with a list of the bidonvilles already "liberated" and outlined the coming "rehousing operations with a view to the liberation of grounds."[63] The notion of liberation, particularly after 1945, held the connotation of reclaiming land from foreign military occupation. An article in *France-Soir* dubbed Asnières's deputy mayor in charge of housing, Lavergne, the "*chef d'état-major* of the antibidonville army." Lavergne himself spoke in terms of battles and operations, remarking that two deaths occurred during the survey projects and that municipal officials found that they "had to fight with [the bidonville residents]."[64] Overt military references may not have been conscious on the part of those who employed them to speak of migration, but they were pervasive. A 1954 Paris police memo exclaimed, "At the very gates of Paris, veritable 'Bidonvilles' have been constituted and progressively this pacific invasion, coming closer and closer, has conquered the near totality of the Parisian agglomeration."[65] A police map illustrating the movement of North African migrants throughout France bore a strong resemblance to military invasion plans (see figure 1.2). A thick arrow crossed the Mediterranean to the port at Marseille and divided into two main prongs—one striking straight for Paris and then through the Nord department and the other running through the Rhône industrial region—before the two finally converged at a point marked "Ardennes" (the weak link of national defense exploited by the German invasion of 1940).[66] Asniérois officials did not explicitly equate North Africans with Nazis; their terminology, however,

FIG. 1.2. Police map of North African migration (1958). Map by Erin Greb. Redrawn from "Étude de la population musulmane d'Algérie implantée à Paris et dans la région parisienne depuis la Libération," December 15, 1958 (AHPP, HA 9).

reflected a definite distinction between *belonging* (in the sense that the land in the northern zone belonged to the city) and *not belonging* (on the part of the migrants, who were seen as illegal and unwanted occupiers of that land).

Asniérois officials' actions—or lack thereof—demonstrated their belief that migrant populations were the responsibility of the state, not the city. Bidonville dwellers whose means were deemed sufficient were listed in the city's HLM records; those found to be badly off were entered into the Seine prefecture's file for the department's *mal-logés* (poorly housed). This bookkeeping strategy kept unwanted populations out of municipal files and left them to departmental authorities. This reflected the Asniérois notion that cities were responsible for their native-born citizens, while working migrant residents (whose claims to welfare benefits were perceived as a drain on city coffers) belonged to someone else. When possible, Asnières's municipality even avoided direct participation in rehousing the North Africans displaced by the renovation projects.[67]

That this marginalized population simply did not belong, in the eyes of city officials, was further illustrated by municipal rehousing policies. SEMERA acknowledged at the outset that all current residents would need to be appropriately rehoused for their plans to proceed.[68] The municipal agenda outlined two processes: offering new opportunities to metropolitan French families and resettling North Africans, preferably far away. Mayor Bokanowski described the renovation project as a renewal effort: the neighborhood overrun by slums and bidonvilles was to be transformed into a new residential paradise. A key component of this transformation was to be demographic: "A new population, composed essentially of young households, will enrich [the neighborhood's] dynamic potential."[69] Bokanowski declared that rehousing would be a priority and that families would soon take residence in new apartment complexes built after the evacuation of the bidonvilles from the land. He did not explicitly link these two resettlements, however. As the use of the phrase "new populations" suggests, those who were rehoused in the northern zone's bold new HLMs were not the same people who had inhabited the area's bidonvilles. City officials planned "the expulsion of North Africans" alongside the destruction of shanties and condemned buildings; young metropolitan families were slated to settle in their place.[70] The renovation project thus sought to give the neighborhood not only a face-lift but also a full transfusion.

This population exchange was grounded in racialized imperial ideas about North African adaptation to metropolitan life—and the belief that this was hindered by concentrated communities of

migrants. The idea of a *seuil de tolérance* (the "threshold of tolerance" that defined housing quotas for foreign families) did not formally enter the French lexicon until 1964.[71] However, officials had
been preoccupied for years with how to establish and manage housing quotas for migrants. Strategies to ensure Algerian integration
in particular were in tension with local desires to maintain what
they believed to be an appropriate separation—and demographic
balance—between foreign laborers and metropolitan citizens. As
much as quota systems were upheld by French officials and experts
as racially neutral—even scientifically objective—population controls, any attempt to disperse North Africans must be understood
as a project to police local belonging and to uphold a vision of
whiteness as a measure of Frenchness.[72]

SONACOTRAL sought to limit the proportion of "Muslim" families in its newly built HLMs to 15 percent;[73] however, the actual size
of the North African population quickly forced them to rethink
this cap. SONACOTRAL appealed to the Seine prefecture to enlarge
the quota significantly in order to make up for the "insufficient"
number of housing units available to displaced Algerians.[74] The
director for construction in the Paris region suggested that a maximum threshold of 25 percent might be acceptable, but Jean Vaujour, then director general of SONACOTRAL, insisted that even
this was too high. Vaujour cited a high Algerian birthrate (claiming it to be twice the metropolitan French birthrate) and warned
that any quota above 15 percent would fail to encourage Muslim
assimilation.[75] French officials worried about the possibility of
emptying the bidonvilles only to create new ghettos within the
HLM complexes. They hoped that proper education and socialization, to be carried out in the cités de transit, would assimilate
North African families quickly and avoid culture clashes in the
new housing complexes. Most of all, they sought to preserve racial
and social boundaries by limiting the presence and visibility of
North African migrants.

SONACOTRAL affiliates faced further opposition over rehousing North Africans from municipalities throughout the Paris
region. Maintaining the 15 percent threshold meant that many

North Africans could not be rehoused in the city they had been calling home. Exchange programs were set up across the region, allowing a city to relocate North Africans to other cities in return for accepting a corresponding number of metropolitan families. These agreements were difficult to implement and enforce.[76] Michel Massenet, Délégué à l'action sociale pour les Français musulmans d'Algérie en métropole, declared in 1959 that Algerians were not being given appropriate access to normal, nontransitional housing options by HLM management offices and that "severe racial discrimination [was] being practiced by these organizations toward Muslim families."[77] The majority of French officials paid lip service to the idea of integration even as they placed the blame for the difficulties North Africans faced on the migrants themselves. Despite a set of safeguards that welfare experts had implemented to prevent the formation of Muslim "ghettos," the reality was that many migrants remained for years in a state of de facto segregation.[78]

Plans for North African expulsion went hand in hand with strategies to assimilate migrants to modern standards. Controlling migrant housing offered the state the best access to foreign households so as to educate and socialize their members. As Amelia Lyons has demonstrated, these programs effectively brought the civilizing mission back to the metropole. In the case of single male workers, foyers enabled employers, police, and government authorities to observe and "correct" residents' behavior. Workers' foyers, however, were deemed wholly unsuitable for women and children. The prefects and other local authorities requested more family housing options for Algerians in the 1950s, even as SONACOTRAL's president, Claudius-Petit, worried that moving beyond single worker housing would be problematic. By 1958, even Claudius-Petit acknowledged the need to provide solutions for families as well as single workers, and the groundwork was laid for SONACOTRAL to begin construction of cités de transit, which would house Algerian families until they were considered "suited" for integration into regular social housing (HLMs).[79]

Careful surveys of bidonville residents, like the census of le Curé in Asnières, assessed whether individuals and families were "assimilated" or "assimilable."[80] In 1966, the Infrastructure Ministry explained that families would be transferred out of the bidonvilles "either, if they are judged suitable, to ordinary HLM units, or, most often, to cités de transit"; single workers would be placed in foyers.[81] While "suitability" was determined in terms of a family's assimilation of French quotidian practices, it also included the ability to pay rent.[82] Though the language of assimilability in these documents remained ethnically neutral, in practice North and sub-Saharan migrants were found to be the least suited to French society.[83] Officials in Asnières and other cities thus developed alternative categories to track racial identities and presumed "sociability" scores, similar to the practices Minayo Nasiali has documented among local experts in Marseille.[84]

The arrival of the *pieds-noirs*, the nearly one million European settlers who fled Algeria after its declaration of independence and created a secondary "Algerian" housing crisis, both compounded the difficulties in rehousing North Africans and accentuated the racialized assumptions that underlay national and local officials' understandings of who could be assimilated into local communities. Initially able to claim status as both French and Algerian (they soon had to choose), these "*rapatriés*" (repatriates) were given HLM slots reserved for Algerians even as their European origins saved them the intervening stay in cités de transit.[85] Ten to 30 percent of the HLMs built in the early 1960s were reserved for repatriates.[86] Emergency housing for North African migrants could also be turned over to repatriate families under the right circumstances.[87] While the pieds-noirs faced their own process of assimilation and integration into metropolitan society, they were still seen by locals as preferable to "Muslim" Algerians.[88] In Asnières, fifty-two HLM units were reserved specifically for pieds-noirs.[89] Asniérois officials' willingness to work closely with the secretary of state for rapatriés to provide resources and policy solutions contrasted starkly with their desire to transfer other North Africans out of the city. European repatriates were embraced as part of the municipal population, whereas other migrant workers and families were un-French and therefore un-Asniérois; they were somebody else's problem.

When they had no choice but to retain some of the North African population, Asniérois officials perceived families to be more assimilable than single males. The mayor declared during a 1963 operation that "only the families could be rehoused" in Asnières, leaving fifty single men to the Paris prefecture.[90] North African workers displaced by the renovation of Asnières's northern zone were regularly sent to foyers in Nanterre, La Courneuve, and other nearby cities.[91] In 1964, the municipality opposed the construction of a North African foyer within the city, securing an agreement with SONACOTRA that it would be built instead "on the territory of any other commune." Asnières would provide funding for the project in return for reserving an appropriate number of rooms for men leaving the northern zone's bidonvilles.[92] Over and again, Asniérois officials ensured that ridding their territory of bidonvilles did not entail the resettlement of unwanted populations within their city's boundaries.

When it came to families, Asniérois officials initially maintained that North Africans would be rehoused "in the same manner as Metropolitan families."[93] Yet in practice, North African families were not dealt with exactly as their "French" (by which officials meant white and metropolitan) counterparts. The commission that oversaw housing attribution explicitly gave priority to families with "French nationality."[94] SEMERA memos on rehousing projects kept separate lists of French and North African families. French families who held municipally recognized property titles or leases were rehoused in municipal HLM units (or in some cases given temporary residences in buildings that would be destroyed as soon as enough new apartments had been built to accommodate these families). Initially, North African families, who rarely had leases for the properties they inhabited, were also moved to older municipal apartment buildings. From there, however, they were slated to move to Asnières's main cité de transit, the Cité du Stade.[95]

SONACOTRAL had agreed to build a cité de transit on municipal land eventually slated for a new stadium.[96] Plans were hastened after predominantly white metropolitan families in one of the new HLMs complained about their continued proximity to "bidonvilles."[97] The Cité du Stade was intended "for the temporary resettlement of North African families."[98] When the municipality faced criticism from "Europeans" who complained that "Arabs" were being offered preferential treatment, officials explained that this was a temporary situation brought on by the rapid destruction of the bidonvilles and held out the possibility that European families would be given a place in a "magnificent apartment building" that would be built.[99] Thus, they implicitly acknowledged that the bulk of the new housing developments would not be assigned to North African bidonville residents, at least not until these migrants were deemed ready.

To this end, local officials tracked the perceived "evolution" of the families in the Cité du Stade and enacted social and surveillance policies intended to promote "development" and assuage neighbors' fears. Deputy Mayor Lavergne, in charge of rehousing operations, declared that North Africans could be moved into HLMs only once "families have learned to be clean, [and] when they acquire the habit of paying rent regularly."[100] As in so many discussions of migrant adaptation to French life, Lavergne directly associated North Africans with dirtiness and delinquency without regard for the circumstances that created these problems. In line with plans to tear down the bidonvilles and erect new, modern structures in their place, the inhabitants of the Cité du Stade would themselves be transformed—modernized—through reeducation and socialization. Cité residents were often reminded of regulations: possessions were not to be left outside of residences, vehicles could only be left in the designated lot, and no animals were to be kept within the cité grounds.[101] Officials were also concerned with residents hosting long-term guests.[102] The cité caretaker was directed to "denounce ruthlessly anyone who violates these instructions" so that infractions could be punished and repeat offenders evicted. The director emphasized that his organization sought "a complete metamorphosis for the cité" and, implicitly, its inhabitants, who were prevailed upon to keep the grounds "in a state of perfect cleanliness."[103] Cité officials were expected "to impose a stricter and more rigorous discipline on the cité's tenants, all by way of inculcating lifestyles more in line with our morals and our habits" so that they could gradually "be inserted into our Society."[104] The Cité du Stade was, in other words, Asnières's municipal extension of the imperial civilizing mission, designed to discipline North Africans and inculcate in them white French norms and values.

Colette Pétonnet's ethnographic work in a cité de transit southeast of Paris suggests that most families viewed these apartments as a "promotion."[105] At the same time, Cité du Stade residents were well aware of the control they were subjected to and how this curtailed their options. The head of one family, who had lived in Asnières since 1954 and was moved to the Cité du Stade in 1963, wrote to the mayor in 1975 to protest that they were still stuck in this supposed "transition." Their four-room unit was totally unsuitable for their eight children. All requests to secure a larger space had gone unheard, circling fruitlessly through local and ministerial services. The father explained that, having explored all other avenues, he had threatened to stop paying rent. Yet at the same time, he recognized that taking that action—the only one he believed was still available—would worsen his family's situation by giving authorities an excuse to designate them as unsuitable. In a telling aside, though his family was constantly shuffled back to municipal services, the writer insisted, "We do not particularly wish to stay in Asnières itself."[106] His frustration was unmistakable: he was caught in a loop of official nonresponse and denials of responsibility even as he and his family were stuck without a means of viable protest, hamstrung by rules and surveillance that seemed designed to make them fail. It is hardly surprising that this family did not identify with or wish to stay in Asnières, as there was nothing to encourage their local belonging.

In the end, nearly all the families who managed to meet officials' standards were eventually placed in HLM apartments within Asnières.[107] Their new neighbors worried that some families would prove less well adapted than hoped. Echoing rhetoric in wide circulation about the supposed backwardness of North Africans, the most common concern was with families who raised chickens or even goats in their residences.[108] City officials, especially Lavergne, lobbied for strict quotas in the city's HLMs, keeping former bidonville residents to only a tenth of a building's units.[109] As elsewhere, these quotas were seemingly justified by the persistent belief that concentrated populations of foreigners, especially nonwhite ones, would re-create ghettos within the city and undo the social education families had been subjected to. At the same time, adherence to these race-based ideas about migrant distribution inhibited rehousing efforts, ironically re-creating the cités de transit as racialized and heavily stigmatized spaces, and kept the Cité du Stade in operation much longer than planned.[110] By 1970, municipal authorities once again saw North African residents as an obstacle to urban development, now delaying the construction of the stadium for which the complex was named.[111] Only in 1974, however, were the last traces of the Cité du Stade removed.[112]

Mayor Bokanowski hailed the SEMERA project as Asnières's "contribution to the important evolution of the Paris region."[113] The renovation of the northern zone was conceived in "a new spirit," "in the light of the principal tendencies of modern life."[114] The bidonvilles nearly always appeared in city documents within quotation marks, holding them visually apart from city affairs; they and their inhabitants not only were foreign but also stood in opposition to the image of a renovated and rationalized city that the Asniérois (and the French Fifth Republic) sought to project. By 1964, Asnières's municipality had managed to eliminate six bidonvilles, leaving only two, which were vigorously patrolled to prevent new residents.[115] When Marc Roberrini began his annual reports on the situation of bidonvilles around Paris in 1969, he found none to mention in Asnières.[116] Asnières's officials had thus achieved their goal of transforming a dilapidated, haphazardly settled area into a meticulously planned urban space with set ratios of inhabitants to hectares and beautified city gardens and parks. City officials' attitudes toward the bidonville residents they evacuated demonstrated their lack of engagement (or any desire to engage) with this predominantly North African population. Their priorities derived from a modernizing mindset; a 1963 description of the HLM les Courtilles declared the complex to be "inscribed in the general context of the renovation of and restoring of order to the banlieue."[117] Central to the municipality's project to restore order was a recalibration of local demographics rooted in distinct racial preferences. City officials managed to chase away most North Africans under the guise of modernization and subjected the minority of migrants who remained to a set of "civilizing" and assimilationist educational programs.

Liberating Lyon's Centre de la Part-Dieu

Looking to the southeast, we find a similar story. Local officials in the Rhône worked with many of the same motivations and assumptions as the Asniérois. While bidonville resorption was as important a facet of local interactions with North African migrants, there are two moments that bookend that process in the Lyon region and offer a clear picture of how ideas about urban renewal and population management informed policy. In the 1950s, the massive Centre de la Part-Dieu was deemed too full of North Africans to be maintained in the middle of Lyon, and a project to open foyers in the suburbs to absorb these migrants predated the region's antibidonville actions. By 1970, just as Asnières was celebrating the final renovation of the northern zone, anxieties about North African "ghettos" in Lyon and its banlieues were becoming overwhelming. When housing and urban policy proved inept at managing migrant settlement to the satisfaction of local officials, the prefecture turned to educational policy for a creative solution.

The Lyon municipality and especially the Rhône prefecture figure more prominently than the smaller suburban municipalities of Vénissieux and Villeurbanne in these stories. In part, this is due to both the size of the cities themselves and the size of local North African populations. Relative to the Paris region, there were many fewer migrants in the Rhône. Municipal officials also proved more willing to cede control over such projects. Villeurbanne's mayor, Étienne Gagnaire, explained in 1960 that he was happy to authorize SONACOTRAL and the local Notre-Dame des Sans-Abris (NDSA) to build and operate foyers for North African workers in his city but expressed no interest in being further involved in these efforts. Moreover, he asserted that he and the Villeurbannais under his jurisdiction were counting on the full support of the prefecture to resolve the "problem" of the bidonvilles, which "only seem[ed] feasible at the departmental, if not regional, level."[118] Georges Martin, Conseiller technique pour les affaires musulmanes (CTAM) for the Rhône, had likewise insisted in 1955 that any successful plan to improve the housing conditions of Algerians in the region would not only rely on national policy but also require "efficient collaboration" among local and national, public and private actors.[119] It is important to highlight that Martin and other prefectural figures were appointed to their positions through the Interior Ministry. They were not elected officials like the various municipalities under discussion and so had a different relationship both with their regions and with the national state. Yet as we will see, this diverse set of local actors articulated many shared aims and assumptions as they cooperated in the region's first major project to house North African migrants at Part-Dieu—as well as in the Part-Dieu center's eventual dissolution.

The Centre d'hébergement des travailleurs nord-africains de la Part-Dieu was created in 1946 to alleviate the housing crisis for North African workers around Lyon. Multiple associations interested in North African issues worked with Rhône prefect Marcel-Paul-Louis Grégoire (1946–47) to establish and fund the center in the former stables of the Caserne de Part-Dieu. The initial bedding was provided by local military offices and the Labor Ministry.[120] In 1948, after an inauspicious start and repeated financial troubles, Part-Dieu was given over to the Association lyonnaise pour l'hébergement des Nord-Africains (ALHNA), run by M. Mouchnino, the Directeur Départemental du Travail et de la Main-d'oeuvre.[121] ALHNA oversaw a number of improvements, adding sanitary facilities as well as a prayer room, canteen, café, small stores, and a barber.[122] The center eventually included a medical clinic for the residents, with the stated aim of preventing diseases from spreading to the broader Lyonnais population.[123] Even with these improvements, one Algerian who was a resident from

1956 to 1958 recalled that Part-Dieu still felt more suited to animals than humans: "There were 140 people sleeping in the same hangar. We washed ourselves in a trough."[124] Moreover, as Émilie Elongbil Ewane details, the center maintained a prisonlike setup, with a single well-guarded entrance.[125]

By 1951, Part-Dieu had evolved in the eyes of local officials from a solution to North African housing to a new sort of problem. The center was filled beyond capacity, housing 1,600 of the Rhône's 7,500 North African workers.[126] Around 90 percent of the residents were Algerian.[127] In 1952, a meeting of local North African social services recognized that 1,600 residents in one facility was perhaps a bit much but that large residences had proved relatively cheap and effective.[128] ALHNA repeatedly asserted a desire to reduce the number of residents to between 1,200 and 1,300; however, there were daily pressures to accept even more residents.[129] Priority was given to workers whose employers had helped fund Part-Dieu's creation and to previous tenants returning from Algeria. Further requests came from local unions, social services, administrative offices, and even political parties. The center had also just accepted 100 men displaced from the slum at rue Chaponnay.[130] This large congregation of North African workers led to plans for "decongestion" by means of foyers with 200 to 250 beds "set up in diverse suburban localities."[131] Part-Dieu's concentration of North Africans, in other words, would have to be dispersed across the region and removed from Lyon itself.

At first, much of the language about reducing and eventually closing Part-Dieu emphasized residents' needs. Their large number wore down facilities and required too many beds to be packed tightly into the rooms.[132] Plans for new foyers would need to take into account the distance to places of work, since this was one of the main priorities for the migrants themselves.[133] Many—though not all—North African workers did indeed seem to prefer the newer, smaller, more comfortable residences, moving away from Part-Dieu's large dormitories as soon as they were able.[134] The new foyers would also allow migrants to cook for themselves, whereas Part-Dieu had required them to rely on the cafeteria—though

earlier reports noted that many of the residents managed to sub-
vert these rules.[135]

In addition to these "material reasons," a 1953 report explained
that housing so many North Africans was a problem "above all, for
psychological reasons. We must facilitate the formation of small
communities, groupings by tribe or family." At the same time,
migrant housing needed to support assimilation; "to avoid the
construction of North African neighborhoods or 'villages,'" residences of 200 to 250 were ideal.[136] The Comité interministériel de
coordination pour les affaires sociales musulmanes also voiced
concerns in 1955 for the ways Part-Dieu impeded North Africans'
"social evolution."[137] These ideas about the ideal limits on North
African habitation reflected both an engrained assumption that the
migrants were socially backward—the inclusion of "tribe" underscored the racial dimensions of this—and the imperial impetus to
encourage their development into modernized urban residents.

Beneath these concerns for the migrants' "social evolution," of
course, were anxieties about what it might mean for other city
residents to contend with such a concentration of North Africans. As many problems as existed inside Part-Dieu, there were
also fears that it was "contaminating" the neighborhood. In 1954,
there were forty-nine cafés, twenty-one restaurants, and seventy
hotels and *garnis* (furnished rooms for rent) that served a predominantly North African clientele in Lyon's third arrondissement, centered around Part-Dieu. Making Part-Dieu "disappear"
would have the benefit of "a very noticeable reduction in the number of establishments frequented by North Africans in the 3rd
arrondissement, which will thus get back to its normal, residential
purpose."[138] CTAM Martin added to the list in 1958, reemphasizing
that the neighborhood was supposed to be "residential" (begging
the question of why North African housing did not count as residential) and that closing the center was necessary "for consider-
ations of social, sanitary, moral, and public order and for urban
development."[139] Just as in Asnières, white French officials around
Lyon perceived the large and dense North African population as
an abnormality—an obstacle to their modern urban ideal—that

needed to be removed or remade. Martin's participation signaled a further shift in how Part-Dieu was understood. In addition to serving as CTAM, he also directed police social services for Algerians in the Rhône. As the Algerian War progressed, Part-Dieu was classed as a danger zone for Algerian nationalist activity, and local actors embraced the notion that large North African populations needed to be broken up for security purposes.[140]

Dismantling Part-Dieu turned out to be a much more difficult and much longer process than anyone had hoped. In 1954, the prefect explained that over the course of a few months, residents would move out of Part-Dieu, bunk beds would be replaced with singles, and occupancy would be halved to eight hundred.[141] Given the plans to close the center, no major renovations would be supported.[142] However, the new foyers and employer housing that this plan relied upon were slow to be built, even as the number of migrant workers in the region continued to grow. By 1958, only one block of beds had been reduced, leaving a total of 1,310 available spaces, of which 1,180 were filled. Mouchnino optimistically noted the regular departures to Algeria, along with workers' rehousing in new foyers or in the neighborhood's other hotels and rooms, to conclude that Part-Dieu was progressing well and that "the needs for [North African] housing are now less imperial."[143] This provoked a startled response at the prefecture, where one reader of the report left multiple question marks in the margin, asking, "And the replacement for the Part-Dieu center, for la Doua? And the bidonvilles? The cellars?"[144] Policies for housing North Africans in the Rhône were, of course, absolutely "imperial" in 1958 (as detailed in chapter 3). Part-Dieu, however, had been joined by the bidonvilles and slums as predominantly North African spaces that needed attention. Some bidonvilliers were even initially rehoused in Part-Dieu.[145] In 1961, a police survey found that there were still 1,397 residents (despite the existence of only 1,310 official beds).[146] It would take until 1965 for Part-Dieu actually to close.

As in Asnières, Rhône officials' rhetoric revealed their underlying assumptions. Multiple documents referred to the "*éclatement*"

or "breaking up" of Part-Dieu.[147] Within the context of the Algerian War, the term seems particularly violent, signifying explosive
ruptures and destruction more than a simple dismantling. It is not
hard to read this attack on infrastructure as one that also targeted
Algerian nationalists. After 1957, the center was a known stronghold for operatives of the Front de libération nationale (FLN), one
of whom headed the Part-Dieu convenience store, ran sophisti-
cated collection schemes, and tried to recruit fighters.[148] In response
to this nationalist presence, it was the local SAT police force, with
its links to imperial administration, who ultimately spearheaded
Part-Dieu's destruction.[149] In 1960, "éclatement" gave way to "suppression," with equally troubling connections to the suppression
of political dissent.[150] For a moment in 1962, there was talk of
"résorption," in line with the emerging national conversation about
the bidonvilles.[151] Soon, though, as in Asnières, discussions revolved
around the idea of "liberation."[152] Indeed, when the process was
finally completed in 1965, Prefect Ricard triumphantly informed
Lyon mayor Louis Pradel (1957–76) that "the City of Lyon, thanks
to the efforts of the Fonds d'action sociale, has seen the Centre
de la Part-Dieu liberated."[153]

Also similar to Asnières, one key to this "liberation" was mass
displacement: pushing North Africans out into the suburbs and,
even there, to the margins of cities and neighborhoods. Ricard
explained, "The 1,200 or so Algerian workers who, even recently,
occupied [Part-Dieu] have been distributed among foyers-hotels
built in the communes of Villeurbanne and Vénissieux."[154] Villeurbanne and Vénissieux had been selected early on as likely hosts for
the new North African foyers.[155] The municipalities were receptive
to these plans, which originally consisted of building two foyers in
Vénissieux (Antoine Billon and Viviani) and one in Villeurbanne
(la Poudrette), as well as a fourth on the outskirts of Lyon itself
(by the Vaise train station). Construction went smoothly, though
there were some funding debates with Villeurbanne's city hall.[156]
Each of the foyers built to hold Part-Dieu residents had 252 beds,
in line with the reigning idea that North African residences should
be limited to about 250 places to support assimilationist aims.[157]

This progress on the construction front did not, however, ensure rapid closure. The rehousing process, which relied heavily on surveillance, disciplinary action, and force, began with a census of Part-Dieu residents, two-thirds of whom responded readily. Other residents resisted attempts at eviction and resettlement. To catch the final third, the SAT Nord police forces set up a checkpoint at the center's entrance; Captain Bertrand, the SAT Nord chief, noted, apparently without irony, "We have the sense that they were reticent and looking to escape our control."[158] Soon thereafter, a group of fifty Algerian workers showed up at the SAT office to demand their right to continue to live at Part-Dieu—to no avail.[159] Residents were assigned to the new foyer closest to their workplaces. Volunteers were moved first, with the help of city trucks. Remaining residents were formally expelled to their assigned residence, with the center responsible for immediately removing bedding and city services and quickly breaking down doors, windows, and walls "to make the evacuated premises unusable."[160] The police were asked to provide special surveillance and other help during these operations.[161] Bertrand expressed concern that FLN supporters among the residents might be able to mobilize discontent about the heavy-handed moving process to spark protests. He also, though, expected the rapid demolition of dormitory space to encourage more residents to overcome their resistance to relocating.[162] In April 1962, largely due to a massive SAT operation in February, Part-Dieu was down to six hundred residents, and eleven dormitories had been destroyed.[163]

Part-Dieu residents' reluctance to leave for the new foyers largely derived from practical concerns. Many migrant workers had a strong preference for being in the city center, and they universally wanted to be close to their workplaces. Some also emphasized the importance of being close to family.[164] The majority of Part-Dieu residents requested to move to Villeurbanne over Vénissieux. Villeurbanne's foyers were closer to the urban core, closer to most workplaces, and better served by public transport.[165] Meanwhile, Vénissieux's existing North African community was largely Kabyle and so seemed less welcoming to Part-Dieu's predominantly Arab population.[166] Ralph Grillo's ethnographic study of North Africans in Lyon further revealed that single workers often preferred private rooms—however run-down—to foyers because of "the relative freedom (to come and go, to receive visitors) that they offer, and their location." Others complained that foyer directors had discriminatory attitudes, and they resented strict rules, particularly those about guests.[167] Refusing to leave Part-Dieu or refusing to take one's assigned rehousing thus pushed back against both the initiative to disperse North Africans beyond Lyon's urban center and the paternalistic structure that foyers shared with the cités de transit.

Meanwhile, Mayor Pradel and Lyon's urban planners were growing impatient. By 1963, plans were in the works to build a new hotel on the Part-Dieu grounds.[168] Given an attractive (to them) alternative to the North African residence, the term *liberation* became much more prevalent, and just as in Asnières, the migrants themselves were referred to as an impediment to urban development. Pradel in particular began to suggest that the migrants were unworthy of occupying this space, claiming, based on "personal inquiry," that the large majority of those remaining in Part-Dieu were unemployed.[169] In fact, a survey of the final 279 residents indicated that all of them were working in the area.[170]

Compounding the problems of rehousing so many residents, antibidonville efforts—many targeting neighborhoods in Vénissieux and Villeurbanne—were ramping up.[171] Single workers from the bidonvilles now had priority access to beds that opened in existing foyers. The final push to close Part-Dieu thus had to wait for the completion of the Foyer Paul Kruger in Villeurbanne.[172] At the same time, negotiations to build "an international class hotel" had finally succeeded, but were being delayed by the continued occupancy.[173] On July 19, 1965, the last of Part-Dieu's tenants left the premises, and the land was given over to the mayor's office.[174] Even with Part-Dieu effectively closed, Mayor Pradel was insistent that no new housing for foreign workers be built in Lyon proper.[175] Lyon's housing problems were thus outsourced to surrounding suburbs.

The process of dissolving Part-Dieu and redistributing its residents across the region was driven by the notion that it was undesirable—even dangerous—to house so many North Africans in one place. In 1959, as part of a national discussion of whether non-Algerian migrants, and even metropolitans, might eventually be admitted into workers' foyers, the Rhône prefect acknowledged that the existence of foyers for "Muslim French" should be "transitory."[176] The Service des affaires musulmanes et de l'action sociale (SAMAS) asserted that the foyers allowed North Africans to remain among themselves, continuing to live "like foreigners within the French population." Housing North Africans with other groups would "favor[] an evolution of Muslims toward integration into our social and economic life, effectively fighting against their shutting themselves away." Dispersing the migrants would counter FLN propaganda and recruitment that fed off of discontent and boost foyer profits by enlarging their clientele. Yet SAMAS insisted that the real object of this eventual policy was to respond to what they perceived to be North African workers' "profound desire to be associated with the life of Europeans."[177] Moreover, both regional and national officials maintained that shared housing would allow North African migrants to enjoy at home the spirit of conviviality that supposedly emerged in mixed workplaces.[178]

Conveniently, the imperative to redistribute Algerians among the broader population—supposedly for their own health, advancement, and assimilation—supported urban officials' desires to rid their cities of North African "ghettos." Liberating Part-Dieu meant unraveling an unwanted knot in the urban fabric to smooth—and effectively whiten—the population. This same argument against concentrated communities of North Africans drove the Rhône prefecture in 1970 to formulate a policy aimed at tearing down another large residence for North African migrants and their families, Villeurbanne's infamous Cité Olivier de Serres.

From Ghetto to Apartheid in Villeurbanne

The Cité Olivier de Serres originated with businessman Victor Simon's 1958 request to build a housing complex on land he had

FIG. 1.3. Residents of Cité Olivier de Serres with CRS police (riot police), Villeurbanne (1980). From *Le Progrès*, in "Olivier de Serres: Radiographie d'une 'cité ghetto,'" exhibition catalog, 2009 (Le Rize, Villeurbanne).

previously used for manufacturing bicycle seats.[179] Simon seized the opportunity offered by national policies to fund residential construction for rapatriés from Algeria; indeed, the first occupants to move into the Cité Olivier de Serres in 1962 were pied-noir families.[180] Simon proved a frustrating landlord: he had no interest in maintaining the hastily erected buildings and yet soon raised rents by at least 15 percent and fees by over 80 percent.[181] These policies chased away most of the white European families, whose places were quickly filled by migrant workers, overwhelmingly from Algeria.

For a time, as with Part-Dieu, local officials saw Olivier de Serres as a good option for rehousing families from the bidonvilles they were demolishing elsewhere in town.[182] A number of businesses in the area likewise reserved apartments for their North African employees.[183] Soon, however, the large number of North African families became a source of great concern for the cité's neighbors. "Olivier de Serres" became a sort of boogeyman for urban development experts.[184] In 1967, Algerian families occupied 237 of the 336 units; 21 units were occupied by Tunisians, 4 by Moroccans, 14 by Spaniards, 6 by Italians, 4 by Portuguese, and 44 by "French."[185] By 1975, the Rhône prefecture reported with alarm that "only" four units were occupied by "French" residents, with "French" here clearly including only whites, not the *harki* and other North Africans with French citizenship living in the cité.[186] Indeed, a report by the Service de liaison et promotion des migrants (SLPM) from 1971 made the distinction between "French" occupants and others even more stark: listing fourteen "Muslim and Jewish families from North Africa," the report clarified that there was "not a single purely French family" in the complex.[187] Racial composition, then, was one of the major priorities for those looking to close the cité.

Similar origins and shared community were, at the same time, a prominent and positive part of residents' experience of Olivier de Serres. In a set of testimonies collected in 1997, Algerians from the cité made frequent reference to being "*entre nous*," which captured a sense of being both "among us" but also left on their own. Driss, who came as a boy with his family, called it "a fantastic neighborhood . . . because we found ourselves with people who had the same roots. . . . Everyone also spoke Arabic. . . . It was reassuring. It was terrific."[188] Karim, who had arrived in 1966 at the age of ten, recalled the joy of celebrations: weddings for which neighbors threw open their own apartments and Ramadan festivities that were well attended and unbothered by noise complaints.[189] Rachid, who spent his early years in the cité but left in his late teens, regretted the loss of openness and togetherness; his family felt much more isolated when they moved to the Nord department.[190]

Adult residents had somewhat more troubled memories. Mme B. expressed relief at being relocated out of the bidonville Gerland—which she remembered as both disorderly and subject to extreme police pressure. Olivier de Serres, though, also became a place where she "suffered," and she repeated the phrase "We were all very unhappy" in her testimony. In part, she was disturbed by the steadily increasing police presence—exactly what she thought she had escaped earlier—but she and others were certainly aware of the deteriorating state of the complex.[191] On one front, the sense of community started to fail: the early 1970s brought internecine conflict (particularly after the arrival of a group of single Tunisian construction workers); Rachid cited an attitude of "everyone for themselves."[192] More threatening, though, were the failures of the physical environment. Most of the former residents had stories about dangerous, even deadly, accidents. A 1983 study noted that official neglect for the site brought on a willingness by some residents to "accelerate the damages" in a deliberate strategy of "*la politique du pire*," where rapid degradation would hopefully force needed change after multiple attempts at more positive action had failed.[193]

Local officials proved more responsive to cité outsiders' anxieties about racial concentration and political activism than they did about the residents' own pressing concerns. When a delegation of Algerians wrote directly to the prefecture to demand that officials press Simon to conduct needed repairs and maintenance, their protests about their living situation had no noticeable effect.[194] City officials, however, did capture the prefect's attention. Beginning in 1966, Villeurbanne mayor Étienne Gagnaire's office was seized by petitions from the areas around the cité.[195] Gagnaire turned to the prefecture for help. Reminding departmental officials of his previous concerns for the neighborhood, he wrote, "Not only is this situation continuing, but it is worsening to the point that one starts to ask, whether, in the coming days, more serious—even grave—problems will arise."[196] The department began to include Olivier de Serres in its discussions of the region's bidonvilles as an example of how even new constructions could rapidly degrade seemingly by the mere presence of North African migrants.[197] In the aftermath of May–June 1968, the Olivier de Serres neighborhood also attracted leftist activists (mostly Maoists), whose presence alarmed the local police, the municipality, the department, and Simon himself.[198]

Deeply concerned by what they saw as an "island of North

Africans," prefectural officials joined Mayor Gagnaire in his quest
to undo Olivier de Serres's demographics. This, however, was far
from easy. As long as Simon refused to change his leasing practices, there were no legal means to force him to do so (though the
mayor and prefecture looked desperately).[199] Their first attempt,
to curtail Simon based on his exploitative rents and fees, got them
nowhere. A departmental report from 1969 even seemed to support Simon on this matter, arguing that he was giving options
to "numerous Algerian families, previously so poorly housed in
the Lyon agglomeration," and that though his rents were high, the
migrants were able to afford the cité's rates given their housing
allowances.[200] Housing and urban development policies, so well
honed in previous years as a tool for closing bidonvilles, were ineffective against an intransigent private landlord.

At this point, the local administrations shifted gears to consider
the effect migration might be having on the region's schools. Many
of the complaints about Olivier de Serres came from white parents and school organizations, echoing Vaujour's earlier anxieties
about the influence of North African children on their "French"
peers.[201] Algerian parents in Olivier de Serres had their own set
of concerns. Mme B., cited above, sent her children away to a private school "to distance them from the neighborhood; that's what
saved them." Driss recalled local teachers' easy dismissals of cité
children and assertions that they could "do nothing with their
lives." Rachid recounted a writing assignment about family practices for Christmas, admiring the bravery of the first student who
said they had none and noting the surprise of the instructor at this
fact.[202] Such everyday prejudice was not, however, addressed by
local officials' inquiries.

In October 1969, the prefecture asked the department's Inspecteur
d'Académie to look more closely at the nearby schools.[203] Both the
boys' and girls' primary schools at rue Berthelot and Jules Ferry
were found to have 64–67 percent foreign students, the vast majority identified as "Arab." Though insisting that parents did not have
pedagogical reasons to worry, the report allowed that their concerns could also derive from racial anxieties, particularly "the

repugnance French families can have for the sometimes insufficient hygiene, cleanliness, and education practices of foreign little ones." The report offered some reassurance to French families worried about their children's learning. In particular, the practice of dividing classes into "normal or strong groups" with a French majority and "weak" groups with a majority of foreigners allowed them "not to lower the level of normal classes" and provided "a progressive and rational integration" for foreigners.[204] The inspector's recommendations emphasized stronger enforcement of hygiene standards as well as launching additional introductory courses, hiring more teachers, and reducing class sizes.[205] Notably, this report did not include a suggestion for limiting foreigners' access to these particular schools, though that would be the ultimate policy result. Yet both the inspector's report and the popular opinions it included displayed a set of racist assumptions about the conduct and abilities of North African children, as well as a continued emphasis on the need to modernize migrants' habits and living standards.

The prefecture surveyed all the schools around Lyon in order to determine which had the largest proportion of "foreign" students. A dozen neighborhoods in the region were identified as having more than 45 percent migrants.[206] Later justifications for the policy maintained that the sociologically sound ratio for foreign students was capped at 30 percent, employing a similar logic to the housing quotas discussed above.[207] The prefect's report to the Interior and Labor Ministries made special note of the "very strong density of the North African population" caused by Simon's property.[208] With ministerial approval, the prefect released a regulation on June 15, 1970, to ban new migrants from these neighborhoods. The policy included a request that local officials also "limit as much as possible the regularization of families arriving to settle in other neighborhoods." The one exception to these new rules was for migrants arriving from the European Economic Community—effectively increasing the policy's weight on African and other non-European families.[209] Indeed, initial correspondence with the national ministries specifically identified the policy as one that concerned "Algerian workers and other North

Africans."[210] While many later discussions would insist that the policy was without any racial bias, it was clear to all that North African migrants were the most affected and that the new rules were meant to benefit the city's white families.

As the prefect explained to Mayor Gagnaire, the new policy "targeted in particular the neighborhood of rue Olivier de Serres."[211] Defending the policy to state ministries, Prefect Max Moulins (1966–72) insisted that the number of North African students in the four neighborhood schools was over 70 percent, which "rendered useless all pedagogical efforts in the schools, to say nothing of the impossibility of teaching." Moreover, things seemed likely only to worsen. According to Moulins, having so many young Maghrebins around "poses problems of social relations and public order in the neighborhood. . . . French families refuse, in fact, to live there and foreign families already resident in France consider living in this neighborhood as a regression."[212] The rhetoric of delinquency appeared repeatedly in popular complaints, in city and departmental discussions, and in correspondence with the local police. Shortly before enacting the school policy, Moulins notified Gagnaire that police were setting up a permanent daily surveillance around Olivier de Serres.[213]

The prefect explicitly maintained that the June circular "did not represent discriminatory measures, but rather measures for public order."[214] Yet later reports reinforced the explicit targeting of North Africans. While the overall foreign percentage remained the main qualifier for schools to make the list, "Arab" or "North African" children were tracked separately for all schools.[215] In a situation where crime—and even place—were so racially coded, distinguishing appeals to order from racial discrimination became essentially impossible. Olivier de Serres families "grievously resented" the segregation they faced and the inability of their supposed allies to prevent the situation from continuing to worsen.[216] A group of Algerian parents petitioned Gagnaire to address school disparities that served as "very large proof that racism exists in France."[217] Indeed, by 1974, with the opening of a new school in the neighborhood to which only white children were initially accepted, the national magazine *Le Point* concluded that a system of "apartheid" now reigned in Villeurbanne.[218]

This new policy seemed to offer Gagnaire and the Rhône prefecture a legal means of denying North Africans the right to settle in Olivier de Serres. Of course, achieving the desired dispersal of North Africans living in that cité alone would have required even more massive investment in social housing; one estimate claimed that a total of 6,400 units would be needed if the quota principle was to remain intact.[219] Moreover, a large number of North African families in the Rhône were coming from within France and so were not subject to the June 1970 regulation.[220] Other families could settle in nearby departments long enough to acquire the correct status and then return to the "high-density foreign neighborhoods that we [the French officials] want to protect."[221] Yet the biggest obstacle to implementing this policy would come from the strength and breadth of public opposition (detailed in chapters 5 and 6).

The case of Olivier de Serres and the June 1970 circular reveal the use of education as a convenient policy lever to enact racialized resettlement projects in the Rhône. But this emphasis on education also points back to one of the underlying logics of all the urban renewal projects discussed here: the desire to mold what French officials and the public would see as an appropriately modernized—civilized—urban population. Moulins, Gagnaire, and their associates repeatedly characterized local North Africans as uncivilized and disorderly. The June 1970 circular sought to impose order by literally and figuratively cleaning up both schools and neighborhoods: creating new educational spaces that, like the cités de transit, were intended to inculcate French values of hygiene, high learning standards, and political conformity. In short, this was yet another attempt to resurrect the imperial civilizing mission in the postcolonial metropole.[222]

For their part, North African residents from Olivier de Serres had a mixed response to this policy of racial redistribution. As much as the younger residents enjoyed their sense of belonging, they had seen it evaporate over time. Driss explained that being together in the cité meant "we weren't completely uprooted, but it became more difficult when demolition began and the inhabitants were scattered throughout the Lyon agglomeration. In one sense, it was a good thing, because we were obliged to integrate, but in another it was difficult; we grew up with these people and from one day to the next we were separated." Karim testified that their "ghetto life" derived from "an abnormal ethnic consolidation"; in his eyes, it would have been better "to disperse these families." A self-professed "intercultural" humanist, Karim later clarified that "there should not have been such a consolidation of the population, despite the advantages it gave people. It had the result of separating two populations, and that is never good; it's contrary to—I wouldn't say integration (I don't know for that matter who should integrate into whom)—but I would say contrary to a necessary pluralism. It's very bad to concentrate minorities and we need to prevent it from happening again."[223] These ideas of community mixing, which deny any racial or cultural hierarchy, clearly derived from a different set of assumptions than those of the policy-makers. Moreover, these former children of Olivier de Serres invoked their sense of belonging in French society in their own right (unlike their parents' long-held desires to eventually return to Algeria).

There is irony in the fact that the HLMs built around Paris and Lyon soon transformed into the new symbol of France's failing banlieues. These constructions never were intended to become immigrant strongholds, as SONACOTRA/L and other quotas made clear, but rather were built as a modern and progressive reply to the endemic housing crisis faced by metropolitan French. Asnières's renovation in particular was directed by progressive urban developers, heirs to Le Corbusier's vision of modern, rational city planning and architecture.[224] Claudius-Petit, in particular, brought to SONACOTRA/L a belief in the centralized promotion of modern values through housing policy and the ability to use construction to affect inhabitants' morals and morale.[225] By the 1960s, public opinion had rejected Le Corbusier's visions for gigantic residential blocks, preferring "the real city, with streets, passers-by, shops and ateliers."[226] Yet most of the HLMs built to absorb the bidonvilles and the rest of the country's insalubrious housing were built as gigantic towers and complexes.

Amid these shifting visions of the modern city, one constant was that North Africans were believed to be an obstacle to achieving the ideal urban community. In each of the cases discussed in this chapter, migrant workers and their families were perceived as less than modern—less than civilized—and certainly less than citizens. That Algerians actually did have citizenship rights after 1949 (and could choose to keep these even after Algerian independence in 1962) did not affect these local officials' opinions—though chapter 3 will discuss how Rhône officials and their allies reinterpreted and limited Algerian migrants' rights during the Algerian War. Formal national citizenship did not entail actual community belonging and therefore did not inspire any sense of obligation or responsibility on the part of municipal actors—particularly when they had their own racialized ideas about who should be considered part of their community.[227] Indeed, part of the imprecision in city records over migrants' identity as North Africans or, more specifically, as Algerians may be connected to this fundamental disinterest in Algerians as citizens. It is precisely on this issue of belonging, however, that experiences in the Parisian suburb of Saint-Denis differed so significantly. As easily as the examples in this chapter fit into the typical national narrative of North African exclusion, many of the stories that follow challenge and reshape that understanding.

TWO

Politics

I n June 1950, Auguste Gillot, the communist mayor of Saint-Denis, hosted a tea for the city's North African residents in honor of the Muslim holy month of Ramadan. The municipality's goal was to ensure "that the North Africans feel 'at home' and to signify as well that the Party respects the traditions and morals of the peoples from the overseas departments."[1] Invitations for the event were printed in French on one side and Arabic on the other.[2] In his address to the gathering, Gillot proclaimed, "For us, the respect for traditions, for religions, for morals, for language, for our Algerian brothers, corresponds exactly with our will . . . for the common struggle against a common enemy: colonialism, fruit of imperialism, the oppressor of colonial peoples." Gillot explicitly linked this broader imperial opposition to the work his municipality had been doing on behalf of migrant workers in the city: "We are taking action in Saint-Denis because we love the Algerian people, who suffer misery, unemployment, and repression."[3] These were not just empty words. The Ramadan tea coincided with a flurry of municipal activity on behalf of North African migrants. City officials helped provide housing, education, welfare, and other social benefits. From 1945 well into the 1960s, Saint-Denis's elected officials were significantly more inclusive in both rhetoric and action than their counterparts in other French cities.

This chapter investigates how elected PCF (French Communist Party) officials anchored their activism for North African rights and welfare within their politics. Where the previous chapter examined local officials—both elected and appointed—whose goals, priorities, and motivations neatly aligned with other state actors, the focus here is on difference from—even resistance to—those prevailing notions. Saint-Denis had long been one of the brightest stars in the Paris "Red Belt," and the decades after World War II were unquestionably colored by the municipality's steadfast communist affiliation. City officials' strident rhetoric in support of North Africans set Saint-Denis apart from municipalities that felt no obligation to work for the benefit of North African migrants. Indeed, migrants were well aware of communist city officials' greater willingness to listen to their concerns and often appealed specifically to PCF municipalities for aid.[4]

From the very beginning of the postwar era, city officials in Saint-Denis articulated a place for North African migrants as members of their working-class city and constituents within their worker-centered politics. In part, this stemmed from a broader ideological solidarity; Dionysien communists' embrace of North Africans as comrades in the international worker's struggle is considered more closely in chapter 6. Yet PCF officials in Saint-Denis also involved themselves in issues of North African rights and welfare with more immediate political goals. First, social services and rhetorical support cultivated local North Africans as potential PCF voters, particularly after the 1947 law granting Algerians full citizenship rights in the metropole. Second, critiquing national policies that failed to adequately support North African migrants provided a convenient vehicle for the communist politics of opposition to the French state.

In their efforts to shore up electoral support, Saint-Denis's officials dedicated a considerable amount of energy to North African initiatives and to making sure those initiatives were well publicized. The municipality commissioned reports to tally their activities and interactions with the local North African community. To make migrants aware of these efforts, the municipal council distributed a "work plan" to the North Africans in the city.[5] Officials looked to launch a bilingual French-Arabic newspaper, supported by the municipality, the unions, and the local PCF sections, "whose goal would be the defense of the North African colony in Saint-Denis." They sought to incorporate North Africans into the local political system, asking that both elected officials and the heads of local PCF sections maintain daily contact with North African workers.[6] They even created a consultative commission comprising ten North Africans and two French communists.[7] As we have seen, not all local leaders cultivated support from—or even deigned to listen to—the North Africans in their communities. Indeed, in Vénissieux, we will see that not even all elected communists engaged migrants in this way. Yet Saint-Denis's elected city leaders worked hard to be perceived by migrants as the guarantors of social benefits and the authoritative means of accessing other governmental services. This intention to speak on behalf of people officials believed could not—or perhaps should not—speak for themselves demonstrates a degree of paternalism, as did the pursuit of priorities set by the municipality and not necessarily by local migrants. However, the fact that North Africans were consulted and included—even that the discussions took place at all—speaks to significantly more direct involvement than may be observed elsewhere during this period.

At the same time, Dionysien communists' political identity was grounded in opposition to the national state. Mayor Gillot and his colleagues never missed an opportunity to lambaste policies and programs they believed to be insufficient, ineffective, and downright imperialist. This combative spirit contributed to municipal difficulties in mobilizing support from the national government for its reconstruction efforts. City officials constantly wrangled over finances, insisting that local funds should not be relied upon to address the housing crisis and demanding greater contributions from departmental and national budgets. Often, Dionysien officials played the role of watchdog: quick to criticize the missteps and failures of the state and insistent in their demands for attention and support from upper levels of government. Political friction exacerbated misunderstandings and poor communication, which in turn led to slower construction and development.

In the end, these two sets of political interests—electoral and oppositional—proved to be at cross-purposes. Endless arguments with state officials hindered municipal efforts to provide meaningful support. The rocky process of bidonville resorption and migrant rehousing contributed to a growing sense of migrant fatigue in the city. Moreover, Algerian independence in 1962 meant that many migrants were no longer participating in French politics, claiming Algerian citizenship instead. By the 1970s, though the municipality had not given up its support for North Africans entirely, Saint-Denis proved less willing to welcome migrants with open arms. Vénissieux's elected communists, already less enthusiastic in their support for local North Africans, also increased opposition to newly arriving migrants and their families.

Cultivating North African Votes

The time, energy, and political capital spent by Dionysien municipal officials on issues of North African welfare signaled their desire to develop and maintain influence within that community. Indeed, a number of election cycles witnessed specific appeals to North African voters. Political groups on the French left had cultivated North African support since the 1930s, both on the mainland and in the empire.[8] At one point, Saint-Denis city officials attempted to register North African migrants as voters, though their status at the time as French subjects precluded their enfranchisement.[9] By the early 1950s, once Algerians had been granted voting rights in the metropole, Mayor Gillot went out of his way to court North African workers. Table 2.1 demonstrates PCF dominance through the 1950s, including a major jump in support in 1959, at the height of the Algerian War (a signature issue for local communists, as shown in chapter 4).

This broad system of migrant support contrasts with the clientelism seen in cities like Marseille. In the first place, as Ed Naylor explains, Algerians in Marseille were "perceived as a non-voting block" and therefore not worth political investment.[10] Dionysien politicians clearly did not share this opinion and devoted significant time and money to North African concerns. At a deeper

Table 2.1. The PCF in Saint-Denis's
municipal government, 1945–59

Year	Members of the municipal council	Percentage of total vote
1945	36 of 36	60.34
1947	23 of 37	58.2
1953	23 of 37	60.87
1959	37 of 37	65.88

Notes: Created by author from Préfecture de la Seine, "Projet de rénovation de la commune de Saint-Denis: Examen des répercussions politiques," April 29, 1961 (AP, PEROTIN 101/78/1–19).

level, Saint-Denis's PCF officials' relationships with migrant constituents seemed to be much richer than the patronage networks described by both Naylor and Minayo Nasiali.[11] Beyond a simple attempt to buy votes, Saint-Denis's municipal leaders incorporated North African workers' demands into their overall political platform. The breadth of challenges facing North Africans in France, and within the empire, resonated with local communists' ideological convictions. Publicly embracing North Africans—even imperfectly—strengthened their political position on nearly all fronts.

North African migrants were considered an important enough voting bloc that other local actors made numerous attempts to turn them against the PCF. "Do not let yourselves be duped or maneuvered by the Communist Party," cried a 1952 pamphlet. "For whom do they take us in Moscow?" demanded another.[12] These counterpropaganda pieces warned that the communists wished to reinstate the infamous North African Brigades from the interwar period and appealed to North Africans not to participate in May 1 strikes or demonstrations. Police ideas about the relations between Algerians and communists may have influenced the decision to designate North African population density on their maps of the Paris region with ever-deeper shades of red.[13] With or without North

African voters, the PCF lost ground nationally in 1951, becoming only the second largest party represented in the National Assembly (behind the Gaullist Rassemblement du peuple français [RPF]).[14] This then raises the question of just how many North African workers voted over the 1950s and '60s.

According to census figures, Algerians did represent a sizable slice of the Dionysien population. In 1954, 4,468 of the city's 80,705 residents were counted as Algerian. In 1962, Algerians constituted 8,101 of 95,072, and in 1968, North Africans (Algerians no longer being counted on their own) were 7,800 out of 100,060.[15] Table 2.2 details the number of Algerians on the local electoral rolls. The registration rate was highest in 1956, around the time that municipal politicos were most actively promoting North African social issues and most outspoken about the war in Algeria. A massive sign-up drive ahead of the 1956 elections added 792 Algerians (and 2,888 others) to the municipal electoral rolls in a single day.[16] The decline shown for 1961–62 likely indicates local Algerians' preoccupation with political developments outside of Saint-Denis, along with a possible hesitancy to engage with a French state grown increasingly suspicious of Algerian residents. In 1958, the police remarked that few North Africans were attending political events or meetings.[17] The numbers dropped precipitously after 1962, with the abrupt change in Algerians' citizenship status: no longer were Algerians citizens with full rights on French soil; their nationality had to be affirmed and voting rights reclaimed.

The election of René Benhamou as municipal councillor stands as one possible marker for the political inclusion of North African migrants. Benhamou was born in France to North African parents, most likely of Jewish origin.[18] Neither Benhamou's religion nor his ethnic origins were ever mentioned in municipal documents or the local press. The municipal council's selection of Benhamou as fifth deputy mayor in 1953 did arouse comment—but only because of his youth.[19] When he first stood for election in 1953, *Saint-Denis Républicain* listed his occupation as an electrician and noted that he was an "orphan of the war '39–'45" whose "parents died for France"; a 1954 letter from Gillot declares that his parents "were assassinated by German Hitler-ites [*sic*]."[20]

Table 2.2. Algerians registered to vote in Saint-Denis, 1956–64

Date	Men	Women	Total
March 31, 1956	2272	26	2298
March 31, 1960	1378	55	1433
March 31, 1961	1393	71	1464
March 31, 1963	264	28	292
March 31, 1964	258	29	287

Notes: Created by author from "Listes électorales: Statistiques sur le nombre d'inscrits d'origine algérienne," April 29, 1964 (AMSD, 37 AC 17). In February 1964, the total number of registered voters was 45,421. "Nombre d'électeurs inscrits," 1969 (AMSD, 10 S 120). Note that up until 1962, the women registered in Saint-Denis would not have been allowed to vote back in Algeria.

The Paris police, however, pegged Benhamou as Muslim, declaring that the North Africans in Saint-Denis "maintained good relations with the municipality, in which one of their coreligionists is deputy mayor."[21] The police may not have been known for their subtlety in distinguishing various ethnic and religious groups from North Africa; however, the greater population often failed to differentiate as well. Local reactions to the Algerian War may be gauged in part by Benhamou's remarkable persistence on the municipal council over the course of the conflict and his promotion to third deputy mayor in 1959 (at its height). For the Dionysien municipality, his presence clearly did not signal any conflict of interest and may have shored up local officials' views. Benhamou worked on many issues with immediate relevance to local North African migrants. His portfolio included housing, urban development, and culture; he also served as vice president for the city's local HLM (Habitation à loyer modéré) office. That a man with a North African name, perceived by many voters and community members as an indicator of Muslim roots, would be elected to the municipal council and then as deputy mayor speaks volumes for the level of North African inclusion in the local political scene.

It is worth asking whether communist activism within the local North African community translated to solid electoral support. Evidence is scant for this sort of evaluation. A police investigation from 1948 suggested that "contrary to their predecessors from before 1939, [North Africans] appear closed to communist propaganda."[22] Records from 1965 suggest that PCF attempts to co-opt sub-Saharan migrants bore little fruit (though sub-Saharan Africans may have already been swayed by their dissatisfaction with the management of foyers in communist towns).[23] Migrants from both North and sub-Saharan Africa seemed less interested in political allegiances than in being left alone to work and live in France.[24] An analysis of North African voting habits in Saint-Denis in the 1980s concluded, "There does not exist an 'Arab vote' any more than a 'Jewish vote.'"[25] If the majority of Algerian workers in Saint-Denis voted with the PCF in the 1950s and '60s, they reflected the overwhelming political color of the city at that time. Certainly, their social position (and perhaps their anti-imperial aspirations) would have made them natural allies for local communists. Local pandering to issues relevant to North African voters did not, however, cause the municipality to veer off of its traditional message and goals; rather, issues of housing, social benefits for workers, and even positioning on foreign affairs flowed naturally from the agenda set by communists in Saint-Denis for decades.

Early Social Activism

As early as 1946, the municipal council debated both the housing of North African workers in France and the lack of freedom in imperial Algeria. The formal vote extended the city's "warm, fraternal salute to the thousands of North African workers arriving in Saint-Denis" and then denounced the terrible and unhygienic living conditions to which these migrants were subjected, emphasizing in particular the dangers of disease.[26] This official welcome and the determination to take direct action came a decade before most other French municipal initiatives (with the exception of the Part-Dieu center in Lyon) and even before most major regional and national programs. Later municipal reports would

highlight their early and sustained attention to the migrant housing crisis even as they denied charges that they were politicizing
reconstruction.[27]

To make good on this first call to action, the municipal council
voted to transform a cluster of barracks—La Grande Caserne—into
a foyer for North African workers. From the start, the city council was frustrated in its efforts. The War Ministry first claimed
it required La Caserne to house German POWs,[28] which led the
municipality to make frequent use of the notion that the government was providing for "Nazis" and "fascists" what they would
not give to their own North African citizens.[29] When plans for a
foyer at the Fort Double-Couronne moved ahead in 1949, Gillot
insisted that the municipality be kept informed about all developments, given their concern for local North African workers
and the "daily" contacts they had with these migrants.[30] He deemed
the French state responsible for the migrants' presence and their
miserable conditions and thus obliged to fund and organize the
projects to alleviate these workers' misery. Meanwhile, the municipality's role was to be the personal interface between individual North Africans and the state. Insisting on the municipality's
right "to participate actively in the direction of the Center,"[31] Gillot staked out a position for the city as the sole authoritative voice
both to lobby upward on behalf of North African workers and to
convey information—and services—downward to those workers. North African issues thus served as a dual political tool. Supporting migrants' rights and welfare was a means to oppose the
state through criticism and demands. It further established a set
of services the city could claim as its own in order to be seen by
the North Africans as the bearers of generous aid and banners of
resistance.

Saint-Denis's progressive policies thus did not entirely escape
paternalism. City officials' attempts to provide services to their
North African inhabitants often followed the city's preferences
rather than those of the North Africans themselves. The PCF's
habit of criticizing the French state for the migrants' poor conditions also required that the city make itself the mouthpiece of

this population and its concerns. Yet Gillot and his colleagues did not operate entirely without input from North African workers. A delegation sent to the War Ministry in 1949 included a few North Africans. The mayor regularly met with individual migrants who sought his help, and he made inquiries on their behalf. When a delegation of residents from the Double-Couronne foyer petitioned the municipality with protests against high fees, a crowded and unhygienic environment, and the practice of expelling unemployed residents, Gillot forwarded these complaints directly to the Seine prefect, using the delegation's own words in the phrasing of the letter.[32]

The municipality also looked to unions for support and input on North African migrant questions. Local workers staged a strike in 1947 to demand that the Caserne be transformed into housing for North Africans employed in Saint-Denis's factories. One strike committee insisted, "It is inadmissible that a people already so oppressed by colonialism is further compelled in our Republic to sleep on the ground. . . . These comrades have always been and will always be good cannon-fodder, profiting only those who oppress them."[33] Gillot and the municipality insisted that unions be involved in governing any North African housing centers.[34] They trusted workers' organizations to act for the benefit of the North Africans even as they shied away from cooperation with the national government. This desire to include unions underlined city officials' allegiance to a workers' party. Union participation may also have been seen as extra weight to balance the needs and rights of the North African workers against the interests of an unknown association and their collaborators, the local employers. In this way, the foyer's committee became a microcosm in the greater social struggle of the working class and its allies against the state and the industrialists.

Saint-Denis's municipal support for North Africans extended far beyond housing. This involvement in a breadth of social welfare concerns further set them apart from other local actors. As staunch communists, members of Saint-Denis's municipality emphasized the central role of labor and workers in their community. As early as

1949, Gillot and the municipal council were agitating to expand a variety of social rights to migrants, especially with regard to employment and welfare benefits. They demanded, for example, that all Algerian workers be included on the unemployment rolls.[35] While this was technically already the case for migrants who had resided in a given community for more than six months, many Algerians were recent arrivals and thus fell through the cracks.[36] Focusing on the effects of the residency clause highlighted the ways that Algerians, though legally French citizens, were subject to subtle forms of discrimination from a national state that demanded their labor but cared little for their welfare. Beyond distributing national unemployment benefits, the city made specific provisions to aid North African workers directly from the city budget. Most of these funds were allocated to various centers and organizations working in the city, while a portion was reserved for "emergency support" to individuals in dire circumstances.[37] Building on traditions of mutual aid, Saint-Denis was willing to devote finite resources to support local migrants.

While money was lacking, paper was not. The city hall received many letters and visits from unemployed North Africans seeking work. In response, municipal officials penned countless letters of recommendation on their behalf.[38] The municipality sent most of the North Africans they met on to the Seine prefecture's Placement Office, run by the department's North African social counselors. This is curious given the municipality's habitual distrust of the social counselors, who operated (if indirectly) under the auspices of the police prefecture. It seems that social counselors' employment placement record was strong enough to override municipal concerns even as housing and educational programs remained suspect. The number of North Africans who made return visits and the letters from employers claiming to have no space suggests that municipal support went only so far. However, these letters attest to the municipality's readiness to deal personally with North African workers—many who wrote asking for aid received invitations to meet with a deputy mayor—and to intercede on their behalf. Occasionally, they even found open positions within the city's own service sector. Municipal officials never missed an opportunity to point out the ineligibility of candidates for unemployment benefits in their missives to departmental and national offices.[39] Their work on individual cases thus supported their overall political platform.

North African petitioners tended to draw from a set of ideals to make their cases. As seen in chapter 1, Algerian workers in particular staked their claim to Frenchness as well as to a city identity. What differed in Saint-Denis was municipal officials' willingness to accept, repeat, and even bolster these claims in their interventions on behalf of these migrants. Moreover, the case for belonging, in particular, supported Dionysien communists' vision of North Africans as part of their political contingent. Many North African petitioners specified how long they had been in the city itself (ranging from two months to forty years) to establish their right to ask for municipal support. Veterans never failed to mention their military service, citing their time in the French ranks (sometimes as POWs) as an affirmation of French loyalty. Migrants further invoked their family situations, both confirming their value as heads of households and eliciting sympathy for their minor children. Though the vast majority of workers who appealed to the municipality for help were unskilled, those who had particular skills emphasized both their training, to set themselves apart, and their willingness to accept any paying job so as not to discourage employers from taking them on at lower rates.[40] All these strategies could be effective not only in garnering municipal attention, which seemed predisposed to their plight, but also in aiding city officials in making their case to other state services and to local employers. In 1952, the municipality announced it would hire a North African interpreter to work in the city hall three mornings a week and "devote himself especially to questions concerning North African workers."[41] This action may be read both as an indication of the numbers of North Africans appealing to the municipality for aid and as further evidence of municipal willingness to work directly with these migrants and ease their interaction with the French state system.

Chronic unemployment was not the only situation for which the municipality offered material aid to North African workers. Migrant workers' abysmal living conditions increased the incidence of disaster, especially fires. These all-too-frequent incidents spurred the municipality to action. In one of the worst of these fires, two decrepit buildings burned down at rue du Landy and rue des Renouillères in May 1956. The following morning, city hall "immediately arranged for monetary aid, . . . distribution of free clothing, [and] a canteen for the children."[42] The municipality requisitioned an unoccupied building on rue Ernest Renan to provisionally house twelve of the victims—single working men—and attempted, unsuccessfully, to convince the Association des foyers nord-africains de la région parisienne (AFNA) to move them to a new foyer at the chemin de Marville, still in Saint-Denis.[43] In November 1956, another fire left eight North Africans homeless on the rue du Canal. The municipality opened a room in one of its own buildings to provide temporary shelter for the men and offered each of them a small emergency grant. The city again looked for placements in AFNA's Marville foyer and requested additional monetary aid.[44] By seeking to keep the men resident in Saint-Denis, the city both hoped to keep local supporters on their soil and attempted to address the migrants' frequent complaints that government plans to rehouse North Africans too often moved them away from their jobs.

The municipality also looked for ways to raise North African workers' social position more permanently. In 1949, the municipal council demanded that the Labor Ministry establish a center for vocational training.[45] By the early 1950s, municipal officials supported measures to further the education of the North African workers in their city. The majority of these workers were poorly educated, spoke little or no French, and were functionally illiterate, all of which curbed their potential for professional advancement. Moreover, it left them ignorant of their rights and unable to argue effectively for access to those rights. Education initiatives could also serve a political recruiting purpose. In 1952, national officials acknowledged that the PCF's "official goal is to fight against illiteracy" but insisted that "the instructions given to those in charge [of courses] remind them to select from their North-African pupils future militants liable to organize their coreligionists."[46]

In October 1950, Saint-Denis struck a deal with the Education Ministry, agreeing to host evening classes for North African workers, provided the ministry funded two-thirds of the operating costs. To advertise these courses and recruit students, the school director for the program held a series of informational meetings in cafés in North African neighborhoods and posted information in various cafés and workers' hotels. He was accompanied on his rounds by a North African bus driver, "completely devoted to the school and especially to these evening classes," who would engage the workers in conversation in Arabic and aid the director in convincing them to attend the classes. In his December report to the municipality, the director claimed success for his recruitment process. Some meetings gathered up to sixty students, though a range of thirty-five to forty was more typical. Regular attendance was rare—many of the students worked changing night shifts—and the director cited high dropout rates. His reports revealed the tension between available material provisions and the desire to reach as many students as possible; even as he lamented the lower attendance, he remarked that classes of more than forty-five were "too large to make for good work" and that the current numbers were more manageable and productive.[47]

This project highlights some of the qualities that the municipality demonstrated more generally in its relations to North African workers. City officials were reliant on upper levels of government for funding these programs and pushed to shift the financial burden out of their own (admittedly much smaller) coffers. At the same time, they were ready to engage individual North Africans not only to bridge the linguistic gap but also to provide a more comfortable entry into the workers' world. One senses that the director would not have had an easy time convincing workers to come to his night classes without help in allaying some of the North Africans' suspicion of representatives (however indirect) of the French authorities. The director's reports also indicated an underlying frustration with the North Africans; if allowances were made for the obstacles to finding time for regular evening classes, there was little understanding of the perceived unwillingness or inability of migrants to struggle through the difficulties they encountered. As was so often the case among those who worked with and hoped to better the situation of North Africans (and other migrants) in France, the line between goodwill and paternalism was almost impossibly fuzzy.

In 1953, the municipality refused to provide a location for a new professional training center run by the Labor Ministry.[48] This was one in a series of rebuffs to other governmental organizations that seem strange in the context of municipal policy toward North African workers. The municipality railed against the state for doing too little and constantly demanded further funding. Yet when presented with the opportunity to cooperate on a program intended to correct problems identified by the city, officials backed away. This reticence derived from their deep distrust of the state's motives. Saint-Denis's municipal officials had long refused to provide the Seine prefecture with an office for a social counselor for North Africans. In 1951, the city rejected the first request for a room in city hall after consulting with Waldeck l'Huillier, the PCF mayor of Gennevilliers.[49] L'Huillier had refused to back the program, worried that the counselors were too closely linked to surveillance operations: "On the one hand, something must be done for the North Africans, but on the other, we don't want to deliver them into the hands of the Police."[50] A decade later, Dionysien officials continued to deny requests for a meeting room for police-run social services.[51] Dionysien concerns over police involvement in North African issues were equally present in their housing debates; only in 1965 did Saint-Denis solicit help from SONACOTRA to deal with the bidonvilles at les Cornillons and les Francs-Moisins.[52] For officials in Saint-Denis, the state's role in questions of migrant welfare was to be solely one of financial backing.

Dionysien unwillingness to collaborate thus comprised both a desire to be perceived as the generous beneficiary to the North African community and an anxiety—not unfounded—that some

of the social programs set up by the French government for Algerians were too closely related to national security and policing policies.[53] When, in 1962, the Education Ministry laid out a proposal
for general and home economics courses for "Muslim" women in
the Paris region, this concern prevailed. The Union of Mayors
in the Seine and the General Council for the Seine entreated Saint-
Denis to accept a role in the program. First, they explained that
they were not seeking physical space to hold the classes; this having proved a problem in the past, the ministry proposed to host
the classes in a mobile truck set up as a classroom. More importantly, they stressed the purely educational motives for the project: "The assurances we have received permit us to affirm that this
does not entail an operation of political or confessional supervision [*encadrement*]."[54] The authors could not have been clearer in
their desire to disassociate the program from policing or population control efforts, suggesting that this issue was the key to the
municipality's concerns and previous rejections. Nevertheless,
Saint-Denis's officials rebuffed the initiative.

The Dionysien city hall continued to promote literacy and other
courses for North African workers into the 1960s.[55] For nearly two
decades, municipal officials were strong proponents of North African rights in matters of housing, unemployment, and education
and even in moments of crisis. This broad interest in and action
for these migrants proves that Gillot's invocation of brotherhood
in his 1951 speech was not empty rhetoric. In every instance, elected
PCF officials framed their engagement with local North Africans
as part of their dedication to fellow workers and emphasized their
policies and positions as part of their broader political platform. It
was largely their politics that helped them make space for North
African migrants.

The Politics of Opposition and the Bidonvilles

Saint-Denis's lengthy project to rid the city of its bidonvilles was
often stymied by the municipality's habit of contesting departmental and national initiatives. The municipal council issued its first
official call for the "resorption of the bidonvilles" in November

1957.[56] Yet despite this early awareness and the subsequent organization of city resources for addressing migrant housing, actual
construction and rehousing in Saint-Denis followed a much slower
pace than was seen in nearby Asnières. The program to rid the
city of its bidonvilles started in earnest only in the mid-1960s,
when Asnières had all but finished the renovation of the northern zone, and was not successful until 1973. This decreased tempo
reflected a number of difficulties facing the Dionysien municipality. In particular, they had a troubled relationship with other state
authorities—the prefectures, the police, the ministries.

Local officials proved more adept at identifying the failings of
state policies than they were at making use of the tools these provided. The Dionysien municipality made demands, not requests.
Elected officials refused to acknowledge work that had been done
by SONACOTRA/L, the Seine prefecture, or other associations and
were fiercely territorial over the city's level of input for new construction. Scholars of French local politics have often remarked
on communist successes in renovating and rebuilding their cities,
which benefited both their communities and their own electoral
records.[57] Tyler Stovall, for example, attributes the staying power of
nearby Bobigny's communists less to their ideological purity and
more to their "ability to solve concrete problems for the community's residents."[58] Construction was not, of course, the sole purview of PCF municipalities. It can be no accident that Asnières—a
political outlier in the Paris region—built a legacy of political stability and support for the Gaullist mayor, Bokanowski, on the foundations of the massive renovation project in the northern zone.
Indeed, one police analysis suggested that only Bokanowski's significant urbanization achievements were holding off a coordinated
attack from the city's socialists and communists.[59]

Asnières's example sheds further light on the contentious communist relationship with other state offices, raising the possibility
that Saint-Denis's difficult experience with bidonville resorption
was rooted in the rockier soil of the Dionysien politics of opposition. Asniérois correspondence with departmental and national
bodies was significantly more congenial. Bokanowski received

letters from other ministries addressed to "Mon cher Michel,"[60] whereas Auguste Gillot was "dear" only to fellow communists. Asnières's renovation and construction files likewise gave no indication of heated debates over the purpose or implementation of projects. Asniérois correspondence typically included espousals of common interest, requests based on mutual understandings, and expressions of gratitude for aid in any given matter.[61] This collegiality was rooted in the shared assumptions and goals of elected city officials and appointed state experts.

In contrast, city officials in Saint-Denis faithfully followed the tenets set out by the Second World Congress of the Communist International in 1920: both attending to "the interests of the poorest part of the population" and seizing "every opportunity to reveal the obstacles raised by the bourgeois state against all radical reforms."[62] Roger Bourderon, historian and former Saint-Denis municipal councillor, affirms that during the decades after World War II, "The politics of the city, its difficulties, its accomplishments, were placed permanently in a relationship with the general platform of the [national] government, which the municipal council's resolutions did not hesitate to criticize on a regular basis."[63] Myriad Dionysien municipal votes castigated government policies on housing, social welfare, and the Algerian War. In many cases, the prefecture then demanded that these votes be rescinded. The police prefect revoked numerous Dionysien municipal council votes and declarations on foreign policy issues.[64] In rare cases, municipal action led to official reprimands.[65] The municipality lodged complaints of its own, running an energetic campaign in 1950 to get rid of the local police commissioner, in part due to rumors that he had allowed an Algerian detained by his officers to be beaten while in custody.[66]

Beyond moments of open political warfare, the timbre of quotidian interactions was marked by disharmony and outright discord. Regular exchanges with the General Council for the Seine offered the impression that the municipality and the prefectures were talking right past each other. This miscommunication did not derive from mere misunderstanding; rather, local communists were engaged in a lively show of political opposition. North African migration provided the Dionysien municipality with an effective means to distance themselves from the state as well as a key issue on which they could voice their discontent. As early as 1949, deputy mayors were denouncing the government's handling of migrant issues through persecution and expulsion instead of offering solutions to migrants' social welfare needs.[67] During the antibidonville projects, political conflict frustrated a number of reconstruction and rehousing efforts. In 1960, Dionysien officials complained that one of the Seine department's bodies had begun construction on a series of 2,500 housing units "without the authorization of the services of the city of Saint-Denis" and thus had begun building on the wrong side of a national highway.[68]

Departmental authorities were not unaware of the potentially destabilizing force of large migrant populations on city governments and their popular support.[69] Political preferences may have influenced prefectural decisions about rehousing programs for bidonvilliers. Asnières had a remarkably easy time shuffling North African bidonville residents out of their municipal system and into foyers in other communities. Saint-Denis was most often on the receiving end of such deals, hence their concerns that migrants were being purposefully directed into their city and their eventual appeal to stop the flow of incoming migrants. Political connections greased the wheels for Asnières's projects, particularly given Mayor Bokanowski's periodic stints in the national government. At the same time, Saint-Denis was better equipped to host migrants, having already built a number of foyers and established a reputation of being open to and willing to support North African workers and their families.

As much as oppositional politics set Saint-Denis's municipal strategies apart, so too did their approach to bidonville residents. Notably, unlike in Asnières, Lyon, or Villeurbanne, the Dionysien municipality did not use rehousing operations to redistribute their North African population across the region. At least at the outset, large numbers of families and single men were accommodated within the city. In May 1967, the municipality fully funded four separate relocations, moving all the residents—North African,

African, Portuguese, and Spanish individuals and families—to the foyer and "familial transit center" at the Fort de la Briche.[70] This is not to say that the municipality provided places for all the migrants displaced by resorption efforts; some single workers were sent to foyers in other cities, but their numbers were relatively small.[71]

Saint-Denis's strategy for rehousing bidonville residents also lacked Asniérois officials' preference for families over single males. Lone workers were easier to house: foyers could be built with reasonably large occupancy rates, and more importantly, these foyers were administered and financed by outside associations. As part of their earlier program for North African welfare, Dionysien officials had lobbied heavily for more foyers for North African workers throughout the region, allowing a number to be built in the city itself.[72] In 1972, five foyers with a total of 1,589 beds for single migrant workers were still open in Saint-Denis.[73] North Africans still made up a large proportion of foyer residents, though sub-Saharan migrants were quickly surpassing them, and two of the foyers also hosted workers from Italy, Spain, and Portugal.[74] By 1973, the number of beds had risen to 1,613, and plans were in the works for a new SONACOTRA foyer at les Tartres.[75]

Along with the workers' foyers, Saint-Denis hosted a number of cités de transit. City officials had no reason to challenge the prevailing idea that dormitories were unsuitable for families, nor did they call into question the importance granted to education and socialization programs for migrants. Local communists viewed these as basic rights. Gillot and his successor, Marcellin Berthelot, signed joint declarations from the PCF mayors in the Paris region, demanding more government support for municipally based social action services for resident migrants (in the areas of lodging, health, and education).[76] Four cités were built by SONACOTRA in Saint-Denis, with a total of 374 housing units.[77] The municipality also opened a temporary office within the Francs-Moisins bidonville to help residents with social, sanitation, and health concerns and even to attempt to run literacy classes for children and adults.[78]

Providing permanent housing for migrant families proved more difficult. HLM construction drew directly from the municipal housing budget, and the allocation of HLM units pitted migrant families against other city residents. In 1965, over 4,500 families appeared on Saint-Denis's municipal HLM lists.[79] In negotiations with SONACOTRA, officials sought a guarantee that LOGIREP, the official housing oversight body for the Paris region, would orchestrate a housing "exchange" for bidonville residents with offices and associations around the region. The draft agreement specifically acknowledged that this exchange would reassure the city's other *mal-logés* (poorly housed) that their rate of rehousing would not be affected by the bidonville projects.[80] A later appeal to the National Assembly following fires at Francs-Moisins used stronger language: "Mindful of defending the interests of Saint-Denis's mal-logés, the municipality has refused to assume the total burden of rehousing immigrants."[81] The city agreed to rehouse one-third of the migrant families evicted from the bidonvilles, having received a pledge from the secretary of state for housing to settle the remaining two-thirds outside of Saint-Denis. In contrast, Saint-Denis accepted the rehousing of all the single males displaced by the Francs-Moisins resorption in foyers within the city.[82] Still, the city was able to rehouse a relatively larger number of North African families within its HLM stock.[83]

In contrast with experiences in Asnières or around Lyon, Algerians and North Africans did not receive separate headers in Dionysien memos about the bidonvilles. On one hand, this reflects long-standing municipal attitudes toward inclusion and the promotion of rights for all workers. For over fifteen years, Saint-Denis had welcomed North Africans into the community and adopted their issues as the city's own. On the other hand, the diversity of Saint-Denis's migrant population—enumerated in table 2.3—prevented the easily bifurcated path seen elsewhere.

Local officials were especially upset when departmental services seemed to usurp the municipal government's role as champions for local migrant rights and welfare. In 1973, even as Mayor Berthelot and others were increasingly concerned with the numbers of migrants in town, the city was offended by the prefecture's precipitate rehousing of a group of African workers from the foyer

Table 2.3. Occupants of Saint-Denis's bidonvilles by nationality, 1965–69

Address	1965	1967	1969
1 chemin des Francs-Moisins	3,221 P-S	3,095 NA-F-S-P	1,028 (276 NA + 752 P-S)
200 rue du Landy/ impasse Sorin	373 S-NA-P	—	20 A families
1 chemin des Cornillons	360 Various	240 S-P	323 P
67–81 rue Daniel Casanova	300 NA	—	—
10 chemin de Marville	225 S-P	209 S-P	272 P
113 boulevard de la Libération	210 NA	—	63 A + 5 A families
73 chemin de Marville	91 S-NA	—	—
60 rue Jean Jaurès	60 NA	—	—
5 rue des Renouillères	21 NA	—	21 A
2 impasse Duval	2 NA	—	—
19 chemin d'Aubervilliers	—	102 NA	122 (includes 30 NA)

Note: A: Algerian; NA: North African; P: Portuguese; S: Spanish.

Source: Created by author. For 1965, "Liquidation des bidonvilles de la région parisienne: projets et perspectives," 1965 (CHAN, F1a 5116); also reproduced in R. Dumay, "Rapport au Bureau municipal: Assainissement d'îlots défectueux—Liquidation des bidonvilles," April 1, 1966 (AMSD, 18 ACW 6). The order of nationality seems to represent relative numbers, with the first listed being the most heavily represented. For 1967: "Etat des bidonvilles recensés dans le département de la Seine–Saint-Denis," March 1967 (ADSSD, 1801 W 432). For 1969, "Liste des bidonvilles de la Seine–Saint-Denis," October 30, 1969 (ADSSD, 1801 W 432).

on the rue du Landy, undertaken without alerting the municipality or involving any of its personnel. Berthelot complained that "such proceedings undermine our relationships in terms of work and mentality, through which the difficult problems facing migrant workers must be treated." Berthelot concluded by assuring the prefect that the city would be the one to oversee the rehousing of another group of African workers from the Foyer Gaston-Phillippe.[84] Such a lack of coordination between the prefecture and the municipality was seen by the Dionysiens as an affront to their jurisdiction and a threat to their special relationship with migrant workers.

Ironically, the Dionysien municipality's long record of promoting expanded rights and welfare benefits for North Africans and other migrants may have been one of the most important factors in creating the difficulties the city faced in rehousing North African migrants and families. Their inability to find—or create—common ground with the prefectures or SONACOTRA/L, given their distaste for these offices' approach to North African issues, ensured that the bidonville resorption process started later in Saint-Denis and was unable to benefit from the push given to earlier projects in cities such as Asnières, Nanterre, Champigny, or even Lyon or from friendlier cooperation with these organizations. Despite Dionysien officials' best intentions, their instinctive turn to a position of strong and constant political opposition left them unable to fulfill many of their promises to the local North African population, while the multiplying burden of new migrants and rocky political support networks eventually led the city to close down migration entirely.

Migrant Fatigue

It is important to recognize that Saint-Denis's municipality did not always live up to its expressions of welcome and shared goals. The 1960s brought a marked reduction in municipal energy and attention directed toward North African workers. Once Algerians could claim citizenship to an independent Algeria, city documents rarely referenced North Africans explicitly. They were instead folded into general discussions of immigration, housing, or the bidonvilles. Where city officials had once harped on the need to treat Algerians like all other French citizens, they now found themselves at pains to make the case that they were like all other immigrants. In addition, the 1960s brought large numbers of Portuguese workers and families into Saint-Denis, as well as many sub-Saharan migrants, truly altering the face of the city's migrant population. The municipality continued to act on behalf of individuals and groups (usually in the context of a particular bidonville or condemned building) but abandoned its specifically North African initiatives.

While Dionysian officials continued to speak on behalf of North African workers, their actions became less frequent. The practice of generalizing about migrant and bidonville populations also obscured emerging differences in their treatment of these workers, particularly between North and sub-Saharan Africans and Europeans. When the municipality finally embarked on a systematic program to resorb the bidonvilles, priority went to Francs-Moisins and Cornillons, both with majority Portuguese and Spanish populations (see table 2.3).[85] Francs-Moisins (figure 2.1) became the symbol of Saint-Denis's immigrants and their housing difficulties: its size dwarfed the city's other slum neighborhoods, and frequent, well-publicized fires drew public and media attention.[86] It was, therefore, an obvious target for much of the city's resorption efforts. However, the secondary focus on Cornillons when the areas around rue du Landy and rue Daniel Casanova were close in size (rue du Landy had even more occupants) raises questions about how a bidonville's ethnic makeup affected the attention it received. By 1969, nearly all Spanish bidonville residents had been moved, with the exception of a group in Francs-Moisins.

Meanwhile, Algerians continued to occupy the bidonvilles at rue du Landy, boulevard de la Libération, rue des Renouillères, and chemin d'Aubervilliers.[87] This relative neglect of North African bidonvilliers in the mid- to late 1960s highlights the importance of electoral motivations for city officials' support for this population. Elected communists' interest waned with the post-Evian disenfranchisement of local Algerians; there was less to be gained

FIG. 2.1. Francs-Moisins bidonville and HLM block,
Saint-Denis (1970). From Organisme public d'HLM (OPHLM)
de Saint-Denis, "25 ans au service du logement social," 1970 (AMSD, 40 C1).

from promoting the platform of a group ineligible to vote. More-over, many more North Africans lived in the city's hotels and foy-ers than in the bidonvilles. National and regional authorities made these slums and "insalubrious habitats" a priority only after the bidonvilles were removed.[88] The North African foyers demanded by Saint-Denis's municipality in the late 1940s and early 1950s were also urgently in need of renovation, yet they did not receive the attention given to the bidonvilles.[89] Adding to the crunch, workers' foyers throughout the region had been saturated as a result of earlier clearance and rehousing projects like in Asnières, which affected North and sub-Saharan Africans more than other groups due to the preponderance of single male workers from those regions. Whatever the practical and logistical forces behind the apparent failure to rehouse North Africans at the same rate as Spanish and Portuguese, table 2.3 suggests that despite municipal rhetoric to the contrary, not all migrant workers were equally received—and city officials' tolerance was increasingly tested.

In 1974, Saint-Denis informed departmental officials that they did not want yet another foyer built in their city.[90] This refusal had less to do with a rejection of single male migrant workers as a group and more with an overall concern that municipal coffers and energies were being unduly spent on migrants, who should have been cared for by the state. Even in 1973, when the municipality evicted 146 North African workers from condemned housing, these men were rehoused in the foyer les Tartres, not sent out of the city.[91] The municipality repeatedly called upon other actors to bear the financial responsibility for migrants and their families. In 1964, the municipal council had demanded that the rehousing of Spanish and Portuguese from the Cornillons and Francs-Moisins bidonvilles be financed by the state, with participation from companies who employed migrant workers.[92] Gillot argued that the city was strapped for land to build much-needed schools and could not provide the sites for new foyers or cités de transit; instead, the prefect should consider properties held by the military or unused land owned by large companies.[93] Municipal officials even negotiated with the local Nitrolac company, offering to swap a parcel of land elsewhere in the city for a piece of the company's land to serve as the site for a new foyer-hotel for former bidonville residents.[94]

Further city reports appealed to SONACOTRA, the Fonds d'action sociale (FAS), and employers to provide funding for rehousing the migrants whose presence resulted from policies pursued by the state and by companies.[95] The municipal council voted in 1968 to have the FAS shoulder all the previous and future expenses for resorbing the city's bidonvilles, which they insisted "developed despite interventions by the municipality."[96] FAS overseers pointed to the substantial contributions they had already made to Saint-Denis's efforts and explained that they could not retroactively meet the city's demands, though they would be willing to help with further projects.[97] The city again asked for reimbursement in the aftermath of devastating—and headline-grabbing—fires in Francs-Moisins in June 1970, arguing that "the City cannot be held responsible for the existence of bidonvilles on its territory."[98] Over and over again, the municipality blamed the development of the bidonvilles and all the problems that ensued on the state (for its irresponsible migration policies) and on employers (for using migrants for their labor but failing to provide for their basic welfare). These demands conformed with the municipality's insistence, dating from the mid-1940s, that better services be provided to these immigrants at the expense of those who profited from their presence in France. These funding battles highlighted a paradox in the city's interactions with the French state: the municipal budget relied on state financing, and municipal officials were strident in their demands for ever-increased funding for their projects. Yet they were equally insistent that the city alone carry out all programs related to social and migrant welfare.

To some extent, the city was a victim of its own successes: its positions and policies on migrant workers meant that many were drawn to Saint-Denis. As the number of migrants rose, some city officials grew less willing to welcome those migrants unconditionally. On one hand, the municipality continued to critique the national immigration system, supporting the communist group's 1967 proposal to the National Assembly, which sought "a democratic and social status for immigrant workers," emphasizing both the "often inhuman living conditions" of the city's migrants and "the burden this situation brings to bear on the communal budget."[99] PCF deputies accused the state of exploiting migrant workers to serve industrial and employer interests. They made the familiar argument that the state and employers should bear the cost of rehousing migrants from the bidonvilles and other slums and demanded that all migrant workers receive the same civil and labor rights as French workers.[100]

On the other hand, this familiar opposition to the French state was linked to new demands to restrict migration—both to France and to Saint-Denis.[101] Demands to redistribute migrant workers and families throughout the region were a marked change from the city's earlier practice of keeping as many migrants as possible in the city. In 1968, the city council specifically linked national policies to the continued growth of the bidonvilles and blamed the government for its inability to provide appropriate housing

for these immigrants.[102] Moreover, Mayor Berthelot and the rest
of the communist coalition complained that their cities had been
unfairly burdened by migrant populations: "These large groupings
of the population pose urban development problems, financial and
sociocultural problems, that even the best run municipalities cannot resolve without external aid. . . . These extraordinary needs,
for housing and social services, hav[e] severely burdened municipal budgets with very heavy charges and add[ed] to the ceaselessly
growing needs of the local populations."[103] Much of the language
here echoed an earlier declaration made by the PCF mayors of the
Paris region, who insisted that migrants came to their cities not only
because they recognized that communist municipalities were dedicated to supporting "the laboring classes" but also because they were
"systematically directed there by state officials."[104] As early as 1962,
municipal reports had raised the suspicion that migrants not only
were coming to the city of their own accord but had been sent to
Saint-Denis by unknown forces.[105] Such accusations were not without basis in fact. By 1975, more than half of France's PCF-led cities
counted immigrant populations over 10 percent (compared with
less than a quarter of socialist and centrist towns).[106] Migrant housing policy, therefore, had become politicized not only as a way for
local communists to assert their opposition to the state but also as
a means for the national government to punish PCF municipalities.

Feeling this pressure, municipal officials in Saint-Denis began
to follow practices more similar to those seen in Asnières and
around Lyon. They first looked to redistribute some of the bidonville population to other cities in the region, citing both the size
of the city's migrant population and the number of nonmigrant
families already on the city's priority lists for rehousing. In 1970,
Deputy Mayor Robert Dumay expressed the desire for "a fairer
redistribution of bidonville residents among the communes of
the Paris region," which would allow the city "to give priority to the
rehousing in Saint-Denis of Dionysien families, currently living
in bad conditions."[107] Dumay had advocated for such a redistribution for years, often relying on prevalent ideas about integration and thresholds of migrant tolerance.[108]

As frustration with migrant housing grew, Saint-Denis's officials invoked a system of quotas for migrant residents in line with national trends but in contradiction to earlier rhetoric on migrant rights. By 1970, the municipal council echoed the demand for a 10 percent *seuil de tolérance* within their own HLM projects.[109] City officials even began to enforce an earlier statute that set the HLM units reserved for migrant families as low as 6.75 percent.[110] In 1973, the city asserted that within one of the new HLMs, "the rehousing of migrant or nonassimilated families should be at a maximum of 15%, with the understanding that it would be very desirable that this maximum is not reached."[111] Despite these efforts, foreign residency in Saint-Denis's HLMs increased over the 1970s (see table 2.4). A 1972 survey of all the HLM complexes revealed a foreign occupancy rate of 10.15 percent, which rose in 1974 to 11.63 percent, and by 1978 had reached 19.7 percent.[112] The number of North African HLM residents, quite small in 1958, rose to roughly one-third of the foreign population and stayed constant through the decade.[113] The HLMs still did not reflect the size of the city's migrant population. The municipality claimed that migrants accounted for fully 20–25 percent of the Dionysien population in the early 1970s,[114] and these numbers ultimately spurred officials to reject the feasibility—and fairness—of rehousing all the city's former bidonville residents.

Thus, in 1974, Saint-Denis joined six other cities in the Seine-Saint-Denis department to petition the prefect to block entry by new migrants into their communities, in effect paralleling the efforts made by the Rhône prefecture in Villeurbanne a few years earlier.[115] The prefect acknowledged the concerns in each of the cities for "the presence of very numerous immigrant families" and, in particular, for the frequent exceeding of migrant quotas in social housing complexes—particularly Francs-Moisins.[116] The new policy forbade the entry of new migrant families into any of the seven cities, whether from abroad or from other communities in France. These new rules explicitly banned rehousing of foreign families in those cities unless they were already residents in said city under insalubrious or otherwise unsuitable conditions.[117] The

Table 2.4. Foreign occupancy in Dionysien HLMs, 1958–78 (percents)

Cité HLM (in order of construction)	1958	1972	1974	1974 North Africans / foreigners	1978
Barbusse (1933)	1.62	5.55	6.2	35.71	10.6
P. Langevin (1951/52)	3.57	7.52	7.74	—	10.7
Fabien (1952/57)	4.75	6.58	8.0	44.44	13.2
Eluard (1955)	1.13	6.57	5.99	5.56	7.9
D. Casanova (1957)	6.67	19.33	8.84	32.56	30.7
P. Semard I (1958)	8.28	13.92	12.50	40.00	17.4
Delaune (1959)	—	4.21	3.60	0	9.7
J. Curie (1960)	—	14.81	19.67	48.24	27.3
P. Semard II (1960)	—	11.7	10.8	24.49	17.4
Delaune (1962)	—	5.5	7.40	20.00	9.7
G. Péri (1962/69)	—	8.28	7.3	35.48	10.4
Romain Rollan (1965)	—	6.61	6.19	19.23	8.2
Marcel Cachin (1966)	—	6.87	10.62	29.41	14.4
Guynemer (1968)	—	8.13	9.37	75.00	13.3
Les Cosmonautes (1969)	—	8.02	12.5	45.45	17.6
Stalingrad (1971)	—	5.55	8.08	25.00	6.6
La Courtille (1970–71)	—	13.77	19.11	43.82	25.05
Saussaie (1971)	—	10.34	16.25	48.94	17.5
Les Francs-Moisins (1971–72)	—	18.33	15.04	38.66	24.15
Total	**3.63**	**10.15**	**11.63**	**36.72**	**19.7**

Source: Created by author. For 1958, Office public d'habitations, Reports by HLM cité, "Loyers impayés au 30 avril 1958" (AMSD, 38 AC 5); calculation of Arabophone names/ total author's. For 1972 and 1974, "Pourcentage des familles étrangères en HLM, Saint-Denis," 1974 (ADSSD, 1801 W 228); figures refer to the number of units occupied by foreign or migrant families; North African / foreign calculations based on list of individuals by nationality (not housing units) available only for this year. For 1978, "Eléments pour une politique de l'habitat," October 1978, p. 17 (AMSD, 261 W 22); of these, one-third were Algerians, one-third Spanish or Portuguese, and one-third "other."

rapid growth of the migrant population, the increase in foreign families, the proliferation of the bidonvilles, and the strain on the municipal budget had all contributed to the municipality's shift away from instinctive inclusion. By the early 1970s, under a new mayor, with an economic crisis looming, Saint-Denis had been overwhelmed by sheer numbers. France itself closed its borders to all new migrants in July 1974 (with the exception of family reunifications) in response to the global oil shock and the deepening national economic crisis. Saint-Denis's municipality went from opposing the state to foreshadowing its actions.

In 1961, the Seine prefecture tried to determine whether regional urban renovation projects might finally wean Dionysiens away from the PCF. The report found that the party was simply too popular: "The particularly active Saint-Denis municipality has pursued for years, and continues to pursue, a considerable effort in multiple domains (the construction of apartment buildings, schools, medical clinics, daycare centers, summer camps, retirement homes, etc.) [that] has delivered tangible results that these people are able to observe every day."[118] Since the 1940s, such "tangible results" regularly benefited the city's North African population as well. Yet Saint-Denis stands as a cautionary tale in which a migrant-friendly environment induced further migration, leading to a sense of overload and a strong backlash.

Vénissieux: When Politics Were Not Enough

Saint-Denis's relative inability to manage its bidonvilles, in stark contrast to Asnières's early and efficient efforts in the same region, raises further questions about politics and political relationships. French communists more generally have a mixed record of relating to migrant populations. Self-proclaimed enemies of imperial powers, they allied themselves with anticolonial movements and avowed support for migrant workers as fellow members of the global oppressed class. Saint-Denis's city officials were well ahead of this curve in their opposition to French imperialism and especially the Algerian War (as discussed in chapter 4). This ideological platform, however, often failed to materialize into concrete improvements for migrants' situations. Indeed, there is ample evidence to support sociologist Olivier Masclet's claim that the relationship between the French Left and immigrant workers represents a "missed opportunity."[119]

Communism alone was not sufficient motivation for local engagement with North African communities. Further south, Vénissieux was no less communist than Saint-Denis. Yet there is no evidence that either of its PCF mayors (Louis Dupic or Marcel Houël) or their colleagues in city government were involved with questions of North African rights and welfare at the level seen in Saint-Denis. In part, the difference in the political calculus can be explained by the relative numbers. There were many fewer North Africans in the Rhône. In 1953, for example, there were 11,500 "French Muslim citizens" in the region, of whom only about 650 actually appeared on the voting lists. In the previous year, only two Algerians had been added to Vénissieux's register. Even Lyon's third arrondissement, where the massive North African Center at Part-Dieu was located, counted no more than 100 "Muslim" voters.[120] These totals were dwarfed by the registered North African voters in Saint-Denis alone, even after 1962.

In the few instances of activity by Vénissian municipal officials, there are echoes of the sorts of arguments seen in Saint-Denis. Houël attempted to recruit North Africans along with the Confédération générale du travail (CGT) in early 1954, though the planning meeting for one event attracted only three North African workers, suggesting that the organizers lacked meaningful contacts with the Rhône's migrant community.[121] A tract put out by the CGT that spring hit familiar themes on the evils of French colonialism and imperialism, particularly emphasizing how these connected to unemployment and poor working conditions in France.[122] In the midst of these efforts to reach out to local North Africans, however, Dupic, as mayor, failed to attend the 1954 grand opening of a foyer for migrant workers at the city's Berliet company. The building itself was in Saint-Priest (bordering both Vénissieux and Bron), whose mayor did attend with his deputies and the full municipal council.[123] Dupic's absence is particularly notable given the long list of attendees, including the Rhône and Isère prefects, other regional officials, representatives from the Centre d'accueil nord-africain and the Maison de l'Afrique du Nord, as well as multiple top representatives from Berliet.[124] Had North African relations been a Vénissian priority, someone from the mayor's office would certainly have made the effort to be at such a high-profile event.

From the mid-1960s, when bidonville resorption and other housing initiatives were in full swing, Mayor Houël occasionally emerged to support housing demands—or to frustrate them. Notably, the city's own discussions about housing, reconstruction, and the Zone à urbaniser en priorité (ZUP) at Minguettes failed to pay any particular attention to North Africans (and rarely mentioned immigrants more broadly).[125] SONACOTRA, LOGIREL, and the FAS all found the city unresponsive—or opposed—to their construction plans in the ZUP Minguettes.[126] Houël did pay some attention to individual requests for aid. He was especially vocal on behalf of a group of women set to be removed from the Foyer Viviani: "It seems abnormal to me that we evict, without prior arrangement for rehousing, Muslim women who opted for French nationality to install foreign workers in their place."[127] Of the women in question, it turned out only one was a French Muslim; the others were Jewish repatriates.[128] Houël's misunderstanding of the women's situation again suggests that his contacts with local North Africans were relatively rare. Moreover, his dismissive tone toward "foreign workers" marked a significant difference from Dionysien rhetoric, which regularly included migrants as fellow workers.

There is some evidence that communist activists outside the municipality had more inclusive instincts. One of the young Algerian residents of Villeurbanne's Cité Olivier de Serres had fond memories of a "grand communist ball" hosted at Minguettes: "They made no difference between native-born French and Maghrebins, and whatever happened during the party, they never called the police. There, we felt like everyone else." He also noted that the Olivier de Serres youth respected the communists who came to coach them in sports.[129] Ralph Grillo's ethnographic account of a

1976 PCF meeting in a nearby suburb likewise highlights the difference between elected PCF officials' positions and those of communist activists. Though one Algerian HLM resident insisted that Vaulx-en-Vélin's communist mayor had asked to "shut the door to immigrants," other Algerian PCF members in attendance repeatedly asserted that activism through the party—and through their own local party cells—was the best way to force the changes they wished.[130] This snapshot reveals that some Algerians were active within local PCF circles but also that their influence on elected municipal leaders was limited. Grillo's own analysis points to PCF politicians' need to speak to popular racial anxieties, which left them "caught between the demands of their ideals and the realities of their constituents."[131] This desire not to lose electoral support by challenging the racist assumptions of their voting base does not, however, entirely explain why Vénissieux looked so markedly different from Saint-Denis on these issues.

Once the Lyon region embarked on its major rehousing campaign in 1965, Vénissieux was one of only two suburban cities not to immediately refuse construction for this purpose.[132] Houël also, on occasion, attempted to intervene on behalf of North African residents in local foyers, particularly in cases where he saw private administrators as part of a larger repressive system. He was particularly concerned about the Foyer Bonnet-Pernet, which was overseen by the Comité des amitiés africaines. Houël received a petition from foyer residents in January 1966 and immediately wrote to Director Brachet to demand a meeting about the charges of "mistreatment and abuse."[133] Though his actions did not get results—or much of a hearing—Houël had made the concerns of these North African residents his own, echoing in some ways Gillot and his colleagues' insistence that communist city officials had obligations to migrant workers.[134] His demands to the Rhône prefecture, however, included a remark that concerns about Bonnet-Pernet made him reticent to sign off on new foyers and migrant housing in the city.[135] The head of the Rhône Service de liaison et promotion des migrants (SLPM), Jean-Pierre Gat, met with Houël to assure the mayor that steps were being taken to remedy valid concerns and plead with him to sign off on the construction of new foyers in the ZUP Minguettes. As an incentive, Gat reiterated a guarantee that 50 percent of the beds in these new foyers would be reserved for "foreign workers (of all nationalities) living in Vénissieux."[136] This promise highlighted Houël's complex vision of his relationship to migrant workers: on the one hand, there is the sense that he felt some responsibility for foreigners within his jurisdiction and wanted to ensure that they were well cared for; on the other hand, rehousing more migrants already within Vénissieux meant fewer places available for those who might be sent to his city from elsewhere in the region.

Such ambivalence remained. In 1970, the Rhône prefect again singled out Houël as one of the only mayors in the region who was willing to accept foreigners into public housing projects.[137] According to *L'Humanité*, the number of "foreign" families in Vénissieux had reached 35 percent of the total population over the previous three decades.[138] The paper praised Houël as one of the few voices to have "fought against the chauvinistic aims" of the Rhône prefecture's June 1970 circular limiting foreign residents in neighborhoods with large migrant populations.[139] Houël had declared the policy "contrary to the traditions of humanism and hospitality in France."[140] He admitted that there were serious problems with foreign families' "large number and excessive concentration in certain locales or neighborhoods" but suggested that the June 1970 policy was not a real solution. He notably did not question the underlying logic of finding a "more equitable and harmonious distribution of foreign families in the Lyon agglomeration" but demanded more funding for HLMs and transitional housing as well as increased numbers of and support for remedial classes (*cours de ratrappage*) for foreign students.

Houël's insistence on more state funding for social programs was well in line with Dionysien demands. Behind the scenes, however, his support for migrant families was less enthusiastic. Around the same time that he was publicly opposing the June 1970 circular, Houël was also expressing concerns about the number of foreign families being rehoused in the ZUP Minguettes, specifically citing

FIG. 2.2. Schoolchildren in Vénissieux (1972). From *Bulletin d'informations municipales*, Vénissieux, May 1972 (AMVén).

"the regrettable repercussions for the community of too great a percentage of foreign families, most of which are large families: overload on schools, rising social aid expenditures, etc."[141] The Rhône PCF was more reticent than even the national party to come to the defense of migrants—and local communists initially did not take part in the movements to oppose the June 1970 policy and other actions against migrants, despite the participation of numerous other groups.[142] Houël's intervention was thus part of a plan to realign Rhône communists with the PCF's central committee without calling too much attention to their earlier inaction. Houël followed up with Gat, whose further clarification on the legality and intentions of the June 1970 circular appeared to assuage the mayor's concerns.[143] Indeed, Houël himself invoked the June 1970 policy just a few years later in order to refuse a housing certificate to an Algerian worker who had procured an HLM unit in Vénissieux.[144] He began to lean into the idea of redistribution, asking, "Why not lodge [migrant families] elsewhere, but decently?"[145] By 1978, the Vénissian municipality insisted that no further "foreign" families be accepted into the city—and especially not into the ZUP Minguettes.[146] While the timeline here tracked with Saint-Denis's similar resistance to accepting further migrants into the city, Houël's response was not an overt departure from his or other Vénissian communists' earlier reticence to promote the interests of local North Africans. In contrast, Dionysien officials' 1974 petition to limit the number of foreign workers entering their community presented a marked difference from earlier actions on behalf of North Africans and a confirmed stance of solidarity with the North Africans as fellow workers and members of a globally suppressed class.

The local activism of PCF officials in Saint-Denis and Vénissieux supports Gillian Glaes's argument that the relationship between migrants and the French Left was "more nuanced and complicated" than usually described.[147] The Dionysien political calculus, which carefully counted both sources of electoral support and opportunities to score points against the French state, further extended to municipal activism surrounding the Algerian War. While anti-war activism in Saint-Denis will be treated at length in chapter 4, it is worth considering here the ways that opposing the war both supported city officials' arguments for enhanced North African rights and welfare and offered them a useful platform to critique national and imperial efforts. When denouncing the "tortoise speed" of national housing projects, for example, Gillot insisted that the real problem lay with the government's priorities: residential construction could easily have been funded by a reduction in the military budget. This increasingly common refrain set the lack of social spending against military endeavors: "To have lodging in Saint-Denis, we must choose between the construction of residences and the fabrication of cannons and other engines of death."[148] Local communists promoted opposition to de Gaulle in 1961, urging citizens to vote no on the president's referendum in part because "the war in Algeria is delaying the construction of the housing you are waiting for."[149] Pamphlets asserted that the funds to build five thousand housing units were equivalent to only five days of war.[150] Political opposition and the pressing need for social benefits and residential construction were intimately related to antiwar activism in Saint-Denis. Here again, Vénissieux's municipal officials were barely, if at all, publicly engaged with questions of imperialism and war. This lack of action further suggests that Dionysien officials' linking of empire and migration encouraged their more substantive work on both fronts.

Anti-imperialism, it turns out, played very well to political audiences in Saint-Denis. It was hardly a coincidence that the 1946 municipal council debate that set the stage for the city's postwar engagement with North Africans included both the question of migrant housing in the metropole and North African rights within imperial Algeria.[151] Speaking to North African workers in 1951, Gillot insisted that all votes for the French Communist Party were votes "against colonialism and for Algerian national independence."[152] The PCF distributed lists of interventions by communist deputies on behalf of North Africans and invoked the long-standing anti-imperialism of party leaders (noting that Maurice Thorez had served eighteen months in prison for his opposition to the 1925 Rif War).[153] Gillot asserted that the PCF's support for Algerian independence had been long-standing and constant, not an issue raised only when it served the party's interest;[154] his municipality's support for Algerian workers was likely perceived in the same light. Again, during legislative elections in 1956, the local PCF declared to Algerian migrants, "The elections in France are also your affair." They claimed Algerian voters should "have confidence in the Party of French workers, your brothers in misery and in combat, in the Party that offers practical support for your social demands and your legitimate right to national independence, and who fights for the union of our two peoples in equality and amity."[155]

Support for North African rights and welfare was an important means to support or oppose France's ongoing imperial endeavors. These efforts will be treated in depth in the following two chapters. They also, however, provide another key to understanding how Saint-Denis's position toward North African migrants shifted over the course of the 1960s. In addition to the overwhelming nature of dealing with the bidonvilles, the ever-increasing number of migrants in the city, the evolving cast of city leadership, and the loss of automatic voting rights for local Algerians, North African issues after the signing of the Evian Accords in 1962 were no longer tied up with the greater project of anti-imperialism. This contributed to waning municipal interest in the plight of the North Africans: the loss of a grand ideological framework for interaction between communists and North Africans translated into a faulty foundation for further action. Algerian independence thus undercut both Saint-Denis PCF officials' impetus to inspire North African voters and their ability to marshal anticolonial arguments against the French state. Without these political motivations, the municipality's support for North African migrants as a specific group declined noticeably.

THREE

In Defense of Empire

On May 15, 1953, an artillery salvo at the La Doua military camp in Lyon marked the opening of another local Ramadan celebration. The Rhône prefect, the mayor of Lyon, the local military commander, and Lyon's Cardinal Gerlier had cooperated to initiate this event—and claimed it as the first such commemoration of the Muslim holiday on the French mainland.[1] The guns were fired again on June 8 and 12 to celebrate the "nuit du Destin" (Laylat al-Qadr, the commemoration of the revelation of the Quran to the prophet Mohammed) and the end of the month. These local leaders also worked with the Maison de l'Afrique du Nord (MAN) to host a "couscous" in honor of the Eid el-Seghir (Eid al-Fitr) feast on the last night of Ramadan (see figure 3.1).[2] Cooperation among this diverse group of civil, military, and religious authorities speaks to the variety of local actors who were invested in supporting North Africans in the Rhône. Yet it also poses a bit of a puzzle: How did a group of civil and military authorities in France's secular republic find themselves working with a high-ranking church official to promote a Muslim holy day?

The picture becomes slightly less muddled once we acknowledge that France had long engaged in many activities to demonstrate their support for the Muslim subjects of their empire.[3] It may not be surprising that the secular republic used faith as a means to shore up imperial power, yet it is a bit strange to see this play out on a local scale. It is not immediately clear how each of the individuals involved (beyond the military commander) played a role within the French

A l'occasion de l'Aïd el Seghir

On a mangé le couscous
à la Maison de l'Afrique du Nord

...et l'on a fait cuire le mouton à la broche

FIG. 3.1. Eid couscous at the Maison de l'Afrique du Nord in Lyon (1953).
From unlabeled press clipping, likely *Le Progrès* (ADR, 248 W 152).

imperial system. While many of them had close relations with the
national government—only Lyon's mayor was locally elected—their
official purviews were quite domestic. Yet the quotidian politics of
Rhône officials, both prefectural and private, were intimately bound
up in these actors' support for maintaining control of French Algeria. While chapter 1 examined cases where rhetoric about North
African welfare was often a bad-faith cover for racial discrimination, here we see how imperial interests—while still rooted in deeply
racist assumptions—required that local services provide real and
meaningful support for Algerian migrants and their families.

This chapter thus focuses on how imperialist ideology drove

engagement with local North Africans in the Lyon region. Delv-ing into the motivations of these local actors reveals a surprising level of concern with the future of the French Empire on the part of officials whose jurisdiction would seem in no way to call for such interest. These were more than personal opinions expressed in familiar company or over a dinner table: municipal and depart-mental agents invoked the empire in their official correspondence, advancing their own foreign and imperial policy agendas even as they managed narrower city and neighborhood problems. In the Rhône prefecture, reports to the national government often included minor treatises on the importance of the empire, particularly Alge-ria, in maintaining France's global presence. Individual prefects and other community players viewed the Algerian migrants in their region through this lens and encouraged both increased social wel-fare for and expanded police surveillance of those migrants (mir-roring their hopes for Algeria itself). While it is not surprising that prefectural officials, who were appointed through the Ministry of the Interior, would support national policies like the repression of Algerian nationalism, what is remarkable is the extent to which Rhône officials articulated their specific local activities as an explicit part of a broader imperial strategy. Prefects Pierre Massenet and Roger Ricard in particular thus revealed how embedded French imperialism was within mainland domestic governance and how local actors made space for the empire at home.

Security and Social Welfare

North Africans' social welfare in the metropole had long been linked to French colonial policy in Algeria. In 1937, speaking on behalf of his legislation for greater Algerian political rights, Mau-rice Viollette declared, "Algeria will remain French only if France maintains the loyalty of its Muslim population."[4] European set-tlers' social action committees played a key role in the creation of early foyers in the metropole, acknowledging that migrant expe-riences on the mainland affected the administration of Algeria itself.[5] In 1944, as World War II came to a close, the French min-ister to North Africa warned that "the maintenance of French sovereignty over her overseas possessions will be disputed." The best chance for France to defend its imperial system would be to ensure that "the autochthonous populations stand in solidarity with her." The only way to garner such support would be through effective assimilation policies throughout the empire: better education, equality for employment and benefits, and a guarantee that "Muslims' living conditions be aligned with the respect for individual dignity."[6] In other words, without proper social services to improve the lot of colonial subjects (in the colonies and in the metropole), assertions of, and support for, French Algeria would falter.

By 1951, the colonial administration in Algeria was particularly concerned with the treatment of Algerian "Muslims" in the metropole and the implications for continued French control of the colony. One report from the Algerian offices declared that the May 1 workers' demonstrations throughout mainland France showed that "too many emigrants are responding to subversive propaganda. A broad employment policy on their behalf, combined with a hardy plan for housing and professional training, is more necessary than ever. If one measures the importance of this factor, which will play for or against us according to whether Algerian workers in France feel welcomed or forsaken, one is tempted to conclude that it is the future of French Algeria that is at stake."[7] For those officials based in Algeria, the repercussions of continuing to neglect North African social welfare were unmistakable. The governor-general of Algeria wrote to the interior minister, "I am overwhelmed with ever more frequent grievances from Algerian Muslims, students or workers, who solicit our help for finding lodging. . . . They claim, rightly or wrongly, to run up against the distrust of landlords, because of their origins." Faced with hostile attitudes, these Algerians became more bitter toward their metropolitan hosts, with potentially dire consequences.[8] If France could not share her bounty with Algerian migrants, if the republic could not convince its Muslim subjects that they were equally respected and cared for, then the premise of French Algeria could not hold. It was in this atmosphere that the French government renewed its support for Algerian social services and Muslim religious practices—as the Rhône prefecture would do with its Ramadan celebrations.

On the mainland, the police were the most forceful of the state institutions to demand enhanced social policies for North Africans.[9] The Paris prefecture argued that an overhaul of the housing situation, particularly the destruction of the bidonvilles, was a necessary instrument of national security policy. The police created the SAT-FMA (Service d'assistance technique aux Français musulmans d'Algérie) in 1958 with the mission to "raise the standard of living for citizens with Muslim origins, in order that they might benefit from conditions of existence analogous to those of their metropolitan compatriots, notably in permitting them to exercise effectively the rights attached to their citizenship . . . [and] to reestablish a climate of trust between the Muslim and metropolitan populations." A draft version of the SAT-FMA's explanation of this mission included a third prong: "to tear the Muslim Algerian population under their watch away from the hold of the FLN [Front de libération nationale]."[10] Lyon received its own set of SAT brigades in 1960.

Conflict in Algeria was directly linked to the growth of the bidonvilles, both in spurring the increased migration—particularly of families—that fed their construction and in providing the French state with an urgent security framework to address the housing problem.[11] Influenced, no doubt, by the reports issued by the police prefecture, the Interior Ministry fought against government reticence to engage the problem by arguing that the bidonvilles would soon serve as the second front for the FLN. These communities, with high numbers of North African residents, stood outside of mainstream French society and, worse, outside standard mechanisms of surveillance and control.[12] Police suspicions did not derive from unfounded paranoia. Benjamin Stora, in particular, has demonstrated the strength of the FLN in France, the extent of its operations, the effects of the "civil war" among nationalists on Algerians in the metropole, and the significance of the funding for nationalist groups drawn from Algerian emigrants.[13] North

African migrants, either living in the bidonvilles or packed into overcrowded foyers and hotels, existed at the margins of metropolitan life. Disadvantaged, destitute, and often disillusioned, many were persuaded by nationalist propaganda, while others were pressured into conforming to nationalist practices or fell victim to racketeering (often accompanied by violence or its threat). Abdelmalek Sayad and Éliane Dupuy describe the bidonvilles as subject to both the control of Algerian nationalists and "the same [state] repression" employed in Algeria.[14] Though many police practices were discriminatory and overbearing, officers also intervened on behalf of migrants seeking protection from nationalists or rival factions. Moreover, as Amelia Lyons explains, Algerian migrants could play both sides by telling "representatives of the French system and the FLN what they wanted to hear in order to survive."[15]

As much as the Paris police prefecture tried to cultivate a public image of goodwill and humanitarianism, SAT-FMA files consistently demonstrated the fundamental relationship between social and surveillance operations. Reports issued on SAT-FMA activities listed the social services they provided and then detailed the political and security "results" of these policies.[16] Police Prefect Maurice Papon also believed that the importance of social/surveillance services for North Africans should persist; in May 1962, he declared, "Whatever the circumstances and the evolution of the situation, and even under the hypothesis of Algerian independence . . . , it will be necessary, for reasons of political safety and public security to control the mass of Muslims assembled in . . . the Paris region." Papon continued to insist that the difficulties they faced were a result of the decision to discontinue the earlier North African Brigade.[17] Lyon's police had likewise lamented the lack of a dedicated North African Brigade, particularly after open conflict broke out in Algeria in 1954.[18] Social services helped the police cultivate stability, contentment, and a positive view of the French state, as well as providing a powerful and effective means of gathering information and maintaining influence over the North African population; Papon and others believed both of these to be crucial to public security. This reasoning provided the greatest impetus for

the police and government ministries to launch the program to
rid France of its bidonvilles with the watershed creation in 1956
of SONACOTRAL.

It is important to emphasize that the development of substantial social housing initiatives to benefit North Africans in
mainland France derived from a logic of surveillance and control
and increasingly from a fear for national security.[19] Marc Bernardot has asserted that one of SONACOTRAL's primary functions
was to exercise control over its residents and to serve "all at once
as an instrument of infiltration, tabulation [*comptage*], and surveillance of the communities of single Algerian 'workers.'"[20] The
evolution of the conflict in Algeria (and the strengthening of
the nationalists' position) actually led to increased French efforts to
integrate Algerian workers as a means of strengthening the claims
to a French Algeria. SAT-FMA files demonstrated the important
links between migrant socialization and public security, with social
services trumpeted as one of the most effective tools in keeping
a close watch on the Algerian population and weaning Algerians
from the influence of nationalists.[21]

Algerian migrants appeared well aware of the state's dual motives.
Certainly, in Algeria itself, the proffered welfare carrots did not overcome the vast harm of the military stick. Despite French authorities' insistence that average Algerians were only ever duped or
seduced by nationalist propaganda—which willfully ignored
the myriad reasons for which national independence could be
embraced—social services and their material benefits did not garner
support for imperial connections.[22] As Amelia Lyons has argued,
Algerian migrants to the mainland proved adept at leveraging the
language of rights and claiming state entitlements they believed
they were owed—from family allowances and employment services to housing benefits and education.[23] This willingness to pull
the state's bureaucratic strings and familiarity with the rhetorical
claims that were most likely to bear fruit is a testament to Algerian
migrants' agency in navigating the late imperial system. Their ability to make the French state work for their own needs can hardly
be read as an embrace of French imperial aims or a rejection of

Algerian nationalism. Indeed, it highlights the overconfidence of French paternalistic policies that denied Algerians the right—or even ability—to determine their own political futures.

Even once Algerian independence looked inevitable, national officials continued to demand fair treatment for Algerian workers, now as a means of strengthening the French diplomatic position in the Evian negotiations. The French were also aware that their economy could not remain competitive without the continued participation of Algerian workers and hoped to encourage future population movements. Thus, social welfare issues went from being an "arm in the war" to a lever in the peace process.[24] With the signing of the Evian Accords and the creation of an independent Algeria in 1962, social policy for North Africans was no longer defined by national security and political repression. However, as historian Jim House maintains, "Social action as supervision [*encadrement*], control, and surveillance stay[ed] firmly in place and target[ed] certain groups more than others, even under the cover of a more 'universalist' policy."[25] North and sub-Saharan Africans remained the majority of residents in SONACOTRA's foyers and cités de transit through the 1970s, even as the HLMs (Habitations à loyer modéré) that the association built were used for Portuguese, Yugoslav, and especially metropolitan French families.[26] Even with the disappearance of the immediate security threat posed by Algerian nationalism and open conflict with France, the French police continued to use social services as a means of surveillance and control of postcolonial migrants.[27]

National and colonial officials, of course, are expected to concern themselves with such issues of security, public opinion, and imperial affairs. The role of the Paris police prefecture in setting up social welfare programs is perhaps more surprising, though not unprecedented. Less expected is the extent to which truly local administrators, like those in the Rhône prefecture, engaged in questions about the future of Algeria and linked their activity within their jurisdiction to their imperial ideals.

Saving French Algeria

The Rhône prefects' monthly reports to the Interior Ministry, first required in late 1953,[28] assumed a marked preoccupation with events in North Africa.[29] Initially, these appeared at the end of the reports alongside discussions of Franco-Soviet and other foreign relations. Whereas other foreign topics were listed by country, one subsection was always devoted to "the North Africans," meaning those migrants living within the prefecture's jurisdiction. The use of this term in this section of the report both marked the migrants as being foreign, or at least apart from the autochthonous population, and refused them—as imperial subjects—a country of their own.

The actual reporting on North Africans was fairly standard, quite similar to the reports on North African activity issuing from other departments or the Paris police. Topics included the number of North African workers in the region, some mention of the social problems faced by these workers (employment, housing, health), and a discussion of the political situation. There were two main aspects to these political concerns: first, the state of intra-Algerian and nationalist politics; and second, the involvement of "French" political groups (usually the French Communist Party [PCF]). By November 1957, the category of "North Africans" was replaced by more specific reports on the FLN, MNA, and "Muslim syndicalists," marking a mindset that no longer considered the migrants as a full population, but rather as discrete and problematic groups of rebel actors.[30] Where the Rhône reports diverge from others, however, is in the consistent invocation of French imperial politics, which often received far more attention than regional or national issues in the reports' opening discussions.

Pierre Massenet first mentioned North African affairs in his prefectural report late in the summer of 1954, with a focus on unrest in Morocco and Tunisia.[31] Soon thereafter, Massenet began to inject his reports with proimperial rhetoric in a tone that verged on chiding. Like many of the elected mayors discussed in this book, Massenet had been active in the French Resistance.[32] After liberation, he was briefly appointed to Marseille as prefect, then as Inspecteur général de l'administration en mission extraordinaire (IGAME).[33] The position of IGAME was created under the Interior Ministry in 1948 to coordinate civil and military actions within jurisdictions defined by existing military districts. The IGAMES' tasks were thus intrinsically linked to keeping social order, and in the 1950s their main focus became containing Algerian nationalism.[34] Massenet arrived in Lyon in 1949 as both Rhône prefect and the IGAME for the eighth district. His role as IGAME largely explains his close attention to local North Africans and his repeated invocation of a broader imperial framework to underline his policies and positions. He was, moreover, a distant relation to Michel Massenet, one of the major players in North African—and later other immigrant—welfare services in France in the latter half of the twentieth century.[35]

Prefect Massenet's report for October 1954, written in the first few weeks of open conflict in Algeria, expressed the hope that the French state would "be able to use all necessary energy and authority to keep North Africa for France."[36] He had been far less concerned with developments in French Indochina, even appearing to oppose military involvement there.[37] In contrast, Massenet demanded that, in North Africa, "rapid and energetic means . . . be established to bring an end to a situation that is detrimental to the prestige France enjoys within the empire."[38] Here, his own imperial agenda became clear: as many future reports would indicate, Massenet was caught up in a worldview wherein France's worth and global power were perfectly congruent with its ability to hold North Africa. That this rhetoric appeared in his reports as Rhône prefect, not only in his IGAME documents, underlines the extent to which imperial administration permeated domestic policies on the mainland.

According to Massenet, Algeria was the key both to France's economic success and to its status as a global power. Any "weakening of French power" in North Africa would result in "dangerous consequences."[39] In the first place, Massenet worried about the local and national economy, asserting that "the repercussions of an eventual loss of North Africa in the realm of business appear[ed] quite considerable." His real fear, though, was that France's global influence would evaporate with the loss of Algeria, that "she would lose at the same time her status as a great power and would have to renounce—on the economic front as well as the political—her seat at every conference of equals with certain other countries."[40] Crucially, Massenet insisted that the imminent economic catastrophe would "mean a notable fall in the standard of living for every Frenchman" and foretold "if not the collapse, at least the inevitable disequilibrium of [France's] economic system."[41] Here, at last, is part of his justification for his outspokenness on imperial issues—Massenet believed that the French quality of life was inextricably bound up in the success and endurance of the empire. Thus, the day-to-day workings of the Rhône department could not, in his eyes, be separated from these larger imperial and global currents. French imperial grandeur was not amorphous or unrelated to his concerns for the citizens in his charge but central to their growth and well-being.

Here, as well, we begin to see why Massenet became so involved in the Ramadan celebration that opened this chapter. The artillery salvos begun in 1953 continued at least through 1956 as a "sign of respect for moral and spiritual values, and in the spirit of liberalism appreciated by the Muslim population of the Lyon agglomeration."[42] Communications to local newspapers sought to educate the public and included a basic summary of the month's meaning for Muslims and its function as one of the five pillars of the Islamic faith.[43] Le Progrès announced the event with gusto, mentioning the region's growing North African population, lauding the prefect and his wife for their considerate approach, and ending with the reminder that "there ha[d] always existed a close relationship [entente sympathique] between the Quran and the Gospel."[44]

At the feast hosted by the MAN, the prefect and his wife were joined by Abdelkader Zitouni, a Muslim of Algerian descent who was very active in local associations for North African migrants and a close ally of the prefecture.[45] Zitouni praised local officials for their "benevolent attention" and declared that this recognition of Muslim holy days "gives us an idea of the true face of France, respectful of Islam, of our customs, and our traditions."[46] He explicitly invoked France's role as "protector and civilizer" and mentioned his French and North African brothers fighting in Indochina "to safeguard our liberty and defend the free world." This was exactly the message that Massenet hoped would issue from the event, with the overtone that North Africans were valued by the French imperial state—and that they were made better through their association with the empire.

These celebrations at the MAN carried on through the 1950s. Yet for all this rhetorical support for migrants' Muslim faith and customs, Massenet refused to get involved with less photogenic rituals, like burial. When asked to help ensure that Muslim migrants had access to appropriate burials, both Massenet and the administration of his predecessor clung to the idea of separation of church and state by invoking the 1905 law.[47] This apparent contradiction serves as an excellent demonstration of just how far Massenet was willing to go in support of the empire. It also reminds us that policies of accommodation and toleration did not always derive from openness—here they were part and parcel of enhanced policing and surveillance strategies.

Just as the French state supplemented its "hearts and minds" campaign with iron-fisted repressive tactics, so too did Massenet embrace the use of overwhelming military force on Algerian soil as "the only effective means to conquer a situation that risks rapidly becoming irremediable."[48] France, he declared, "must put everything on the line in order to conserve her overseas departments." Indeed, Massenet insisted that "force be rapidly deployed in order to avoid our departure from North Africa, as should have been done in Indochina."[49] This implicit critique of national policy grew more pointed as the conflict wore on and the overall imperial situation evolved.

In November 1955, as a response to Mohammed V's return to the Moroccan throne, Massenet complained, "The common opinion does not understand and accepts with difficulty that the French government can so rapidly abandon former positions that one hopes were carefully thought through." Some of Massenet's barbs were better couched—for example, his statement in early 1956 that "one ardently wishes that the politicians who have the evidently difficult charge of resolving this delicate problem succeed in serving the best interests of the nation."[50] By April 1957, Massenet had grown impatient, diagnosing "a certain pessimism . . . as regards the evolution of our [France's] Algerian policies."[51] He charged that "the situation in North Africa is currently dominated by great confusion" and accused the press of "sowing uncertainty by diffusing points of view that are too diverse, often badly informed, and always unverifiable."[52] Against those who called for the "liberation" of Algeria, Massenet charged that such action "would equal not only losing it, but also delivering its population over to massacres and reprisals."[53] As national popular opinion and governmental policy slowly began to turn away from holding on to French Algeria, Massenet preferred to see misunderstanding in the place of actual disagreement over imperial policy.

Massenet's approval of the use of force applied not only to the Algerian departments but also to his own. Both he and his successor oversaw massive police operations against Algerians living in the Rhône in their shared role as IGAME for the eighth region. Massenet asserted that the public was fully behind his actions and quite satisfied with the authorities' treatment of "individuals who, even as French citizens, still worry them." Massenet's nod to Algerian citizenship here was thoroughly undercut by his exclusion of local migrants from the "metropolitan population" he claimed to protect and serve. This rhetorical tactic of keeping North Africans apart from metropolitans differed markedly from how Saint-Denis's municipality spoke of its Algerian neighbors. Massenet further explained, "For their part, honest Algerians, holding down a regular job and often forced, through fear, to financially contribute to the Nationalist Movements [s added in pen here] watched without displeasure as the Police Services concerned themselves with suspect elements and troublemakers"—honesty in Algerians being defined for him as opposition to the nationalists.[54]

In January 1955, Massenet assured police intelligence services that from the moment that "the events occurred in Algeria . . . the North African colony in the Rhône department (around 15,000) ha[d] been the object of special surveillance." In those first two months of the conflict, fifteen separate police raids were carried out: most in Lyon, but one each in Villeurbanne and Vénissieux. Massenet later explained that many of the Rhône's Algerian migrants had come from "rebel zones" (Kabylia and northern Constantine), which made the region "particularly sensitive to the evolution of the situation in Algeria." Police surveillance followed individuals out of the Rhône as well, keeping tabs on many of those who returned to Algeria and corresponding with French administrators there to continue to track their movements and political activities.[55] Local police services made both implicit and explicit requests to reconvene a North African Brigade.[56] In 1956, they boasted of a "considerable" uptick in operations targeting Algerians on the streets, in the slums, and in North African cafés; they tripled the number of individuals stopped for questioning (from nearly four thousand in 1955 to over twelve thousand in 1956).[57]

Massenet framed the surveillance work as necessary "at once to reassure the metropolitan population, who worried about anti-French intrigues, and to protect the North African workers who wanted to keep away from the agitation."[58] Massenet insisted that the methods employed were all "carried out within the framework of legality," apparently to defend the region's police work against some negative press reports circulating in 1955. He believed that the "preventive measures" were successful at "identifying troublemakers, discovering weapons and tracts, disrupting clandestine meetings." Most of all, Massenet declared, the work they were doing in the Rhône ensured that the "most active nationalists" operated in insecurity, unable to act in public, and with the knowledge that those "hostile to France" put themselves at great risk. Massenet's concerns included the possibility that the area's metropolitans, witnesses to demonstrations and "assassinations," might be provoked to take violent measures on their own.[59]

Massenet left Lyon—and, it seems, imperial politics—in 1957 to join the Ministry for Public Works (in 1959, he was named

president of the Régie autonome des transports parisiens [RATP],
which operates public transport in the Paris region). His successor, Roger Ricard, held somewhat less strident views on empire,
though no less of a professional connection. Ricard also jointly
held the Rhône prefect and IGAME positions but came to Lyon
with more experience in the empire. During the Second World
War, he served in the imperial administration in Morocco and was
a subprefect in Algiers. After rising through posts in Brest, Sarthe,
Isère, and two ministers' cabinets, he was named IGAME for the
DOM (Départments d'outre-mer, or overseas departments) in 1955.

Ricard's reports repeated assertions that Algeria should remain
French but allowed that the relationship might evolve and that the
war was becoming more of a problem than a solution.[60] In early
1958, Ricard explained that "while fully hoping that France's legitimate interests are not in any way betrayed, the population desires
more and more a rapid end to this conflict."[61] Under Ricard, the
Rhône experienced growing levels of violence; thus, while Ricard
may not have embraced Massenet's advocacy for French Algeria, he
had no qualms about furthering police action in the department.
Ricard saw curbing "North African terrorism" as his first duty,
seized immediately upon entering office, and regularly asserted
that he personally oversaw operations against local Algerians.[62]
In the wake of continued violence, he noted, "Though the efforts
deployed night and day by the police forces are largely known,
public opinion wants us to go further still."[63]

Ricard continued to step up police presence and action in and
around Lyon as the population grew ever more uneasy about the
possibility of attacks on "metropolitans" (intra-Algerian violence
did not seem to concern them). In early 1958, Ricard again assured
the Interior Ministry, "The measures for prevention and repression that I am personally directing have been again reinforced:
over two hundred arrests were made in the preceding months (during which sixty attacks had been made or attempted)."[64] In the following years, Ricard would oversee the creation of the Lyon region's
SAT police forces, modeled on the Paris police prefecture's work,
which furthered the surveillance and control of Algerians in the

region. Detention was a common practice. By the end of the war, more than 400 Algerians were detained "for political motives" in a camp at Thol (in the nearby Ain department), while another 240 were held in the region's prisons.[65] Fully in line with the national developments discussed above, the Rhône prefecture linked these repressive actions with a massive program of outreach and social welfare to win the hearts and minds of Algerian migrants.[66]

In the summer of 1958 (following de Gaulle's assumption of power after the attempted coup d'état in May), teams were sent into hotels and *garnis* to work on improving living situations, help with formal documentation needs, and nurture "détente in psychological relations through direct and human contact with public offices, associations, and the Muslim population, who can, at times, have the feeling of being abandoned to itself." These visits were deemed successful, as the migrants who met with the teams "understood the humanitarian and social aims of the actions taken on their behalf and welcomed [the teams] with confidence." Moreover, the prefecture claimed that the host of services offered to migrants was winning individuals over and putting the FLN on the defensive in the region.[67]

Migrant, and specifically Algerian, responses to the police and prefectural services suggested a nuanced engagement on their part. Lyon's SAT reports repeatedly lamented the reticence of their Algerian visitors to discuss politics or the war.[68] For the migrants, however, this would have been an effective strategy for avoiding problems (or outing their own allegiances); earlier police discussions acknowledged—with much frustration—how effectively Algerian nationalists used silence as a tactic to obscure and deflect from their activities.[69] SAT commanders regularly insisted that migrants cared only about retaining their ability to work and their access to social services, particularly as independence became the likely outcome.[70] It is indeed likely that many migrants—who, after all, came to France precisely for employment opportunities (see chapter 5)—were invested in ensuring that they retained their jobs and other benefits. Yet there are also distinct traces of wishful imperial thinking on the part of the Lyon police, not to mention a long-standing prejudice that nourished disbelief in Algerian political agency.[71]

Most Algerians who came through the SAT welfare offices (or who worked with Georges Martin, discussed at length below) sought specific forms of aid, especially in navigating French bureaucratic systems. These did not differ markedly after the outbreak of the Algerian War or with the creation of new services. These habits aligned closely with Danielle Beaujon's analysis of how Algerians made use of police services in Algiers and Marseille. As much as the French police, in Beaujon's words, "served as bearers of France's 'civilizing mission,' imposing behavioral norms on Algerian colonial subjects," Algerians long proved to be savvy consumers who mobilized police forces toward their own ends whenever possible.[72] Algerian visitors to Lyon's SAT offices generally sought help with housing and employment. They came for aid in acquiring or replacing their identification papers, ensuring the proper disbursement of family allocation funds, and getting travel authorizations to visit Algeria. Algerian women stood out as a group to the SAT reporters; they came for administrative support and, occasionally, personal advice.[73] A growing number of wives, as well as white women with Algerian partners, approached the police for help with finding men who had abandoned their families.[74] Others sought repatriation to rejoin husbands who had been sent back to Algeria because of their political activities.[75] Young women in particular seemed to drop by in order to read or collect copies of the *Femmes Nouvelles* magazine available in the waiting room.[76]

While only a small number of North Africans came to the SAT in its first few months of operations, by the beginning of 1962 hundreds of visits were clocked each month. The relatively large number of visits to the Lyon-Nord office was especially significant, as they were located right by the Centre de la Part-Dieu. Given the impressive extent of FLN influence there, this serves as evidence that even committed nationalists were willing to engage police services to their own ends—though they did launch their own countersurveillance of the newly appointed head of the Lyon-Nord office, a Captain Bertrand.[77] At the same time, a notable number of Part-Dieu residents vented their frustrations with FLN control and collections, though these complaints were unlikely to be as indicative of pro-French sentiments as the officers seemed to hope.[78] SAT visits dropped precipitously after the Evian Accords were signed, and by 1963 the soon-to-close SAT was forwarding migrants to the Algerian consulate.[79] Bertrand, who oversaw all three Lyon SAT offices as the units closed down, spoke strongly on behalf of harkis, veterans, and other pro-French Algerians, emphasizing the state's responsibility to these groups even as formal imperial ties dissolved.[80]

Alongside these massive surveillance and welfare operations, the Rhône department oversaw a massive propaganda push. According to Massenet in 1955, the region's migrant workers were avid programming consumers. They had no trust in the French National Radio's Arabic programs, however, which they believed obeyed the state's desire to leave out important news and information. Algerian listeners were also, unsurprisingly, insulted by the French radio's consistent use of the pejorative "fellaghas" or even the simple correlation between North African and "terrorist." Instead, the migrants listened to foreign sources. Radio Cairo was audible in the Lyon region, Radio Budapest was a favorite (even though the migrants were wary of its procommunism), and if French-language programming was sought after, it was often Radio Luxembourg.[81]

In order to overcome this pattern, and to ensure that migrants were exposed to the French state's perspective and purported goals, Ricard's prefecture oversaw the distribution of photographs from Algeria—of both Muslim and "European" areas in the major cities—to all the housing centers; they acquired the images from the military in hopes of promoting better metropolitan-Algerian relations.[82] Local officials then worked to get television sets in each of the area's foyers and housing centers to ensure that "the excellent propaganda offered by *Télévision Française* programs" would reach more Algerian migrants. Finally, in a more targeted action, they printed eighteen thousand brochures in French and Arabic to highlight the major points of de Gaulle's speeches during his first trips to Algeria (in June and July 1958) and disseminated these among the region's North African housing centers, cafés, *garnis*, and even individual homes (see figure 3.2).[83]

The prefecture was equally instrumental in disseminating information about the end of the war, sending out a brochure, "L'Algérie de demain" ("the Algeria of tomorrow"), to detail the points of the Evian agreement to all the local associations working with migrants (including the MAN, SONACOTRAL, and other foyers).[84] Ricard was assured that the region's Algerian workers, upon hearing news of the Evian Accords, were "satisfied" by the idea of independence but that "they cannot conceive of this independence except within a close cooperation with France, the only guarantee of their continued survival in the Metropole, whose advantages they appreciate."[85] Ricard himself seemed to have moderated his stance once de Gaulle had taken office and begun to evolve the imperial agenda.

On June 27, 1959, Jean Jacques Servan-Schreiber, director of *L'Express* and a vocal critic of the French state's Algeria policy, held an open meeting in Lyon. Ricard faced significant pressure to ban the meeting. Former soldiers warned that they would "do the impossible to prevent him from speaking."[86] The Comité d'information France–Afrique du Nord, which worked "for the health and the renewal of French Algeria," insisted, "We believe it superfluous that once again our army will be insulted, our Government hindered in its so delicate operations in North Africa."[87] The Union Gaulliste called Servan-Schreiber a "defeatist" and pleaded with the prefect to cancel the meeting "and thus avoid very possible incidents and also stop the harmful work of this individual in its tracks."[88] A settler group, the Association nationale des Français d'Afrique du Nord, sent Ricard a copy of their resolution, citing the French prime minister's declaration that the state would not tolerate any apologism for illegitimate Algerian violence.[89] The settlers' representative further explained that Servan-Schreiber's calls for the state to negotiate directly with the "so-called Algerian government" were an "attack on the morale and honor of the army," warning the prefect that "local branches of national

FIG. 3.2. Flyer promoting de Gaulle's
Constantine Plan (1958). ADR, 437 W 91.

organizations will not allow [Servan-Schreiber] to speak here,"
and moreover, "police measures will be insufficient to prevent
order from being disrupted."

Despite such strong pressure to uphold the glory of French Algeria, Ricard did not give in to the military and settler groups. In his

report to the Interior Ministry, he explained, "I refused to pro-
hibit this meeting, respectful of the principles of liberty."[90] Even as
the French population began to drift away from supporting the
war, Ricard had begun to balance the imperial imperative with
his faith in basic republican rights and values. This is not to say
that Ricard gave up his imperial ideals. In 1965, after Algerian
independence, the French Consul in Algeria wrote to the Rhône
prefecture to request brochures and guides about the department
in order to pass them along to those interested in traveling there
(either settlers looking to relocate or Algerians "concerned with
preserving traditional links with our Country").[91] Ricard responded
with delight, sending a package of information on Lyon and the
various departments of the Rhône-Alpes along with the hope "that
these documents will aid you in keeping alight the beacon of French
culture in Algeria."[92] Though the formal empire had been torn
apart, Ricard's vision of French glory had not waned entirely.

Rarely did the prefects include alternative or opposing view-
points in their reports: they described a Rhône population united
in its support for French Algeria; the only outliers were rebellious
North African migrants and quarrelsome communists (neither of
whom were believed to truly belong to the community). In contrast, when the Interior Ministry's aggregated reports for this period
did discuss general national trends in opinion on the subject of
Algeria, the Rhône's particular stance barely appeared. Instead, the
national reports noted growing reticence to support the war. In 1957
the ministry was already concerned that segments of the French
public questioned the right of French sovereignty over a territory
whose majority supported independence from France.[93] It is quite
clear, however, that the Rhône officials took a decisive stance
in favor of the French Empire (or at least French Algeria) and
used their reports and other policy options as a means of expressing
their imperial desires. The Rhône prefects' habit of holding forth
on imperial and international issues suggests that Massenet and
Ricard closely linked the administration of the region to France's
place in the world, both through their professional position as
IGAME within the national administrative structure and through

their personal investment in the idea of the French Empire. Massenet, in particular, did not approve of the national government's willingness to soften its Algerian policy as the situation changed: his fervent belief in the need to keep Algeria French inspired his critiques of imperial policy.

The Local Imperial Office

The prefects were not the only local leaders with an affinity for French Algeria and a belief in the importance of controlling the North African migrant population. Those who ran services for North Africans either through the prefecture or as independent organizations expressed similar admiration for imperial tactics. Within the Rhône prefecture, the one official whose charge came directly through the French imperial administration was Georges Martin, the Conseiller technique pour les affaires musulmanes (CTAM). Martin was one of the original four CTAMs posted to metropolitan prefectures by the Interior Ministry in 1954.[94] The CTAMs were selected by the Government General of Algeria and recruited from the Algerian imperial administration; all were former heads of the "communes mixtes," who had had expansive oversight over Algerian populations in regions with few European settlers.[95] By 1958, the CTAMs had authority over "all questions related to Muslim affairs."[96] In the Rhône, this meant Martin also directed the region's SAT-FMA forces[97] as well as coordinating all SONACOTRAL projects and serving as vice president for Logement et gestion immobilière pour la région lyonnaise (LOGIREL) upon its formation.[98] Sociologist Françoise de Barros describes the CTAMs as part of a "parallel" administration within the prefectures, with their own networks of colleagues and associations—a sort of implant from the empire.[99] Historian Fatiha Belmessous specifically situates Martin's daily work within a framework of imperialism inside the metropole.[100] Unsurprisingly, given this position as a local imperial official, Martin's adherence to French imperial structures mirrored that of the prefects, and he too found avenues to assert his opinions on the need to hold on to Algeria even as he concerned himself with local North Africans.

Martin was born in Algeria and spoke Arabic fluently. He had served in the Algerian branch of the French infantry in 1939–40 and spent a number of years in the colonial administration before being posted to the Rhône.[101] He came from a settler family who employed Algerians in farm and domestic work; his father and brother were mayors.[102] He described his job as CTAM in 1953 as a "social mission" with programming, orientation, and information services, as well as an important liaison role among all the interested government agencies (and, of course, with the North Africans themselves). However, he also held a clear view of his surveillance role, explaining to the secretary general in Algiers that "in addition, [the Algerian civil service administrators sent to the metropole] pay discrete but close attention to the attitudes of the North African migrants, their political behavior, [and] union or party activity in all its forms" in order to relay this information to the imperial administration. At the same time, he undertook an "active" propaganda campaign "to make France's civilizing work in Algeria known and appreciated fully [à sa juste valeur] and the efforts undertaken by the Administration of this country to improve the living conditions of its populations."[103] Here, Martin stressed the links between his work in the Rhône department and the overall French imperial mission. Belmessous emphasizes the importance of this colonizing ideology in Martin's activities, particularly in relation to labor and employment.[104]

During the period of the Algerian War, Martin was particularly impressed by Robert Lacoste's actions as resident minister in Algeria, which relied heavily on military force. He likewise believed in enhanced police activities targeting Algerians on the mainland. Martin concluded a report on the department's social services for North African migrants with a strong note of support for local police action: "The surveillance and repressive measures taken against Algerian agitators to neutralize their dangerous antinational plots," he wrote, "provide the necessary preconditions for improving the Muslim workers' state of mind and for making more efficient the social actions taken on their behalf."[105] Indeed, early in 1958, the mission of all French CTAM officials was expanded beyond mere social concerns to include "all questions related to Muslim affairs." Martin and his colleagues were warned, however, that their political and policing work should be discreet so as not to disrupt their social programming.[106]

In January 1957, Martin wrote to Lacoste to thank him for his support of the civil administration in Algeria (to which he had long belonged) and to declare his "total and faithful devotion to your person and to the actions you have courageously taken to keep Algeria and all her children, without distinction, within the framework of the French community."[107] Soon thereafter, Martin joined forces with a number of local leaders—including both Massenets (the prefect's wife represented the MAN), Jacques Soustelle (former governor-general of Algeria), and the mayors of Lyon and Villeurbanne—to create a Comité France–Afrique du Nord in Lyon, with the stated goal of "maintaining French sovereignty in Algeria and French presence in Morocco and Tunisia." The group worked mostly in the realm of public opinion and sent informational flyers to U.S. congressmen in hopes of swaying them in advance of one of the UN General Assembly votes on the Algerian conflict. The group explicitly described their local work as "completing and concretizing" national ideals and encouraged activities "on either coast of the Mediterranean." In evidence of their unwavering support for French imperial presence in North Africa, one of the committee's main goals was to "combat all defeatist propaganda at the regional level."[108]

Martin, and the other CTAMs, had personal links to French Algeria and, as de Barros argues, should themselves be understood as trans-Mediterranean migrants. Travel back to Algeria served as an additional way for these agents of empire to refresh their colonial expertise and to ensure that Algerians in the metropole were handled similarly to those in North Africa.[109] Martin took one such trip back in the summer of 1957. Upon his return, he wrote to Soustelle to share his insights gleaned from interactions with the "Muslims" who approached him in the streets and markets, suggesting that these interactions provided a better window into the "reality" of the Algerian situation than could be gleaned from the French mainland. Metropolitan perceptions were, he felt, too colored by the "tragic" events of the conflict, whereas on the ground he witnessed "the continuity of human and economic life of a whole country."[110] Martin's conversations, he explained, "reinforced my belief in the possibility for coexistence between Muslims and Europeans and the desire for peace on both sides." Martin described an Algerian population weary of fighting and desiring ever closer ties to France. His invocation of a singular country and system reinforced the logic of colonial presence. As Belmessous asserts, his support for military action in Algeria derived from his insistence that this "was necessary for the well-being of the *Muslims* themselves."[111] In this way, he channeled his own dedication to French Algeria; his work on behalf of North Africans in the Rhône was thus part of an overall vision of coexistence—and tutelage. He concluded, "In the Algerian affair, there is no medium-term, we will be either victors or vanquished, and true peace can only come from ourselves."[112]

In March 1959, Martin spoke to a Rotary Club meeting about the situation of the Muslim population in the Rhône.[113] He insisted on the need for both social and psychological strategies in wooing migrants away from the FLN by developing fraternal ties and pacification programs. Martin's task, and that of his service, was to "stress the spiritual, moral and material human values of our Western civilization. Offer objective information to counterbalance nationalist propaganda. Convince [migrants] of the interest and sincerity of efforts to bring together the two communities." To accomplish these goals, Martin highlighted programming for radio, film, and television that targeted the local North African population, such as the campaigns Ricard was promoting. Martin was also invited to speak to police and military groups, audiences that de Barros identifies as active participants in validating and legitimating Martin's specifically colonial knowledge.[114]

Within the realm of social services—housing, in particular—he cautioned against any sort of "discrimination between Muslims and metropolitans."[115] Martin concluded with a reminder of how important North Africa had been to France: "We owe a debt of gratitude to the Muslims who fell for the country [*pays*], for those who fight at our sides. This encourages us to pursue a course of action whose purpose is to serve the people [*les hommes*] and France." With this, Martin expressed a clear sense of continued French obligation to its colonial subjects—with distinct echoes of the civilizing mission—even as he built on the notion that the French and the North Africans share a future as well as a past. These ideas dovetailed perfectly with those expressed by Prefects Massenet and Ricard. This particular notion of the French imperial system also supported Martin's own dual role as a social services administrator for CTAM and a surveillance director for the SAT-FMA.[116] Martin's imperial frame of reference did not disappear with Algerian independence. As head of the LOGIREL housing association through the 1960s, he maintained close ties with the prefecture's Service de liaison et promotion des migrants (SLPM) office (which replaced the CTAM position) and continued to monitor and report on North African residents' conduct.[117]

Imperial Associations

The Maison de l'Afrique du Nord (MAN) and its director general, Colonel Marcel Le Page, were also very much involved with regional surveillance and control efforts. Indeed, the MAN was one of the regional associations most closely linked to CTAM Martin.[118] Marthe Massenet, wife of the Rhône prefect, had been a founding member of the MAN Association in 1951. Le Page came to the MAN in August 1958 after a distinguished military career in the colonies, mostly in Morocco.[119] Le Page's first tour of service was the Rif War, after which he remained in Morocco with the Service des affaires indigènes (for a total of more than twenty years). He fought on the Italian front in the Second World War and spent five years in French Indochina (1949–54), during which he was imprisoned by the Vietminh. Le Page claimed expertise in ethnography and "Muslim sociology"; he spoke Arabic as well as a bit of Berber.[120] His trajectory was emblematic of all those imperial military officials who found positions within French migration services during and after decolonization.

Both Le Page and the MAN Association advocated for stronger social services for Algerians (and later other migrants) in the Rhône. The MAN's mission was to "maintain the reciprocal sentiments of esteem and confidence between French Citizens of the Metropole and from North Africa, to provide in a fraternal spirit its support for those of the latter who arrive on metropolitan soil to participate in the Nation's economic activity." The first MAN center opened in July 1952, offering medical assistance, clothing, education, housing, and help with administrative processes—in essence, everything needed to "hasten the adaptation of those concerned to metropolitan life." They also ran a housing center at the La Doua military camp in Villeurbanne. A report on their 1953 activity opened with a strong statement of their humanitarian ideals; the association existed to "bring together all those who, in a fraternal spirit and for simple social justice, want to offer our Muslim friends all the moral, material, and social aid that they need."[121] Yet their development over the years, particularly after the outbreak of the Algerian War in 1954, calls attention to their deeply imperial roots. From the start, MAN funding drew from a variety of offices that showcased public and private investment in the imperial system: the Interior Ministry, the Gouvernement générale de l'algérie, and military authorities partnered with the Lyon municipality, local business owners, the Conseil Général du Rhône, and a host of other associations.

By 1955, the MAN was recognized as a central actor in migrant services in the Lyon region.[122] In addition to the first two centers, they ran a welcome desk at the Lyon-Perrache train station jointly with the Comité Lyautey,[123] were building the new Foyer Inkermann in Villeurbanne,[124] and regularly demanded funding for the urgent housing needs of North Africans in the Rhône.[125] Once Le Page joined the MAN, he became a strong proponent of housing initiatives to benefit North African migrants, which he saw as a crucial means of ensuring the future of Algeria.[126] In addition to playing a role in the closing of the Part-Dieu housing center in Lyon, the MAN was also instrumental in bidonville resorption processes throughout the region.[127] Le Page and other MAN officials oversaw the emptying of the bidonville des Poilus in Villeurbanne in 1962 and 1963, rehousing individuals as well as closely monitoring evacuation, reporting on bidonvilliers' reticence to relocate, and recommending stricter control measures by the prefecture to ensure that premises emptied on time.[128] Le Page's efforts in closing the bidonvilles were recognized in 1967 as particularly "dynamic and competent," while the association was given credit for much of the success of local housing initiatives and the resorption of the bidonvilles.[129] Le Page continued advocating for migrant housing even after the area's bidonvilles had disappeared. He insisted that Algerians and others were doing the sorts of work that no one else in France was willing to do and that officials needed to do a better job of communicating their contributions to the public.[130] He consistently coupled these expressions of support and his desire for deeper French–North African connections with an unswerving allegiance to ideas about discipline and the use of housing and other services as a means of control.

Throughout his time in the Rhône, Le Page maintained strong connections with the military. He was a regional delegate for the Comité des amitiés africaines, which organized and looked after African veterans of the French army.[131] In that role, he consistently advocated for programs that would bring African and metropolitan veterans together. He sought to encourage "union" between these communities, very much in line with imperial ideals of integration. Mixed gatherings could also help Algerian veterans meet without facing reprisals from the FLN.[132] Le Page was involved in recruiting Algerian migrants (as well as interested metropolitans) for the French army's 3ème Régiment de Tirailleurs Algériens. He claimed to be approached "frequently" by former soldiers and young men, often those who had been "threatened by terrorism" or without work for a long period, and promised that he would offer them all "useful propaganda" and recommend likely candidates directly to Martin.[133] With the end of the war, Le Page took a special interest in the plight of the *harkis*, Algerians who served in the French army. He received personal requests from other officers to look after their former "protégés."[134] In June 1962, Le Page

wrote to Martin to express his own concerns for these former soldiers, insisting that it was "unthinkable that those who loyally gave
their service to France and who, for that reason, are now on the
receiving end of prosecution by those who chose rebellion, should
be abandoned." This obligation to the harkis derived from their
service to the empire, and Le Page's comments reveal his objec-
tion to those who fought to end the imperial system. This sense of
responsibility did not disappear with decolonization; MAN reports
included special mention of harki support at least through 1965.[135]

Beyond their connections to French armed forces, Le Page
and the MAN were specifically recognized by Lyon's SAT forces as
supporters of and collaborators with police activity.[136] Le Page oversaw a strong network of surveillance within the foyers operated by
the MAN. In 1959, Le Page arranged to have police patrol inside the
Inkermann foyer in Villeurbanne on Friday and Saturday nights.[137]
From January 1960 to October 1961, there was a dedicated police
post at the Inkermann foyer, which closed only for cost concerns
(and was replaced by heavy patrolling in the area).[138] Foyer residents were closely monitored by MAN employees as well. From
1960, all applicants to the Pressensé foyer in Villeurbanne were
screened by the prefecture in hopes of preventing "partisan" activity, and annual reports tracked the number of arrests made within
the foyer itself.[139] In May 1962, Le Page sent Martin a list of "militant nationalists" living at the Bonnet-Pernet foyer in Vénissieux,
noting that other long-term residents had left to escape pressure
from Algerian nationalists.[140] He sent a similar list of Inkermann
militants in June, explaining that the MAN planned to refuse to
renew contracts for those individuals, but gradually and with the
excuse of rule infractions so as not to spark protest.[141] MAN residents were thus subject to multiple levels of policing, and Le Page's
dedication to quelling any and all political activity within the foyers demonstrated both the links between housing and surveillance
and the reliance of French state officials on private individuals and
associations to support imperial practices.

Le Page provided a series of special reports on MAN residents'
reactions to various propaganda efforts and televised official

remarks, paralleling Ricard and Martin's interest in promoting formal information campaigns. This was not, however, a common practice of social associations in the region and stands as a clear example of how Le Page saw his and the MAN's work as a means of furthering French imperial goals. When requesting funds to purchase a television for the Inkermann foyer, he specifically cited TV programs and monitoring as effective "psychological, cultural, and educational action."[142] His reports detailed how many residents watched or otherwise received these messages as well as a sampling of responses—though Le Page noted that most were reticent to "externalize their sentiments."[143] Without fail, Le Page ascribed a desire for peace to all his North African residents, but he also included some of their political hopes (freedom for Ahmed Ben Bella, Algerian independence, etc.).[144] Following de Gaulle's September 26, 1959, speech, Le Page insisted that migrants felt burdened by the financial pressures of forced FLN dues and were predominantly awaiting the "end of hostilities." He assured the prefecture that "General de Gaulle's prestige ha[d] again grown," while FLN militants risked losing all support if they did not accept the terms for autodetermination.[145] For de Gaulle's June 14, 1960, speech, Le Page reported "a real satisfaction and hope for an imminent peace"; one of the residents was particularly impressed by de Gaulle's invocation of "l'Algérie Algérienne" (an Algerian Algeria).[146] For an April 1961 press conference, Le Page noted optimistically that Algerian migrants "are inclined as a whole toward association with France" and that de Gaulle benefited from "unconditional admiration" as the only leader capable of bringing peace.[147] A February 1962 report was less positive; residents seemed upset de Gaulle had not mentioned a cease-fire in his speech, though they were happy to hear condemnations of the OAS. Le Page suggested at this point that many migrants lacked strong enough French skills to follow these broadcasts closely—showing both his paternalistic attitudes and his search for reasons that response was lackluster.[148] While these reports reflect the growing realities of decolonization, Le Page's habits of political surveillance revealed that imperial methods of control were still firmly entrenched in the MAN's social services.

Algerian independence hardly marked an end to these practices. Le Page closely followed the number of residents who registered to vote in the independence referendum, emphasizing the role of the FLN in getting Algerian migrants engaged.[149] The MAN even reported on the independence celebrations held at the foyers they ran. While the directors signed off on the use of common rooms and allowed flowers, cakes, and banners, they also prohibited nonresidents in most of the foyers. At Bonnet-Pernet in Vénissieux, the foyer director argued with the FLN representative who spoke at the festivities.[150] Along with so many other migrant services in France, the MAN did change its name to reflect a broader constituency; in 1963, they added "du Travailleur d'Outre-Mer, (for workers from overseas)," and by 1965 they had become simply the Maison du travailleur étranger (MTE), or the foreign worker's house. Yet Le Page and other staff continued to monitor their residents closely for political activity. They forwarded tracts found circulating in the foyers,[151] reported on all disciplinary measures and police contacts,[152] and set up interior regulations specifically to prevent political agitation.[153] At the same time, their reports denied much political agency or interest on the part of their North African residents. Algerians after independence were described as focused on keeping their jobs.[154] In 1965, Algerians were said to be surprised by the ousting of President Ben Bella, though anti-Boumédiène sentiments faded quickly due, according to MTE, to the facts that the new regime was more "liberal" and that "relations with the French [were] better."[155] Le Page and his colleagues displayed some lingering allegiance to the empire, declaring that "after 3 years of independence and anti-colonialism, it seem[ed] that Algerian migrants [were] becoming aware of the vital importance of French aid and the sentimental ties born of one hundred years of co-existence."[156] Their residents, in other words, were supposedly coming to see the benefits of the imperial system they had rebelled against (erroneously, the tone of this report suggested).

This idea that French aid was vital to these postcolonial migrants—and that surveillance and control remained the best ways to ensure this support—clearly comes through MTE's approach to governing foyer residents. Indeed, the MTE was specifically directed by Michel Massenet (the national Délégué à l'action sociale pour les travailleurs étrangers) to avoid "paternalism" in 1965, following a series of local critiques of their policies.[157] The response that the MTE now dealt with all migrants "without distinction by nationality" was somewhat telling: rather than dropping the imperial practices that had targeted Algerians, these regulations were brought to bear on all migrants.[158] A few years later, Le Page defended the practice of communal housing for migrants at a time when national figures were promoting a shift away from group housing and toward individual rooms. Though he argued that the dormitory-style foyers were still required to manage the sheer number of migrants in the Rhône, his position seemed also to stem from his belief that communal living offered foyer directors better avenues of control.[159] Speaking directly to critiques of MTE regulations, Le Page asserted that "a certain discipline is, in a community, the safeguard for individuals' liberty" and, moreover, a foyer is a "*maison familiale,*" or family house, in which the director must play the role of the "good father."[160] Le Page had likewise defended the strict enforcement of the rules in the Amitiés africaines foyer at Bonnet-Pernet in Vénissieux, which had been the target of one of Mayor Marcel Houël's rare campaigns on behalf of North African migrants.[161] Le Page blamed that controversy on the actions of a "cabal" whose leader was a well-known agitator, a "fellagha," and a communist/syndicalist militant (who had fortunately returned to Algeria).[162] Thus, Le Page and the associations with which he worked exemplified the enduring presence of imperial ideology in migrant welfare: migrants required firm discipline, political activity was to be rigorously suppressed, and problematic individuals were to be expelled.

This interest in and consistent invocation of empire sets these various local leaders apart. Other local actors involved in North African affairs rarely invoked imperial logics so openly. Asnières's Mayor Bokanowski, for instance, left such larger-scale issues entirely out of city discussions—indeed, he and his colleagues regularly stressed that even migration was a national issue, not a local one, and therefore out of their purview. Aid to Algerians before 1962 was, of course, often undergirded by the goal of shoring up the French Empire and undercutting Algerian nationalism. Yet day-to-day work at the local level mostly focused on narrowly defined issues of housing, health, and employment, with little attention to the greater purposes these might serve. The actors examined here, however, foregrounded those larger goals and articulated their local actions explicitly within a proimperial framework.

The Lyon region was generally associated with a higher degree of intolerance toward North Africans (and other migrants) than one finds in Paris or Marseille—gaining a reputation as the capital of French racism by the end of the 1960s.[163] Officials in the Rhône maintained a number of close ties to the settler population of Algeria—in addition, Lyon and its suburbs saw a large influx of *pieds-noirs* after Algerian independence.[164] The events and individuals discussed in this chapter suggest that local actors in Lyon and its suburbs were particularly affected by their allegiance to the French Empire and imperial ideology. Housing initiatives, employment programs, and even holiday celebrations were promoted with a view to showcase French support for Algerians and inspire North African loyalty. Martin and Prefects Massenet and Ricard were professionally linked to the empire in their respective roles as CTAM and IGAME. Both prefects, as well as Colonel Le Page and the private associations with which he was affiliated, brought imperial ideas and practices out of the national government and into their local work. All were deeply embedded in the imperial project—and its afterlives. Notably, Ricard's successor Max Moulins (prefect, 1966–72) also brought imperial experience to the job. Moulins served in the Algerian administration (1959–61) before being named general secretary for the Administration of the Overseas Departments (1961–66). Though Algerian independence fundamentally reframed welfare and services for North African migrants in France, Moulins's expertise in the logics of empire informed his involvement in restricting North African settlement and shutting down Olivier de Serres.[165]

As the next chapter will demonstrate, the municipal government of Saint-Denis took a similarly cosmopolitan view of their community politics, though in this case, elected local officials vociferously protested against the French state's attempts to retain the empire. Remarkably, these Dionysien city officials seemed to dedicate even more of their time and energy to imperial questions than did the Rhône prefecture and its allies. Certainly, they were more outspoken in public forums on the questions of Algerian nationalism and independence. They also engaged more directly with the North Africans in their community and fought—both rhetorically and physically—to protect these migrants from exactly the sorts of policing policies that Massenet, Ricard, Martin, and Le Page championed.

FOUR

Anti-imperialism

On October 2, 1961, Mayor Auguste Gillot and his colleagues marched to Saint-Denis's police commissariat at the head of a demonstration protesting police suppression of protests against the Algerian War (1954–62). The officer who met them in front of the building refused to recognize the municipal officials and gave orders to disperse the crowd; these orders were carried out violently. By Gillot's estimation, at least three city officials were physically attacked. In the aftermath, the Paris police prefect sought (but did not secure) the mayor's suspension. This confrontation proved to be exemplary of Saint-Denis's experience of the Algerian War. Gillot and his elected colleagues had long been outspoken in their opposition to the war, to the French Empire, and to the state's (mis)treatment of North African migrants to the French mainland. In stark contrast to the Rhône prefecture's support for French Algeria, the communist municipality of Saint-Denis was vehemently anti-imperialist. Not only did Dionysien city officials champion the cause of Algerian nationalists, but they also sought to protect local North African migrants from the police and demanded that their rights and welfare be upheld by the French state.

This chapter examines how anti-imperialism drove municipal actions, connecting Dionysien officials' commitments to their city's North African residents with their deeply held opposition to colonial violence. Most historians now include the metropolitan front in their discussions of the Algerian War. In this and the previous chapter, I demonstrate that the fighting over Algeria within mainland France was not limited to direct partisans. Even as intra-Algerian struggles crossed the Mediterranean and the French state marshaled repressive forces against Algerian migrants, local actors also used the Algerian War as a lever to move policies in a variety of areas. Both the Rhône prefecture and the Saint-Denis city council advocated positions based on specific foreign and imperial policy objectives, which had real effects on the local policies and programs they launched. Their very reasons for acting were grounded in their understandings of the French Empire and its future, which were neither distant nor irrelevant for these local actors.

In both places, local actors upheld stances very much in line with their broader ideologies and with long-standing local traditions. The Rhône department had been feeling the burden of North African workers since the interwar period, and their relations with newcomers grew ever more strained. While the prefects and their allies briefly elevated Algerian concerns in a bid to win them over to the imperial system, they were fundamentally uninterested in cultivating or supporting—or even understanding—Algerian politics or nationalism. Saint-Denis, in contrast, had long been more open to migrants. City officials had made a habit of involving themselves in foreign policy matters important to these newcomers, going out of their way, for example, to support Spanish Republicans (and communists) during the Spanish Civil War. Gillot and his colleagues had begun working with local North Africans immediately after the end of the Second World War and thus enjoyed a much closer and more congenial relationship with their city's migrants than any of the officials in the Rhône prefecture. In fact, though in the case of the Rhône prefecture, it is clear that imperial notions shaped Massenet and Ricard's ideas about migrants, in Saint-Denis anti-imperial ideology developed alongside these close relations with local North Africans. The links between Gillot and Dionysien migrants cannot have been incidental in the municipality's approach to the Algerian conflict, nor could these have remained unaltered by the shared experience of the Algerian War, particularly the battles fought on French soil.

Certainly, the local officials discussed here were at the extreme end of imperial engagement—Massenet and Gillot, in particular, held forth on the value/shame of the French Empire much more frequently than other local actors. One should not, however, entirely discount the role that notions of empire must have played for other metropolitan officials. Notably, both Gillot and Massenet were most outspoken when they disagreed with the direction of governmental policy (in Saint-Denis's case, this was, of course, almost always). This helps explain why these two men's imperial rhetoric was so strident: while other officials toed the state (or party) line, these two had bones to pick and so seized any opportunity to register their disapproval.

French Communists and the Algerian War

At its Sixteenth Party Congress in 1961, the French Communist Party (PCF) boldly declared, "Since the first days of the Algerian War, communists have fought for the recognition of the right to independence."[1] The actual record is less clear. The PCF's most controversial move came in 1956, when it supported the Special Powers Act that imposed severe restrictions on Algerian activities and organizations. Some historians have questioned the depth of party support for that vote.[2] Others cast it as a defining moment in the creation of extralegal opposition networks in France, when many finally lost faith in the PCF's anti-imperialist credentials.[3] The PCF did mount some opposition to the war in Algeria, but only when they could fit it into their greater policy goals. Their support of the 1955 protests by young draftees followed decades of antimilitarism and peace campaigns.[4] The most useful rubric was that of antifascism, though this cut in two directions. Initially, the PCF read the fall of the Fourth Republic and de Gaulle's assent to power as an extremist putsch from the Right, fueled by the Algerian crisis.[5] Certainly, Dionysien communists freely associated de Gaulle with fascism in their opposition to his government. The catalyst for the PCF to pivot to their 1961 declaration of the right to Algerian independence, however, was the development of the OAS (Organisation de l'armée secrète), a group of extreme right-wing military officers who vehemently opposed de Gaulle's movement toward Algerian independence. Their operations included many terrorist acts and assassinations, both in Algeria and in metropolitan France; these actions convinced the party that the OAS, not de Gaulle, was the graver fascist threat.[6]

By 1961, the broader French population was starting to turn against the war, as was international opinion (January 1961 was the first UN vote on the Algerian conflict). In response to torture allegations following the Battle of Algiers, the major antitorture campaigns were led not by PCF officials but predominantly by former or non-Communist intellectuals.[7] The party's allegiance to independence was also called into question when the PCF allowed their hatred for de Gaulle to color their reaction to the general's call for self-determination, though their initial reluctance dissolved after Khrushchev came out in support of the Gaullist policy.[8] Taking all of this into consideration, one sees how easily the PCF could be cast—both by contemporaries and by many later scholars—as a party that did nothing concrete to support the decolonization of Algeria and thus betrayed earlier claims to anti-imperialist leadership. Indeed, the engagement—or lack of engagement—by communist officials in Vénissieux largely follows this pattern.

Yet the party was never monolithic.[9] Nor was the broader constellation of workers' movements; Laure Pitti calls attention to how CGT (Confédération générale du travail) activists at Renault's Billancourt factory invoked Algerian national rights, while PCF operatives continued to speak of French national interest.[10] What emerges from a closer look at individual actors is a complex scale of resistance, in and out of the PCF, into which Saint-Denis's municipal officials might fit. The major force for opposition within the party was anti-Stalinism, closely aligned to anticolonialism and spurred by the Soviet reaction to the attempted Hungarian revolt in 1956.[11] Dionysien communists, however, did not break with the Stalinist lines in the PCF on this or other issues.[12] Other factors must then have been in play to bring the municipality of Saint-Denis to voice their disapproval of France's stance and conduct in the conflict and later seek to mitigate the state's policing power over North African residents in their community. Remarkably, there is little indication that this divergence induced friction between local communists and the national party; in fact, Gillot sat on the PCF's central committee throughout this period (1945–64).[13]

In Saint-Denis, opposition to French Algeria was voiced loudly and early. Gillot and other municipal officers made countless public statements condemning continued colonial presence in Algeria as well as the conduct of the war. Their activism on issues of social welfare for North African migrants was explicitly connected to an anti-imperial stance.[14] Many of their pronouncements did follow milder PCF rubric and favored antifascist and anti-OAS rhetoric over overt support for Algerian nationalism. Police records charting public participation in and reaction to municipal rallies and demonstrations suggest that Gillot's views on the Algerian conflict were more radical than the population's. It is therefore likely that members of the municipal council consciously toned down their declarations over time to avoid alienating their supporters. Yet there were many moments, particularly Gillot's 1951 address decrying "racist colonial oppression" and affirming Algeria's right to national independence, where local communists displayed much more strident views than those espoused by the national party. Certainly, city officials were aware that the PCF's stance was perceived as problematic. Gillot's strong words often seemed to implicitly address the charge, made in various leaflets and posters distributed by anticommunist parties in the city, that the PCF was neither a friend to the Algerian workers nor a true supporter of Algerian nationalism.[15] Dionysien actions throughout the war and the peace process remained robustly critical of colonial policies and more willing than the PCF to embrace the national aspirations of the Algerian people. Most striking, Dionysien officials did not waver in their support for individual Algerians whose civil and social rights were curtailed by state policy and police actions. It may be no coincidence, then, that the party's 1961 statement—embracing Algerian independence for the first time—was issued from a congress held in Saint-Denis.

Antiwar Activism in Saint-Denis

Dionysien engagement in international affairs did not begin with the Algerian War.[16] In the 1920s, for example, the Dionysien population participated, in large numbers, in a series of strikes and demonstrations against the Rif War in Morocco (1919–26).[17] That period saw a steady rise in local support for communist candidates even as the party platform, driven by Jacques Doriot (elected mayor in 1930) and the Jeunesses communistes, focused increasingly on international and specifically anticolonial issues.[18] Clearly, anticolonialism resonated with Dionysien voters, and municipal leaders were unafraid of involving themselves in hotly contested global issues.

Municipal activism related to the Spanish Civil War (best described by Natascha Lillo) set an even stronger precedent.[19] When the economic crisis of the 1930s hit, and most communities began to turn on their migrant residents, Saint-Denis remained open to Spanish workers. Under Doriot the municipality pursued an ambitious social aid program for all who were resident in the city for more than three months, regardless of their nationality.[20] A number of Dionysiens left to fight for the Spanish Republicans, while many of those who stayed participated in political solidarity efforts within France. The municipality supported the Spanish Communist Party (PCE), hosting their meetings and events even after the French government outlawed PCE activism within France in 1950. Dionysiens engaged in further anti-Francoist agitation, organizing publicity campaigns and collecting petitions.[21] As late as 1975, the municipality hosted a rally to condemn Franco's execution of five Basque separatists.[22] Lillo concludes that Saint-Denis's deep connections with Spanish politics were due both to the presence of the large Spanish community and to "the existence of a municipality susceptible [*sensible*] to international questions and inclined to unite behind them all the inhabitants living on their territory."[23] Municipal involvement in the Algerian conflict was linked to a similar inclination to mobilize residents of all nationalities in their community.[24]

Dionysien officials did not strictly limit the scope of their outrage over international developments to regions from which their
largest migrant communities originated, but they engaged such
issues with significantly more energy and to a much greater extent.
In line with their communist platform, Gillot and the others often
spoke against the "dirty war" in Vietnam, German rearmament,
nuclear proliferation, and American hegemony. However, not one
of these produced the vast files of documentation or the long lists of
municipal activities that were sparked by those events that directly
involved international members of the Dionysien community.[25]

Of all the debates in the decades after the Second World War, the
Algerian War resonated most deeply. From the earliest moments
of Algerian national rumblings, the municipality stood solidly in
opposition to French policies in Algeria and often explicitly linked
Algerians' social ills in the metropole to French colonial conduct.
This strong antiwar stance was grounded in a sense of solidarity
with the Algerian people as victims of imperialist repression and
extended to the city's advocacy for the rights of North Africans
living in the community. Soliciting Algerian workers' support for
the PCF lists, Gillot cast the 1951 election as a "great political battle
between the forces for independence and peace and the forces for
oppression and war," invoking both the militarism of the French
Empire and the Algerian right to independence—a full three years
before the nationalist rebellion officially launched.[26] Gillot connected the contemporary situation in North Africa with French
violence in Syria, the Rif War, and the Sétif massacres—he claimed
that this last saw the murder of forty thousand Algerians.[27] Gillot explicitly linked French colonialism in Algeria to the plight
of Algerian workers in France. Driven out of their homes by the
"misery resulting from 120 years of colonialism" and "racist colonial oppression," Algerian workers were greeted on French soil
with low salaries, poor lodging, unemployment, "bullying [bri-
mades] by the racist employers [and] the police," and "repression."
All of these ills resulted from decisions by the "French colonialist government" to oppose Algerian independence and persecute
Algerian militants. Gillot also went to great lengths to associate

colonialism in Algeria with fascism, a full decade before the PCF made this central to their platform.[28] Already in the 1940s, Gillot had argued for better housing for North African migrants by emphasizing the better treatment of German prisoners, implicitly accusing the state of coddling fascists while ignoring the plight of French citizens and protected subjects.[29]

Calling what was happening in Algeria a "war" was the first sign that communists in Saint-Denis deviated from the majority perception.[30] Throughout the conflict—indeed, well past its end—the French state refused to recognize a state of "war." Partly, this was a semantic issue: wars take place across international borders, and in the eyes of the French government, Algeria was an integral piece of the French state. More important, however, was the propagandist power of assigning labels such as "terrorist," "law and order problem," and "pacification" to Algeria and Algerians.[31] To invoke "war" was a conscious denial of the government's "rationalization" of the conflict as a question of basic domestic security. Opponents described atrocities taking place in Algeria, especially the use of torture, many freely associating these actions with Nazi activities during World War II.[32] "War" runs through the Dionysien record of the conflict, proving their willingness to accept the "events in Algeria" as acts of aggression by the French state.

Saint-Denis's police commissioner documented municipal activity over the course of the Algerian War, making frequent reference to protests organized by Gillot and his officials.[33] Dionysien communists made numerous attempts to reach out to the general population and involve them in the antiwar effort: they gave speeches, put up posters, flew banners, and organized assemblies and demonstrations. The municipality often used soldiers' funerals as platforms for their opposition. Gillot's city hall cultivated a close relationship to residents sent across the Mediterranean: publishing the *Bulletin du soldat Dionysien*, a news-from-home journal for these soldiers;[34] sending election reminders and political tracts;[35] and even eliciting responses from the young men.[36] In March 1956, the municipality hosted a reception to honor new conscripts, boldly asking the men to sign petitions against the "war in

Algeria."[37] Dionysien communists carefully tracked the number of local soldiers serving in Algeria and publicized their deaths as a stark reminder of the cost of the war in terms of French lives.[38] When a soldier died in Morocco that spring, the municipality put up posters announcing his funeral, which also referenced a municipal council vote for a "cease-fire" in Algeria.[39] Weeks later, Gillot spoke at another funeral, explicitly calling for recognition of the Front de libération nationale (FLN), while other officials distributed information for a "day of action" organized by the municipality.[40]

Local officials also did not hesitate to air their antiwar activism in city hall proceedings. The Dionysien municipal council convened an "extraordinary meeting" on May 30, 1956, to discuss the need for a cease-fire in Algeria and negotiation between parties. The council had already issued votes demanding a cease-fire and "free elections in Algeria" on March 30 and April 27 but claimed that this special session derived from the demands of various community groups for a forum to discuss the Algerian question at length. In his opening remarks, Gillot declared that it was the duty of the municipal council, "as elected representatives of the people, to act with the population, and with labor and political organizations, for Peace in Algeria." Refusing criticism that the council members were overstepping their bounds in debating the war, Gillot insisted that they could not "content [them]selves with going to *papas* and *mamans* to announce the deaths of their sons in Algeria, and then organizing burials for the bodies returned to Saint-Denis."[41]

While the request for a cease-fire and the insistence on negotiation track other blander PCF positions at this time, Gillot went significantly further to denounce French imperial presence in North Africa and support Algerian nationalism. After announcing, to applause, that he believed it was the state's duty to bring back the soldiers, given that they stood no chance of winning in Algeria, Gillot continued, "It is not possible, in 1956, to continue . . . this colonialism led by French imperialism. . . . The Algerian nation exists, it must be recognized."[42] The municipality collected petitions at this meeting from forty-seven delegations, comprising over nine thousand signatures from workers, neighbors, and union members.[43] The council, "owing to the deep current animating the Dionysien population," organized a delegation to deliver the petitions to the president of the republic.[44] The Seine prefecture, however, disapproved of municipal meddling in foreign affairs. The prefect wrote to Gillot announcing that the deliberations from the May 30 meeting were null and void: "Communal assemblies cannot deliberate matters other than those concerning the direct interest of the city, or those expressly placed by law under their control and jurisdiction."[45] As Gillot had set out in his speech, and as future actions by the council would attest, Dionysien officials believed to the contrary that the Algerian War did indeed command the "direct interest of the city" and its population.

In March 1957, the Dionysien section of the PCF organized a public assembly against the war, to be held, symbolically, in the municipal Salle de la Résistance. Their announcement for the meeting included a handful of articles on their concerns about the war and its effects, which echoed and extended the themes of Gillot's 1956 speech. An essay entitled "So That Algeria 'Remains French,' Will We Ruin France?" charged that France, alone among nations, had been waging unbroken war for eighteen years, the conflict in Algeria being the latest in a series that began with the Second World War and continued through Vietnam and North Africa.[46] Pacifism joined with anticolonialism to indict the state's history of belligerence and imperial repression.

The cost of the war was regularly weighed in terms of forgone social services. War spending for 1956 was tallied at 485 billion francs: "With the money spent in *one day of war*, it would be possible to build: the new hospital, the high school, [and] the vocational training center [*centre d'apprentissage*] of which Saint-Denis has need." The cost of ten days of war was equivalent to ten times the money spent building two of the city's recent large housing developments—that is, enough to cover the construction of "the 6,000 residences indispensable for making the slums in Saint-Denis disappear." Addressing the question of why Saint-Denis had become home to so many Algerians, the tract cited the "great misery that reigns in Algeria." Algerian workers crossed the Mediterranean in search of jobs they were told were abundant but that translated into poor salaries for the most difficult labor; further "deprived of the affection of their families and friends, they live like dogs in horrible, inhuman conditions." The notion that unemployment in France resulted from the presence of Algerian workers was merely "the employers' endeavor to create division between French and Algerian workers." All workers stood to gain "real satisfaction" only from an end to the war.[47]

The Dionysien population did not always react as favorably toward the Algerian cause as the municipality must have hoped. Initially, officials were able to build on the momentum of the May 1956 meeting; in October 1956 the petition drive for "peace in Algeria" topped 18,000 signatures, and by January it had reached 21,482.[48] This success was likely due in part to the ability to mobilize existing social networks in the neighborhoods and especially through the industrial unions.[49] In October 1957, Dionysien communists organized another "day of action." The town hall flew a banner demanding "Peace in Algeria"—which was quickly removed by the police—while Gillot and his deputy René Benhamou gathered a crowd near the train station to march back to the city center, chanting pacifist slogans. This time, police records noted that the crowd never topped two hundred.[50] It is, of course, easier to gather signatures than it is to convince people to descend to the streets. By the end of 1957, Dionysiens had been confronted with growing OAS terrorism on French soil as well as high levels of intra-Algerian violence, and concern for their own security began to overtake their disapproval of French pacification methods. During this period, a local graffiti artist scrawled "Gillot, *bicot*" on a bridge near the train station; the same bridge bore the slogan "Self-determination, peace in Algeria."[51] Even as some in the community stood fast for Algerian independence, others saw Gillot as sullied by the depth of his engagement.[52]

By 1961, antifascism had practically become the sole framework for opposition to the war (and the Fifth Republic). The municipal council met on April 24 to discuss the failed coup in Algiers. They lauded the creation of twenty-five committees for the "antifascist struggle" in local workplaces and neighborhoods. Gillot wrote to Dionysien soldiers on the anniversary of the Nazi surrender, praising them for their "courageous attitude . . . in the face of the coup by factious generals in Algiers" and expressing his hope that said generals would be brought to justice and that "the Republic will remain republican and peace will come soon to Algeria."[53] The municipality also released a series of flyers. Most of these claimed that the coup intended to "prevent peace negotiations in Algeria and institute fascism in France"; however, one addressed to former Resistance fighters stepped beyond standard antifascist rhetoric to accuse the generals of trying "to prevent the application of the Algerian people's right to self-determination."[54] The assumption was that those who had "fought against the German fascist hordes" were equally opposed to a new "terrorist regime" in France and so were more susceptible than others to calls for Algerian independence. This flyer also revealed that beneath the mobilizing antifascist arguments, the municipality had not quite lost sight of the Algerians' own liberation struggle. This new campaign appears to have reignited popular participation in the protest movement. The local PCF paper *Saint-Denis Républicain* reported a massive turnout for a rally at the city hall in April 1961: sixteen thousand attendees by their count, many of them young activists.[55]

After the cease-fire, the municipality co-opted soldiers' mothers into their movement. By this point, the tide of French popular opinion had mostly turned toward peace and even Algerian independence, with the OAS violence souring most loyalty to the notion of a French Algeria. Gillot sent an open letter to "the *mamans* of young Dionysiens currently in Algeria," claiming to write on behalf of concerned mothers who had shared with him their "anguish . . . at the thought that after the cease-fire their child finds himself in danger because of the criminal acts of the OAS" and inviting all other mothers to a meeting at which they could draft a letter to President de Gaulle.[56] The mothers' letter invoked their "anguish" but also their "indignation and anger" upon learning that the OAS had begun to attack French soldiers. They called upon de Gaulle to bring imprisoned OAS members and their conspirators to rapid

and harsh judgment. They also demanded the return of young soldiers whose terms of duty were up.[57] The municipality provided
transport for a delegation of the mothers, accompanied by Gillot and his deputy, Paulette Charpentier, to meet with the president and present their grievances. The mothers' declaration did
mention their desire, "with the entire country," for peace in Algeria, but their main concern—understandably—was the protection
of young French soldiers from OAS attacks. Local communists had
found an antiwar stance around which a majority could rally. It
may seem that the officials' position on the war had been diluted
over the length of the conflict. Yet the moderated tone of later
years served their original goals by attracting broader support for
peace and even independence.

Despite the vehemence of their pronationalist stance, Gillot and
his colleagues did not explicitly weigh in on intra-Algerian political struggles during the war, nor did they appear to take sides. Initially, Messali Hadj and his parties (the Parti du Peuple Algérien
[PPA] and the Mouvement national algérien [MNA]) were claimed
as allies. The October 1946 municipal council vote on migrant welfare and imperialism included both the insistence that Messali Hadj
be allowed to return to Algeria and demands for freedom and legal
recognition for "all Algerian national parties, including the Parti
du peuple algérien."[58] Gillot again denounced the persecution of
MNA activists and press in his 1951 speech to Algerian workers.[59] In
1955, Messali Hadj's "Appel au peuple français" was carefully kept
in the city's files on the Algerian War.[60] In January 1956, L'Humanité
printed an Algerian communist (PCA) declaration on the importance of unity within the national struggle.[61] Thereafter, most of
the sources lean toward the FLN, though this development was
never addressed explicitly by city officials. Gillot heavily marked
up a piece by Ferhat Abbas in December 1960, underlining phrases
about "race war," "exterminations," and "the era of barbarity" as
related to French conduct in Algeria.[62] PCA documents kept by
the municipality painted Messali Hadj as a potential French pup-
pet in 1961 and accused the MNA regularly thereafter of being anticommunist, even "counter-revolutionary and . . . [complicit] with

French colonialism."[63] The Paris police asserted that immediately after the cease-fire, the Saint-Denis municipality had quickly hired "multiple FLN militants freed from prison or internment camps," in part to cultivate communist sympathies.[64]

Certainly, both Messalist and FLN forces were active in Saint-Denis, and there was strong competition for allegiance (and financial contributions) among the local Algerian population.[65] Between 1957 and 1959, there were at least forty-two attacks perpetrated in the city.[66] While one of these was attributed to the MNA[67] and a few to FLN crackdowns and extortion,[68] police reported the vast majority simply as attacks by "coreligionists." For the local police and the local press, violence between North Africans was subsumed under a general rubric of nationalist action.[69] Municipal officials' relative silence suggests that they too paid little attention to the intricacies of intra-Algerian politics. Rather, their interest was first in using Algerian nationalism as a means of opposing the French state and second in the practical effects the war had on their local populations. In a similar vein, Gillot and his colleagues never commented on violence by the FLN (or MNA)—the violence that troubled them was that perpetrated by the French state, especially in the guise of the local police.

Two years after the signing of the Evian Accords, Gillot sent a letter of congratulations and warm wishes to the diplomatic representatives of the new Algerian state, acknowledging the anniversary of the "celebration of the Algerian Revolution."[70] This letter included a request to find the Dionysiens a twin city in Algeria (though municipal records do not contain evidence that such a connection was made). The municipality's embrace of the nationalists and city officials' castigation of French imperial practices was ingrained in their standard operations. Municipal officials' connection with their North African residents, however, extended beyond their commitment to an anti-imperialist, proliberation ideology. Elected officials often crossed from rhetoric to action, particularly in cases where they believed the Algerian members of their community to have been singled out to have their basic social and civil rights abridged. Just as strong proimperial desires

led Rhône officials to support vast surveillance operations, municipal anti-imperialism in Saint-Denis translated antiwar activism
into local actions against the police.

Standing against the Police

An antiwar stance presupposes an aggressor, and for the Dionysien municipality, French soldiers on the Algerian front were
not guilty—in fact, they were subject to their own brand of state
oppression. Rather, it was the French police who were accused of
belligerence and repressive action against North African residents
in the metropole (especially around Paris). French police forces
were directly administered by the Interior Ministry, which deep-
ened the perceived divide between officers and locals. Workers'
party governments in Saint-Denis had always had an antagonis-
tic relationship with local police forces.[71] Gillot and his contemporaries therefore followed a long tradition of confrontation with the
local police forces and certainly were not the first Dionysien officials to fall victim to police actions. While municipal officials had
already demonstrated their wariness in ceding too much power
over North Africans to the police in matters of social welfare (see
chapter 2), the Algerian War heightened their concern for direct
police infringement of migrants' civil rights. The municipality was
especially troubled by three common police tactics in this period:
the widespread use of racial profiling, the mass detainment of
Algerians at facilities like the camp at Vincennes, and the presence of members of the "Auxiliary Police Force" (FPA; police officers recruited from the Algerian population). Each of these tactics
was also employed in the Rhône region and supported by the proimperial officials there. In Saint-Denis, however, municipal anti-
imperialism targeted the police as an imperial force within their
city limits.

Profiling

Racial profiling by the police was high on the list of charges put
forth by Dionysien communists. As early as 1952, Gillot and others
called upon the General Council for the Seine to make the police

prefect answer questions about discriminatory practices. Their concern was spurred by a series of police raids.[72] One of these operations targeted a series of Algerian cafés in Saint-Denis and culminated with the detainment of over a hundred men. In true workers' party fashion, the criticism was twofold: the police were guilty not only of "discriminatory procedures" but also of impeding these workers' rights to work (and to repose).[73] Racial profiling grew increasingly common as FLN networks became active in France. When Gillot took issue with the arrival of police reinforcements, including riot police (CRS), the police commissioner informed Gillot that "there are many North Africans in Saint-Denis and we fear for the population."[74] The mayor replied that were any violent incidents to ensue, he would hold the police themselves responsible. *L'Humanité* claimed that the population backed Gillot's protests and that workers in local industries "demanded the retreat of the Saint-Denis police forces, thus affirming their solidarity with their Algerian brothers."[75]

Police presence led to police violence. In July 1959, a young man, headed to work early in the morning, was shot by police who believed he "resembled a North African" and was attempting to flee. *Saint-Denis Républicain* lambasted this explanation: "Let us admire the argument, 'We thought he was an Algerian.' French or Algerian, he was a man whose life should have been respected. Does it suffice to have lightly tanned skin and curly hair to risk being the target of a police officer . . . ?"[76] A week later, an Algerian man was asked for his papers, then pushed against a wall and shot. A communist flyer questioned press reports that the man was armed and suggested that "war-mongers" were seeking to create an atmosphere of civil war in order to stoke fears and quell opposition.[77] Local officials viewed the discriminatory policies pursued by the police both as a direct affront to Algerians' civil rights and as a policy aimed at deepening divisions between the Algerian and metropolitan populations to allow for the use of ever harsher repressive tactics. In contrast, they continually set forth their own image of a Saint-Denis "where French and North Africans have lived together for years in the fraternity that reveals

itself in the shoulder-to-shoulder labor of workers of all nationalities to earn their bread."[78]

As critical as local communists were of the police before the fall
of 1961, the massive demonstration of October 17 and the harsh
methods used to suppress it ushered in a new phase of condemnation and action. The overseas war had unmistakably come to
the mainland, and never had the police role in enforcing imperial ideas been clearer. The demonstration was itself a response
to police repression and discrimination, especially the restrictive
curfew placed on "French Muslims from Algeria" in the decree of
October 5, 1961.[79] On October 17, tens of thousands of Algerians,
including women and children, filed peacefully into Paris (the FLN
had given strict instructions that no one should come armed). The
police, on Prefect Maurice Papon's orders, met the crowds with
violence and intense repressive tactics.[80] Well over 10,000 participants were arrested, and the death toll reached 120 by the end of
the month.[81] On November 3, the municipal council issued a declaration against the violence, noting that three hundred Dionysien
Algerians had been arrested during the October 17 demonstration
and worrying that "some have not returned, and we do not know
where they are."[82] On November 7, Gillot and others addressed the
General Council for the Seine, decrying the police reaction and
demanding that the curfew for North Africans be repealed, that
the arrests made that night be overturned, and that the master-
minds of the repression be sanctioned by the Interior Ministry.[83]

Even members of the local police forces began to speak out
against violent and discriminatory practices: in the aftermath of
the repression, a group of "republican police officers" directed an
open letter against "the odious acts that risk becoming common
currency and overwhelming the honor of the entire police force."[84]
Beyond the violent repression of the demonstration, they listed
other tendencies, including the "systematic" beating of Algerians taken to the Dionysien commissariat for questioning: "The
death toll from a recent night was particularly murderous. Thirty
unhappy individuals were thrown, unconscious, into the canal after
being savagely beaten." The officers also described the practice, in

Saint-Denis, of officers working in split patrols, the first group to stop Algerians for questioning and take their documents for verification, the second to follow immediately in order that the individuals could be detained for failure to produce these same documents. Such accusations added to the municipality's list of grievous sins committed by the police. Looking ahead, and ever mindful of the possibilities for continued links between France and an "autonomous" colony, the national Communist Party warned that "the repression of Algerians living in France further compromises the future relations between France and Algeria."[85]

For the PCF, and certainly for Saint-Denis's elected officials, October 17 was yet another reason to bring the conflict to an end. Two weeks before the demonstration, the PCF sections of Saint-Denis had launched a membership drive, linked to mounting opposition to the presence of special police forces (the FPA) in the city, with a four-page leaflet calling the "workers and inhabitants" of the city to "union and action against the fascist menace [and] to restore and renovate democracy." While most of the articles discussed worrying fascist tendencies in general and the actions of the FPA in particular, the list of demands concluded with an appeal for "the end to the violence and abuse of which the Algerian and French population is victim."[86] Note that "population" here was singular, overcoming division between the French and the Algerians and signaling that both groups were members of a single (local) community. Such phrasing signals just how far Gillot and his colleagues were from the Rhône officials of the previous chapter in the way they envisioned the role of Algerians within their city.

Detainment

On many occasions, municipal officials also intervened on behalf of individual North Africans who were taken into police custody. Over the course of the war, more than thirty thousand Algerians, roughly 12 percent of those resident in France, were imprisoned.[87] Families and friends of detained Algerians solicited intervention by municipal officials, in some cases to gain material aid, in others simply to learn the whereabouts of the missing individual. The vast majority of these cases were raised in the aftermath of October 17, 1961. One of the first cases involved two municipal employees; the director of the local housing office wrote to the deputy in charge of social welfare to ask if the municipality could intervene on their behalf "in the capacity as their employers."[88] Gillot and his colleagues' work on detainment issues proved another means of combating injustice perpetrated on North Africans in the name of imperial necessity and another platform on which they could call the entire project of French Algeria into question.

As requests for aid in locating Algerians piled up, Gillot instructed his first deputy to figure out the best way for the city to acquire useful information.[89] The municipality sent numerous demands to the Interior Ministry and the regional prefects while cooperating with the Commission de sauvegarde des libertés and working closely with the Secours populaire français (SPF) and the unions.[90] The municipality's letters, signed by the mayor or one of his deputies, emphasized the men's legal working and living situations, asserting that all documents were in order at city hall and therefore little could be held against the men on these charges. Often, they focused on the families left behind as a way to generate sympathy for the detained individuals. Indeed, the municipality kept families in the loop throughout the petitioning process, sending updates and, in successful cases, receiving letters of thanks. In one case, the city's hospital mobilized their own Comité antifasciste et de défense des libertés on behalf of two detained employees, enlisting Gillot to support their demands to the police prefect.[91] A December 1961 letter to the Interior Ministry clarified the municipality's perception of their relationship with these detained men—and, by extension, with the Algerian population of the city—by asserting that the mayor was appealing on behalf of "one of my constituents [administrés]."[92] Here Gillot invoked his responsibility toward these Algerian men and their families as integrated members of the Dionysien community.

The municipality began to focus on the social and financial repercussions of the prolonged detainment of Algerian workers. The city's social welfare bureau met in October 1961 to discuss the large number of arrests of Dionysien Algerians. They resolved to call attention to "the consequences of massive arrests," particularly the effects on families and the burdens placed on the local welfare services that ended up caring for affected families.[93] As with many of the social policies discussed in chapter 2, municipal officials expressed dismay not only at the abysmal situation in which families found themselves but also at the state policies that created these situations, even as the cost fell to the city.

Merely releasing those detained did not solve all problems. Many Algerians left camps like Vincennes only to find themselves unwelcome at their previous jobs and even denied social welfare aid. Gillot appealed to the General Council for the Seine to provide Algerian workers with documentation upon their release that would ensure their rights to their former employment and to social security benefits.[94] After the cease-fire, Gillot and other regional communists complained that released Algerians were still subject to discrimination, with so many employers refusing to rehire them that it seemed "as if they were obeying received orders." The group demanded to know what would be done "to permit these workers to find work and to live like all other workers," a formula that emphasized solidarity on the basis of class and a lack of distinction by nationality (even as Algerians lost their automatic claim to French citizenship).[95] Gillot and others were further concerned for the livelihood of Algerian café and hotel owners: many who had been detained for lengthy periods returned to find their businesses threatened either by ministerial decrees closing them for security purposes or by failure to pay rents and taxes while in custody.[96] In each of these cases, the police and the state were accused of denying basic social rights to Algerians—who incurred great individual costs—on the basis of political or security questions in which these individuals may or may not have been involved.

Such social rights were intimately linked to Algerians' civil and political rights, and the municipality often called into question the practice of arresting and holding individuals for their political beliefs. A municipal council decree from November 1961, spurred by a motion on behalf of municipal employees, demanded that the "Algerians detained in camps and prisons for their actions in favor of an independent Algeria" be designated political prisoners, not criminals.[97] After Evian, in the spring of 1962, many Algerians were released from the internment camps, and their rights to social security payments were reinstated. Municipal officials were quick to point out that though many of the political prisoners had been granted amnesty, they were still ineligible for social aid.[98] Gillot himself investigated the cases of continued detention in the following year. The municipal council adopted his recommendations and called on the president of the republic "to offer, on the occasion of the great national holiday of 14 July, a measure of general amnesty to those who are still in prison for having wanted Peace and Friendship with the Algerian people."[99] Holding political prisoners was not a practice worthy of the French Republic, especially after the signing of the Evian Accords, which had essentially validated the Algerian nationalist cause and overthrown the imperial system Gillot and his colleagues had contested for so long.

FPA "Harkis"

The municipality's distaste for police practices was magnified by the introduction of Auxiliary Police Force (FPA) officers into the city. By the fall of 1961, much of their energy was directed toward chasing the FPA, whom they (mistakenly) called *harkis*, out of Saint-Denis. The term *harki* is most often used to refer to North African soldiers who fought in the French army during either the World Wars or the colonial conflicts. Dionysien officials, however, applied it freely to the FPA. Their protests against FPA presence in the city proved to be some of the most inflammatory of the war years, culminating in the violent showdown between police and municipal officials featured at the opening of this chapter. The PCF had begun to single out the FPA over the summer: *L'Humanité* launched the campaign in August 1961 with a full-page spread in which two Algerians related their experiences of violence and deprivation while in the custody of FPA forces; photographs were included of the wounds on their backs and arms.[100] PCF members would not be the only critics of the use of FPA patrols; in July the three Muslim senators from Algeria (Abdelkrim Sadi, a former police officer from the Gaullist camp, and Youssef Achour and Mohamed Larbi Lakhdari, both from the Gauche Démocratique) vociferously denounced FPA practices on both sides of the Mediterranean and provided the Dionysiens with extra fodder for their own demands.[101]

Gillot joined the chorus of protests from the communist mayors of Ivry, Montreuil, Nanterre, and other Parisian banlieues by penning a letter to Police Prefect Papon in August 1961 to complain that "harkis" with submachine guns (*mitraillettes*) had "invaded" the Quartier Pleyel and the cafés along the rue du Landy.[102] Gillot insisted that the large Algerian population in the neighborhood was peaceful and had never caused problems for the other inhabitants; moreover, the residents themselves had come to believe that the police and the FPA were greater potential threats to their security than the migrant workers. He placed the Pleyel incident within the context of FPA activities around Paris and asserted that "the municipality considers that the presence of these harkis in the commune could provoke incidents and trouble the public order." This formula of blaming the FPA for violence and chaos mirrors the more general denunciation of police actions as well as the Dionysien tradition of resisting the police. Gillot declared that the municipal council found the FPA question "so alarming" as to schedule a discussion for their next meeting. He closed the letter by declaring, "It is in the interest of France that the harkis return to their homes and that negotiations are resumed to reach peace in Algeria as soon as possible."[103] Not only did Gillot link local policing practices directly to the Algerian War, but here he also created a parallel between his beliefs on the illegality of FPA presence in Saint-Denis and the similarly insupportable presence of French imperial forces in Algeria.

At the municipal council's September 15 session, Deputy Mayor Manuel Velasco presented a report on the presence of the FPA in Saint-Denis.[104] He drew extensively on the testimonies of Senators Sadi, Achour, and Lakhdari to set the local FPA raids into context. He emphasized that though the "harkis" were intended primarily as a tool for the oppression of Algerians in Algeria and the metropole, they had also acted against "French citizens"—a national distinction rarely seen in Dionysien municipal dialogue up to this point. Velasco enumerated four different occasions in the past month where armed "harkis" had entered stores and cafés, not only "searching and manhandling the passersby," but also brutalizing individual Algerian workers or detaining them for days without due cause.[105] According to Velasco, such incidents had left all Dionysiens "indignant" and concerned for their safety.[106] Residents insisted that the community had been peaceful up until the arrival of the "harkis." Accordingly, the municipal council issued a formal protest against the presence of the FPA in the city on the grounds that these officers posed a threat to "public order" and demanded "the immediate dissolution of these reprehensible units." These exhortations for the removal of FPA patrols were clearly linked to growing perceptions of threats to the metropolitan population in Saint-Denis. However, the municipality was unsettled more generally by the use of FPA officers as a particularly violent force for repression of Algerian political sentiment. Each description of events treated the detainees as innocent bystanders subject to arbitrary repression; of course, given the municipality's stance on the Algerian conflict, one presumes that had any reasons been offered for the arrests of these men, these would have been rejected as unfounded charges.

Gillot did not limit his anti-FPA activism to his own jurisdiction. In October 1961, he was part of the communist group who criticized the treatment of Algerians in Nanterre during a hotel search. Gillot also headed a delegation to the police prefect over allegations of "harki" impropriety in Aubervilliers, where the population was particularly concerned that FPA officers had been stationed near a local school. The police responded to these charges with a list of weapons stocks discovered in the aftermath of the Nanterre operation as well as the processing of numerous individuals through Vincennes; "these results . . . constitute the best response to the habitual detractors of the auxiliary forces, who would do better to save their indignation for the extortion by the FLN and the assassinations they commit."[107] Papon remained unapologetic in the face of mounting criticism, viewing his work as effective and necessary for maintaining order and protecting citizens. Meanwhile, Gillot's opposition stemmed both from his support for Algerian nationalism and from his concern for the well-being of Algerian individuals in his community. Here and in other correspondence between the police and the Saint-Denis municipality, the two parties talked right past each other, neither accepting the foundations for the other's opinions or actions.

Gillot's opposition to the presence of FPA brigades in Saint-Denis eventually brought him and his colleagues into their direct confrontation with the police. On October 2, 1961, the municipality received word of a number of FPA operations in the city and led a host of delegations to the police commissariat.[108] They alleged that even as nearly fifteen thousand children were walking home from school, groups of armed "harkis" had lined the city's sidewalks, training their guns on passersby. Gillot himself was called into a café after FPA patrols had passed through; he found a young Algerian man lying unconscious on the floor and drove him to the hospital. On his return to city hall, the mayor was met by a group of residents angered by another FPA raid on a public bus, during which, they claimed, a pregnant woman who argued with the officers had been slapped and a seventy-seven-year-old woman had been manhandled.

Gillot then led a second delegation to the commissariat, demanding that "public order" be returned. As mentioned in the opening of this chapter, the officer who met them refused to recognize the municipal officials, and orders to disperse the crowd were carried out violently. Gillot claimed that at least three city officials were attacked, one of whom spent the night at the hospital. Gillot maintained that the municipality's intervention had been crucial in curbing an escalation of violence. His portrayal of city officials as a force for calm contrasted sharply with the habitual characterization of the FPA as a lawless force of repression and served as his main defense against the counterproceedings launched by Papon, who sought the mayor's suspension on the grounds that by contributing to the disorder, Gillot had neglected his public duties.[109]

Papon was particularly upset by the anti-FPA slogans that municipal officers had chanted during the demonstration. Deputy Mayors Persancier and Benhamou were charged along with Gillot for conduct unbecoming of their offices as well as for the municipality's behavior on October 3.[110] That day, a meeting had been convened at city hall to discuss "peace in Algeria, the dissolution of the FPA, and the restoration and renovation of democracy." One flyer proclaimed, "Terror will not reign in St-Denis," and compared police actions to "those values worthy of Hitler's occupation."[111] Discontent and opposition were on the rise; in Aubervilliers and Montreuil, workers had banded together to chase out the FPA. Given the tone of these tracts, it is not surprising that the police attempted to break up the meeting.[112] Benhamou's presence, though unsurprising given his municipal role, is notable given that the Paris police believed him to be a North African Muslim.[113]

Further violence did not ensue, but the city commissioner and Papon were determined that the municipal officials should be reprimanded—and temporarily suspended—for their role in inciting public fervor and leading demonstrations against the forces of order.[114] Had order and calm been their foremost objectives, Papon affirmed, city officials should have themselves called on the police for aid in dispersing the crowds, not taken the lead in protesting. Gillot and his deputies met the charges of disorder with accusations of police violence.[115] Deputy Mayor Benhamou claimed to have been hit in the face and elsewhere during the confrontation in front of the commissariat. Each of the letters to the Seine prefect affirmed the parties' own commitment to public calm and to the desires and interests of the populace; they each claimed to have acted only in response to the general public outcry over FPA operations.[116] In the end, the mayor and his deputies received only "a very severe warning letter, notifying them that a renewal of such actions would entail an immediate suspension."[117] The reversal of opinion likely owed to the public furor surrounding the events of October 17, 1961. In the aftermath of the demonstration, police likely wished to rein in stories implicating their forces in unduly violent and repressive actions.

This debate over the meaning of the municipality's actions on October 2 highlights the conflicting notions of political order held by local communists and the police in these final stages of the Algerian War. At each turn, the police and the prefects asserted their crucial role in maintaining security for the population, just as municipal officials rejected that very notion of security, which they believed was an illegitimate stifling of political opposition. Where the police were obliged to defend the community from those they perceived as terrorists, the municipality claimed to be holding the line against fascism and state terror. Indeed, the Dionysien use of the term *harki* blurred the distinction between the police and the military, reinforcing the idea that the so-called events in Algeria constituted an actual war, not a domestic security operation, and emphasizing that this war had been brought into France itself. Moreover, criticism of the FPA is one area in which the Dionysien municipality revealed their own penchant for discrimination on racial grounds. They did not view the "harkis" as valid police officers, and when calling for the FPA's disbandment, the municipality demanded that they "return home." The FPA invasion of Saint-Denis was, for Gillot, as illegitimate as the French army's invasion of Algeria.

Dionysien officials' conduct over the course of this incident suggested that they were willing to risk their positions—in some cases to suffer bodily harm—to oppose the actions and direction of the French state. Protests against the FPA fit neatly into the municipal record of opposition to the police as a force for repression, and their denunciation of police tactics, particularly in targeting Algerian workers in the city aligned with their greater opposition to the continuing conflict in Algeria and their support for equal social and civil rights for Algerian individuals and their families. When yet another FPA raid inflamed the municipality's anger in January 1962, Gillot and his communist colleagues at the General Council for the Seine denounced the ongoing "hunt for Algerians."[118] They further linked the FPA practices to the boldness of

OAS bombers by "creating a climate of disorder and danger." They noted that even as police forces took stronger and stronger measures against Algerians living in the metropole, "the arrests of the bombers, so few, are often followed by evasion and acquittal, and at the same time members of the police who protest against the striking [*matraquage*] of Parisians who demonstrate against the OAS are sanctioned." They concluded, "The population has enough worries of all kinds; with these officials, they desire public order, tranquility and security, which requires peace in Algeria." An end to conflict—and to police repression—was the only viable means to ensure the freedoms and rights of Algerians and metropolitans alike under the Fifth Republic.

In April 1957, the three Socialist members of Saint-Denis's overwhelmingly communist municipal council lodged a formal complaint against Gillot and the rest of the councillors. They were upset because "at nearly every meeting we are forced to attend or participate in debates over international politics lasting whole hours . . . the time spent in arguing endlessly over matters not under our jurisdiction is time lost for municipal questions."[119] While these sentiments seem reasonable—even expected—for city officials, the mayor and his PCF colleagues hardly shared them. In the decades following the Second World War, they regularly issued votes and decrees on far-flung global matters; organized marches, rallies, petitions, and delegations; and raised their concerns in local and national assemblies. For them, these international issues were unequivocally municipal questions—just as the Rhône prefects believed imperial policy to be part of their purview. Gillot and his colleagues, in line with previous Dionysien governments, clearly believed that the boundaries of their concerns lay far beyond the city's own borders. While the prefects for the Seine and the Paris police consistently rejected Dionysien votes and petitions to intervene on global matters on the grounds that such issues were beyond the scope of a city government, municipal officers anchored themselves in these global debates through their ties to communist internationalism as well as to local migrants whose lives were directly linked to these matters, whether they were anti-Francoist Spaniards or nationalist Algerians.

Here again, Vénissieux serves as an interesting foil to Saint-Denis. Just as chapter 2 revealed significantly less Vénissian municipal engagement on North African welfare issues, so too did Vénissian communists take a much less active role in opposing the Algerian War. Certainly, there are few traces of the overt action seen in Saint-Denis; the war just didn't seem to be much on the minds of local Vénissian officials.[120] Moreover, in the few moments where Vénissieux's local officials were involved in antiwar efforts, their tone aligned with milder PCF rhetoric emphasizing peace, negotiation, and autodetermination without explicitly acknowledging Algerian nationalism or calling for independence. Where Gillot and his colleagues were ready and willing to face off with local police as part of their antiwar protests, Vénissieux's Mayor Louis Dupic ducked out of a meeting about Algeria when it seemed it would become contentious.[121] Other cities in the Rhône, like Givors and Oullins, appear to have had more engaged antiwar activists than Vénissieux, while local politicians like Jean Cagne and Pierre Cot (both National Assembly deputies) were significantly more outspoken than their Vénissian counterparts.[122] Both the CGT and CFTC (Confédération française des travailleurs chrétiens) had a strong presence in recorded antiwar activity in the region, as did a number of student organizations.

Much of the antiwar activity in the Rhône was directed through the Mouvement de la Paix.[123] At the 1956 meeting of Rhône PCF delegates, speakers (especially Jacques Duclos) insisted that opposing the Algerian War needed to be a central part of party activity and applauded the success of the Mouvement de la Paix on this front.[124] Henri Drogue, who presented the report from Vénissieux, claimed that the "battle for Peace in Algeria" was going well in the city, citing coordinated action with local socialists within the Mouvement de la Paix.[125] In October 1960, in the leadup to a regional protest and work stoppage coordinated by local union branches, the Mouvement de la Paix hosted a demonstration in Vénissieux that culminated at city hall and was addressed by Mayor

Dupic.[126] While Dupic offered his gratitude and support for such activism, his more passive role in the movement is quite a contrast to Gillot's much more active participation. Dupic likewise stressed negotiation and not independence.

As much as the Algerian War forced all of the actors discussed above to confront the presence of North Africans in their communities and to invent policies and programs to support these migrants, the end of the war also affected the relationship between locals and migrant issues. Indeed, the waning attention to North African migrants after 1962 proves just how important imperial (and anti-imperialist) ideologies were in motivating even local officials to support migrant rights and welfare. The impetus for both the national government and the Rhône officials to pay attention to North Africans was intimately linked to the Algerian War; welfare initiatives were coupled with security efforts. Programs created within this environment of mixed social and security motivations were highly efficient (and had significant moral and monetary support) and did result in a distinct rise in migrant welfare.[127] Yet Algerian independence in 1962 had profound ramifications for Algerian migrants: at the same time that Algerian nationalists became much less of a security threat, all Algerians lost their automatic right to French citizenship. These changes curbed proimperial officials' and agencies' motivations for social engagement with these migrants and thus led to a loss of urgency and focus (especially as the welfare programs expanded their mandates to include all migrants). The 1960s furthered the pattern of excluding migrants from the community; by the 1970s, tensions were regularly boiling over into violence.

Ironically, Dionysien municipal reactions to migrants after 1962 paralleled these changes. Where the state had been invested in the Algerian question for security purposes, Saint-Denis's municipality was drawn to local migrants for ideological and political reasons. Agitating on behalf of North African workers' rights in France—and Algerians' right to independence—aligned with the municipality's long-standing anti-imperialism and offered municipal officials yet another front for their combative opposition politics.

These motivations for engagement dwindled with the signing of the Evian Accords and the creation of the new Algerian state. It was no longer necessary—or possible—for municipal officials to rally with local Algerians around anti-imperialist opposition to the French state. Algerian independence signified the loss of a common enemy, leaving local communists with an ideological framework into which Algerian workers no longer fit so neatly.

From the mid-1960s, confrontation over migration in Saint-Denis occurred mostly between the PCF and the rising Far Left, and the contested field was more likely to be immigrants from sub-Saharan Africa than those from the Maghreb.[128] At the same time, the preoccupation with migrant housing and the bidonvilles in the 1960s and '70s expanded the municipality's interactions to other migrant groups, particularly the Portuguese, which meant that municipal advocacy became less focused in its scope and vaguer in its recommendations. As seen in chapter 2, Saint-Denis was slowly being overwhelmed by this growing migrant population, and communist officials were realizing that the city might not be able—or willing—to live up to the internationalist ideas that they had long espoused. In short, the context of the Algerian War had raised interest in the North African population for both pro- and anti-imperial actors who, for various reasons, saw benefit in promoting migrant welfare. However, by the 1970s, this context had changed dramatically, and the onset of a global economic crisis made the presence of migrant workers more—and more broadly—problematic.

FIVE

Profit

I n 1970, businessman Victor Simon launched a series of strongly worded attacks against the Rhône prefecture, accusing departmental authorities of racism, discrimination, and violating the fundamental values of the French Republic. The catalyst for this barrage of criticism was the department's attempts to close down the apartment complex Simon owned in Villeurbanne, the Cité Olivier de Serres. The large number of North African families living in Olivier de Serres was the source of ever-increasing anxieties about the presence of migrants in the Rhône—and had inspired the prefect's June 1970 circular capping the number of foreign children allowed in neighborhoods around Lyon (as discussed in chapter 1). In the contentious debate that followed with both city and departmental authorities, local governmental actors might have been expected to take up the language of migrant rights against this exploitative proprietor, who rented badly deteriorating apartments at exorbitant prices primarily to Algerian migrants. Simon, however, effectively employed the rhetoric of rights and antiracism in order to fend off attempts to shut down his housing business. North African welfare, in other words, could be used as a shield for private profit.

This chapter examines a variety of local actors whose involvement in North African migrant affairs supported their own financial interests. The potential for profit was, of course, what brought many North Africans to metropolitan cities in the first place. The need to rebuild France—literally—after the Second World War pulled workers across the Mediterranean. Those who employed North Africans were well aware of the needs for and of this workforce, both the extent to which they propelled the national economy and the basic living conditions they required in order to perform this crucial work. State and local officials worked closely with employers to ensure proper working and living conditions for North African migrants (and, once the Algerian War had begun, to access additional means of surveillance). In both the Seine and Rhône departments, employers were invested enough in their North African workforce to intervene on their behalf, most often in the realm of housing. Property owners and builders were likewise drawn into the debates over North African migration and migrant welfare. For many of these actors, making space for North African workers was simply good for business.

Industrialists, Employers, and Business Owners

Even before World War II, the 1938 Ollive-Laroque report on North African workers in the metropole had asserted, "France has need of North African labor."[1] North African workers at the time did not compete directly with metropolitans but were concentrated in "rough, difficult, and unhealthy jobs that repulse national [French] laborers." Given these needs for labor, Ollive and Laroque recommended an enhanced role for employers in housing North African migrants, even suggesting that lodging and food be included as part of workers' salaries "in order to combat the natural tendency of these workers to live in slums and be under-nourished."[2] Recognizing the vital links between migration and industry, the national ministries involved in North African migration issues (primarily Interior, Labor, Reconstruction, and Urbanism) sought support from French employers to address the massive housing shortages. They began by working with local business associations, though found this inefficient. In the early 1950s, the Interior Ministry worked closely with the Confédération nationale du patronat to set up a building society (a precursor to SONACOTRAL).[3] Later, employer contributions to social housing projects (Habitations à loyer modéré [HLM]) reserved 1 percent of the new apartments for their migrant workers. Bosses and business owners were themselves aware of the importance of decent housing and the effects that poor living conditions could have on recruitment and productivity.[4]

While employers were active in both regions, their role was more prominent in the Rhône. In part, this resulted from the greater general attention to the Paris region's much larger North African population. As we have seen, there were more groups and agencies available and willing to address migrants' needs around Paris. Table 5.1 enumerates the migrant workers housed by their employers in the Seine and the Rhône. While the total Rhône numbers go from half to three-quarters of the Seine totals, the actual number of workers in the Seine was much higher, making Rhône employers relatively more involved.

Already in 1947, the Rhône prefecture estimated that there were at least six thousand North African workers in the region, 90 percent in the Lyon agglomeration. Thirty-eight of the largest factories around Lyon employed a total of 1,612 North Africans (30 of them worked at the SOMUA factory in Vénissieux).[5] By 1953, it was clear that Rhône employers were becoming more willing to hire North African workers.[6] North Africans took part "in all the dominant activities of the Lyon economy. . . . They are efficiently used in a wide variety of industries." A third of North Africans in the Rhône worked in metallurgy, nearly another third in construction, 12 percent in the region's textile manufacturing, 10 percent in chemical industries, and the rest in diverse industries.[7] As the labor supply grew, some "unscrupulous" factory foremen in the Rhône padded their own profits by demanding hiring fees directly from North African workers seeking employment.[8] Police, the prefecture, and the local press alike denounced this practice. Relatively small numbers of North African women also earned their living in the metropole, though less often in industrial settings.[9]

The profitability of North African labor was believed to be shared with the migrants themselves, who came to the metropole for better wages, social services, and money to send home. Through their remittances and those who returned with savings to invest,

Table 5.1. Number of North Africans
housed by employers, 1959–63

Department	1959	1960	1961	1962	1963
Seine					
Single men	1,800	2,000	2,000	2,000	2,000
Families	300	320	320	340	380
Family members	1,200	1,300	1,300	1,450	2,000
Total	3,000	3,300	3,300	3,450	4,000
Rhône					
Single men	1,160	1,112	1,112	1,371	1,800
Families	115	216	216	217	240
Family members	460	864	864	867	1,100
Total	1,620	1,976	1,976	2,238	2,900

Source: Created by author. All figures taken from SAMAS, Statistiques de logement (CHAN, F1a 5115).

Algeria in particular was expected to prosper. A 1949 Rhône police report explained that those who had already fought or worked in the metropole were "the most active propaganda" for recruiting their compatriots and claimed that each village that managed to send a few workers to the metropole saw a marked improvement in their local economy.[10] This purported mutual benefit was central to imperial ideology; given the marked proimperial stance of Rhône officials (as discussed in chapter 3), it is not surprising that officials there took extra care to encourage hiring North Africans. The local Conseil social de la main-d'oeuvre nord-africaine "aim[ed] above all to convince employers to make one or more North African personnel attempts and not be discouraged by sometimes disappointing results." Working with industry, the prefecture and its associates did not rely only on imperial duty; they also emphasized the payoff in productivity for those who ensured their North African workers were provided for: "Good housing conditions make discipline and cleanliness [*propreté*] easier and encourage rapid education for the most retrograde tenants."[11]

Local employers were an important force in the creation of the Centre de la Part-Dieu to house North Africans in Lyon.[12] The ALHNA (Association lyonnaise pour l'hébergement des Nord-Africains) board, which oversaw the project, included three representatives from employers. For the initial construction, ALHNA raised funds from local businesses, asking for six thousand francs for each North African employed, a total of over three million francs. In 1948, employers contributed another three hundred thousand francs for works and renovations in the Centre. The municipalities of Lyon and Villeurbanne also contributed directly to both rounds, since each employed thirty North Africans in their respective highway departments.[13] Likewise, in the Seine, the Association des foyers nord-africains de la région parisienne (AFNA) had close relationships with employers, who reserved beds for their migrant workers. In fact, workers had no right to their beds outside of their labor contract; they had to agree to leave if they were let go from the business, and only employers could designate replacement tenants.[14]

The Société Automobiles Berliet, which had a factory in Vénissieux and steadily employed large numbers of North African workers (at least seven hundred by 1960), stands out as one of the Rhône businesses most involved with migrant housing.[15] Notably, more than half of the company's North African workers were specialized, or semiskilled.[16] In 1952, Berliet put forward a plan to build collective housing for two hundred North Africans, or roughly 40 percent of its Vénissieux workers.[17] Prefect Massenet was particularly happy with Berliet's initiative on this front, and the Interior Ministry also expressed a desire to support the company.[18] Opposition arose, however, from the mayor of Saint-Priest, since the land for the project was technically over his city line. His initial resistance, qualified as "absolute," eroded over time, especially as Berliet negotiated to build in alternative open plots.[19] Construction finally began in April 1954, once the mayor and the company reached an agreement.[20] The first building, with 51 of the planned

216 beds, was inaugurated that October in a well-attended ceremony, presided over by Madame Massenet.[21] Berliet then planned
a project to support private ownership of family housing; however, after an appeal from the prefecture, the company first built an
additional facility for North African workers and families.[22] Berliet was one of the main partners (and funders) for Vénissieux's
municipal construction society, SACOVIV (Société anonyme de
construction de la ville de Vénissieux), in the early 1960s.[23] Later,
in 1969, Berliet joined forces with both the Maison du travailleur
étranger (MTE) and Notre-Dame des Sans-Abris (NDSA), with
some national Fonds d'action sociale [FAS] funding, to build a new
foyer of four hundred beds.[24] This was after former prefect Ricard
retired from government service to join the company.[25] In 1971,
Berliet was still receiving notice as a company with an unusually
high commitment to the welfare of its migrant workers.[26]

Besides Berliet, ten other Rhône businesses housed twenty or
more North African workers in the early 1950s (including Elec-
trodes Savoie, also in Vénissieux), and 130 companies housed fewer
than twenty each.[27] In 1953, 1,573 Algerians were housed by their
employers in the Rhône.[28] After 1950, a number of employers shifted
their housing efforts to rely less on Part-Dieu, which had become
overcrowded and problematic, and build their own facilities (or
reserve places in smaller foyers).[29] By 1955, 1,072 North Africans
were in company lodging (in addition to those at Part-Dieu).[30] A
"Foyer des Employeurs" was built in Villeurbanne, on the avenue
Léon Blum, with room for 330 workers.[31] Employer housing did
not necessarily fill up—the Rhône prefect observed in 1961 that
Berliet and others' facilities had empty beds, even as other foyers
in the region were heavily overpopulated.[32] Yet employers did work
to improve the quality of their quarters, providing more individual rooms in the place of large dormitories.[33]

The arrival of more and more workers' families challenged
employers as much as other housing offices, and very few employers were able to offer housing appropriate for families.[34] From
the late 1950s, many employers who could not adequately house
their workers' families added their support to individual housing

requests (most often for new HLMs), emphasizing individuals' hard work and seriousness.[35] Employers tended to approve of family resettlement, which made workers less likely to leave abruptly or travel for lengthy home visits, and voiced concern over the negative economic implications of the June 1970 statute that limited family settlement in certain neighborhoods around Lyon.[36] In 1973, for example, the Société lyonnaise pour l'exploitation de véhicules championed the cause of an Algerian worker, whose ability to bring his family to France was stymied by the mayor of Vénissieux on the basis of that policy.[37]

Some large companies further lobbied against the use of "*seuils de tolérance*" in HLMs, claiming the policy made their contributions to HLM construction effectively worthless, since their workers were regularly denied entry. Delle-Alsthom, an electrical equipment manufacturer in Villeurbanne, complained of "insurmountable difficulties for lodging immigrants, Maghrebins for the most part," particularly longtime workers who hoped to finally bring their families over to join them.[38] The Rhône-Poulenc textile company in Vénissieux was more direct, "insist[ing] on the regrettable economic consequences that the absence of housing and thus the impossibility of recruitment cannot fail to have for the future development of our factory in Vaulx-en-Vélin" and demanding an exception to the 15 percent rule.[39] While the prefecture categorically refused to lift the quotas, employers' insistence on the need for good family housing as a necessary precondition for hiring migrant workers—and thus a crucial foundation for economic growth—further demonstrated the connection between profitability and migrant welfare.[40]

Employers also sought educational opportunities for their North African employees, hoping that training would "make them more invested in the business."[41] Migrants, Algerians in particular, were often criticized for lacking professional skills (including French language abilities).[42] General professional training centers around Lyon did accept some North Africans, though many migrants had difficulty meeting entrance requirements. The Centre d'accueil de la Doua ran a special program for construction training. Yet the majority of North Africans received their training in the workplace. Berliet, for example, offered special professional courses for welders. Employers further supported general education and literacy. North African students were most likely to succeed (or simply complete their studies) when employers provided incentives like flexibility to schedule working hours around class times or even financial bonuses for those who performed well. Some workplaces hosted their own courses, such as an experimental literacy program at Berliet in 1972.[43] Employers also gave North African social service workers access to their factories and businesses.[44] Sometimes this was to follow up directly with individuals previously helped. In other cases, officials interviewed owners or bosses with the hopes of turning these supervisors into additional arms of the North African welfare services.

Political concerns further affected employers' support of North African needs. Company bosses worried from very early on that North Africans were being recruited by communist operatives in the Maghreb. They feared that "the high cost of living, [in the metropole] rapidly disillusioning these workers, would come to increase the mass of discontented," which in turn would make them easy to "infiltrate by the parties of the far left," who would turn them into "'shock troops' to be used in case of mayhem."[45] This concern was echoed in the aftermath of the Algerian War. Lacking the previous imperial support structure, large numbers of unqualified Algerian workers would be adrift, and the Paris police asked, "To whom will they go? Won't they be easy prey for the Communist Party?"[46] By the late 1960s, additional anxiety came from the attempts by leftist groups to gain migrant followers.[47] In other words, some support for North Africans came from employers as a means of staving off leftist political gains that they feared would be bad for the bottom line.

North African workers' participation in leftist politics and workers' movements varied widely. As discussed in chapter 2, political allegiance can be difficult to pin down. Union membership and workplace activism left more traces. North Africans, like all other migrant groups, were often presumed by their contemporaries—and by later scholars—to be reticent to engage in actions that might jeopardize their already precarious positions.[48] This meekness, however, is vastly overstated, and there is considerable evidence that North African workers were willing to demand fair treatment. In June 1951, for example, North African employees at the Mandy chemical factory in Lyon went on strike to demand higher wages, garnering support from CGT (Confédération générale du travail) union activists. Workers in Givors filed complaints leading to the arrest of a manager who required bribes from new hires.[49] While the Lyon SAT officers repeatedly asserted that there was little syndical engagement by Algerians—given their attention to the Algerian independence struggle and the fees collected by the FLN (Front de libération nationale)—by 1961, they reported to the contrary that most of their North African visitors were card-carrying members of the CGT.[50] Berliet's North African workers were known to be particularly engaged in leftist political and syndical actions.[51]

Through the 1950s and early '60s, of course, Algerian workers were indeed attentive to the independence struggle. Factories like Renault's in Billancourt, outside of Paris, saw not only Algerian activism within existing—predominantly CGT—labor organizations but also the founding of an official "section MTLD [Mouvement pour le triomphe des libertés démocratiques]" and early forms of what would be the FLN's Fédération de France.[52] Algerian workers participated in regular FLN-initiated strikes around both Paris and Lyon. Their employers reacted by increasing their aid efforts in hopes of dissuading Algerian strikers. An FLN strike in the fall of 1957 was a source of "serious apprehension" among industrial circles in the Rhône, including a concern that some factories might be forced to close for the fortnight.[53] Some North African workers were preemptively taking their sick leave to cover the period.[54] While contracts and company policies made clear that striking would result in sanctions—and likely loss of the job—workers were expected to follow the strike orders anyway, as crossing the FLN seemed a much graver danger.[55] We should assume, contrary to official assumptions, that many Algerian workers partook in strike actions out of actual solidarity and not just due to external pressure. The Comité interprofessionel lyonnais (CIL) worried that "employer measures will be perfectly ineffective if the right to work and protection for individuals are not assured by the responsible authorities."[56] The CIL and the Rhône prefecture called upon local forces of order: the police to provide additional surveillance as well as direct protection for workers' transport and the army to offer bedding and linens for factories who wished to keep their North African workers on the premises for the duration of the strike.[57]

In rare cases, employers provided active support to Algerians caught up in the political conflict. Police were unhappy that "certain company managers [went] so far as to endeavor to redeploy employees banned from the Paris region to the provinces (sometimes to other branches)."[58] This circumvented security efforts and kept individual migrants employed in the metropole when they might have been forced back to North Africa. Other employers intervened directly on behalf of detained workers.[59] Employer activity during the war was not only aimed at supporting workers; some also took disciplinary action against politically active Algerians. Berliet, for example, fired one of its employees in 1955 for being a "nationalist propagandist."[60] Most owners and industrialists complied with the police.[61]

Employers did not embrace North African workers wholeheartedly. Over the decades, many complained about the migrants they hired or refused to engage North Africans at all. Up until their legal status changed with decolonization, North Africans were supposed to be hired before "foreigners," given similar qualifications. In the immediate postwar period, this meant that North Africans competing in the Lyon region with a new wave of Italian workers should have had a competitive advantage, though many employers did not see it that way.[62] Moroccans were generally preferred to Algerians. Ollive and Laroque noted already in 1938 that Moroccans were perceived to have equivalent productivity to "French" workers, while Algerians' "productivity and conscientiousness are generally esteemed to be well below average."[63] The requirement to pay these workers equal wages heightened dissatisfaction with this perceived productivity gap—attributed largely to poor adaptation to metropolitan life.[64] Employers also claimed that North Africans lacked French language skills and other education.[65] Algerians were furthermore considered unsuited to work requiring any sort of formal training: "Having come down from their mountains . . . their adaptation is longer and more difficult, in the end more costly."[66] Within Algerian groups, Kabyles were seen as better qualified (especially in metallurgy) as well as more stable.[67] Consistently, employers expressed dissatisfaction with North African workers' transience—whether in a particular job or in the metropole.[68]

Once the Algerian War had begun, employer ambivalence about their North African workers rose. The Paris police observed in 1959, "Employers are generally happy with their FMA [Français musulmans d'Algérie] employees. . . . They are interested in them and defend them."[69] Bosses tended "to judge their workers strictly on their professional conduct," though some were starting to express a preference for hiring Moroccans, who were less likely to be arrested and miss work.[70] A 1960 survey of Rhône employers showed wide vacillations. On one side, Algerians were called "well-managed and integrated" and "indispensable, despite their difficulties with adaptation given the small number of metropolitans disposed to undertake this disagreeable physical labor." On the other side, there were familiar complaints about the lack of education—"a minority understand French"—and instability: "Many keep returning to the country and, to pay the costs of the trip, . . . eat badly." One Rhône boss invoked both positions at once, complaining that this "regular and hard-working personnel" was often "troubled" by political events, and "this manifests in the request for an unusually large advance, and from then on, the individual disturbs the workplace with ill humor and laziness."[71]

Fellow workers had similarly mixed reactions to Algerians in their midst. In some cases, "a certain comradery" existed on the factory floor, particularly in contexts with very few North Africans. The "events" in Algeria, however, often worsened relations: "Suspicion, contempt, fear, sometimes hate manifest more or less openly once European workers have a friend or a family member killed in Algeria or victim to aggression in the Metropole."[72] This friction with metropolitan workers added to employer reticence, particularly as strikes, sabotage, and terrorist attacks increased in 1957 and 1958. Problems were less acute, however, when Algerians were relegated to "difficult or dirty positions not sought after by metropolitan or foreign workers."[73]

As the war continued, and especially as policing within the metropole heightened, employers, "irritated by the repeated absences of FMAs caught up in the rebellion and apprehended by the Police," grew less likely to renew contracts for Algerians—even those whose work they appreciated.[74] Some employers asked officials to refuse travel authorization to Algerians outside of annual factory closings.[75] Moreover, Algerian workers themselves began to lodge more complaints about discrimination in the workplace.[76] One white-passing transport worker feared for his job security in the event his "ferociously anti-Muslim" boss discovered his ethnic origins or his more visibly North African wife.[77] By 1961, the Interior Ministry worried that "certain businesses who make a point of employing French Muslims over foreigners will no longer consider themselves bound by this moral obligation once Algeria is independent." As the Evian Accords loomed, employers did grow hesitant, some "for sentimental reasons" based in political, imperial, or nationalist beliefs but others for the more pragmatic concern that Algerian workers would leave en masse at the moment of independence.[78] Businesses were especially wary of hiring new Algerians, even if they retained those they knew.[79]

Following Algerian independence, it became more difficult for Algerian migrants to find work in the metropole. Those Algerians who had work were more careful: they spoke little of politics, and many did not travel home for their annual leave but brought their families to the metropole.[80] The Paris SAT police observed in 1964, "In every business, we are met with the same *outcry*, 'No Muslims, they are only good for playing with knives and straining social security budgets.'"[81] Business owners offered a litany of complaints: "Their unsuitability for any promotion; their quasi-chronic instability and their apathy [*lymphatisme*] (it requires two Algerians for one Moroccan or Portuguese); their insufficient productivity which creates conflict on worksites or in workshops with their better performing [*plus habiles*] comrades: French, Moroccan, Portuguese; . . . their propensity for criticism and systematic demands and their readily quarrelsome spirit; their deficient state of health."[82] Algerians who opted for French citizenship were given some preference by employers who demanded proof of nationality as part of the hiring process, but usually only over other Algerians.[83] More and more Spanish and Portuguese workers were taking North African places in factories and other workplaces, and Algerian rates of unemployment surpassed other migrant groups.[84]

By 1966, Algerian workers were "less and less considered" for employment; the Paris police asserted, contrary to the evidence, "Certainly, we cannot speak of racism," though they wondered "whether this ostracism did not result from a watchword [*mot d'ordre*] or a concerted effort by business bosses who hire Portuguese, Spanish, or Italian workers."[85] Industrialists appeared to be hiring these European migrants as direct replacements for many Algerians.[86] Algerians' poorer job prospects also coincided with a shift toward more skilled labor for which they mostly lacked the training.[87] Short tenures and frequent job changes also left Algerians with fewer and weaker references.[88] Moreover, employers associated Algerian migrants with high rates of delinquency due to the bias toward North African criminality in the press.[89]

Some union leaders distanced themselves from Algerian workers in the 1960s, even actively opposing their hiring.[90] Others, however, continued to engage. The CGT remained an important vehicle for North African workers' demands, hoping to build upon "the solidarity that sometimes existed on the production line." One Algerian CGT militant disputed the idea that the factory floor was exempt from racism but acknowledged that "in the factories people are sometimes forced to accept us." An Algerian metalworker explained, "I personally support the trade unions," but clarified that he did not participate in street demonstrations where police "generally grab the Arabs" for detainment (even deportation).[91] By the

1970s, North Africans were also more involved with the Confédération française démocratique du travail (CFDT) union. One CFDT
operative explained that the experience of colonialism had made
North African workers more familiar with France and therefore
more liable than other migrants (like the Portuguese) to support
social movements.[92] A group of Tunisian workers at the Caluire-
Légumes factory north of Lyon organized a protest of their working conditions, sending delegations to local and national officials
before making contact with CFDT militants who supported and
publicized their eventual strike.[93] Another predominantly North
African strike at Penarroya in Lyon showcased the CFDT's willingness to follow migrant workers' lead in both setting their demands
and choosing their modes of action.[94] Though workplaces were
not without their own prejudices and challenges, North African
workers found ways to make themselves heard. Their own activism on their rights as laborers—to fair wages, to safe conditions,
to social services and benefits—underscored both their personal
economic motivations for remaining in France and their willingness to use French laws, policies, and systems to attain their goals
and assert their value as humans as well as workers.

North African Entrepreneurs

North African migrants to France did not only labor for metropolitan bosses. Some established themselves as small business owners, particularly in stores, cafés, bars, and hotels. Cafés, shops, and
other businesses flourished even within the bidonvilles.[95] Not sur-
prisingly, these migrants were among the most financially successful.[96] They also proved more economically mobile, able to enlarge
their shops, purchase additional businesses, or often start their
own hotels.[97] In the late 1950s, around ten thousand North Africans owned businesses in the metropole.[98] In 1951, there were fifty
cafés, bars, and restaurants owned by North Africans in Lyon; one
in Villeurbanne; and eight in Vénissieux and St. Fons.[99] Counting
cafés, restaurants, bars, grocery stores, and hotels together, Saint-
Denis had thirty-five North African–owned businesses at that time,
and Asnières had seventeen. Records for the Paris suburbs show

that the majority of North African–owned businesses in Asnières catered to a "European" or mixed clientele, while in Saint-Denis the majority of North African owners served the North African population exclusively.[100]

Already in 1946, Rhône officials had worried about the influence café owners had on local North African workers; in fact, a push to create a central North African canteen came in part from the desire to remove migrants from the influence of those business owners "who cleverly get their clientele to adopt their ideas."[101] Likewise, in the Paris region, Algerian business owners were "notorious" for their community leadership: "Most of the time, it is to one of these storekeepers, originating from the same town, that the immigrant presents himself on arriving in Paris . . . It follows that a whole series of information or impulses can be given." This significant role as the main contact for migrants, and especially for newcomers, was well known to nationalist groups as well. In 1951, the MTLD conducted a full census of North African–owned businesses to cultivate their ties to the Algerian emigrants in the metropole.[102] These venues came under growing police surveillance during the Algerian War.[103] By 1957, there was a noticeable surge in Algerian café ownership, connected to the conflict. Most of the new owners were believed to be working with the FLN, "who seems to want to create by these means new centers [foyers] for recruitment and propaganda in the metropole."[104] Some FLN activities within North African communities were thus as profit driven as the initiatives by employers and other business owners.

"Sleep Merchants"

Beyond the direct profits of North African labor, there was plenty of money to be made from housing migrants and their families. Previous chapters have discussed the development of state-funded housing projects, but private owners also opened or expanded their market for renters (from very short- to rather long-term). Many of the North African business owners in the metropole opened hotels and other lodging services, building on the tendency of new migrants to seek these people out as established figures whose contacts and information could be invaluable for establishing a new metropolitan life. Just like café owners, North African landlords often acted as "tutors or leaders" for other migrants.[105] As Abdelmalek Sayad and Éliane Dupuy point out, these migrant elites acted out of a sense of "solidarity" that was "not exempt from calculation, nor self-interest, nor even . . . exploitation."[106] Even smaller proprietors within the bidonvilles engaged in a brisk trade in materials and constructions.[107] These landlords were a concern for many officials and organizations. Not only might they exercise undue political influence, but they could also easily exploit migrants' desperate needs for shelter. In addition, French police worried about the impact of such haphazard housing on surveillance activities and complained about the difficulties of controlling slum areas.[108] This enhanced their own desire to support better housing for North African migrants throughout the metropole.

Nineteenth-century migration from the provinces into French cities introduced the term *sleep merchants*, which was used more and more often in the postwar era to capture concerns about migrant—especially North African—housing. These concerns were often raised in terms of North Africans' own welfare. A Rhône police report in 1946 warned that North African café owners might lodge for the night "30 to 40 of these sprawled, without covers, on the very tiles." As bad as the experience was, the optics were even worse: North Africans did "not fail to compare [their situation] to that of the Italians, nourished and housed on their arrival at the Centre Lumière. The favorable treatment applied to these ex-enemies seems to them a great injustice, many of them having been mobilized and having campaigned against Italy."[109] At a time when France felt its imperial debt more acutely, and when officials at all levels were determined to prove that North Africans would fare better with France than apart from it, this housing crisis—compounded by a similarly better treatment of Italians in the workforce—threatened to cleave North African migrants from pro-French sympathies.

The Paris police recognized that migrants were often driven to the sleep merchants by lack of other options. French landowners

(and other migrants) also operated many of the hotels and furnished rooms that worried local officials less for political reasons
than for public health and welfare. Many landlords were "wary,
if not hostile" in their response to North African renters, even
those willing to pay unusually high prices. Migrants, in turn, recognized this as "a manifestation of racism and fe[lt] a deep bitter-
ness": "They pile up, as you know, in furnished flats of the worst
category, in cafés, in stores, even in attics and cellars."[110] Another
report claimed that hotels in Asnières and Gennevilliers were
"invaded by a North African clientele, who lodge on the ground
in bars, in kitchens, in cellars, in attics, in rabbit huts. One sees
women and children living together with animals, with goats."[111]
The domain of the sleep merchants was thus coded as crowded,
dangerous, and less than "civilized"—drawing again on racialized
tropes about the presence of animals.

Migrants themselves were regularly—if unjustly—blamed for the
deplorable state of these residences, regardless of who owned them.
The Catholic group Mouvement populaire de familles (MPF)
launched complaints about hotels on the rue de Landy in Saint-
Denis, declaring that "premises occupied by North Africans are
transformed into slums due to the laziness and negligence of their
occupants" and that French families were not so destructive.[112] The
MPF also voiced moral concerns, accusing the hotel owner of renting some rooms by the hour and allowing half-naked women to
dance for audiences in the café.[113] The police investigation found
"a cosmopolitan population, North Africans working in France,
Spanish refugees, unstable Metropolitans" living in terribly dirty
and unhygienic conditions, though they did not find evidence of
prostitution.[114] A follow-up report found improvements, including
the hiring of a cleaner for the bathrooms, though it also asserted
that "the North African clientele refuses to observe the most ele-
mentary hygiene rules."[115] Of particular interest for our consideration of profit motives, the hotel owner had been charged with
"illicit raising of rents" in February 1947 and was sentenced to eight
months in prison and a fine of fifty thousand francs.[116]

Landlords were not the only group to profit from housing North

Africans. Builders marketed products specifically for use in resorbing the bidonvilles and other insalubrious areas. The ALGECO cor-
poration contacted the Rhône prefecture in 1962 to extol the virtues
of its "transit-bungalows," which had already been used at various
times by the Maison de l'Afrique du Nord (MAN) and by the prefecture itself during the resorption of the bidonville des Buers in
Villeurbanne.[117] These mobile constructions could be used to prevent both a worsening housing crisis triggered by bidonville dwellers' demands and "exploitation by unscrupulous landlords of those
persons displaced from precarious and insalubrious housing, as is
the case in Vénissieux and Saint-Fons." ALGECO was concerned,
though, that Labor Ministry officials were overzealous in enforcing
laws about dwelling size (despite having supported the use of the
ALGECO bungalows in previous years) and appealed to the prefect
for support in this matter. Here, as with Victor Simon and Olivier
de Serres, a company adeptly used the rhetoric of North Africans'
best interests—safe, hygienic, and affordable housing—to support
their business plan. In this case, the prefect did indeed intervene
on ALGECO's behalf.[118]

In the late 1960s, both slum dwelling and slumlord profits began
to rise as an unintended consequence of bidonville resorption programs. Marc Roberrini's 1972 report on migrant housing in the
Paris region called attention to "microbidonvilles" and slums that
had been ignored throughout the '60s. Bidonvilles and slums alike
offered a chance for profit: whether on public or private land,
"exploiters pull substantial gains from renting the makeshift dwellings they erected."[119] Roberrini warned that about 7.5 percent of
migrants around Paris lived in "locales not suited for habitation,"
while just over 12 percent were in hotels and furnished rooms.[120]
Roberrini emphasized that migrants often turned to the sleep
merchants by choice, unhappy with rehousing options they were
provided by state officials and believing that by finding their own
alternatives, they would pay lower rent, have more freedom, and
maintain closer community ties. Indeed, no bidonville operation
ever resulted in all the occupants being rehoused as planned.[121]

Roberrini worried, though, about how much more difficult it

would be to reduce slum housing than it had been to get rid of the bidonvilles: "Using a bulldozer to demolish a bidonville evacuated by its occupants, after rehousing them, is something that only outrages the exploiter; to force a loss, tear out the windows, smash the floorboards, wall up the entrances—to make a slum uninhabitable—is to violate property." Respect for private ownership was becoming a barrier to ensuring safe and healthy housing for migrants and their families. Moreover, Roberrini observed that both migrants and slumlords were adept at marshaling their legal rights to preserve their homes or their rental income: "A new race of exploiters is born, and a new race of the exploited as well," both supported by lawyers, by press reports, and "by good works and good souls too."[122] Nowhere was this confrontation of profit and comfort, choice and mandate, rights and well-being so clear as in the controversy over the Cité Olivier de Serres.

A Slumlord with a Heart of Gold?

The Cité Olivier de Serres, owned by Compagnie Victor Simon, was significantly larger than the average operation run by sleep merchants and hotel owners. The complex of eight low-rise buildings comprised 336 apartments of three to five rooms each.[123] At first, one resident recalled, Simon himself was "well-liked": the young boys thought he looked like Charles de Gaulle and admired his big black Cadillac. He lived nearby and would come to the complex to chat with residents.[124] As soon as the first leases came to term, however, Simon raised rents and fees sharply, then expelled the residents who organized against these policies. Renters were subject both to neglected upkeep and to regular price hikes. Families with viable alternatives were quick to flee the complex, creating a situation where recent arrivals from North Africa were the majority of—and eventually the only—residents. Simon required a lease deposit of a full three months' rent.[125] Migrant workers signed leases for Olivier de Serres in order to establish living conditions that allowed them to bring their families over from Algeria. Many families moved once they received their relocation permits, providing a regularly rotating clientele to line Simon's company pockets.[126] Certainly, turnover in the buildings was fairly high; a 1968 report showed that eighty-four units—nearly one-fourth of the complex—had changed occupancy over the course of the previous year.[127]

As seen in chapter 1, Villeurbanne's mayor, the Rhône prefect, and other neighborhood residents grew increasingly anxious about Olivier de Serres over the course of the 1960s. Mayor Gagnaire explained in 1966 that the cité was becoming a "multi-level bidonville [*bidonville à étages*]" and that he was disturbed not by the presence of North African migrants but rather by "their exploiters who have them come [to France] without contracts or lodging."[128] Gagnaire's umbrage at those who would take advantage of North African migrants was somewhat undercut by his assertions that Olivier de Serres was overseen by a "veritable mafia" of North Africans who organized the rotation of multiple migrant families and his questioning of whether North African labor was truly "indispensable." Gagnaire did, however, see fit to warn the Algerian Consul about the cité's "lamentable conditions" and "shameful exploitation" of Algerian workers, hoping for help in dissuading new arrivals.[129] Ultimately, as we have already seen, Gagnaire and the Rhône prefecture turned to educational policy to help resolve the situation, with the June 1970 circular restricting migrant relocation to neighborhoods whose schools had large "foreign" populations. Simon did not receive the news of the new policy lightly, given that it would deplete his revenue stream. He launched a letter campaign to the prefecture and eventually to a number of ministries and national figures in order to force them to renew his supply of residents.

In his attempt to fend off prefectural policies to shut down the cité, Simon articulated an intriguing vision of French migration policy and the role of his Algerian residents within the republic. Responding to the prefecture's charges, Simon claimed to be "astonished," particularly by the accusation that he was driven by "highly mercantile interest." He asserted that, to the contrary, he worked very much in line with the *national* interest by providing much-needed housing, for which he had received government funding.

Intriguingly, Simon objected to the idea that he brought "disorder" into his own properties by allowing so many "foreign" families: "These foreign families—having been legally admitted into France and for *France's needs*—must they be crammed into the bidonvilles? Have we not heard, just recently, Monsieur the Prime Minister declare that he will take urgent measures to ensure that *apartment buildings be built* without delay, to house the populations of foreign origins crammed into the bidonvilles around Paris? Will Monsieur the Prime Minister face the same reproaches as we do?"[130] Simon here put a remarkable emphasis on the migrants' position as desired individuals, serving the good of the French Republic. In essence, he reminded the prefect, as other migrant rights activists would often do, that foreign workers had been invited—even needed—and thus deserved to be well hosted.

Simon also played with the idea of national belonging later in the letter, referring to his first pieds-noirs residents as "French," his own quotation marks calling into question what made those migrants more French than the others he housed.[131] A later assertion was even more striking: he described his residents as "a numerous population of North Africans including many children (who will be perhaps the French of tomorrow)."[132] Simon, in effect, claimed these North African children for the republic, endowing them with a Frenchness that—though legally clear—was rarely admitted by other officials and certainly not by the neighborhood petitioners.

Simon directly confronted the prefecture's new policy, insisting that "when you announce that you will refuse residency permits to North African families living in our buildings, it is above all a *discriminatory* measure against us."[133] Simon clearly felt singled out among other property owners (no other complex was subject to such restrictions). Yet it cannot be coincidental that he employed the term *discrimination* and underlined it without an intention to also call attention to the discrimination against prospective North African residents—especially given that the cité's high North African population was the only means of differentiating his properties from others in the region. Indeed, his use of "us" may be strategically ambiguous in this context, referring to the members of the company but also potentially including his current and prospective residents.

As proof of his "anti-racist sentiments," Simon emphasized his role in providing "wholly new" housing options for North African migrants.[134] Moreover, he claimed (contrary to some of his earlier statements) that his renters were respectful and would live peacefully if not for the presence of "foreign elements" looking to stir up trouble.[135] Simon clearly positioned himself against the political agitators and leftists that so worried the police and other local governments. Indeed, his use of "foreign" to describe the political operatives in contrast to "his" renters was telling. He painted the neighborhood socioeducational organization (the Association socio-éducative Villeurbannaise [ASEV]) as a subversive element with no useful educational programming and demanded that, instead of continuing to outsource this work, the Rhône prefecture spend real resources to enhance the presence of both the police and members of the Service de liaison et promotion des migrants (SLPM) in the neighborhood. More importantly, he explicitly separated the troublemaking Maoists from his residents, asking, "Are our North Africans responsible [for this political activity]?"[136] This "our" once again brought the North African residents into Simon's rhetorical community and marked the leftist agitators as the troublesome other, whom he assured officials he would be happy to remove from the premises.

The prefecture certainly did not appreciate being the brunt of such attacks and struck back where it could. Neither departmental nor municipal actors, however, managed to reclaim the moral high ground on migrant welfare. To the contrary, as Simon's rhetoric became strategically more inclusive, theirs seemed ever more defensive and intolerant. Again and again, officials accused Simon of being at the root of the neighborhood frictions. In June 1970, the prefecture wrote, "It is unfair to force educators or their director to bear responsibility for a situation that you, yourself, have created. . . . By allowing [*favorisant*] the installation of foreign families above the 15% rate sociologically recommended for their proper insertion into our modern life, you have created an explosive situation."[137]

Descriptions of Simon's business practices sounded like admonishments to an industrial polluter: he should have known that his residents were problematic (by virtue of their foreignness) and taken measures to avoid allowing their concentration to disturb the neighborhood's previously flourishing social system. Another memo, sent to the Labor Ministry, complained that "while most apartment administrators in the Lyon agglomeration show little enthusiasm for renting family units to North African workers, the V. Simon management presents itself as very welcoming to them." This "welcoming" attitude was not advantageous, as such hospitality was not cheap: "Public opinion is shocked and protests against this massive immigration of North Africans, whose presence raises numerous social problems."[138]

Simon, in turn, insisted that he was providing crucial solutions to real-world problems, while the city and department clung to delusions. He explained in a letter to Paul Dijoud (Sécretaire d'État aux travailleurs immigrés) that his company's difficulties began at the moment when "some utopian bureaucrats relying on the advice of sociological dreamers decided that they needed to establish within our complex a cohabitation of North Africans and Europeans." Meanwhile, even as the French state called for better migrant housing and the region faltered in its ability to provide social housing for anyone on their lists, "modern apartments partially financed with public funding . . . remain empty by the will of the Rhône prefecture."[139] Dijoud's office sided with Simon, suggesting to the prefect that "it would be good to find a way to end the inoccupation of between sixty and eighty units belonging to the Compagnie Victor Simon, given the serious shortage of social housing suffered in the Rhône department."[140] This overall housing crisis was key to how the end of the Olivier de Serres affair played out.

Any satisfaction the city and department derived from turning down residency applications and slowly bleeding Simon of his clientele was short-lived. The overall number of Algerian families in the complex did begin to drop: by September 1971, fifty of the units were empty.[141] After another two years, though, there were still 320 families living in 292 of the apartments.[142] A group of sixty residents refused to pay the exorbitant housing fees.[143] One former resident explained that they would easily have had a legal case against Simon, but in addition to "not being aware of their rights at the time," they were wary of engaging the French judicial system, given their memories of the Algerian War. He further explained that families' energies were caught up in keeping work and feeding their children.[144] Meanwhile, the school situation had only worsened, and more families went on strike to protest their exclusion from the newest neighborhood school.[145]

Simon and the authorities had reached an impasse: Olivier de Serres was still a North African ghetto in the heart of Villeurbanne, but Simon's profit margins had slimmed to the point that he too began to look for a way out. Simon repeatedly asked local housing offices to send him "Europeans" to house and did not hesitate to point out the fundamental flaw in the administration's plan to normalize the residency rates in the cité as it stood: "We have tried to rent the vacant units to Europeans—French or foreign—without success; these potential renters do not wish to live alongside North Africans."[146] For a while, he used his empty units as further proof of the prefecture's discriminatory practices toward his company and North African migrants. Eventually, however, the complex became more of a burden than a boon, particularly as leftist groups became active in the neighborhood, and in 1975 Simon asked the local authorities to help divest him of the Olivier de Serres property.[147]

With some relief, the city and the prefecture laid plans to purchase, then level, the cité in the next year.[148] Collaboration among four construction offices enabled the transfer of ownership but did not help with the overly optimistic time frame.[149] Since white families were unwilling to move into the complex—and even other North Africans were put off by the reputation of Olivier de Serres—the families in the complex would have to be rehoused elsewhere. The majority of residents, by this time, expressed their own desire to leave.[150] To hold to the 15 percent threshold on the number of North Africans in a given housing development, departmental planners realized that they would need to disperse the cité's families across a total of 6,400 social housing units (many of these yet unbuilt).[151] Public and private leasing organizations often refused to take on any families from the infamous complex, and prospective neighbors petitioned to prevent Olivier de Serres families from moving in.[152] An even greater obstacle to the project was the size of the families. Olivier de Serres was unique in that most of the apartments were well suited to large families (in stark contrast to the majority of social housing). During the lengthy rehousing process, departmental officials even resorted to asking Simon to shuffle large families within his own available units—since there were no options elsewhere in the region that could offer sufficient room.[153]

1977 brought some changes to Villeurbanne. Additional public attention was called to the cité's plight when Victor Simon's son, then the building manager, was kidnapped that September.[154] More importantly, socialist Charles Hernu succeeded Gagnaire as mayor, with a promise to make Olivier de Serres one of his priorities. One young resident remembered Hernu as "a courageous man [who] came to the neighborhood in the evenings to see what was happening. He welcomed you if you asked for a meeting."[155] Where Gagnaire had repeatedly insisted that Villeurbanne's HLM had no space for families from the cité, Hernu gave them precedence.[156] This meant, though, that he refused residency requests for North African families who were coming from anywhere but Olivier de Serres—and was often frustrated when neighboring suburbs refused to admit cité residents into their own housing programs.[157] He questioned the assumptions behind the 15 percent rule for foreign occupancy, even as he cited them as reasons to fund even more social housing construction.[158] Hernu further worked to resolve the status of family members who had taken up residence after clandestinely entering France.[159] There were also some attempts to bring residents and their concerns into the process, their voices having been treated as incidental to city and prefectural officials up to this point. Nine North African delegates were elected by residents to be part of the commission overseeing the cité's closure.[160] In November 1979, with 130 families still to rehouse, Hernu convened a meeting with Olivier de Serres residents to address some of their own concerns, including unemployment, funding to reduce new rents, and police harassment of workers heading out in the mornings.[161]

In 1978, the first of the buildings to empty entirely was destroyed—setting a precedent in the region for dynamiting poorly conceived social housing, the best-known incident being the destruction of Vénissieux's ZUP (Zone à urbaniser en priorité) Minguettes in 1984 (see figure 5.1). Both Hernu and Gagnaire attended the demolition launch, along with multiple other departmental and city officials and Lyon's long-serving imam, Bel Hadj Ben Maafi.[162] Ninety percent of the residents of that first building were rehoused within Villeurbanne.[163] The majority of the families from the second building to fall in March 1979 also remained in the city.[164] The municipal council voted in November 1980 to rename the neighborhood Jacques Monod in an attempt to erase the stigma of "Olivier de Serres."[165] In 1984, the last of the Olivier de Serres buildings finally came down. Three-quarters of the families had indeed been rehoused within Villeurbanne itself—in contrast to earlier instincts to shuttle migrants around the region.[166] This official commitment to keep families within the city was met with popular resistance; Le Progrès observed halfway through the process that "after demanding that we make the ghettos disappear, residents fear the consequences."[167]

Simon's voice largely disappeared from the record after 1975. Having decided to offload the property and its problems, he lacked a motive to speak on behalf of his North African residents. Clearly, he had not crusaded for migrant rights out of the goodness of his heart. Indeed, the "heart of gold" in this section's title should be taken less as a metaphor for kindness but rather as a literal indication of Simon's commitment to his bottom line. Threats to his profits drove Simon to fight against local migration restrictions, just as opportunities for profit had brought him and so many other employers and landlords into the business of North African welfare in the first place.

FIG. 5.1. View of the demolition of Cité Olivier de Serres, Villeurbanne.
From *Le Progrès*, in "Olivier de Serres: Radiographie d'une
'cité ghetto,'" exhibition catalog, 2009 (Le Rize, Villeurbanne).

Throughout the decades following World War II, there was plenty of
money to be made from North African migrants' labor and serving
their basic needs. The fascinating lesson from the Olivier de Serres
example is not so much Simon's financial motivations for opposing discriminatory measures but rather his ability to draw effectively on a language of migrant rights and welfare that embraced
North Africans as part of the local community and sharply criticized French policies on these fronts. That he did so in Lyon in
the early 1970s was even more remarkable. As the litany of neighborhood protestations and prefectural policies demonstrates, this
was a tense moment for migrants in the region. Indeed, in 1971,
Lyon earned the title of the French "capital of racism" from the
national press.[168]

Local officials seemed to suit that mold, given both the policies
they enacted and the terms with which they so often described
Simon's tenants. Their concern for Olivier de Serres residents was
hardly ever articulated as a desire to improve their living situations;

rather, Gagnaire's constituency in particular proved to be the petitioning neighbors from around the cité. Even the discussions about the effects on schooling focused on the problems faced by teachers, the disservice to white "French" children, and the anger of white "French" parents—the migrant children's own difficulties appeared in the background, if at all. This made it even more surprising that Simon would choose to fight on the rhetorical background of migrant rights (which seemed to have such little place in the municipal and prefectural calculations). At the same time, this choice to invoke ideas about migrants' rights suggests that even in a racially charged Lyon, the prevailing norm was a belief in migrant workers' dignity and their place within the community. This ideal—though far from reality—was powerful enough to alter policies and practices.

Simon's most effective tactic, perhaps, was his ability to play national actors off local ones. This kept the Cité Olivier de Serres in operation long past the city and prefecture's wishes and then served as additional pressure on local officials to buy the land away from Simon. In the late '60s and into the '70s, Simon received support and even praise as a rare proprietor so willing to help the state with the migrant housing problem. A 1969 report from the Rhône's own Social and Sanitary Action Board backed Simon against other local government actors: though the mayor was doing his best to prevent more families from settling there, "given that the Algerians face particular difficulties, due to their origins, in finding sufficient family housing, the Compagnie Victor Simon offers them housing possibilities at rue Olivier de Serres, which other proprietors are reticent to provide."[169] Here Gagnaire came off as having questionable motives, while Simon looked generous and tolerant. Distant national officials were more likely to be drawn to the sort of rhetoric Simon employed (consider Dijoud's support above)— especially since he claimed to be aligning himself with the best principles of the republic. Local officials had more difficulty with this, as they faced a host of angry neighbors to whom they were more directly responsible.

Even on the practical level, Simon was able to argue that he filled a vital gap in the French migration system by providing decent housing to North Africans who would otherwise be lost in the slums and bidonvilles and add ever more weight to the local social housing rolls. There is some irony in that many concepts Simon invoked seemed to be borrowed directly from the playbook of the leftist activists he regularly deplored as troublemakers. Simon's drive to maximize his profits hardly aligned with our image of the perfect champion for migrant rights. However, he proved to be a highly effective critic of local and national migration policies, keeping public attention on migrant housing and integration.

By the 1970s, a host of individuals had become embroiled in a struggle over North African rights—and their place within local and national communities. Motivations for getting involved in these issues were myriad, and in the struggle over the Cité Olivier de Serres, we find the fascinating example of a slumlord led deep into the language of radical inclusion and rights within the French Republic. This language of migrant rights was thus powerful currency in France at the dawn of the 1970s. Not all those who invoked these ideals, however, did so for self-serving reasons. Indeed, their very power was rooted in a set of values that were vigorously defended by a diverse set of actors in French communities. The next chapter turns to these true believers, the local leaders whose experiences and worldviews shaped a decidedly nonnational understanding of community relationships and thus a humanist obligation to stand with migrant workers and their families in defense of their basic rights and welfare.

SIX

Solidarity

I n July 1970, local Catholic and Protestant leaders around Lyon joined the chorus of protests against the Rhône prefecture's June circular limiting the number of "foreigners" allowed to settle in particular neighborhoods. They and concerned members of their congregations warned that the discriminatory education policy was a move toward overt segregation and away from the humane treatment of migrants. Unlike Victor Simon's clearly self-interested critique of the circular, which we saw in the previous chapter, these voices seemed to emanate from a real sense of human solidarity. Indeed, local Christian actors had provided services and support to North African migrants in the region for decades, emphasizing their obligations to serve fellow humans and carefully avoiding any activity that might be seen as proselytizing or aimed at religious conversion.[1]

This final chapter examines the role of solidarity rooted in creed, class, and community. Along with Christians, communists and other leftists also offered strong support—both real and rhetorical—to North African migrants. While Christians and communists are rarely seen as natural allies, all of the groups and individuals discussed in this chapter shared a decidedly nonnational understanding of community and belonging.[2] These actors were moved by worldviews that defined migrants not by their otherness but rather through their connections: they were comrades, neighbors, children of god. Such activists regularly invoked their sense of brotherhood or fraternity—a value encoded in the French Republic's vision of *liberté, égalité, fraternité*. Their results were not perfect, and at times they certainly fell back on patronizing and paternalistic ideas and practices. Their motivations, however, stemmed from their sense of justice and a desire above all to do the right thing by these new members of their communities.

Previous chapters have considered baser motivations for involvement in North African affairs: concerns about modernity and diverse urban populations, political calculations, adherence to imperial and anti-imperial ideologies, and even opportunities to make money. However, politics, profit, and ideas about empire do not explain all instances of local French engagement with North African migrants. Even in cases where some of these motives were present, they cannot always on their own answer satisfactorily the question of how and why certain individuals became so involved with the migrants in their community, particularly given the larger number who did not bother. Though it can be difficult to discuss in scholarly terms, we should perhaps leave some room for basic human empathy. In addition, with each of these groups of activists, we find evidence for larger ideological frameworks within which there was space to embrace migrants.

Each of the ideologies discussed in this chapter gave certain actors a vocabulary and a method for working with North Africans. Members of these political and religious communities were not automatically more likely to embrace local migrants; indeed, plenty of communists and Christians had no dealings with (or even stood opposed to) North African migrants.[3] What these worldviews offered, however, was the possibility for action on the part of individuals likely or able to rally for migrants' causes. If we delve beneath traditional state-level inquiries into migration policy (itself a transnational issue), we can shed light on the interplay of internationalist ideologies and day-to-day local concerns and thus discover important, direct connections between local and global currents.

Christian Charity

One of the most active proponents of North African welfare in the Rhône was the private Association du Foyer Notre-Dame des Sans-Abris (NDSA). NDSA played a major role in housing local migrants and especially in getting rid of the region's bidonvilles. NDSA was founded by Gabriel Rosset, with the support of Cardinal Gerlier, and a handful of like-minded friends.[4] Rosset was a teacher from a peasant family and a social Catholic who fervently believed in the sanctity of charitable work. In 2006, the diocese of Lyon began the process of beatification and canonization for Rosset on the basis of his work with NDSA. Gerlier too was closely associated with social Catholicism as well as the worker-priest movement and a more ecumenical activism. Named archbishop, then cardinal, of Lyon in 1937, Gerlier was an outspoken advocate for and supporter of Jews under Vichy (despite having supported Pétain as a fellow veteran) and argued for a humanist response to the "odious excesses" of racist policies.[5] In 1951, Gerlier penned an appeal to all French Catholics to learn to "[respect] and [comprehend]" migrants, "[triumph] over prejudices," and accept North Africans as brothers and sisters in the "true spirit of Jesus Christ."[6] This spirit of brother- and sisterhood ran through much of NDSA's activism and activities.

Rosset characterized the association as having "Christian inspiration" and being supported by various church authorities and religious orders, though it was not properly a religious charity.[7] They opened their first shelter of two hundred beds on Christmas Eve in 1950, at a converted café on 3 rue Père-Chevrier in Lyon's seventh district.[8] Their clientele expanded rapidly, from 11 that first night to 150 at the end of their first month of operation. Rosset and his team redoubled their outreach as they found themselves forced to turn people away for lack of space.[9] In 1954, Rosset expanded NDSA's reach by partnering with the Comité Lyonnais de secours d'urgence aux sans logis et mal-logés to begin building transitional housing in the banlieues for families moving out of the region's bidonvilles.[10] By 1964, NDSA was operating thirty *cités d'urgence*, or emergency housing centers. Such cités d'urgence were operated throughout France from 1954, following Abbé Pierre's national crusade on behalf of all "*mal-logés*" during that year's exceptionally hard winter, which had raised public awareness about the French housing crisis.[11]

The original shelter was predominantly staffed by volunteers, and NDSA recruited youth for help with building and maintenance and (on Sundays and holidays) for partnering with and mentoring the children they housed.[12] Starting in 1959, NDSA organized groups of young "*compagnons bâtisseurs*" (French and foreign—Dutch, Italian, German) to volunteer during the summers to build new housing units and renovate NDSA's main buildings, all of which were used to close down the region's bidonvilles.[13] Indeed, by 1959, NDSA had taken the lead in providing transitional housing for former bidonvilliers in the Rhône. The association believed that for the vast majority of cases, a "transplant" directly from the bidonville into social housing was "too brutal" and left the migrants unable to adapt. NDSA proposed instead to create small cités de transit incorporating both an architecture that supported supposedly traditional collective living arrangements and—more importantly—a staff trained to control, observe, aid, assist, and educate the residents.[14] NDSA had as much trouble as any other service in successfully transitioning families out of supposedly transitional housing. Rosset's frustration with the lack of good housing options pushed him to request that NDSA form its own HLM (Habitation à loyer modéré) office, launched by the prefecture in 1972.[15] In his 1974 eulogy for Rosset, Lyon's Mayor Pradel went so far as to declare that "it is thanks to Monsieur Rosset that there are no more bidonvilles."[16]

The association's initial mission statement did not explicitly mention migrants, yet the majority of those housed by NDSA were not listed as French, and a sizable number were North African.[17] In December 1956, Rosset wrote to the Interior Ministry to raise specific concerns about the "distress faced by North African workers and the disinterest of the public authorities on their behalf."[18] Though the Rhône prefecture vehemently denied the factual basis of many of Rosset's charges, his concern for North African welfare was clear, and his association became ever more involved in providing housing and socioeducational services for these migrants.[19] Rhône CTAM (Conseiller technique pour les affaires musulmanes) Martin reached out to Rosset in 1957, after reading one of NDSA's bulletins, to express his appreciation for Rosset's "courage, devotion, and efficiency." Martin also wanted to be sure Rosset had a more comprehensive view of what was being done for North African housing needs in the department (by the prefecture and by employers) so that he might see the prefectural services as sharing the same goals.[20] NDSA became a major partner for the prefecture, recognized officially as a nonprofit organization serving the public good in 1957.[21] NDSA applications for national funding received strong departmental support: the prefecture wrote in 1965 that the association was Lyon's "most important and most supportive charity for the homeless" and had the Rhône administration's "total support."[22]

This intense cooperation, where NDSA at times appeared to be a direct extension of departmental services, does not fit entirely with the supposedly strident secularism of the French Republic.[23] Yet in official correspondence with the prefect and his staff, Rosset and his colleagues never invoked tenets of faith. Many of the reports sent were purely statistical, with little of the qualitative evaluation seen from other organizations (especially the Maison d'Afrique du Nord / Maison de travailleur étranger [MAN/MTE]). Dealings with state ministries and other offices were also devoid of religious content (not even a discussion of the religious affiliation evident in the name of the association). Yet the association's Christian roots were never far from the surface and were more apparent in NDSA's other publications. The shelter on rue Père-Chevrier held a monthly Mass for the homeless.[24] One Easter, Rosset compared rehousing to resurrection and the housing crisis to a crisis of faith.[25] An NDSA brochure, calling on citizens and public officials alike to act on the "agonizing" problem of housing, closed with the invocation "God help us! And Notre-Dame so that hope might be reborn among those unhappy families in search of a roof!"[26] Rosset himself claimed to be inspired by Saints Vincent de Paul, Antoine Martel, and Joseph.[27] The association's links with the prefecture were matched only by their ties to the diocese, especially under Gerlier, of whom Rosset wrote, "We had in him a protector, a guide, a father."[28] Gerlier, in turn, said of visiting the main shelter, "Here, one is fully in the gospel."[29]

Despite Rosset's openness about his religious inspiration and these regular reminders that the association itself was animated by faith, there were few, if any, traces of proselytizing among their residents. Notably, when a series of complaints was lodged against the association in the mid-1970s, there wasn't a single mention of religiosity. Rather, the critiques focused on the material conditions in NDSA's buildings, a lack of response to resident concerns, the paternalistic attitudes of cité directors and welfare workers, and the difficulties of transitioning out of these supposedly temporary spaces.[30] Rosset did assert, in a 1965 newsletter, "If God wishes us to house the homeless, he wants us at the same time to bring them into his Love."[31] This loving, however, was more about the heart of the host and not the soul of the resident. NDSA's role was to alleviate suffering, to provide a safe bed and a warm meal, and to offer access to more stable housing and even to education and employment. Rosset cited scripture, particularly the parable of the good Samaritan, and asserted that hospitality to the poorest was a form of receiving Christ. Moreover, one always had to be open to criticism, to hearing from those one served that their needs had not truly been met. To do this divine work, each resident—North Africans included—was met as "a human person with their dignity as a creature of God."[32] Basic human dignity was the foundation for all NDSA activities.

This perspective on Christian charity aligned well with the church's own evolving sense of its role in a decolonizing world. The Second Vatican Council's 1965 *Ad Gentes* decree on missionary activity included calls for greater humanitarian engagement. It specified that "Christian charity extends to all, without distinction of race, creed, or social condition, it looks for neither gain nor gratitude. . . . The faithful should in their charity care for the human person himself." Education, which could be used to promote Christian values, was also "a valuable public service . . . working toward the uplifting of human dignity and towards better living conditions." Christians furthermore were charged to "take part in the strivings of those people who, waging war on famine, ignorance, and disease, are struggling to better their way of life and to secure peace in the world."[33] As historian Darcie Fontaine suggests, these particular directives created a broader sense of Christian "solidarity with the poor and oppressed."[34] They also potentially enlarged the sphere of charitable action. Rosset himself certainly looked beyond providing basic humanitarian care. He declared that offering aid did not remove the obligation to "search scientifically and politically to destroy the cause of suffering." People of faith looking to serve those in need were equally responsible for influencing leaders and policy-makers and for bringing about "the most just reforms on the social and international plan."[35] This appeal to social justice further revealed the capacious definition of human responsibility and community engagement that drove NDSA, in line with an expansive Christian worldview.

While Rosset does not appear to have explicitly criticized imperial practices, other local Christians certainly did. Those who opposed the war in Algeria provide the clearest example. In March 1957, amid the ongoing Battle of Algiers, the Assembly of Cardinals and Archbishops of France (ACA) made a declaration against the war's conduct—objecting (with much of the population) to the use of "torture, collective reprisals, summary executions, [and] arbitrary internment." Much of their opposition was based in the evident changes in "moral sense" suffered by young men returning from the Algerian front. More locally, a group of Lyonnais "Christians from various milieus and with different political leanings" insisted to the Rhône prefect that "a government worthy of the name must and can immediately cease, if it so wishes, all reprehensible practices."[36] These individuals, and the ACA itself, as Fontaine observes, primarily objected to the effects the war had on French Christians and French morality and stopped short of actually supporting Algerian nationalism or independence.[37] Cardinal

Gerlier regularly invoked "the Algerian problem" in his public appearances, and a number of local clergy cultivated support for North African migrants; some even worked closely with known FLN (Front de libération nationale) militants.[38] Concerns about French conduct and about the material conditions of Algerians on both sides of the Mediterranean laid the groundwork for Christian critique of imperialism and its aftermath, with a particular focus on alleviating suffering and providing the basis for a universal human dignity. This approach would be carried forward by other local activists, most notably Christian Delorme, a priest who became one of the most outspoken white advocates for North African rights in the 1980s.[39]

As mentioned at the start of this chapter, Christian groups in the Rhône also mobilized against racial discrimination in the wake of the June 1970 prefectural policy restricting migrant residency in certain neighborhoods. The circular's designation of only Algerian families as subject to the new rules not only made Algerians more "foreign" than other (European) migrants, but it also seemed to signal to Christians that other—predominantly non-Christian—communities would be targeted and that therefore this was not a matter to concern them. To the contrary, the prefect was soon besieged by "the strongest protests on the part of religious authorities, unions, and political groups as well as associations with a social mission, working on behalf of the reception and integration of foreign workers." The Confédération française démocratique du travail (CFDT) union, whose statutes invoked the principle of "Christian humanism"—and whose members included a number of the social assistants in the region—took the lead by holding open meetings for all migrant-focused associations as well as speaking out in the local press (Le Progrès and Christian papers).[40]

Local Christian leaders quickly joined in the wider protest against this new policy. Cardinal Renard, Gerlier's successor, wrote to the prefect after receiving "letters upon letters that fear segregation."[41] Renard, a former teacher, had been elevated to his position through his commitment to social morality, with a focus on family and children.[42] Much of the religious protest against the new policy invoked the detrimental effects on migrant families and children and thus aligned with Renard's own priorities. Willing to concede that high concentrations of migrants in certain neighborhoods "[do] not favor reciprocal comprehension," the cardinal still felt that the policy was ill conceived. Pastor Monsarrat, president of the regional council for the Protestant Church, was more forthright in his concerns. Monsarrat's own background was migratory: born in London, he attended high school in Casablanca and conducted his religious studies in Paris, New York, and Saint-Andrews.[43] Monsarrat said, "As much as I understand the concern that you undoubtedly have to combat the transformation of certain sectors of our agglomeration into overpopulated slums, it seems to me just as disastrous to envision measures that deprive the men whom we ask to come for the good functioning of our economy of the presence of their families." Monsarrat asked the prefect to reconsider his approach, to find methods less "repressive, policing and, in the end, inhumane."[44] Monsarrat, incidentally, would later become a major critic of racism in French politics, especially with the rise of the Front national (FN).[45]

Rhône prefect Max Moulins responded defensively, emphasizing that the policy affected very few neighborhoods, its aim was "educational and social," its purpose was to avoid impenetrable "medinas" within the urban fabric, and finally, the restriction was created in collaboration with local mayors and others.[46] To Monsarrat, Moulins included a request for a meeting to prove the prefecture's good faith in its treatment of migrants and its reliance on "neither repression nor police action."[47] To both, the prefect made sure to point out that "there is no French agglomeration that could rival Lyon in the domain of welcoming foreigners and, in particular, North Africans," given the good work done by a host of public and private associations (Notre-Dame des Sans-Abris was first on the list).

The most interesting piece of the prefect's letters to Renard and Monsarrat, however, was his veiled question about their interest in the matter. Among the region's foreign populations, Moulins explained, "the Algerians are, as you know, more numerous than the Spanish, the Italians and the Portuguese, and more willing to group together in well-defined areas of the agglomeration."[48] Here, Moulins was not merely listing four of the largest migrant groups in France; he was also drawing an unmistakable line between mainly Christian Europeans and Muslim Algerians (ironic given his insistence that this policy was articulated to avoid easy segregation). In short, Moulins appeared to be wondering why either the cardinal or the regional head of the Protestant church was interested in this issue in the first place, as its targeted population lay outside their presumed fold.[49]

Neither Renard nor Monsarrat—nor the concerned followers they invoked in their letters—would have granted this simplistic division of peoples. An article in *L'Essor* was quite clear: "A Christian must not remain indifferent to the fate of his foreign brothers. A Christian must fight with them and for them! . . . Christ knew no borders nor races."[50] This notion echoed the public letter sent by a number of local organizations in direct response to the policy: "We consider that every man, thus every worker, has the fundamental right to live with his family." The CFDT and its supporters repeatedly denounced the regulation as racist and insisted that "it is absolutely abnormal for migrants to pay the cost" for misguided policies.[51]

Moreover, these organizations returned to familiar critiques that the terrible living conditions of migrant families (targeted by this new restriction) resulted from state policies that encouraged migrant workers to come to France without taking responsibility for their housing, education, and health.[52] The proper approach would be for the prefecture and other public powers to expand social housing and to punish—if anyone—the landlords who overcharged or allowed their properties to fall into disrepair.[53] Perhaps even more importantly, the CFDT and others demanded more immigrant participation in the processes that governed them. Ultimately, the CFDT argued, "French immigration policy exists only to serve immediate capitalist interests and in no way takes account of the human beings who bear the cost."[54] Here again, as in Rosset's rhetoric about the work of NDSA, North Africans were supported by Christian (and Christian-inspired) groups by virtue of their shared humanity. Drawing on older traditions of charity and newer perspectives on the role of the faithful in global society, a diverse group of Christian clergy and lay believers offered aid, advocated for migrant rights, and spoke out against policy they deemed unjust—all out of a sense of obligation to North Africans simply as fellow human beings.

Communist Community

Communist actors in Saint-Denis were guided by a similarly enlarged worldview. They embraced North Africans as fellow workers and as allies in the fight against the colonial system. In this, they followed a strand of French communism that had since the 1930s advocated a "union" between French workers and Algerians as two exploited groups.[55] This inclusion of North Africans may also be read as a bid for political support, as seen in chapter 2. Yet attempts to cultivate political allegiance should not be written off merely as cynical or tactical. Politics is driven by the search for support, and myriad policies are enacted in the hopes of securing votes from one group or another. The act of soliciting votes is, in the end, inherently inclusive: it brings individuals into the political community. That municipal officials in Saint-Denis sought out North African support—and pursued policies beneficial to local North African residents—revealed a penchant for perceiving this migrant population as an integral piece of the Dionysien political community.

Saint-Denis had a tradition of including migrants as vital members of the city community. Questions of foreignness and citizenship certainly affected administrative procedures and the extension of benefits. However, the self-image promoted by city officials did not recognize such hard boundaries. Municipal relations with Spanish migrants had already established an alternative idea of local belonging. Spanish migrants had benefited both from a "mythology" of common struggle against fascism and through the strength of the ties between French and Spanish communists (and the two countries' communist parties). As historian Natacha Lillo explains, Dionysien communists built on their experiences of aiding Spanish Republicans during their civil war and acknowledged the role Spanish migrants had played during France's own resistance fight—to the point that "Saint-Denis's communist city hall strived for the inclusion of the entire [Spanish] colony into the life of the city."[56] Portuguese migrants arriving in large numbers in the 1960s were also received as new allies for local communists, particularly in the struggle against fascism and imperialism.

Anti-imperialism, particularly opposition to the war in Algeria, provided a similar set of experiences and goals shared with North African migrants, as seen in chapter 4. Algerians made for a special case, given their French citizenship for much of the period. Algerians were not only fellow workers, brothers suffering under French capitalist/imperialist oppression, but they were also "French like us," as the refrain went. This shared citizenship provided municipal officials with extra ammunition in their fight against the state (on the grounds that the suffering of fellow Frenchmen was being ignored), but Dionysienness did not function merely as a subset of Frenchness. The city continued to espouse an inclusive community identity through the late-1960s and early 1970s, after the Algerian War and the change in Algerians' citizenship status. Algerians and other North African migrants were embraced by the municipality because of a larger sense of solidarity.

From an ideological standpoint, Saint-Denis's communist officials saw Algerians as fellow members of a unified global working class, allies in the struggle against capitalism and imperialism. Mayor Gillot in 1961 declared his allegiance to a shared battle: "By helping the Algerian people to crush their enemies, we are sure to help in the crushing of our own. . . . Consequently, the danger for the working class would be not to react, not to defend itself, not to fight with the Algerian people." He aligned the Algerian struggle with the history of French rebellions, explaining that the generals who led the conquest of Algeria had used this experience to crush the "revolutionary proletariat" of Paris in 1848. This reading of the historical record served to assimilate Algerian nationalists into a grand narrative of proletarian revolutionary movements. Dionysiens and Algerians were to fight "elbow-to-elbow, hand-in-hand, for all the demands made in Saint-Denis: an increase in salaries, the defense of liberties, and the defense of the Independence of France and of Algeria."[57] Gillot's inclusion of Algerian independence here, alongside more standard economic and political demands, clearly connected North African interests and those of French workers. His was a vision of class solidarity that readily crossed national frontiers.

While Gillot and his colleagues used Algerians' Frenchness in their criticism of departmental and national policies, their discussions of local initiatives more often emphasized their status as laborers. For example, a 1950 report on outreach to North African migrants explained that "like all unemployed workers," North Africans had received a free package of living supplies during the winter of 1949–50. Moreover, North Africans on strike were offered the same support as "other workers fighting for their just demands."[58] Carefully stressing the formula "like other workers" and acknowledging migrant participation in social movements emphasized the ties between North African and French workers and built a public discourse about their roles as brothers on the same side of a greater social struggle.

A sense of shared humanity showed up in subtler ways throughout Saint-Denis's discussions of migrant housing and managing the bidonvilles. As seen in chapter 1, officials in Asnières and throughout the Rhône tended to view North African migrants as impediments to urban development. Dionysien reports, in contrast, foregrounded migrants' suffering and the humanitarian dimensions to the housing problem. They discussed the specific difficulties faced by North Africans, their occupation of slums and bidonvilles as a last resort ("chased from everywhere else, they have no choice but to be exploited"), and the need to change their social situation in order to overcome the bidonville problem.[59] Dionysien officials were no less concerned with getting rid of the bidonvilles, speaking of "making them disappear" or "liquidating" them. However, unlike the prevalent use of "liberation" in Asnières and

Lyon, Saint-Denis's communists most often described a process of "absorption" or "resorption." These terms invoked a more integrative approach to the bidonvilles and their migrant inhabitants; the land and people were to be brought into—or even brought *back* into—the local or national body in a manner that did not imply conquering so much as incorporating. Instead of focusing their discussions on the creation of shiny, new, modern neighborhoods, Saint-Denis's municipality opened most conversations with the question of how to rehouse bidonville residents and how to "ameliorat[e] the quality of life" in foyers and hotels.[60] Getting rid of the city's bidonvilles was primarily billed as a humanitarian project, not a land reclamation process.[61]

Migrant residents also appeared in city publications, events, and promotions. In 1967, the municipality published a booklet to celebrate three decades of communist stewardship by both Gillot and Fernand Grenier (deputy to the National Assembly).[62] *Saint-Denis: Hier, aujourd'hui, demain* presented the history of a city closely bound to its working-class politics, overcoming great odds (treachery, war, poor planning, population growth, de-industrialization) to construct an ever more welcoming city, with the promise of a soon-to-be renovated historic city center. One striking page featured a series of photographs of smiling infant Dionysiens, a tribute to the creation of the city's new maternity services that offered "childbirth without pain" (see figure 6.1).[63] The diversity of these young faces sent a strong message about who the city was and would be.[64] Migrations long characterized by images of single male workers, temporary visitors with no roots, had developed into pictures of happy babies. Babies signified families, the setting down of new roots, and a population who fell to the care and concern of the municipality (the page was titled "Protection of Childhood"). Accepting these young children would also require accepting the adults these children would become. Migrant inclusion was inscribed in the narrative of progress and local development. The future of Saint-Denis was diverse; race and ethnicity were not to be markers of separate community identity—at least, if this bit of political publicity were to be believed.

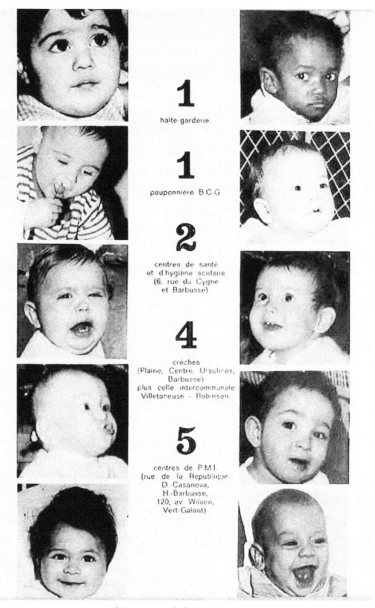

1
halte-garderie.

1
pouponnière B.C.G.

2
centres de santé
et d'hygiène scolaire
(6, rue du Cygne
et Barbusse)

4
crèches
(Plaine, Centre, Ursulines,
Barbusse)
plus celle intercommunale
Villetaneuse - Robinson

5
centres de P.M.I.
(rue de la République,
D.-Casanova,
H.-Barbusse,
120, av. Wilson,
Vert-Galant)

FIG. 6.1. Faces of Saint-Denis's future (1967). From *Saint-Denis: Hier, aujourd'hui, demain*, November 1967 (AMSD, 38 C 4).

A 1970 exhibit, "Saint-Denis, demain," that showcased the renovation of many city neighborhoods, including the center, did not embrace migrants quite as enthusiastically. A snapshot of the city's population included a section on the "Immigrant Problem," explaining that migrants comprised 20 percent of the city's population.[65] Migrants also appeared in discussions of reconstruction, as part of the text on resorbing the Francs-Moisins bidonville. If, on the one hand, this framing still included the city's migrants as part of Saint-Denis's population, on the other hand, they were treated as problematic and associated with bidonville misery. Popular reactions to the exhibit also revealed frustration with the city's migrants—often as complaints that "foreigners" were given priority access to social housing.[66] The 1971 municipal election campaign was similarly marked by anxiety about difficulties posed by migration, and Gillot's successor, Marcellin Berthelot, aligned himself with appeals to distribute migrants more "fairly" across the Paris region—echoing the dispersion logic seen earlier in Asnières and Lyon.[67] Deputy Mayor Maurice Manoel reported in 1972 that though the city had always taken more migrants than neighboring towns—he listed Hungarian refugees, Poles, Italians, Spaniards, and North Africans—the latest waves of African and Portuguese workers threatened to drown the city's good efforts: "This elevated number of foreigners in Saint-Denis poses important problems for the municipality, especially in its attempts to ameliorate their often miserable living conditions."[68] He later worried about backlash from the rest of the population; the presence of so many migrants "does not favor the development of understanding between the autochthonous population and immigrant workers, and risks becoming fertile ground for the development of racist ideas."[69] This policy position reflected the image of migration at the "Saint-Denis, demain" exhibit and echoed the decline in solidarity over time that historian Tyler Stovall traces for nearby Bobigny.[70]

Yet 1972 also brought the "Quinzaine de l'immigration" to the city. The program was conceived in cooperation with the Mouvement contre le racisme, l'antisémitisme et pour la paix (MRAP) and intended to "[establish] a better reciprocal knowledge between migrants and the French population."[71] Local migrants took part in the planning phases.[72] Events and publications showcased the diversity of Saint-Denis's migrant communities, and advertisements were multilingual. Migrants led some of the discussions and debates. There were exhibits of artisanal work from North and sub-Saharan Africa, Spain, and Portugal.[73] A series of photographs at the city hall chronicled the migrants' daily lives, and there were open houses at two migrant foyers.[74] The film series drew large audiences that included local migrants.[75] Most of the selected films centered on themes of liberation from colonial or capitalist oppression.[76] The most vibrant discussion took place after a film about contemporary Algeria, in a predominantly Algerian audience, with one speaker denouncing anti-Arab racism in France, while another detailed the heavy involvement of Algerian workers in French unions (particularly the Confédération générale du travail [CGT] and CFDT).[77] At the closing ceremony, badges were sold with the slogan "yellow=black=white=man."[78] The "Quinzaine" was unquestionably an exercise in political posturing. Yet the decision to allocate funding and energy to raise public awareness about local migrants' challenges and contributions suggests both that local officials still sought connections with local migrant populations and that they believed migrants to be part of the city's history and future.[79] Together, the events of the "Quinzaine" supported the municipality's traditional vision of the city's migrants as fellow workers whose social welfare and rights needed to be protected and who were natural allies against both the French state and employers.

These snapshots of municipal engagement reveal local communists' belief that they had an obligation to North Africans as laborers and as members of a shared community, particularly when considered alongside their strong record of fighting for migrants' social services and civil rights. Certainly, officials failed to follow through on all their promises of and aspirations for improved migrant welfare and a welcoming city community. Declarations of support for migrant causes were linked to demands that the state, the employers, and others bear the cost of hosting migrant workers.

Still, the very fact that migrants were spoken of—and with—sets Saint-Denis apart from most French cities, which did not even pay lip service to the real troubles encountered by migrants or seek to solve them. It would therefore be neither naïve nor unreasonable to take city officials at their word (at least to some degree). While the political calculus involved in the articulation of Dionysien policies cannot be ignored, officials also appeared to be motivated by human empathy—a desire both to better the condition of a particularly precarious population and to build a community identity grounded in the ideals of working-class unity and internationalism.

Comradeship from the Left

Communists were not the only political activists to claim North African migrants' goals and concerns as their own. Indeed, it was the French Communist Party's (PCF) failure to live up to the solidarity they espoused that opened space for yet another set of actors who claimed to understand and support North African and other migrants: the *gauchistes*, or new leftists. Throughout the 1960s, many French radicals—especially youth—grew disenchanted with the PCF. Initially frustrated with most communists' response to the Algerian War, these new leftist groups flourished in the unrest and aftermath of May–June 1968.[80] Their revolutionary ideologies—typically Maoist in inspiration—were explicitly transnational in their strategies and their goals, which raised the profile of migrant communities within their programs.[81] Though not as invested in a local city identity as the communist municipality in Saint-Denis, these groups nevertheless supported North African rights and demands through a broad sense of human solidarity and working-class alliance.

Migrants played a dual role in 1968: as inspiration and as actors in their own right. Historian Daniel Gordon details migrant participation in protests and strikes, roughly equivalent to the rates of French participation.[82] He also explains that the "French New Left was interested in migrant workers because they were both nationally marginal *and* proletarians"; for these activists, "immigrants were workers first."[83] Nanterre's university campus, a central site for student protest, abutted one of the city's bidonvilles. This proximity stoked student perceptions of injustice and their frustration with the inadequacies of that city's communist leaders.[84] For their part, younger bidonvilliers who were initially attracted by the potential for change and revolt soon grew disillusioned with the Nanterre students. Some migrant residents were offended at being considered objects of charity and troubled by the heightened police profile brought on by the university protests.[85] In Saint-Denis's bidonvilles, social unrest disrupted services like trash collection and even rehousing operations or caused wage losses during the strikes.[86]

Despite municipal communists' attempts to stave off criticism from farther left, radical organizers remained active in Saint-Denis in the years following 1968.[87] Leftists had been struck by their encounters in migrant foyers during their 1968 activities and militated for reforms of both the living conditions and the harsh regulations imposed on residents.[88] Maoists, mostly members of the Gauche Prolétarienne, reached out to North and sub-Saharan African migrants living in the foyers. They offered support to these workers, whom they understood as having been uprooted from their traditional social system, with weak ties to French society, suffering from poor material standards, and increasingly feeling the pinch of rising unemployment.[89] Gauche Prolétarienne devoted one page out of each of its bulletins to the problems in migrant foyers.[90] Leftists organized literacy classes in Saint-Denis and Ivry.[91] Some of the most successful leftist campaigns were organized rent strikes in migrant foyers, with their intervention in Saint-Denis being "particularly virulent."[92] Indeed, gauchiste groups met with migrants more frequently in Saint-Denis than in any other Parisian banlieue.[93] Gillian Glaes explains that leftists were drawn to the rent strikes as concrete and familiar social actions that supported their critique of "capitalism, colonialism, and neocolonialism." Migrant activists, meanwhile, "found in leftist politics a message that described their experiences as immigrant workers in France" and which they could use to their own ends.[94]

Leftists in Saint-Denis specifically contested city communists' claims to promote the causes of the working class. Things came to a head in 1970, when the municipality attempted to evacuate ninety-six North African workers from the foyer at the impasse Saint-Jean, citing insufficient hygiene and structural safety. Dozens of leftist militants arrived on the first date set for eviction, causing the city to delay.[95] Gauche Prolétarienne activists held forth in neighborhood cafés and distributed copies of their bulletin including a declaration purportedly from the residents: "We won't take it anymore. We are foreigners, we do the hardest jobs, we are the worst paid, we are the worst housed, in Saint-Denis as elsewhere we are crammed into rooms that are too small and dark, often for quite a high price. THIS IS NOT A LIFE. . . . The sole remedy proposed by the people at City Hall is to send us to Porte des Lilas to be crammed 40 into a room and to be rid of us. . . . WE ARE FIGHTING AGAINST THE CONSPIRACY BETWEEN THE CITY HALL AND THE EMPLOYERS."[96] The plea for recognition and improved conditions was coupled with a strong indictment of the municipality—echoing the charges the municipality had laid against the state for decades and positioning Gauche Prolétarienne as the true allies for migrant workers. These activists foregrounded the migrants' own voices, amplifying them instead of speaking for them.

The fight for the Saint-Jean residents was further linked to leftist solidarity with Algerians during the Algerian War and their continued dedication to anti-imperialism.[97] This too echoed the communist practice of associating North African migrant concerns with Algerian nationalism: support for either of these required a dedication to dismantling imperial and capitalist structures. The perception that leftists and migrants were fighting on the same side of a transnational conflict reappeared that summer when Gauche Prolétarienne organized protests outside the Francs-Moisins bidonville. Local communists, they insisted, were "not on the side of the workers." In contrast, the demonstration embodied the idea that "we are all united in the street: Portuguese, Arabs, Maoist militants."[98] Here again, the gauchistes called upon a solidarity of workers struggling to overthrow local, national, and even international forces of oppression.

Leftist groups also hoped to make inroads among migrant populations in the Rhône. Unsurprisingly, Villeurbanne's Cité Olivier de Serres was seen as prime recruiting ground. A former resident recalled that students had arrived in the neighborhood in May '68, with signs that encouraged residents to stop paying rent to Simon, the "crook." Another group of students came with cars to bring twenty cité children to lunch at the university campus. The young Algerians seemed more perplexed about these incidents than engaged by them.[99] Gauchiste groups, most prominently the Maoist Secours Rouge, continued their campaigns with weekly actions targeting the cité through the fall of 1970. This was part of the reason for increased police presence in the neighborhood—made more urgent in the prefecture's eyes by the fact that much of the leftist propaganda painted the police as Simon's personal protectors.[100] Just as the cité's residents seemed ideal partners for leftist rebellion, so too was Simon a perfect personification of the capitalist forces the activists sought to overthrow, with the police as his army.[101] In July, as part of their case for a shared fight against miserable housing conditions, militants distributed flyers celebrating "popular victories" at foyers around Paris.[102] The *Journal inter-foyers la cause du peuple* included a "Partisans' Hymn" for this alliance of the exploited:

All immigrant workers are our brothers
United together with them we declare war.
Violence is everywhere, you taught us that
Bosses who exploit and cops who beat [*matraquez*]
But to your oppression we cry resistance.
You expel Kader and Mohamed rises
Because you cannot expel the people's revolt
A people ready to take back their arms
That the traitors stole from them in forty-five
Yes, bourgeois, against you the people desire war.[103]

This vision of shared struggle offered migrants—particularly North Africans—a place at the heart of the movement. They further clarified the global stakes of their campaign by attempting

to stage protests in support of Palestinian nationalism and calling on Olivier de Serres residents to resist "like the Fedayin" both
rhetorically and with actual violence.[104] The Palestinian cause was
broadly popular among French leftist groups but here served as
an extra way of signaling shared values with a pan-Arab struggle
they assumed would resonate with local North Africans.

While leftist activity waned significantly by the mid-1970s, their
expressions of solidarity drew on ideas of shared values, shared
oppression, and shared enemies. Much of this activism was explicitly antiracist, refuting both policies and beliefs (that had popular
traction) that marked migrants as other. As with local communists,
other leftist groups sought to include North Africans and other
migrants as part of their communities for action—both allies in
and inspiration for the global fight against capitalism, lingering
imperialism, and state oppression. As Glaes argues, leftist involvement with migrant issues and actions further points to a "greater
society-wide acceptance" of these communities.[105] Not all parties
were welcoming, certainly, but activists across the political spectrum took notice of migrants and their concerns in ways that signaled that these communities were going to remain within France.
Engaging with—and learning from—migrant activists further
pushed segments of the French Left from their earlier anti-imperial
positions into postcolonial antiracism.[106]

What these disparate examples ultimately point to is that many
of those local actors willing to take a stand on migrant rights had
notions about belonging that were not bounded by national borders.
Migrants in Saint-Denis were nearly always spoken of as part of an
"us," as full Dionysiens even if they were not French.[107] At Gillot's
funeral in 1998, Robert Hue—then a leading PCF figure—attested
to the former mayor's "profound humanity and his undiminished
enthusiasm for the ideal of human liberation."[108] These humanist ideals shored up a communist commitment to all workers.
The work undertaken by NDSA and other religious leaders in the
Rhône was guided by a similar sense of connection—even across
the boundaries of faith. Notably, Rosset's passing was also met

with testimonies in the press to his "human fraternity" and his "commitment to justice."[109] These religious actors, of course, are best understood within the broader context of Christian progressivism and social Catholicism. Among French Protestants, those who were active in supporting migrants and opposing imperialism were also tied into global ecumenical movements like the World Council of Churches (WCC).[110] In Saint-Denis and in the Rhône, both leftist politics and Christian faith offered more inclusive ideas of community, based in a global proletariat or human fellowship.

At the core of the relationships these local figures established with their North African neighbors, we find not only grand ideological tenets but also a familiarity rooted in regular contact. Rosset's vision for Christian charity required giving not only aid but also oneself to those in need.[111] Presence in the shelters and interactions with residents were crucial parts of the mission. NDSA publicity relied heavily on photographs (often featuring children) and descriptive language to evoke a response (and preferably direct action) from readers.[112] Gillot's daily contacts are not quite as easy to trace. It hardly seems coincidental, though, that one of the city's bidonvilles (and the first neighborhood officially classified as "insalubrious") surrounded the historical city center and its basilica. This meant that Gillot and his colleagues could not walk into city hall without crossing dilapidated streets and witnessing the daily difficulties faced by neighborhood residents. For them, the bidonvilles and slums did not exist in a far-flung, theoretical space at the fringe of municipal jurisdiction.

Over the years, Dionysien advocates for North African rights repeatedly appealed to the visual, insisting that others come bear witness to the misfortune and suffering of the city's migrants. In 1948, Gillot made an impassioned plea to the General Council for the Seine, asking the members to come see the living conditions of the North African migrants in the city's center: "You can stroll around the Saint-Denis Basilica or the City Hall; you will see how the café owners move the tables and chairs at night to organize sleeping space for Algerians, on the floor, even directly on the ground. . . . I would like the Council General's Commission in charge to enter into these cafés, particularly the one at 10, rue du Landy." At the heart of his argument was the demand that departmental officials and especially the prefect "come see."[113] A decade later, Gillot made the case for the Seine prefect to provide greater support to municipal social welfare programs by invoking the prefect's recent visit: "A large part of this [city's] poor, laboring population lives, as you were able to see on site and as is shown in the attached photographs, in quite ancient and insalubrious buildings."[114] Leftists too echoed the call for direct witnessing; the "Partisans' Hymn" discussed above opened with a demand to "come stroll a bit through the putrid foyers / Where we sleep on rotation while we work our eight-hour shifts."[115]

Seeing migrant suffering or, better still, working alongside migrants toward a common goal imbued larger moral and political allegiances with depth and personal meaning. Proximity was an impetus for action. In this way, we see that Christianity, communism, and even Maoism made the space for new understandings of community, while regular contact made foreigners into neighbors. In each of these cases, interacting with migrants also encouraged greater awareness of and action on international questions—all of these groups connected their support for North African migrants to opposition to French imperialism and solidarity with liberation movements.[116] The local actors discussed in this chapter believed that they had the responsibility to stand up for North African rights and welfare, an obligation to make space for them in their communities.

Conclusion

There is one last visit to make to the Stade de France in Saint-Denis, this one far more somber than the football victories that opened this book. On November 13, 2015, a Friday night, France and Germany were playing a friendly match at the stadium, with French president François Hollande and German foreign minister Frank-Walter Steinmeier both in attendance. At 9:20 p.m., a suicide bomber triggered the first of three explosions near an entrance to the stadium. Within the next twenty minutes, gunmen and bombers launched attacks on four Parisian bars and restaurants and the sold-out Bataclan concert venue. One hundred thirty people were killed and hundreds more wounded. President Hollande declared the attacks to be an "act of war," closed the country's borders, and initiated a formal state of emergency.[1] The Islamic State claimed credit for organizing the coordinated set of attacks. Many of the suspects held French or Belgian citizenship. French police organized a massive search, raiding locations throughout the Paris region and in Brussels, Belgium. Five days after the attacks, Saint-Denis was the site of a major police operation targeting the suspected mastermind (who was killed in the raid).

In the face of this violence, Saint-Denis's PCF mayor, Didier Paillard—who had also been at the Stade de France during the attack—responded much the way we might imagine Auguste Gillot would have done decades earlier. In his very first statement, Paillard called on his city not to "give way to fear."[2] That Sunday, he elaborated, "By attacking the northeast of Paris and the neighborhood around the Stade de France, the terrorists targeted sites of diversity, of social inclusion, youth, tolerance, and openness to others." If coexistence was the real target of the attack, then "coming together" would be a crucial part of the response: "Let us reject the confusion and the hatred of others that encourage turning inwards, racism, the lure of radicalism, and violence. Let us stand in solidarity."[3] Paillard's vision of Saint-Denis remained one of belonging and inclusion—indeed, he repeatedly invoked these values of openness as the reason the city was targeted by the attackers. Notably, his immediate response was to insist that Saint-Denis embrace its tradition of solidarity. His actions followed suit. Most of the city's public spaces were closed down in the days after the attacks, but the city hall was kept open, inhabitants were invited to come speak or write about their experiences, and a special psychological support clinic was opened at a local medical center.[4] This local response to a national tragedy tracks with Beth Epstein's findings in Cergy, a northwestern suburb of Paris, where "positive demonstrations of the city's cultural diversity . . . serve an important social function, as they both encourage and display the city's capacity for tolerance."[5] Paillard's insistence on diversity and tolerance as explicit local values grew out of a lengthy local tradition that could be marshaled in this moment of crisis and mourning.

Given Gillot and his colleagues' castigation of police tactics, Paillard's response to the police raid on the apartment building at 48 rue de la République, just four hundred meters from the city hall, bears further examination. The mayor received no advanced notice that the assault would take place; in fact, he first heard about the operation from inhabitants alarmed that they were hearing gunshots in the city center. After checking in with the police commissariat, the municipality resumed its role as the primary venue for communication, giving regular updates to the population. The city hall hosted families fleeing the area and made space for residents to meet and talk.[6] Paillard applauded police efforts to ensure the safety of Dionysiens throughout the operation.[7] He specified that "terrorist networks" needed to be "eradicated."[8] This at first seems quite different from Gillot's era. Paillard, however, was quick to note that the targeted apartment had only recently been rented out; the suspects, in other words, were strangers, not Dionysiens.[9] This assertion that the attackers could not be considered part of the community reinforced the notion that such violence was anathema to Saint-Denis. The city was represented by the residents who helped one another through the trauma, embracing solidarity and rejecting panic. "More than ever," he declared, "Saint-Denis is a working-class city, tolerant and open. It is this inexhaustible coexistence that allows the 110,000 Dionysiens from more than 130 different nationalities, to live, work, and thrive together."[10] Whereas Gillot had stood with North African migrants as members of the community against police surveillance, profiling, and detention, Paillard here stood with tolerant Dionysiens against the outside attackers and supported a targeted police operation.

Even though the Saint-Denis municipality of 2015 was willing to cooperate with police to remove a specific external threat, Paillard consistently asserted that the most important response to the attack was to adhere to and uplift Dionysien and republican values. Aligning with the efforts to keep the city hall open to residents, the mayor insisted that gathering and discussing were vital: "The question of fraternity has been posed. . . . The best response is really to face up to it together."[11] Other local leaders, including the bishop of Saint-Denis and the director of the Théâtre Gérard Philipe likewise asserted that violence and fear could be beaten by embracing the city's diversity.[12] The threat to Saint-Denis, to France, was one of intolerance and extremism. Raids and repression could not therefore be the sole response. Speaking at the ceremony at the Stade de France on November 19, Paillard again insisted that the attackers took aim at "young people who are passionate about liberties, diverse and tolerant." The best response, then, was to double down on openness: "It is our task, together, to combat division and obscurantism, to refuse hatred of the other and radicalism, to reject racism and fanaticism. It is our task, together, to aim for more tolerance and humanity, to consolidate a fraternal and united society, to affirm the values of the Republic. In Saint-Denis, in Paris, our best weapon in the face of atrocity is to affirm—to acclaim—liberty, equality, and fraternity. Our only response, our only weapon, is to raise ever higher the values that unite Dionysiens and unite the French."[13] Paillard's rhetoric moved naturally between local and national communities, invoking Dionysienness alongside Frenchness in ways that linked the two but also recognized the distinctions between them. Ultimately, he seemed to suggest that France's best path forward after the attacks was to become more like Saint-Denis.

Soon, Saint-Denis had other, familiar enemies to contend with—those on the political right. In the aftermath of the attacks, a regional Front national (FN) candidate accused the communist municipality of "delivering" the city to "radical Islam"; their years of local control had "stripped Saint-Denis of its identity, deliberately and gradually left its neighborhoods to violence, to drug-dealers and to radical Islamism, and encouraged the establishment of associations of politico-religious extremists."[14] The FN demanded that Saint-Denis be placed under state guardianship to disarm and secure the city.[15] Another FN official conflated a veiled Dionysien woman with terrorists on social media.[16] The national PCF responded that these FN attacks on Saint-Denis were "indecent" and linked to their own form of "insidious violence"; the city itself needed to be defended.[17] Paillard himself responded that Saint-Denis's tolerance and diversity made it an obvious target for the FN.[18] These responses more subtly aligned the FN with the terrorists, as forces seeking to undermine the city's core values and identity.

In another familiar move, the municipality also launched critiques against the national government on the issue of constituents' welfare. The apartment building raided by the police had been rendered uninhabitable. Seventy-one residents had been evacuated, and the city temporarily housed them in a gymnasium. The prefecture had planned to rehouse only the one family whose apartment had been riddled with bullets, but the mayor and his deputy protested that the state was responsible for all twenty-nine families. They hosted a meeting in front of the Seine-Saint-Denis prefecture and publicly called on the prime minister to take charge of the situation, recognize all the affected households as victims, and assure their proper rehousing.[19] Paillard even suggested that the existence of such poor housing had made it easier for the suspected attackers to rent the apartment that was raided.[20] The echoes of earlier housing battles could not be clearer. Once again, Saint-Denis's municipality claimed a position as the advocate and supporter of forgotten local residents while insisting that the French state was responsible for providing sufficient living conditions.

There is a striking consistency in the rhetoric and attitudes of Saint-Denis city officials, from Gillot's invocations of brotherhood and municipal demands for North African rights and welfare in the years just after World War II straight through to Paillard's response to the November 2015 attacks. The city's experiences of the 2005 riots offer yet another perspective on how well Saint-Denis has lived up to this image of openness. The Seine-Saint-Denis department was one of the hardest hit by the urban unrest that stemmed from the deaths of two high school boys of African descent who were hiding from the police in Clichy-sous-Bois. And yet the city of Saint-Denis did not have a single violent incident.[21] Just as they would in 2015, the municipality (then headed by a recently elected Paillard) hosted open meetings and decried prejudice. In fact, in October 2015, mere weeks before the attack on the Stade de France, the city hosted a three-day series on the 2005 unrest. The tagline: "My *banlieue* is not a problem. It's the solution!"[22]

It can be all too easy to get caught up in a genealogy of twenty-first-century violence and urban unrest. There is a common litany that begins with the 2005 riots, followed by another round of rioting in 2007 (after a motorcycle accident involving two young men of African heritage and a police car in Villiers-le-Bel), then two nights of stone throwing and tear gas in Trappes in 2013 (triggered when police performed an identity check on a veiled woman). From these moments of communal outrage at oppressive police actions, one transitions to individual acts of terror, including the January 2015 *Charlie Hebdo* attack, the November attacks that same year, the truck that drove through the crowds in Nice on Bastille Day in 2016, and the gruesome October 2020 murder of a schoolteacher in Conflans-Sainte-Honorine. Scholars of minority populations in France, particularly Muslim populations, do seek to explain the societal exclusion, the global conflicts, and the structural factors that produce extremism. Certainly, these are the moments when we are publicly called upon to share our expertise.

And yet we also have an obligation to explain day-to-day existence, the myriad ways that inhabitants of French communities make their way through their lives, the ways that communities on the ground make space for all their members. As I suggested in the introduction, taking the view from the field means that when we think of the Stade de France, even on the night of November 13, 2015, we should remember to look to the stands, to the crowds of attendees from all backgrounds who came together in Saint-Denis for entertainment and for celebration. Each of those people lives within a neighborhood and finds ways to connect, to make their own place. We must also find ways to account for how all players within the field of French society project their own ideals and aspirations onto others.

For Paillard, one of the most urgent messages to convey in the aftermath of the November 2015 attacks was, "This violence is not our everyday life."[23] We cannot only look at burning or bloody spectacles if we hope to understand the deeper social and personal relations at play in contemporary France. For decades, Saint-Denis has maintained an identity that is part of yet also different from—and more open than—simply being French. Local experiences, local belonging, and local community are all vital facets of migrants' lives and the lives of their families in subsequent generations. Paying attention to local communities and their relationships with migrants offers us not only a more diverse picture of the migrant experience in France but also a set of alternatives for managing migration, for promoting inclusion and belonging, for reimagining Frenchness.

Throughout this book, I have sustained two major contentions: that local experiences affect migration at least as much as national policy and that individual actors concern themselves with migrant rights and welfare for a variety of reasons. From these follow four further claims: that understanding motivations reveals modes for action, that there can be a mismatch between motivations and effects, that nonnational frameworks open the most space for migrant inclusion, and that we need to recognize the racist and imperialist structures still operating in France today.

First, understanding local actors' motivations for engaging with migrant communities creates more effective advocacy for those migrants and better opportunities to influence local outcomes. Scholars of contemporary France like Jean Beaman, Beth Epstein, Andrew Newman, and Paul Silverstein foreground nonwhite French agency.[24] More historical work in the vein of Abdellali Hajjat, Félix Germain, Gillian Glaes, and Minayo Nasiali is needed to delve into the ways that migrants themselves navigated various approaches and practices, how they were able to make French systems work to their benefit, the ways they found to influence and change the spaces they were given, and how they made their own spaces within these contexts.[25] Yet throughout this book, we have seen examples of local actors advancing claims and proposals in ways that aligned with particular visions of modernity, urban development, politics, empire, markets, and morals. These attempts were always more successful when they found common ground—to the point that actors with quite different motivations could find themselves promoting similar solutions to, for example, the housing crisis for North African workers and families.

This leads to the second point: we need to pay attention to the ways that motivations and results can fail to align. One of the more spectacular failures of French migration policy has been the creation of vast suburban cités heavily populated by nonwhite families, despite committed efforts to prevent such concentrations. Builders of the new immense housing complexes failed to account for the population's strong preference for individual over communal housing.[26] Many of France's migrants also preferred the independence of bidonville shanties to the HLMs (Habitations à loyer modéré) and especially the strictly regulated cités de transit. Despite the high hopes of modernizers and builders, the HLMs proved to be undesirable, even unhealthy. Most had been built on the cheapest land available, away from city centers and from convenient public transport, "areas bereft of the small shops, cafés and street markets which create the individual ambience of the French *quartier*."[27] Early edifices, built under conditions of urgency, displayed the signs of shoddy construction and quickly began to degrade.[28] During the 1960s, pundits diagnosed "sarcellitis," a collection of maladies associated with high-rise living, named for the mega-complexes built in the city of Sarcelles.[29] As regulations loosened to encourage construction of individual houses and better-quality apartment buildings, early residents fled as quickly as they were able.[30] In their wake arrived many migrant families for whom the HLMs were still an improvement over their desperate living conditions.[31] In Saint-Denis, the cité inhabitants who could afford to live in the renovated Basilica neighborhood rushed back to the center, away from the perceived dangers of Francs-Moisins and other HLM parks, leaving empty spaces in the HLMs for the migrants pushed out of the renovated neighborhoods.[32] Across the country, migrants—North Africans more than others—retreated to the farthest-flung, most poorly maintained HLMs, and the ghettoization officials had hoped to curtail reached new extremes.[33] The desire to disperse North Africans evenly among white French households, coupled with supposedly progressive but ultimately mistaken urban development ideals, ultimately led directly to the "problems" of the banlieues and the deterioration of HLMs.[34]

We see further ironies in the outcomes of local policies and programs, which did not always live up to their initiators' ideals. In Asnières, where officials were relatively successful (and ahead of the curve) at removing North Africans from the city, those few migrants and their families who were rehoused likely enjoyed a better standard of life (certainly of housing) than their counterparts in Saint-Denis, who had to wait much longer to escape slum conditions. Moreover, by the mid-1970s, Asnières's municipality agreed to the construction of a new migrant workers' foyer in the city.[35] The successful reconstruction of the northern zone meant not only that the municipality's sense of crisis had faded but also that the number of local North Africans in need of rehousing had declined. Asnières even saw the establishment of both a mosque and local branches of two Moroccan banks.[36] It was in this same period, in the early and mid-1970s, that Saint-Denis's municipality was suffering from migrant fatigue, backtracking on its policies of openness to migrant workers. Brimming with good intentions, Dionysien officials faltered in the face of mounting challenges. Later reconstruction efforts in the city center and the Basilica neighborhood effectively displaced the most visible of the city's migrant population, while the municipality argued for greater "social diversification" in order to attract more middle-class residents.[37] In other words, the rhetoric of belonging could be difficult to sustain when welcoming policies were so successful as to create a backlash. Practically speaking, Saint-Denis stumbled on its commitment to migrants in the 1970s and '80s. And yet as the testimony from 2015 reveals, the city continues to imagine itself as a diverse community.

Third, the experiences discussed throughout this book indicate that belonging and inclusion come more easily when nationalism is not the driving force for identity. To begin with, admitting to local difference undercuts national visions of a universal republicanism or a monolithic French identity. Deeper connections and stronger support emerged when people were able to imagine alternative communities rooted in neighborhoods and cities or as workers, believers, or simply human beings. Cultivating these local and transnational communities—and the links between them—recasts migration less as an exception than a norm and makes meaningful space for migrants within human collectives. As Beth Epstein demonstrates local urban communities where the reality of French racial and cultural diversity is lived day-to-day can embrace that diversity as "the 'wealth' of France."[38] These relationships at a local level can promote engagement with larger questions: antiwar efforts, broad political movements, arguments for a real expansion of rights and welfare. Ironically, imperialist ideology also made a case for a larger community. In practice, of course, the empire's claims to supporting all its members were undercut by the discriminatory use of force, by paternalism, and by racist assumptions.

This leads to the final point: we need to recognize the ways that racial and imperial ideas continue to operate in French society. Far from the touted color-blind republic, France is subject not only to structural racism but also to structural imperialism.[39] These remnants of empire not only exist at the highest levels of the national government but permeate local administrations, business practices, and even private associations. Much of the impetus to provide social welfare services to Algerian migrants was tied to the desire to safeguard French Algeria. Many of these programs were effective in that myriad migrants found employment, received education and training, and often moved to better living conditions. The need to control the bidonvilles as a matter of national security led directly to the vast construction projects of the 1960s and '70s. Yet there is no denying the incredible harm done by the French forces of order. The war years witnessed the massive internment of Algerian migrants (often with little or no due cause); horrendous levels of violence, torture, and even death; and the repression of October 17, 1961, and subsequent attempts at denial and evasion. It is crucial, therefore, to admit the intimate, perhaps inescapable relationship between two apparently contradictory state agendas—social welfare and public order—and recognize that this tension lies at the foundation of the contemporary French immigration and welfare systems.

It has become common for antimigrant voices within France to blame migrants for their own exclusion. We can see examples from the Front national response to the 2015 attacks to the more centrist responses to the riots of 2007 that invoked an "anti-French ethno-cultural bias from a foreign society" and even in scholarship that emphasizes migrant socioeconomic assimilation without considering migrant experiences of exclusion.[40] This understanding of the dangers of migration is misdirected. The history of French interactions with migrant workers—particularly from formerly colonized territories in North Africa—reveals a pattern of social and economic marginalization as well as outright racial discrimination. Despite homage paid to universal republican ideals and the insistence that allegiance to these ideals erased—or at least overcame—social, cultural, and even racial differences, the French confronted numerous postcolonial challenges to their flexibility and tolerance. Migrant marginalization resulted from many factors, mostly external to their communities: discrimination and xenophobia, as well as the social hurdles inherent to starting at the bottom of the labor ladder, and a gradual spatial distancing that left migrants—and families with migrant roots—both at the outskirts of French towns and at the distant edges of the French political agenda.

Far from being twenty-first-century inventions, questions about France's ability—and will—to fulfill the promise of liberty, equality, and fraternity for all of its citizens permeated policy discussions throughout the twentieth century. Challenging the common portrayal of a monolithic French state, this book has uncovered variations in the way community actors and officials implemented and responded to national and imperial policies—which were themselves the subject of vigorous debate. I have traced the different trajectories of the capital Paris region and Lyon as the center of the Rhône department. Over the course of the decades examined here, which included the violence and turmoil of the Algerian War, both national and local agendas evolved—sometimes dramatically, sometimes incrementally, and often contradictorily. Disagreement was driven by differing conceptions of community and of French responsibility for colonial populations and the migrants who crossed the Mediterranean. This multiplicity of experiences evident at the local level indicates that there are viable understandings of Frenchness that cross ethnic and cultural lines and contradicts a version of French migration history that reads the urban unrest of recent years as preordained.

Both local communities and the French state can accomplish quite a lot when they decide their fundamental interests are at play. Some of the actors from the preceding chapters offer us positive models (though there are also a number of examples of what not to do). When leaders and policy-makers commit to a vision that makes space for all members of their communities, they offer a revised, perhaps a radical, understanding of identity. To truly embrace all its citizens and make good on its promises of universal values, the French Republic must look to those of its members who have already understood that racial integration, acceptance, and belonging are equally vital.

NOTES

Introduction

Unless otherwise noted, translations of cited works in French are the author's.

1. Dubois, *Soccer Empire*, 1–3. Notably, Smaïl Zidane was still in Saint-Denis for the violent police repression of the Algerian nationalist demonstration on October 17, 1961.

2. The original articulation of the national drive to make Frenchman is Weber, *Peasants into Frenchmen*.

3. Dubois, *Soccer Empire*, 168. Thuram, a Black Frenchman, was born in the overseas department of Guadeloupe.

4. Lecroart, "Regenerating the Plaine Saint-Denis," 10.

5. On their similar focus on the effects and implications of French actors' words and deeds, see Scott, *Politics of the Veil*, 10; and Vulbeau, "Roubaix," 13.

6. André, *Femmes dévoilées*; Lyons, *Civilizing Mission in the Metropole*; and Nasiali, *Native to the Republic*, serve as valuable models for uncovering migrant perspectives and experiences within archives that (often purposefully) sought to obscure them.

7. Particularly useful were Grillo, *Ideologies and Institutions in Urban France*; Hajjat, *La marche pour l'égalité et contre le racisme*; Pétonnet, *Ces gens-là*; Sayad and Dupuy, *Un Nanterre algérien*; and Annie Schwartz, *Olivier de Serres*. See also Beaman, *Citizen Outsider*, on the experiences of second-generation Maghrebi-French; Glaes, *African Political Activism in Postcolonial France*, on how Black African migrants also shaped French policy and politics; and Pitti, "La main-d'œuvre algérienne dans l'industrie automobile," and so on, on Algerian labor mobilization.

8. This approach is inspired by some of the principles of critical whiteness studies. See especially Beaman, "Are French People White?"; Cohen and Mazouz, "White Republic?"; and the rest of the special issue edited by Cohen and Mazouz on "Whiteness in France" for *French Politics, Culture & Society*. On "vanilla history," see Shepard, *Sex, France, and Arab Men*.

9. Lyons, *Civilizing Mission in the Metropole*.

10. Nasiali, *Native to the Republic*; Naylor, "'Un âne dans l'ascenseur'"; André, *Femmes dévoilées*; Belmessous, "Du 'seuil de tolérance' à la 'mixité sociale'"; Vulbeau, "Roubaix." On the Paris region, see especially Bernardot, *Loger les immigrés*; Blanc-Chaléard, *En finir avec les bidonvilles*; Cohen, *Des familles invisibles*; David, "Logement social des immigrants et politique municipale en banlieue ouvrière"; Hmed, "Loger les étrangers 'isolés' en France"; and Masclet, *La gauche et les cités*.

11. Lewis, *Boundaries of the Republic*.

12. Shepard, *Invention of Decolonization*.

13. De Barros, "Contours d'un réseau administratif 'algérien,'" "Des 'Français musulmans d'Algérie' aux 'immigrés,'" and "Les municipalités face aux Algériens." See also Belmessous, "Georges Martin."

14. Beaujon, "Controlling the Casbah" and "Policing Colonial Migrants"; Blanchard, *La police parisienne et les Algériens*; House, "Contrôle, encadrement, surveillance et répression"; House and MacMaster, *Paris 1961*; Prakash, "Colonial Techniques in the Imperial Capital"; Rosenberg, *Policing Paris*.

15. See especially André, *Femmes dévoilées*; de Barros, "L'État au prisme des municipalités" and "Les municipalités face aux Algériens"; Lewis, *Boundaries of the Republic*; Nasiali, *Native to the Republic*; Naylor, "'Un âne dans l'ascenseur'"; Sayad and Dupuy, *Un Nanterre algérien*; and Vulbeau, "Roubaix." On other immigrant groups within particular communities, see Blanc-Chaléard, *Les Italiens dans l'Est parisien*; Lillo, *La petite Espagne*; Masclet, *La gauche et les cités*; Moch, *Pariahs of Yesterday*; and Volovitch-Tavares, *Portugais à Champigny*.

16. Mary Lewis observes that "migrant rights developed dialectically, as central authorities placed limits on migrants' civil liberties and social rights, migrants tested these limits, local officials responded, and national authorities in turn reacted to decisions made at the local level. . . . Through improvisation and negotiation, local authorities and immigrants established the boundaries of inclusion and exclusion along quite different lines than those intended by state policy." Lewis, *Boundaries of the Republic*, 10 and 14. Arnold Hirsch makes a similar argument for the utility of studying a city, Chicago, instead of taking a "top-down" approach to the history of urban renewal in the United States: "Local initiative and power not only controlled urban renewal efforts but also helped frame the laws under which it proceeded." Hirsch, *Making the Second Ghetto*, 272.

17. Jim House and Andrew Thompson emphasize the way that the physical spaces of postcolonial migrants' housing mirrored the construction of racialized social identities. House and Thompson, "Decolonisation, Space, and Power."

18. On the benefits of comparative studies of migration, including the form of "mezzo" comparison used in this book, see Green, *Repenser les migrations*, 27–32.

19. Epstein, *Collective Terms*, 3 and 6.

20. Saada, *Empire's Children*; and Wilder, *French Imperial Nation-State*. Saada in particular identifies a transition from an ideal of citizenship "defined, as at the time of the Revolution, in terms of voluntary adhesion to a shared political project" to

one that represented "the culmination of a process of internalizing French civilization and mores." Saada, *Empire's Children*, 109.

21. Fernando, *Republic Unsettled*, 36 and 89.

22. Mazouz, "White Race Blindness?"

23. Newman, *Landscape of Discontent*, 67 and 93.

24. The intersection of local and national identities has been debated, often in the context of regional experiences (and usually at moments considered to be formative in the development of nation-states). See Applegate, "Europe of Regions," on historians' habit of framing their analyses through a national lens. Peter Sahlins insists, "Local society was a motive force in the formation and consolidation of nationhood and the territorial state." Sahlins, *Boundaries*, 8. Alon Confino likewise makes an appeal "to reject [the] separation between localness and nationhood" and operate within the assumption that "localness and nationness simultaneously and reciprocally interact." Confino, *Germany as a Culture of Remembrance*, 23–28.

25. This is the fourth definition of identity outlined by Frederick Cooper and Rogers Brubaker: "Understood as a product of social or political action, identity is invoked to highlight the *processual, interactive* development of the kind of collective self-understanding, solidarity or groupness that can make collective action possible. In this usage, found in certain strands of the new social movement literature, identity is understood both as a *contingent product* of social or political action and as a ground or basis of further action." Frederick Cooper and Rogers Brubaker, "Identity," in Cooper, *Colonialism in Question*, 65 (emphasis in original).

26. According to Patrick Weil, "Nowhere else, but in colonial Algeria, did the French advance so far the confusion between the words of the law and the experiences lived, or empty of all meaning the very terms 'nationality' and 'equality.'" Weil, *Qu'est-ce qu'un Français?*, 275.

27. Quandt, *Revolution and Political Leadership*. For a thorough examination of French settler colonialism and the conquest of Algeria, see Sessions, *By Sword and Plow*.

28. Sayad and Gillette, *L'immigration algérienne*, 15 and 24.

29. Sayad and Gillette, *L'immigration algérienne*, 33–34. For an overview of nonwhite migrant experiences in France during the First World War and, in particular, the racial violence sparked by their presence, see Stovall, "Color-Line behind the Lines."

30. For a broad survey of interwar labor migration to France, see Cross, *Immigrant Workers in Industrial France*; for a chronicle of public opinion toward migrants during this period, see Schor, *L'opinion française et les étrangers en France, 1919–1939*; for a focused examination of migrant rights and immigration policies, see Lewis, *Boundaries of the Republic*; on policing practices in the capital, see Rosenberg, *Policing Paris*; and on the Algerian migrant community, see Stora, *Ils venaient d'Algérie*, 13–22.

31. Sayad and Gillette, *L'immigration algérienne*, 34.

32. Gérard Noiriel asserts that "legislative measures throughout the 1930s were replete with cheap concessions to the prevailing xenophobia." Noiriel, *French Melting Pot*, 65.

33. Charles de Gaulle addressed the Consultative Assembly on March 3, 1945, with his concerns about France's "lack of men" and outlined a plan to encourage French birthrates and "to introduce into the French collectivity, over the coming years, with method and intelligence, good elements of immigration." Cited in Weil, *La France et ses étrangers*, 69.

34. Law no. 47-1853, September 20, 1947, "Portant statut organique de l'Algérie" (CHAN, F60 192, "Questions politiques et Administratives: Afrique du Nord: Algérie"). Article 4 of the law stands as one of the most contradictory rulings in the French Empire, extending the right to vote to Algerian women in the metropole, though not to their counterparts in Algeria.

35. Sayad and Gillette, *L'immigration algérienne*, 40.

36. The number of deaths, particularly on the Algerian side, has long provided fodder for polemics and propaganda. The Algerian state claimed that 1.5 million Algerian lives were lost; the French state acknowledged 150,000 to 200,000. Guy Pervillé, who has devoted much time to resolving this question, concludes that the final toll was roughly 300,000 Algerians and 30,000 French (or Europeans). Pervillé, "Combien de morts?," 94–95.

37. Lequin, "Les vagues d'immigration successives," 398; and Viet, *La France immigrée*, 185.

38. James Le Sueur describes the effect of this violence on altering intellectual and public perceptions of the relationship between France and Algeria. Le Sueur, *Uncivil War*.

39. Morocco and Tunisia were granted independence in 1956, the rest of France's African territories in 1960. The French had withdrawn from Indochina after the disastrous battle at Dien-Bien-Phu in May 1954, leaving the field to the United States.

40. Vincent Viet offers a thorough examination of the evolution of state policies and programs to deal with Algerian migrants during the war. Viet, *La France immigrée*, 163–230.

41. Circulaire no. 490, Interior Ministry to Inspecteurs généraux de l'Administration en mission extraordinaire et Préfets en Métropole, "Directives nouvelles concernant l'aide aux migrants algériens," September 17, 1963 (CHAN, F1a 5126).

42. Seine prefect to mayors of Paris arrondissements and suburbs, "Mise à jour des listes électorales," October 1962 (AMSD, 37 AC 14). The Ordinance of July 21, 1962, settled the status of both populations from Algeria: European settlers would automatically retain their French citizenship (even if they also took Algerian citizenship), while "Muslim" Algerians had to submit to a more complicated, and ambiguous, judicial process. See Shepard, *Invention of Decolonization*, 236–37.

43. Sayad and Gillette, *L'immigration algérienne*, 46.

44. SAMAS, "Bilan des réalisations effectuées au cours des dix-huit mois du Gouvernement présidé par M. Pompidou et récapitulation des résultats obtenus de 1958 à 1964," November 28, 1963 (CHAN, F1a 5055).

45. See especially House, "Contrôle, encadrement, surveillance et répression"; Spire, *Étrangers à la carte*, 205–22; Viet, *La France immigrée*, 221–30; and contributions by

Laure Blévis, Tom Charbit, Françoise de Barros, Choukri Hmed, and Sylvain Laurens to "La colonie rapatriée," *Politix* 76 (December 2006).

46. Gastaut, *L'immigration et l'opinion publique*, 282.

47. Gastaut, *L'immigration et l'opinion publique*, 284. On the Algerian decision to nationalize hydrocarbons as a sort of economic decolonization following the political decolonization of 1962, see Naylor, *France and Algeria*, 74–100.

48. For a catalog of major acts of violence, see Gastaut, *L'immigration et l'opinion publique*, 282–97.

49. Sayad and Gillette, *L'immigration algérienne*, 48.

50. A number of European states—Germany, Denmark, Belgium, the Netherlands, and Austria—had already closed their borders in 1973. For further analysis of the decision to halt immigration and the debates surrounding the policy, see Wihtol de Wenden, "Une logique de fermeture, doublée de la question de l'intégration."

51. See Hajjat, *La marche pour l'égalité et contre le racisme*.

52. For the history of the development of French banlieues, see Merriman, *Margins of City Life*.

53. Lyon was more of a Christian epicenter than Paris, however. Beaune, "Saint-Denis," 44.

54. Hacquemand and de Peretti, "Franciade (1789–An VIII)."

55. "M. Auguste Gillot, maire communiste de Saint-Denis, ne semble plus jouir de la confiance du PCF," May 2, 1968 (AHPP, GA S 12). See also Gillot, *Un forgeron dans la cité des rois*.

56. Gillot and his wife, Simone, who was also a devoted CGT militant and PCF member, cowrote a memoire of their World War II experiences, *Un couple dans la Résistance*.

57. This literature tends to read the problems of the 1970s back through the previous decades to maintain that communist municipalities were as dismissive of migrants in the 1950s as they proved to be by 1974 (and since). See especially Masclet, *La gauche et les cités*, on Gennevilliers's rehousing projects in the 1970s and a "confidential" municipal plan from 1972 that detailed how the city could reduce its foreign population. For more general studies of communist activism, see Bacqué and Fol, *Le devenir*; Bellanger, "Administrer la 'banlieue municipale'"; Brunet, *Immigration, vie politique et populisme en banlieue parisienne (fin XIXe–XXe siècles)*; David, "Logement social des immigrants et politique municipale en banlieue ouvrière"; Fourcaut, *Bobigny*; Schain, *French Communism and Local Power*; and Stovall, *Rise of the Paris Red Belt*.

58. See Byrnes, "French like Us?"; Byrnes, "Liberating the Land or Absorbing a Community"; and David, "La résorption des bidonvilles de Saint-Denis."

59. "Ville d'Asnières," undated (ADHS, 1308 W 3).

60. "Asnières," *La France sociale et municipale* 6 (4th trimester 1958), 4.

61. Jouan, *Asnières-sur-Seine et son histoire*, 85.

62. Jouan, *Asnières-sur-Seine au cours des siècles*, 124–25.

63. Series of memos, "Remise de la Croix de Guerre 1939–45 à la ville d'Asnières," November 3, 7, and 9, 1952 (AHPP, GA 17). Then socialist mayor Jean-Auguste Huet

(1947–59) chastised communist municipal councillors for refusing to participate in the ceremony (the communists boycotted to protest the presence of the police prefect).

64. Jouan, *Asnières-sur-Seine au cours des siècles*.

65. *Saint-Denis: Hier, aujourd'hui, demain*, November 1967 (AMSD, 38 C 4).

66. "Asnières," March 1972 (ADHS, 1308 W 3).

67. "Etude de la Population NA à Paris et dans le Département de la Seine," 1955 (AHPP, HA 8). One 1959 report lists Asnières with 3,500 Algerians and Saint-Denis with 10,000, but these numbers seem too high to be credible and do not correspond with most evidence. "Dénombrement des Français Musulmans Algériens de la Seine," 1959 (AHPP, HA 8).

68. This argument is fully developed in Byrnes, "French like Us?" and "Liberating the Land or Absorbing a Community."

69. Moreover, there is excellent scholarship on Marseille by Minayo Nasiali, Ed Naylor, and others.

70. Françoise de Barros, for instance, makes fruitful comparisons between the Nord and Rhône departments. More recently, Janoé Vulbeau has conducted in-depth studies of the Lille suburb of Roubaix.

71. Lewis concludes that Lyon's earlier North African services differed from those in Paris, "not only in kind, but also in substance," given significant budget constraints and a different political landscape. Lewis, *Boundaries of the Republic*, 189–90.

72. Gastaut, *L'immigration et l'opinion publique*, 286.

73. A group of famous rose cultivators lived in Vénissieux in the early twentieth century and are buried there, including Jean-Pierre Guillot, who created the Vénissiane rose in honor of the city. Gérard Petit, "Les rosiéristes vénissians," Viniciacum, fall 2001, https://viniciacum.fr/rosieristes_venissians/. For a history of rose production in the region, see Ferrand, *Créateurs de roses*. On Vénissian wine, see Alain Belmont, "Une mer de raisins," Expressions: Les Nouvelles de Vénissieux, September 16, 2010, https://www.expressions-venissieux.fr/2010-09-16-une-mer-de-raisin/.

74. Berliet bought up a total of 732 small plots to create his industrial campus. Alain Belmont, "Février 1916: Berliet choisit Vénissieux," Expressions: Les Nouvelles de Vénissieux, January 27, 2016, https://www.expressions-venissieux.fr/2016-01-27-fevrier-1916-berliet-choisit-venissieux/.

75. Local and military authorities set up a heavy regime of regulation and surveillance. Alain Belmont, "Terre d'Afrique à l'arsenal," Expressions: Les Nouvelles de Vénissieux, November 29, 2016, https://www.expressions-venissieux.fr/2016-11-29-terre-dafrique-a-larsenal-en-cours/.

76. Alain Belmont, "Le Moulin-à-Vent, au coeur de la révolte," Expressions: Les Nouvelles de Vénissieux, February 27, 2017, https://www.expressions-venissieux.fr/2017-02-27-le-moulin-a-vent-au-coeur-de-la-revolte/; "Une éphémère expérience communarde," Expressions: Les Nouvelles de Vénissieux, August 28, 2015, https://www.expressions-venissieux.fr/2015-08-28-ephemere-experience-communarde/; and "1936, l'année du grand combat social," Expressions: Les Nouvelles de Vénissieux, June 1, 2016, https://www.expressions-venissieux.fr/2016-06-01-1936-lannee-du-grand-combat-social/.

77. For a thorough accounting of the march and Vénissieux as its place of origin, see Hajjat, *La marche pour l'égalité et contre le racisme*.

78. This destruction followed the bulldozing of a Malian workers' foyer by the PCF municipality of Vitry-sur-Seine in December 1980.

79. Meuret, *Le socialisme municipal*, part 1, chap. 1, para. 1.

80. Bonneville, *Naissance et métamorphose d'une banlieue ouvrière*.

81. Bonneville, *Naissance et métamorphose d'une banlieue ouvrière*, part 2, chap. 1, paras. 91–92.

82. Bonneville, *Naissance et métamorphose d'une banlieue ouvrière*, part 2, chap. 1. There was also continued growth in leather production and the rising prominence of rubber.

83. Bonneville, *Naissance et métamorphose d'une banlieue ouvrière*, part 1, chap. 2, para. 24.

84. Bonneville, *Naissance et métamorphose d'une banlieue ouvrière*, part 1, chap. 1, para. 53.

85. Mitterrand would later act as a witness in Gagnaire's 1948 wedding. Yannick Ponnet, "Étienne Gagnaire est devenu maire 23 ans avant Charles Hernu," *Le Progrès*, August 22, 2015.

86. Meuret, *Le socialisme municipal*, part 5, chaps. 3 and 6. Gagnaire served another stint as deputy (1973–78), taking Marcel Houël's seat (Rhône 6e; Houël himself moved to the seat for Rhône 11e).

87. Begag served as minister for the promotion of equality of opportunity (2005–7) in Dominique de Villepin's government.

88. Annexation was first suggested in 1852, just after both cities were incorporated into the Rhône department (they first belonged to Isère), and multiple proposals for full or partial integration into Lyon were made throughout the early twentieth century. See Alain Belmont, "Quand Lyon lorgnait le Moulin-à-Vent," Expressions: Les Nouvelles de Vénissieux, May 18, 2012, https://www.expressions-venissieux.fr/2012-05-18-quand-lyon-lorgnait-sur-le-moulin-a-vent/; and Meuret, *Le socialisme municipal*.

89. As Ed Naylor notes in his overview of social welfare scholarship, "The type of solidarity that has characterized post-war welfare states like the French one relies as much on calculations of self-interest as on any loftier egalitarian ideal." Naylor, "'Solidarisme ou Barbarie,'" 472.

90. On the fraught imperial ideals of tolerance and integration, see Le Sueur, *Uncivil War*; and Shepard, *Invention of Decolonization*.

91. On the municipal hopes for economic development from the stadium, see Bacqué, "Le Stade de France à Saint-Denis," 6.

1. The Mission to Modernize

1. "Inauguration du quartier nord d'Asnières," June 1970 (AMASS, Brochures diverses).

2. Police memo, "M. Chaban-Delmas, Premier ministre a procédé, le 19 juin, à l'inauguration de la zone nord rénovée d'Asnières," June 20, 1974 (AHPP, GA A 17 and ADHS, 1308 W 3).

3. "Inauguration du quartier nord d'Asnières."

4. This tracks, for example, with Janoé Vulbeau's findings that urbanization policy, especially building renovation and social housing projects, "aimed principally to control and limit the Algerian population" in the Lille suburb of Roubaix. Vulbeau, "Roubaix," 13.

5. On the imperial civilizing mission, see Conklin, *Mission to Civilize*. On the transition to a modernizing framework, see Cooper, "Modernizing Bureaucrats, Backward Africans, and the Development Concept"; and Connelly, *Diplomatic Revolution*, 54. On the extension of modernizing ideas into the metropole and the postcolonial period, particularly with reference to welfare and citizenship, see Naylor, *France's Modernising Mission*. On modernizing as a goal within Marseille's postwar urban development, see Nasiali, *Native to the Republic*.

6. See especially Cupers, *Social Project*; Newsome, *French Urban Planning*; and Rudolph, *At Home in Postwar France*.

7. Lewis, *Boundaries of the Republic*, 195.

8. Rosenberg, *Policing Paris*, 171.

9. Bernardot, "Une politique de logement," 37n.

10. Lyons, *Civilizing Mission in the Metropole*, 128–29.

11. See Blanc-Chaléard, "Les immigrés et le logement," 5; and Viet, *La France immigrée*, 204–5.

12. Lyons, *Civilizing Mission in the Metropole*, 120.

13. On Claudius-Petit's Resistance and religious background, see Lyons, *Civilizing Mission in the Metropole*, 123; on his championing of modernism—and his friendship with Le Corbusier—see Cupers, *Social Project*, 16; Newsome, *French Urban Planning*, 69; and Rudolph, *At Home in Postwar France*, 36. On how Christian humanist ideas shaped social and racial hierarchies in housing and urban development policy, see Vulbeau, "Reloger les familles populaires dans les années 1960."

14. Sayad and Dupuy, *Un Nanterre algérien*, 56.

15. Viet, *Histoire des Français*, 333n9.

16. Blanc-Chaléard, "Des baraques aux bidonvilles," 89. For more on these linguistic adaptations, see Topalov, "Naming Process," 41–42 and 47.

17. Lewis, *Boundaries of the Republic*, 36–38 and 61.

18. Bernardot, "Une politique de logement," 66. Vincent Viet notes officials' awkward adoption of the term and early uncertainty about its spelling. Viet, *La France immigrée*, 198.

19. See chapter 3.

20. Blanc-Chaléard, "Des baraques aux bidonvilles," 89; and de Barros, "Des 'Français musulmans d'Algérie' aux 'immigrés,'" 30. See also Blanc-Chaléard, *En finir avec les bidonvilles*.

21. McDonnell, *Europeanising Spaces in Paris*, 62–65.

22. De Barros, "Des 'Français musulmans d'Algérie' aux 'immigrés,'" 30. For more on imperialism at the local level, see chapter 3.

23. Lyons, *Civilizing Mission in the Metropole*, 197; and Nasiali, *Native to the Republic*, 80–82.

24. Blanc-Chaléard, *Histoire de l'immigration*, 69.

25. Blanc-Chaléard, "Les immigrés et le logement," 6.

26. De Barros, "Des 'Français musulmans d'Algérie' aux 'immigrés,'" 30. On the gradual adoption of *bidonville* as a global term for slums and shantytowns, see Topalov, "Naming Process," 42.

27. Sayad and Dupuy, *Un Nanterre algérien*, 51.

28. Sayad and Dupuy, *Un Nanterre algérien*, 56.

29. Sayad and Dupuy, *Un Nanterre algérien*, 32–33.

30. Pétonnet, *Ces gens-là*, 61.

31. Sayad and Dupuy, *Un Nanterre algérien*, 76–80.

32. Sayad and Dupuy, *Un Nanterre algérien*, 42–46, 48–64, 92–94, 96–97.

33. Sayad and Dupuy, *Un Nanterre algérien*, 42.

34. Sayad and Dupuy, *Un Nanterre algérien*, 89.

35. Sayad and Dupuy, *Un Nanterre algérien*, 50.

36. Memo, "L'implantation nord-africaine dans le Département de la Seine," June 2, 1955 (AHPP, HA 7).

37. "Loi no. 64–1229 du 14 décembre 1964," *Journal official de la République française*, December 15, 1964, 11139 (AP, 36 WR 3).

38. Modeste Zussy, Senate report, no. 1, Annex to Procès-verbal du 2 octobre 1964 (AP, 36 WR 3), 1.

39. The government insisted that municipal reticence hindered SONACOTRAL in the Paris region. Question écrite no. 500 du 26 mars 1959, *Journal official*, Débats parlementaires du 8 avril 1959, 262 (CHAN, F1a 5054).

40. Bernardot, "Une politique de logement," 71–72.

41. Both local and national construction projects emphasized the importance of providing green spaces; see the Senate report by the Commission des finances, "Note d'information budgétaire, financière et économique: Le problème de l'aménagement de la région parisienne," May 10, 1961, 68 (AMSD, 37 AC 11).

42. "Asnières, ville en pleine rénovation," *Asnières: Votre nouveau quartier*, June 1963 (AMASS, Brochures diverses), 11; and "La transformation des banlieues," *Le Moniteur des travaux publics et du bâtiment*, no. 34, August 26, 1961 (AMASS, 3 Durb 58).

43. On the broader phenomenon of using antislum campaigns to disperse African migrants throughout the Paris region, see Glaes, *African Political Activism in Postcolonial France*, chap. 6.

44. Huet, the preceding mayor, opposed the renovation of the northern zone on the basis of its displacement of residents and small businesses. Huet to "Mes chers concitoyens," June 4, 1960 (AMASS, 3 Durb 61).

45. SEMERA, "Assemblée constitutive du 20 décembre 1961" (AMASS, 3 Durb 37).

46. "Compte rendu de la séance d'information de l'aménagement du quartier nord d'Asnières," undated but likely fall 1959 (AMASS, 3 Durb 58).

47. "La transformation des banlieues"; and Bokanowski, "Témoignage," *La vie de la construction moderne française*: 3 (January–February 1963), 14 (AMASS, Brochures diverses).

48. "Asnières et ses Maires de la Révolution à nos jours," brochure for exposition, Ville d'Asnières-sur-Seine, October 9–20, 1995 (AMASS).

49. Flyer, "L'habitat à Asnières," 1971 (ADHS, 1308 W 3).

50. For a sense of scale, out of a set of 471 municipal interventions on housing between 1959 and 1983, only 17 appear to have been on behalf of North Africans. See AMASS, 3 D 241 and 242.

51. Letter from A., March 1959 (AMASS, 3 D 241). Usines Chausson was a major manufacturer for automakers, with factories around Paris, including in Asnières and in Gennevilliers.

52. Frenchness here was invoked in a way to suggest a local belonging—more typically, migrants emphasized their local connections as a means of establishing Frenchness. See chapter 2 on how this functioned in Saint-Denis. On similar claims to belonging in Marseille, see Nasiali, *Native to the Republic*, 49. On the right to comfort, see Nasiali, *Native to the Republic*, 43–50; and Rudolph, *At Home in Postwar France*.

53. Director OPHLM Asnières to Bokanowski, March 1959 (AMASS, 3 D 241).

54. "Recensement au 25 décembre 1959: 3ème groupe" (AMASS, 2 I 63). A single metropolitan man was listed as unemployed.

55. See, for example, speeches by city officials and bus-tour guides for visits in November–December 1964 to the new Descartes school campus (AMASS, 3 Durb 80); also Lavergne to Bokanowski, February 14, 1967 (AMASS, 2 I 63).

56. Meeting minutes, "Commission Voirie-Architecture-Urbanisme-Logement," September 14, 1959 (AMASS, 3 Durb 58). Note the use of *French Muslims*, a term juridically applicable only to Algerians, to cover a general population of North African migrants; Algerians made up less than half the population of the bidonville le Curé.

57. Compte-rendu de la réunion à la Préfecture de la Seine, "Expulsion des Nord-Africains de la zone nord," September 30, 1960 (AMASS, 2 I 63).

58. Comité d'Etude de la Famille, "Etude des problèmes familiaux se rattachant à la zone nord d'Asnières," March 29, 1962 (AMASS, 5 Q 144).

59. A. to Maire, December 18, 1959 (AMASS, 2 I 63).

60. Clery to A., May 4, 1960 (AMASS, 2 I 63).

61. A. to General de Gaulle, April 1, 1961 (AMASS, 2 I 63).

62. On the habit of writing directly to de Gaulle when local appeals went unheard, see Pétonnet, *Ces gens-là*, 299.

63. "Compte-rendu de la réunion du 1er octobre 1963," Oct. 1, 1963 (AMASS, 2 I 63).

64. Maurice Josco, "Bidonvilles," *France-Soir*, November 11, 1965 (AMASS, 3 Durb 148).

65. Note pour M. le Préfet, "Le problème nord-africain dans le Département de la Seine," July 1954 (AHPP, HA 7).

66. Préfecture de police, "Etude de la Population Musulmane d'Algérie implantée à Paris et dans la région parisienne depuis la Libération," December 15, 1958 (AHPP, HA 9), 2.

67. See, for example, Commission Voirie-Architecture-Urbanisme-Logement, September 14, 1959 (AMASS, 3 Durb 58).

68. SEMERA, Assemblée constitutive, December 20, 1961, "Cahiers de Charges," Article 7 (AMASS, 3 Durb 37).

69. Maurice Bokanowski, "En tête à tête," *Asnières: Votre nouveau quartier*, June 1963, 1.

70. Compte rendu, September 30, 1960, "Expulsion des Nord-Africains de la zone nord d'Asnières" (AMASS, 2 I 63).

71. MacMaster, "Seuil de tolérance," 17.

72. For a discussion of how social scientific discourses surrounding the *seuil de tolérance* obscured racist bias, see Minayo Nasiali, *Native to the Republic*, 99–106. On the use of the *seuil* as a means of shoring up white French comfort, see Shepard, "Comment et porquoi éviter le racisme." On the intersection of racialized fears about criminality and demography in the discussion of quotas, see Byrnes, "Criminal Fertility."

73. Note from Commissaire à la construction dans la région parisienne to Préfet de la Seine, February 27, 1961 (AP, PEROTIN/1011/69/2–112).

74. Note from Commissaire à la construction dans la région parisienne, February 27, 1961.

75. Compte rendu de la réunion tenue le 14 avril 1961 à 10h30 au Service départemental du logement au sujet du brassage des familles musulmanes et des familles métropolitaines logées par les Organismes d'HLM (AP, PEROTIN/1011/69/2–112). Vaujour served as director for general security in Algeria from 1953 to 1955, where he was involved in attempts to quell the nationalist insurrection. See Hmed, "'Tenir ses hommes,'" 16–17.

76. See Lyons, *Civilizing Mission in the Metropole*, 197–99.

77. Massenet to Dulière, June 9, 1959, cited in Lyons, *Civilizing Mission in the Metropole*, 192.

78. Lyons, *Civilizing Mission in the Metropole*, 204–5.

79. Lyons, *Civilizing Mission in the Metropole*, 125–26.

80. House, "Contrôle, encadrement, surveillance et répression," 155.

81. Ministère de l'Equipement, "Circulaire No 66-15 du 31 mai 1966 relative à la résorption des bidonvilles" (CHAN, F1a 5116). For an analysis of the key role of such memos, as opposed to parliamentary legislation, in defining French immigration policy in the interwar years, see Lewis, *Boundaries of the Republic*, 123–33.

82. Secrétaire d'Etat au Logement, "Etat actuel de la résorption des bidonvilles," February 7, 1966 (CHAN, F1a 5116).

83. One government report divided bidonville residents into three types (those bound for HLMs, those bound for cités de transit, and those needing particular attention) and asserted that these categories often corresponded to ethnic origins: "North Africans, Black [Sub-Saharan] Africans, Portuguese, Spanish, Italian, and, among the French, gypsies . . . demand particular measures." Secrétaire d'Etat au Logement, "Etat actuel de la résorption des bidonvilles."

84. Nasiali, *Native to the Republic*, 71–77.

85. Lyons, *Civilizing Mission in the Metropole*, 201–2.

86. Secrétaire d'Etat au Logement, "Etat actuel de la résorption des bidonvilles." For a detailed discussion of *pieds-noirs* housing issues, see Scioldo-Zürcher, *Devenir métropolitain*.

87. Président du Conseil Général to Préfet Benedetti, July 12, 1963 (AP, 1027 W 18). This was a rare practice, however; the Seine prefect rejected one such request because "these rapatriés are all of European origin. It is therefore not possible to envision, under such conditions, their settling into barracks intended for North Africans, and even partially occupied by them." Scioldo-Zürcher, *Devenir métropolitain*, 271.

88. For a discussion of the reception of pieds-noirs, see Scioldo-Zürcher, *Devenir métropolitain*; and Shepard, *Invention of Decolonization*, 218–24. On the related case of the *harkis*, see Miller, "Algerian, French, Refugees, Repatriates, Immigrants?" On both these populations, see Eldridge, *From Empire to Exile*; and on the pieds-noirs, harkis, and the special case of North African Jews, see Choi, *Decolonization and the French of Algeria*.

89. Commission municipal du logement, January 12, 1968, and "Opérations de relogement sur Asnières," January 1968 (AMASS, 3 Durb 72).

90. Bokanowski to Benedetti, August 1, 1963 (AP, PEROTIN 101/78/1–11).

91. "Bidonvilles d'Asnières"; and Lavergne to Bokanowski, February 14, 1967.

92. Rollin to Directeur Général SONACOTRA, July 7, 1964, "Construction d'un foyer-hôtel" (AMASS, 3 Durb 148).

93. Commission Voirie-Architecture-Urbanisme-Logement, September 14, 1959.

94. "French" clearly applied only to white metropolitan families, not all those with French citizenship. Commission municipale chargée de l'attribution des logements mis à la disposition de la ville d'Asnières, January 12, 1968 (AMASS, 3 Durb 72).

95. SEMERA, Conseil d'administration, February 5, 1964, "Notes sur les opérations de relogement" (AMASS, 3 Durb 39).

96. SEMERA, Conseil d'administration, November 29, 1962 (AMASS, 3 Durb 38).

97. SEMERA, Conseil d'administration, November 29, 1962. Another petition was lodged in December, insisting that the existence of a bidonville of three hundred to four hundred North Africans "posed a major problem of cohabitation as well as viability. There exists nothing, absolutely nothing, in terms of hygiene on this land." Petition addressed to Bokanowski, December 19, 1962 (AMASS, 3 Durb 148).

98. SEMERA, Conseil d'administration, November 29, 1962.

99. Josco, "Bidonvilles."

100. Lavergne further specified, "In general, it takes two years to render them as capable of confronting daily life as everyone else. A single year is sufficient for those North Africans who have taken a French wife." Quoted in Josco, "Bidonvilles." The special consideration of a—presumably white—French wife reinforced imperial and paternalist notions of racial hierarchy and the domestic sphere.

101. Etring to Cité residents, May 22, 1970, and Etring to Lazarus, January 5, 1971 (AMASS, 2 S 2-30).

102. Correspondence between Lavergne and Etring, October 5 and 19, 1970 (AMASS, 2 S 2-30).

103. Etring to Salanon, May 25, 1970 (AMASS, 2 S 2-30). In previous years, concerns had been raised about the conduct of certain cité caretakers and their unresponsiveness to residents' needs and concerns. Lefebvre to Grosmaire, February 29, 1967; and SEMERA, Service de gestion, to Foure, September 25, 1968 (AMASS, 2 S 2-30). Though one of the caretakers asserted that she was doing her best and the fault lay with the residents, she was soon let go. Correspondence between SEMERA and Foure, September–December 1968 (AMASS, 2 S 2-30).

104. Etring to Lazaru, January 5, 1971.

105. Cité residents took care to decorate their homes and were proud to acquire refrigerators and televisions—the latter being a particular mark, in their eyes, of social integration. Pétonnet, *Ces gens-là*, 61, 114–15, 278–89, and 301–4.

106. K. to Maire, July 17, 1975 (AMASS, 3 D 242).

107. Lefebvre to Caubet, March 8, 1968 (AMASS, 2 S 2-30).

108. On a similar invocation of livestock as a means of underscoring migrants' supposed inadaptability to French life, see Naylor, "'Un âne dans l'ascenseur,'" 115. On a variety of food practices that "irritated" cité de transit neighbors, see Pétonnet, *Ces gens-là*, 64. On the "bidonvillization" of new housing as a product of residents' making the space serve their needs, see Sayad and Dupuy, *Un Nanterre algérien*, 112. On the broader phenomenon of all sorts of residents "not using their homes in the manner that architects had anticipated," see Rudolph, *At Home in Postwar France*, 128.

109. Josco, "Bidonvilles."

110. On stigma and the cités de transit, see Cohen and David, "Les cités de transit."

111. SEMERA to FAS, February 25, 1970 (AMASS, 2 S 2-30).

112. Rouseau to Etring, February 5, 1974 (AMASS, 2 S 2-30).

113. Bokanowski, "En tête à tête."

114. "Asnières, ville en pleine rénovation," 13.

115. "Bidonvilles d'Asnières," November 7, 1964 (ADHS, 1308 W 3).

116. However, 1972 and 1973 showed some regression with the development of a few "microbidonvilles" (gone again by 1974). Roberrini, Reports to Préfet de la Région parisienne, 1969–74 (BAVP).

117. "Le grand ensemble des Courtilles," *La vie de la construction moderne française*, no. 3, January–February 1963 (AMASS, Brochures diverses), 19.

118. Gagnaire to Préfet du Rhône, March 8, 1960 (ADR, 248 W 263).

119. Procès-verbal de réunion, November 1955 (ADR, 248 W 253).

120. "Centre d'Hébergement des Travailleurs Nord-Africains de la Part-Dieu," undated (ADR, 248 W 303); and Mouchnino to Ministre du Travail, November 17, 1951, "Problèmes posés par l'immigration NA dans le département du Rhône" (ADR, 248 W 253).

121. ALHNA was run by a committee led by Mouchnino, with representatives from the prefecture, the Lyon mayor's office, industrial employers, and the main labor unions (CFTC, FO, and CGT). Mouchnino to Ministre du Travail, November 17, 1951. The committee was supposed to include three North African representatives; only two served, the center's interpreter and its imam, Bel Hadj el-Mafi.

Émilie Elongbil Ewane, "Hébergement et répression: Le Centre de la Part Dieu," in Branche and Thénault, *La France en guerre*, 420.

122. Zeller, *Arriver et se loger à Lyon*.

123. See André, *Femmes dévoilées*, 111.

124. Jacques Barou, "Ghettos et bidonvilles," in Bancel, Bencharif, and Blanchard, *Lyon, capitale des outre-mers*, 139.

125. Ewane, "Hébergement et répression," 420.

126. Commission régionale de l'action sanitaire et sociale de Lyon, Compte-rendu de réunion, December 19, 1952 (ADR, 248 W 253).

127. Ewane, "Hébergement et répression," 420.

128. A cap of five hundred seemed to be their goal. Commission régionale de l'action sanitaire et sociale de Lyon, Compte-rendu de réunion, December 19, 1952.

129. Hornung, Directeur du Centre, to Président de l'ALHNA, September 25, 1951 (ADR, 248 W 253).

130. Hornung to Président de l'ALHNA, September 25, 1951.

131. Ministre du Travail to IGAME du Rhône, June 7, 1951, "Hébergement des salariés originaires des départements algériens dans l'agglomération lyonnaise" (ADR, 248 W 253).

132. Préfet du Rhône to Ministres de l'Intérieur et du Travail, November 12, 1954, "Habitat des Citoyens Français Musulmans en Métropole" (ADR, 248 W 253).

133. Délégué Interdépartemental to Ministre de la Reconstruction et de l'Urbanisme, April 17, 1953.

134. IGAME pour la 8e Région to SAMAS, January 20, 1959, "Occupation des centres d'hébergement réservés aux travailleurs Français de souche algérienne" (ADR, 248 W 253).

135. IGAME pour la 8e Région to SAMAS, January 20, 1959. On residents' cooking, see Centre d'Hébergement Nord-Africain, "Rapport sur la situation des travailleurs nord-africains au centre de la Part-Dieu," 1949 (ADR, 437 W 83).

136. Délégué Interdépartemental to Ministre de la Reconstruction et de l'Urbanisme, April 17, 1953, "Logement de la main-d'oeuvre Nord-Africaine" (ADR, 248 W 253).

137. Martin, July 5, 1958 (ADR, 248 W 303).

138. Préfet du Rhône to Ministres de l'Intérieur et du Travail, November 12, 1954. The same language also appears in the Département du Rhône report, "Logement des Travailleurs Originaires d'Algérie—SONACOTRAL" (ADR, 248 W 263).

139. Martin, July 5, 1958.

140. Ewane, "Hébergement et répression," 422. For more on the Rhône prefecture's policies during the Algerian War, see chapter 3.

141. Préfet du Rhône to Ministres de l'Intérieur et du Travail, November 12, 1954.

142. Comité de liaison pour l'action sanitaire et sociale en faveur des Nord-Africains, Compte-rendu de réunion, January 14, 1954 (ADR, 248 W 252).

143. Mouchnino to Ministre du Travail, April 6, 1958, "Amélioration de l'habitat des Travailleurs Nord-Africains" (ADR, 248 W 263).

144. Marginalia on Mouchnino to Ministre du Travail, April 6, 1958.

145. Martin, undated, "Rapport relatif aux opérations d'assainissement des hôtels, meublés, immeubles, et îlots insalubres ou menaçant ruine réalisées dans l'agglomération lyonnaise pendant la période du 1er Janvier 1958 au 1er Mars 1959" (ADR, 248 W 358).

146. Bertrand (SAT-Nord) to Préfet du Rhône, May 2, 1961, "Recensement des locataires du Foyer d'Hébergement N.A. de la Part-Dieu" (ADR, 248 W 303). Of those surveyed, 1,274 were Algerian; 121 were Tunisian; and 2 were Moroccan.

147. Mouchnino commented in 1959 that the Labor Ministry had been referring to "l'éclatement de la Part-Dieu" for years. Mouchnino to Ministre du Travail, April 16, 1959 (ADR, 248 W 263). The prefect and other national bodies adopted the phrasing too: see Préfet du Rhône to Ministres de l'Intérieur et du Travail, November 12, 1954; Mouchnino to Préfet du Rhône, March 25, 1955, "Création de foyers d'hébergement de travailleurs nord-africains en Métropole" (248 W 252); and Commission consultative nationale pour l'étude des questions nord-africaines, Comte rendu de réunion, April 5, 1955 (CHAN, F1a 5043).

148. André, "Les groupes de choc du FLN," 24–25.

149. Ewane, "La guerre d'Algérie à Lyon," 2–4. For more on imperial policing in the region during the Algerian War, see chapter 3.

150. See Cabinet du Préfet, "Note relative au problème du logement des Musulmans (célibataires et familles) originaires de l'Algérie," July 29, 1960 (ADR, 248 W 252); and Programme d'action pour la suppression du Foyer de la Part-Dieu, June 26, 1961 (ADR, 248 W 303).

151. Bertrand to Préfet du Rhône, February 23, 1962, "Résorption du Foyer d'hébergement nord-africain de la Part-Dieu" (ADR, 248 W 282).

152. The earliest use of the term seems to be in 1963. See A. Chaffangeon, Société d'équipement de la région lyonnaise (SERL) to Préfet du Rhône, September 20, 1963, "Part-Dieu, Libération tranche 'Centre Nord-Africain'"; Préfet du Rhône to Bonfils (CTAM), January 22, 1964, "Libération du Centre Nord-Africain de la Part-Dieu"; and G. Belorgey to Secrétaire Général, February 14, 1964, "Libération du Centre Nord-Africain installé sur les terrains de la Part-Dieu" (ADR, 248 W 303).

153. Ricard to Pradel, December 14, 1965 (ADR, 248 W 263).

154. Ricard to Pradel, December 14, 1965.

155. Mouchnino to Préfet du Rhône, March 25, 1955. Vénissieux already hosted two SONACOTRAL foyers (243 beds at Francis de Pressensé from 1959 and another 243 at Bonnet Pernet from 1960); Antoine Billon was finished in October 1961 and Viviani in March 1962. Villeurbanne's foyer de la Poudrette was finished in January 1961.

156. Julien to IGAME, June 3, 1960, "Suppression du Centre de la Part-Dieu"; and Julien to Maire de Villeurbanne, Service de la Voierie, May 30, 1960 (ADR, 248 W 263).

157. Cabinet du Préfet, June 7, 1961, "SONACOTRAL" (ADR, 248 W 251).

158. Bertrand to Préfet du Rhône, May 2, 1961, "Recensement des locataires du Foyer d'Hébergement N.A. de la Part-Dieu" (ADR, 248 W 303).

159. Bertrand, Rapport trimestriel, July 5, 1961 (ADR, 248 W 74).

160. "Programme d'action pour la suppression du Foyer de la Part-Dieu," June 26, 1961 (ADR, 248 W 303). The Part-Dieu director reported with relief that the policy of removing bedding immediately had not sparked any protest among the remaining residents. Directeur du Centre, Memo, November 16, 1961 (ADR, 248 W 303).

161. "Programme d'action pour la suppression du Foyer de la Part-Dieu."

162. Bertrand to Préfet du Rhône, February 23, 1962.

163. Préfet du Rhône to Directeur Général du SONACOTRAL, April 6, 1962, and Bertrand, February 5, 1962, "Instructions de détail concernant le relogement de 540 locataires" (ADR, 248 W 303).

164. Bertrand, Rapport mensuel, April 7, 1961 (ADR, 248 W 74).

165. Bertrand, Rapport mensuel, April 7, 1961, and Rapport trimestriel, October 6, 1961 (ADR, 248 W 74).

166. Bertrand, Rapport trimestriel, July 5, 1961. In addition to the ethnic difference, Bertrand also noted that North Africans in Vénissieux also tended to be more skilled workers and so socioeconomically more advantaged.

167. Grillo, *Ideologies and Institutions in Urban France*, 104. The frustration with rules about guests in shared housing echoes the initial student protests that set off the "events" of May–June 1968. Marc André describes a number of Algerian women who transitioned through Lyon's banlieues after 1962, but most chose this path on their own and none stayed long. André, *Femmes dévoilées*, chap. 8, paras. 49 and 52. On the strict regulations in the Foyer Double-Couronne in Saint-Denis, see Byrnes, "French like Us?," 173–74.

168. A. Chaffangeon to Préfet du Rhône, September 20, 1963.

169. Pradel to Préfet du Rhône, October 12, 1964 (ADR, 248 W 303).

170. Recensement nominatif des 279 locataires du centre de la Part-Dieu à reloger, May 17, 1965 (ADR, 248 W 303).

171. For details, see SLPM, "Bilan de résorption des Bidonvilles dans le département du Rhône de 1958–1971" (ADR, 759 W 40).

172. Belorgey to Secrétaire Général, February 14, 1964, and Préfet du Rhône to Maire de Lyon, April 6, 1965 (ADR, 248 W 303).

173. Pradel to Préfet du Rhône, April 15, 1965 (ADR, 248 W 303).

174. Note à l'intention de M. le Secrétaire Général, July 13, 1965 (ADR, 248 W 303).

175. Pradel to Ricard, January 6, 1966 (ADR, 248 W 263). Pradel's phrasing includes an odd invocation of the feudal system of tenure.

176. Préfet du Rhône to SAMAS, February 11, 1959 (ADR, 248 W 252).

177. SAMAS, March 6, 1959, "Note au sujet de l'admission éventuelle d'ouvriers français de souche et étrangers dans les foyers de travailleurs français d'Algérie" (ADR, 248 W 252).

178. SAMAS to Préfet du Rhône, December 16, 1958, "Admission dans les foyers d'hébergement construits pour les ouvriers Français originaires d'Algérie d'ouvriers de souche métropolitaine ou étrangère," and Mouchnino to Préfet du Rhône, February 11, 1959 (ADR, 248 W 252).

179. Berthet, *Mémoire du renouvellement urbain*, 11.

180. Ricard to Ministère des rapatriés, "Prêts complémentaires pour le logement des rapatriés," September 10, 1963 (ADR, 759 W 318).

181. Berthet, *Mémoire du renouvellement urbain*, 11.

182. Chessel to Commission Divisionnaire, "Expulsion de locataires. Bidonvilles, 15 rue Marie Antoinette à Villeurbanne," April 20, 1965 (ADR, 248 W 361).

183. Deputé Cousté to Préfet Pelissier, April 12, 1973 (ADR, 759 W 318).

184. See, for example, warnings that a new cité de transit might "become, sooner or later, a 'Petite rue Olivier de Serres.'" Balay to President d'OPHLM de Villeurbanne, November 7, 1978 (ADR, 759 W 311). For a useful discussion of how Olivier de Serres, which was an exceptional case, was employed by state officials to fan anxieties about a supposed broader trend, see Cohen, *Des familles invisibles*, 263–64.

185. Gagnaire to Préfet, "Enquête sur les logements de la Régie Simon," February 28, 1968 (ADR, 759 W 318).

186. Préfecture du Rhône, "Au sujet de la Cité Victor Simon."

187. SLPM, "Note sur l'immigration étrangère dans le Rhône," August 15, 1971 (ADR, 248 W 93).

188. Schwartz, *Olivier de Serres*, 15.

189. Schwartz, *Olivier de Serres*, 31.

190. Schwartz, *Olivier de Serres*, 46.

191. Schwartz, *Olivier de Serres*, 33, 35–36, and 51.

192. Schwartz, *Olivier de Serres*, 6 and 35.

193. Brachet and Mayère, "Détruire les ensembles récents," in Schwartz, *Olivier de Serres*, 6.

194. Schwartz, *Olivier de Serres*, 6.

195. See AMVill, 2 D 94. For a discussion of earlier panic surrounding the North African residents of Villeurbanne's Tonkin neighborhood, see Byrnes, "Criminal Fertility."

196. Gagnaire to Moulins, September 15, 1966 (ADR, 248 W 356).

197. SLPM Rhône, "Note sur les bidonvilles verticaux," undated but around 1966 (ADR, 759 W 318 and 248 W 91).

198. See police reports and correspondence in ADR, 248 W 93 and 759 W 100–102.

199. In response to the first disagreements over high rents, the prefect corresponded with both the Directeur Départemental du Ministère de la Construction (August 30, 1963) and the Ministère des Rapatriés (September 10, 1963) with the conclusion that "the Administration has no means to force the Societé [Simon]." In 1968, the prefecture corresponded with the Ministère de l'Équipement (October 21, 1968), invoking the previous findings and complaining, "I had to leave the Compagnie Victor Simon free to recruit its renters as it wished among the families that, for diverse reasons, were ready to accept its exorbitant renting conditions" (ADR, 759 W 318).

200. Rouvièle (Directeur de l'Action Sanitaire et Sociale) to Préfet du Rhône, "Immigration de familles de travailleurs Algériens dans les logements dépendent de la Compagnie Victor Simon," June 19, 1969 (ADR, 759 W 318).

201. See Compte rendu de la réunion tenue le 14 avril 1961 and Procès-verbal de la réunion du jeudi 25 mai 1961 (AP, PEROTIN/1011/69/2–112).

202. Schwartz, *Olivier de Serres*, 16–18.

203. Préfet du Rhône to Inspecteur d'Académie, October 31, 1969 (ADR, 759 W 318). The prefect insisted that this was a problem of language ability, though the inspector's response listed very few children as having a weak or nonexistent knowledge of French. L'Inspecteur d'Académie to Préfet du Rhône, December 1, 1969, "Scolarisation des enfants étrangers—Problème posé par les enfants de la Régie Simon à Villeurbanne" (ADR, 759 W 53).

204. The inspector insisted that this arrangement was based in no way on racial categories. L'Inspecteur d'Académie to Préfet du Rhône, December 1, 1969.

205. L'Inspecteur d'Académie to Préfet du Rhône, December 1, 1969. The hiring points included the suggestion that only male instructors be hired for the boys' schools, "because Arab boys accept poorly the authority of women."

206. Préfet du Rhône to Ministre de l'Intérieur and Ministre de Travail, de l'Emploi et de la Population, May 11, 1970, "Admission en France des familles de travailleurs algériens et autres Nord-Africains" (ADR, 759 W 261). These neighborhoods were in Lyon's first and fifth arrondissements, Villeurbanne, Décines, Vaulx-en-Vélin, Saint-Cyr-au-Mont-d'Or, Oullins, and Givors.

207. Préfet du Rhône, November 30, 1970, "Contrôle de l'admission des familles étrangères" (ADR, 759 W 261).

208. Préfet du Rhône to Ministre de l'Intérieur and Ministre de Travail, de l'Emploi et de la Population, May 11, 1970, "Admission en France des familles de travailleurs algériens et autres Nord-Africains" (ADR, 759 W 261).

209. Moulins, "Limitation de l'admission des familles étrangères—Refoulement," June 15, 1970 (ADR, 759 W 261). The special EEC status had been in place since October 1968 and was a condition for the Interior Ministry to support the local policy. Ministre de l'Intérieur to Préfet du Rhône, May 26, 1970, "Admission en France de travailleurs nord-africains" (ADR, 759 W 261).

210. Préfet du Rhône to Ministre de l'Intérieur and Ministre de Travail, de l'Emploi et de la Population, May 11, 1970. Jean Dours, directeur de la police générale, had raised concerns about racial targeting and insisted that the final language "apply to all foreign families arriving for the first time in France." See Cohen, *Des familles invisibles*, 267.

211. Moulins to Gagnaire, December 9, 1970 (ADR, 759 W 318). Moulins also clarified that European migrants—at least those from EEC countries—were exempt from the policy.

212. Moulins to Ministre d'Equipement and Ministre de Travail, de l'Emploi et de la Population, May 8, 1972, "Doléances de la Compagnie Victor Simon" (ADR, 759 W 318).

213. Moulins to Gagnaire, June 9, 1970 (AMVill, 2 D 94). Moulins also assured Gagnaire that the school policy was about to be approved.

214. Moulins to Compagnie Simon, October 23, 1971 (ADR, 759 W 318).

215. See "Recensement des élèves étrangers, 72–73" (ADR, 759 W 53) and "Liste des écoles du département du Rhône ayant plus de 45% étrangers à la rentrée scolaire 74–75" (ADR, 759 W 261).

216. Schwartz, *Olivier de Serres*, 8.

217. Pétition de parents d'élèves algériens pur une école "mixte," October 1, 1974, in "Olivier de Serres: Radiographie d'une 'cité ghetto,'" exhibition catalog, Le Rize, 2009.

218. Antoine Silber, "Villeurbanne-les-deux-écoles," *Le Point* 169, December 15, 1975 (ADR, 759 W 318).

219. Mangeot to Secrétaire général du groupe interministériel permanent (GIP) pour la Résorption de l'Habitat Insalubre, June 11, 1974, "Groupe d'immeubles constituant la cité Simon" (ADR, 759 W 318).

220. Préfet du Rhône to Ministre de l'Intérieur and Ministre de Travail, de l'Emploi et de la Population, May 11, 1970.

221. Préfet du Rhône to Ministre de l'Intérieur and Ministre de Travail, de l'Emploi et de la Population, July 10, 1970, "Admission en France de familles étrangères" (ADR, 759 W 261).

222. Lyons, *Civilizing Mission in the Metropole*.

223. Schwartz, *Olivier de Serres*, 15, 47, and 52.

224. Harouel, *Histoire de l'urbanisme*. For an overview of Le Corbusier's work—in particular, his participation in a Vichy commission on residential construction—see Fishman, *L'utopie urbaine au XXe siècle*. For a detailed discussion of modernism's role in developing social housing in France, see Cupers, *Social Project*.

225. Rudolph, *At Home in Postwar France*, 36–45.

226. Harouel, *Histoire de l'urbanisme*, 108. See also Cupers, *Social Project*, 269–316.

227. For a detailed examination of how this mismatch between social belonging and legal citizenship persists into the second generation, see Beaman, *Citizen Outsider*.

2. Politics

1. The city also planned an "artistic evening" for the Eid-al-Kabir feast that July. "Plan de travail concernant les travailleurs Nord-Africains de Saint-Denis," May 31, 1950 (AMSD, 37 AC 16). On the interplay of French secularism and Ramadan celebrations, see Byrnes, "Ramadan in the Republic."

2. Invitation, June 17, 1950 (AMSD, 37 AC 16).

3. Auguste Gillot, notes for speech given June 16, 1950 (AMSD, 37 AC 16).

4. For example, a group of North African workers in Asnières appealed directly to neighboring Gennevillier's PCF mayor in their frustration over local employment services. Letter addressed to Waldeck l'Huillier, April 14, 1954 (AMSD, 37 AC 17). The workers had paid a 5,000 FF fee to city hall employment services but received no job offers and were refused a refund of their money. They called upon l'Huillier to "put an end to this scandal of paying for employment."

5. Bureau municipal, Séance du 31 mai 1950, Décision no. 19, "Nord-Africains" (AMSD, 37 AC 17).

6. "Plan de travail concernant les travailleurs Nord-Africains de Saint-Denis."

7. It was expected that four of the North Africans would be PCF members but that the other six would hail from "all inclinations." At least one of the French members was an activist well known and liked by the city's North African community. "Plan de travail concernant les travailleurs Nord-Africains de Saint-Denis."

8. On communist initiatives in Algeria and the development of the PCA, see Drew, *We Are No Longer in France*.

9. "Rapport de MM. Laroque et Ollive, auditeurs au Conseil d'État sur la main-d'oeuvre nord-africaine," March 1938 (AHC, JU 11), 68–70.

10. Naylor, "'Un âne dans l'ascenseur,'" 443.

11. See Nasiali, *Native to the Republic*, 50–53.

12. "Note aux travailleurs algériens," undated, and "Travailleurs algériens: Pour qui nous prend-on à Moscou?" April 1952 (AMSD, 37 AC 16). Unfortunately, the municipal archives did not document the sources of these pamphlets, which could come from local socialists or parties further to the right. The word *maneuver* in French lends itself to a pun on *main-d'oeuvre*, or manual laborers, the very workers communists saw as their source of legitimacy and power.

13. Police report, "La population nord-africaine de Paris et du Département de la Seine," 1952 (AHPP, HA 7).

14. The PCF took 26.9 percent of the vote in 1951, following a 1946 high of 28.6 percent. Bell and Criddle, *French Communist Party*, 79 and 191.

15. "Evolution de la population de Saint-Denis," 1969 (AMSD, 10 S 120).

16. "Inscription sur liste électorale," December 10, 1955 (AMSD, 10 S 10).

17. R. Guenne, "Compte rendu relatif à la physionomie de la circonscription au cours du mois d'Octobre 1958," November 3, 1958 (AHPP, GA S 12).

18. René Maurice Ben Hamou, b. July 5, 1926, in Versailles (Seine-et-Oise). "Membres du Conseil municipal," 1953 (AMSD, 6 AC 1). Nearly all other documentation unifies his surname as "Benhamou." While Benhamou is used as a family name by both Jews and Muslims in the Maghreb, his parents' names (Judas and Rachael on his birth certificate) make it quite likely that the family's origins were Jewish.

19. Conseil municipal de Saint-Denis, "Election du 26 avril 1953: Membres du conseil municipal" (AMSD, 17 ACW 38).

20. *Saint-Denis Républicain*, "Dans 9 jours les élections municipales," April 17, 1953 (AMSD, 13 AC 16); and Gillot, Letter to Conseillers Municipaux de la minorité, December 25, 1954 (AHPP, GA S 12, "Saint-Denis: Activité Municipale, 1948–1978").

21. "Etude de la Population NA à Paris et dans le Département de la Seine," 1955 (AHPP, HA 8). The police's belief that Benhamou was a Muslim raises some questions about the local controversy in October 1961, when Benhamou was reportedly struck in the face and elsewhere while leading the protest against the presence of FPA forces in the city. See chapter 4.

22. Police memo, "Situation actuelle des Nord-Africains dans la Région Parisienne," June 19, 1948 (AHPP, HA 7).

23. Police memo, July 12, 1965, "Les travailleurs africains de la région parisienne se montrent peu perméables à la propagande du Parti Communiste Français" (AHPP, GA S 12).

24. SAT-FMA, "Note au sujet des problèmes qui se posent actuellement au Service d'Assistance Technique," March 10, 1967 (AHPP, HA 60).

25. Kelfaoui, "Le comportement électoral des Français d'origine maghrébine à Saint-Denis," 366.

26. Conseil municipal, "Voeu concernant les libertés en Algérie." For more on the connection between imperial and metropolitan treatment of Algerians, see chapter 4.

27. "Rapport à M. le Maire sur l'activité de la Municipalité et du Conseil municipal en faveur des Nord-Africains," May 26, 1950 (AMSD, 37 AC 16); and Gillot, October 12, 1948, Théâtre Municipal, "Saint-Denis exige des logements" (AMSD, 37 AC 2).

28. "Rapport à M. le Maire sur l'activité de la Municipalité et du Conseil municipal en faveur des Nord-Africains."

29. For example, in a debate in the General Council for the Seine, Gillot charged that the French General Staff "prefers to lodge the Krauts [les boches] more decently than the Algerians." BMVP, Conseil Général de la Seine, Débats, November 24, 1948, 620.

30. Gillot to the Ministre de Travail et Sécurité Sociale, September 13, 1949.

31. Gillot to Briat, March 19, 1951 (AMSD, 37 AC 17).

32. Memo to Gillot, July 13, 1950 (AMSD, 37 AC 17).

33. Comité de grève, Section Syndicale Molton, Résolution, 1947 (AMSD, 37 AC 70).

34. Gillot to the Secrétaire du Centre Intersyndical, October 25, 1949 (AMSD, 37 AC 17); and "Rapport à M. Gillot sur la situation des Nord-Africains à St-Denis."

35. This demand represented a continuation of interwar activism. When the government had ruled in 1927 that North Africans would be required to register for unemployment benefits at the office on rue Lecomte instead of at their local town halls (with everyone else), then mayor Jacques Doriot tried to keep control of the city's right to determine who would be eligible for the benefits. Dionysiens were particularly upset by the underlying intention of the state ruling, which was to allow the government to deny these benefits to known Algerian nationalists. As Neil MacMaster points out in his discussion of the interwar period, this incident serves as an illustration of how "both colonial and anti-colonial movements . . . fought to control the purse strings and access to welfare as part of a broader contest for the hearts and minds of the Algerians." MacMaster, Colonial Migrants and Racism, 164–65. Vénissieux's municipality also fought for North African unemployment benefits in the late 1930s. Lewis, Boundaries of the Republic, 309n114.

36. Préfet de la Seine (Direction des Affaires Sociales) to Gillot, September 14, 1949, "Situation des travailleurs nord-africains" (AMSD, 37 AC 17); and "Rapport à M. le Maire sur l'activité de la Municipalité et du Conseil municipal en faveur des Nord-Africains." A report from the following year noted that of the three hundred unemployed North African workers known to municipal administrators, the majority were newcomers. "Rapport à M. Gillot sur la situation des Nord-Africains à St-Denis," March 28, 1950 (AMSD, 37 AC 16).

37. "Rapport à M. le Maire sur l'activité de la Municipalité et du Conseil municipal en faveur des Nord-Africains."

38. See AMSD, 37 AC 17. Municipal services kept particularly substantial records for 1954 and 1955.

39. See, for example, letter to Directeur, Etablissements Francolor, September 9, 1954 (AMSD, 37 AC 17).

40. See correspondence on employment and housing in AMSD, 37 AC 17, and on a broader range of administrative requests in AMSD, 3 AC 7 and 8.

41. Barron to Chefs et Responsables de Service, February 18, 1952 (AMSD, 37 AC 17). By the following year, the Seine prefecture's official translators included three new Arabic speakers as well as a Polish and an English translator/speaker. The returning list including Armenian, Turkish, Annamite (Vietnamese), Deaf-Mute, German, Hebrew, Russian, Latin, Serbo-Croatian, Ukrainian, Slovenian, and Bulgarian. Memo, "Modification de la liste de Traducteurs jurés," 1953–54 (AMSD, 37 AC 70).

42. Nonmigrant neighbors also rushed to help save belongings and even care for the children of the families affected. *L'Humanité*, "Incendie monstre au Quartier Pleyel à Saint-Denis," May 30, 1956 (AMSD, 37 AC 17).

43. Gillot to president of AFNA, June 15, 1956 (AMSD, 37 AC 17). AFNA offered instead to place them in a foyer in Stains, though the men did not want to move so far from their workplaces. Note for Barron, February 18, 1957 (AMSD, 37 AC 17).

44. Letters to the Director of North African Affairs (Préfecture de la Seine) and to the Préfet de la Seine, November 15, 1956 (AMSD, 37 AC 17). This time, the prefecture sent certificates for a foyer in Nanterre.

45. Préfecture de Seine (Direction des Affaires Sociales), September 14, 1949, "Situation des travailleurs nord-africains" (AMSD, 37 AC 17).

46. Memo, "Activités de la Commission Coloniale du Parti Communiste," Janvier 14, 1952 (CHAN, F1a 5060).

47. "Cours de soir—Nord-Africains: Rapport trimestriel—Oct–déc. 1950," December 12, 1950 (AMSD, 37 AC 16).

48. Note de Conversation, December 15, 1953, "Préformation professionnelle pour Nord-Africains" (AMSD, 37 AC 17).

49. L'Huillier had been born in Saint-Denis and was active in his youth as a member of the city's Jeunes communistes. Brunet, *Saint-Denis*, 275.

50. L'Huillier cited in note to Gillot, October 29, 1951 (AMSD, 37 AC 17).

51. Pierre Didiot, "Demande de salle de permanence pour le service social pour les travailleurs algériens," July 23, 1962 (AMSD, 37 AC 17). One call, to the Service de la main-d'oeuvre, resulted in a declaration that "everyone wants to take care of the Algerians. However there is only one service with the capacity, that's the Labor Ministry." Note, August 1, 1962 (AMSD, 37 AC 17). This sentiment differed significantly from the common association of North African workers with the Interior Ministry.

52. Bernardot, "Une politique de logement," 68n. The association, as SONACOTRAL, had already been involved with managing some of the North African foyers in

Saint-Denis, but municipal officials did not offer to aid or cooperate in SONACOTRAL projects (53).

53. For more on this connection, see chapter 3.

54. Charles Deutschemann and Georges Dardel to Gillot, February 29, 1962 (AMSD, 37 AC 17).

55. In 1964, the municipality offered space for CGT evening classes for a group of around sixty "workers of Algerian origin." The lack of debate over these particular courses likely stemmed from the trust—and ideological kinship—between the municipality and the union leaders. Vialla to Charpentier, January 7, 1964 (AMSD, 37 AC 17).

56. "Saint-Denis—Interventions—1957–1972" (AMSD, 37 AC 52). The municipality had first observed "a 'bidons-ville' block" on rue Martin Deleuze in 1953—a cluster of "tarred cardboard shanties in which a group of North Africans (at least forty) reside, with no toilet, no water."

57. For a detailed portrait of the "builder-mayor," see Bellanger, "Administrer la 'banlieue municipale,'" 1248–49. See also Schain, French Communism and Local Power, 1; and Sydney Tarrow, "Party Activists in Public Office: Comparisons at the Local Level in Italy and France," in Blackmer and Tarrow, Communism in Italy and France, 166.

58. Stovall, Rise of the Paris Red Belt, 142. Interwar Bobigny—like postwar Saint-Denis—demonstrated the importance of basic municipal services and improvements to winning and retaining community support: "Paved streets may not have brought the revolution nearer, but they made life easier." Stovall, Rise of the Paris Red Belt, 178.

59. Police memo, "Fiche B," January 30, 1965 (AHPP, GA A17).

60. See correspondence with Francois Missoffe, minister for rapatriés, from Bokanowski's term as minister of industry (AMASS, 3 D 276).

61. See, for example, Bokanowski to Préfet de Seine Benedetti, August 1, 1963 (AP, PEROTIN 101/78/1–11).

62. PCF, "Le parti communiste et le parlementarisme," Thèses, manifestes et résolutions adoptées par les Ier, IIe, IIIe, et IVe congrès de l'Internationale communiste (Paris, 1919–26), 68; cited in Stovall, Rise of the Paris Red Belt, 111.

63. Roger Bourderon, "La Renaissance (1949–1970)," in Bourderon, Histoire de Saint-Denis, 302. Bourderon emphasizes the opposition role of special municipal councils held in May 1958 to denounce the generals' coup in Algiers and Charles de Gaulle's return to power. The municipal council rulings may be found in AMSD, 37 AC 17. The referendum on the 1958 Constitution, which founded the Fifth Republic, only barely passed in Saint-Denis: 21,175 yes votes to 19,144 nos. Police memo, "Elections 1965," undated (AHPP, GA S 12). Volovitch-Tavares identifies similar "political jousts" in Champigny's dealings with departmental and national bodies during the resorption of their massive bidonville. Volovitch-Tavares, Portugais à Champigny, 109.

64. See "Ville de Saint-Denis, Années 1950–51" (AHPP, GA S 21) for multiple examples.

65. Gillot was suspended from office for a full three months after closing the city hall to support PCF strikes against the arrival of Dwight D. Eisenhower as NATO Supreme Commander. Bourderon, "Renaissance," 302–3.

66. Series of police memos, 15 April–August 26, 1950 (AHPP, GA S 21). For more on city arguments with police during the Algerian War, see chapter 4.

67. Police memo, November 11, 1949, "Compte rendu de la réunion du Comité local (de Saint-Denis) pour l'Entente entre Français et Immigrés" (AHPP, GA S 21).

68. Bulletin municipal officiel de la ville de Paris, April 5, 1960, p. 183 (AMSD, 37 AC 72).

69. See, for example, "Le PCF dans les Hauts-de-Seine, a révisé, fondamentalement, la politique qu'il conduisait naguère, à l'égard des immigrés" (ADHS, 1346 W 17). The undated report argues that the PCF increased their criticism of the government's handling of migration to combat accusations that their desire to redistribute migrants around the region stemmed from racism or intolerance.

70. Paris prefecture, Memo, May 8, 1967 (AMSD, 18 AC 14).

71. For example, during the 1969 resorption of Francs-Moisins, three Algerians were sent to the foyer run by the Paris prefecture in Nanterre, nineteen were sent to the SONACOTRA foyer in Pierrefitte, and two were sent to the Centre d'accueil gratuit in the twentieth arrondissement of Paris. Police memo, September 24, 1969, "Opération de résorption d'un bidonville à Saint-Denis" (AHPP, GA S 12).

72. Not all of these were welcomed into the city wholeheartedly; in 1955, officials had hoped to prevent the Labor Ministry from purchasing land on the chemin de Marville for a new foyer. In the end, AFNA built one of their foyers on avenue Romain-Rolland, a continuation of the chemin de Marville; this was likely the same project. Correspondence, particularly handwritten note from Roussel to Gillot, September 1954–November 1955 (AMSD, 23 AC 11).

73. Roberrini, "Rapport," March 15, 1973, 23. One of these foyers was operated by the department (rue de l'Yser), one by SONACOTRA (La Courtille), two by the Association des foyers de la région parisienne (AFRP; Fort de la Briche and avenue Romain-Rolland), and finally one, reserved for African migrants, by the Association Sociale pour les Travailleurs Africains (ASSOTRAF; rue Pinel).

74. Manoel, Rapport au Bureau municipal, "Annexe," May 5, 1972 (AMSD, 261 W 37).

75. Handwritten notes on "Fiche: Foyer de travailleurs migrants" (ADSSD, 1801 W 401).

76. Déclaration des maires communistes de la région parisienne et des élus de Paris, "Pour la liquidation des bidonvilles/Pour le relogement humain des travailleurs immigrés," October 25, 1969; and "Déclaration des maires communistes," 1972 (AMSD, 37 AC 52).

77. "Foyers des travailleurs migrants et cités de transit en Seine-Saint-Denis," January 1973 (ADSSD, 1801 W 401). The vast majority of cité de transit residents in Saint-Denis were Portuguese families from Francs-Moisins. On the treatment of these Portuguese families and their rate of transition into Saint-Denis's HLMs, see David, "La résorption des bidonvilles de Saint-Denis: Un noeud dans l'histoire d'une ville."

78. BMSD, Extrait no. 11, "Installation d'un baraquement au bidonville des Francs-Moisins pour la permanence du service social," October 21, 1966; and Memo from Mano to Conseil municipal, "Bidonville Francs-Moisins—Installation du Service Social et d'un service de soins," November 24, 1966 (AMSD, 18 AC 14).

79. Extraits du registre des délibérations du Conseil municipal de Saint-Denis, "Acquisition d'un ensemble immobilier," December 28, 1965 (AMSD, 18 ACW 6).

80. "Convention pour l'assainissement des îlots défectueux," November 1967; earlier drafts with identical wording date as far back as July 1966 (AMSD, 50 ACW 37).

81. Communiqué de la Municipalité de Saint-Denis, June 24, 1970 (AMSD, 50 ACW 37).

82. Compte rendu de réunion, "Opération 'Les Francs-Moisins': Contraintes de relogement," June 29, 1970 (AMSD, 101 ACW 11).

83. See David, "Logement social des immigrants et politique municipale en banlieue ouvrière." David notes that Algerian families of some means were more easily accepted, particularly when they had multiple children.

84. Berthelot to Préfet de Seine-Saint-Denis, September 13, 1973, "Relogement des travailleurs migrants" (ADSSD, 1801 W 430).

85. Work in these two areas provided the vast majority of municipal documentation on the bidonvilles (AMSD, 50 ACW 37 and 18 ACW 22).

86. One particularly damaging fire, in June 1970, allowed for "the drastic application" of antibidonville laws as well as an "acceleration of the possibilities to rehouse foreign workers." Bolotte, prefect for Seine-Saint-Denis, to Secrétaire d'Etat auprès de l'équipement et du logement, October 6, 1970, "Situation de logement en Seine-Saint-Denis" (ADSSD, 1801 W 400).

87. Marc Roberrini's 1971 report to the Paris prefect mentioned the particular difficulties of "cleaning up" the slum on Landy, citing the "communitarian and tribal" tendencies of its African residents. Roberrini, "Rapport," February 15, 1972, 22 (BAVP).

88. Roberrini's 1973 report referred to "Résorption de l'habitat insalubre et les problèmes des migrants" instead of "Résorption des bidonvilles et les problèmes des migrants" (BAVP).

89. See folder on "Programme de restauration des foyers existants" (ADSSD, 1801 W 229).

90. "Visite de M. Dijoud du 19 Septembre 1974" (ADSSD, 1801 W 223). The foyer was to be built in the ZAC Delaunay-Belleville and would have housed 488 individuals evicted from insalubrious buildings, mostly around the centre-ville. "Fiche: Foyer de travailleurs migrants."

91. Note to Direction Départementale des Polices Urbaines, "Résorption de garnis clandestins à Saint-Denis," undated, but all actions listed occur in September 1973 (ADSSD, 1801 W 430).

92. CMSD (Conseil municipal de Saint-Denis), "Voeu demandant la suppression des bidonvilles . . . et le relogement des travailleurs espagnols et portugais qui les occupent," December 22, 1964 (AMSD, 50 ACW 37). The council noted that the state had negotiated an immigration agreement with the Portuguese government.

93. Gillot to Préfet de Seine, March 26, 1965 (AMSD, 50 ACW 37).

94. Dumay, Report to BMSD, "Problèmes posés par la migration des travailleurs étrangers," October 7, 1965 (AMSD, 50 ACW 37).

95. For example, "Projet de Convention avec la SONACOTRA pour la résorption des bidonvilles," July 7, 1966 (AMSD, 50 ACW 37).

96. CMSD, "Voeu du Conseil municipal concernant une subvention au Fonds d'Action Sociale pour les Travailleurs migrants," December 17, 1968 (AMSD, 50 ACW 37 and AMSD, 18 AC 14). Similarly, in June 1957, the municipal council insisted that "sufficient funds be accorded to the OPHLM for the city of Saint-Denis in order to quickly finish buildings in the process of construction and to construct new ones." Conseil municipal, "Voeu adoptant les revendications des locataires de Saint-Denis," June 27, 1957 (AMSD, 38 AC 4).

97. Ministre d'Etat chargé des Affaires Sociales, Direction de la Population et des Migrations to Gillot, May 23, 1969 (AMSD, 50 ACW 37).

98. CMSD, "Remboursement des dépenses supportées par la Commune à la suite de l'incendie du bidonville des Francs-Moisins survenu le 15 Juin 1970," October 20, 1970 (AMSD, 50 ACW 37).

99. CMSD, "Voeu pour un statut démocratique et social des travailleurs immigrés," September 29, 1967 (ADSSD, 7 W 34).

100. Assemblée Nationale, 1968–69, Ordinary Session 1, No. 235, published September 24, 1968, "Statut des travailleurs immigrés" (AMSD, 37 AC 52).

101. See folder "Propositions des lois," especially 1968–69, Ordinary Session 1, No. 325, "Statut des travailleurs immigrés," September 24, 1968; 1969–70, Ordinary Session 1, No. 1011, "Relative à la liquidation des bidonvilles et au règlement des travailleurs immigrés," December 16, 1969; and 1969–70, Ordinary Session 2, No. 1220, "Tendant à renforcer la garantie des droits individuels et des libertés publiques des travailleurs immigrés," June 3, 1970 (AMSD, 37 AC 52).

102. CMSD, "Voeu du Conseil municipal concernant une subvention au Fonds d'Action Sociale," December 17, 1968. In this, they echoed the findings of Marc Roberrini, whose 1970 report to the Paris prefecture declared that France must choose "between an excessive liberalism that opens the door to all excesses and a policy of reasonable firmness that permits us to put an end to exploitation and to impose on migrants our lifestyle norms [*norms d'habitat*], which they do not always want to accept." Roberrini, "Rapport," February 21, 1970, 57 (BAVP).

103. Assemblée Nationale, 1969–70, Ordinary Session 1, No. 1011, published December 16, 1969, "Relative à la liquidation des bidonvilles et au règlement des travailleurs immigrés" (AMSD, 37 AC 52).

104. Déclaration des maires communistes de la région parisienne et des élus de Paris, October 25, 1969, "Pour la liquidation des bidonvilles/Pour le relogement humain des travailleurs immigrés" (AMSD, 37 AC 52).

105. Note to BMSD, "Constitution d'importants bidonvilles sur Saint-Denis," October 25, 1962 (AMSD, 50 ACW 37). The accusations in the report are vague but presumably were meant to suggest the working of some political actor seeking to destabilize the Communist municipality.

106. Schain, *French Communism and Local Power*, 78.

107. Compte rendu de réunion, "Opération 'Les Francs-Moisins,'" June 29, 1970.

108. Dumay, Report to BMSD, "Assainissement d'îlots défectueux," April 1, 1966 (AMSD, 18 ACW 6).

109. Communiqué de la Municipalité de Saint-Denis, June 24, 1970.

110. "Visite de M. Dijoud du 19 Septembre 1974."

111. Compte-rendu de réunion, "L'attribution des logements construits par la société LOGIREP, 2ème tranche des Francs-Moisins à Saint-Denis," June 22, 1973 (AMSD, 28 AC 7). For this particular complex, SONACOTRA was given a 10 percent share of units to allocate to migrant families—that is, 25 out of 252.

112. For 1972 and 1974, "Pourcentage des familles étrangères en HLM, Saint-Denis," 1974 (ADSSD, 1801 W 228); for 1978, "Eléments pour une politique de l'habitat," October 1978, p. 17 (AMSD, 261 W 22).

113. In 1958, North Africans represented roughly 3.63 percent of HLM occupants in Saint-Denis (Office public d'habitations, Reports for each Cité HLM, "Loyers impayés au 30 avril 1958" [AMSD, 38 AC 5]; based on the percentage of Arabophone names). The prefecture's 1974 report lists the nationality of individuals in the HLMs; North Africans comprise 36.72 percent. "Pourcentage des familles étrangères en HLM, Saint-Denis." Finally, the 1978 report estimates that of the foreign population, one-third were Algerians, one-third Spanish or Portuguese, and one-third "others." "Eléments pour une politique de l'habitat."

114. Manoel, Rapport au BMSD, May 5, 1972 (AMSD, 261 W 37).

115. Four of these cities were under PCF mandate (Aubervilliers, Aulnay-sous-Bois, La Courneuve, and Montreuil); the other two were led by the Socialist Party (Neuilly-sur-Marne and Sevran).

116. Préfet de Seine-Saint-Denis to Maires, "Introduction en votre commune de nouvelles familles étrangères," October 1, 1974 (ADSSD, 1801 W 223 and AMSD, 37 AC 52).

117. Préfecture de la Seine-Saint-Denis, Note de service, no. 74–100, "Stabilisation de la population étrangère dans six communes du département," December 9, 1974 (ADSSD, 1801 W 223). Aubervilliers was later added to the list.

118. Préfecture de la Seine, "Projet de rénovation de la commune de Saint-Denis: Examen des répercussions politiques," April 29, 1961 (AP, PEROTIN 101/78/1–19).

119. Masclet strongly condemns the communist municipality in Gennevilliers for housing policies that worked to exclude immigrants from the community and marginalize those who remained—policies that predated and even presaged the bulldozing of a foyer for Malian workers in communist Vitry in 1980. Masclet, *La gauche et les cités*.

120. Massenet to Ministre de l'Intérieur, March 7, 1953, "Inscriptions de citoyens français musulmans d'Algérie sur les listes électorales" (ADR, 437 W 79).

121. "La CGT et le PCF s'occupent activement d'organiser une campagne de propagande dans les milieux nord-africains," March 30, 1954 (ADR, 437 W 79). This group actively looked to forge ties with the local activists of the Mouvement pour le triomphe des libertés démocratiques (MTLD).

122. The CGT listed demands including equal pay, equal family allocations, better housing, and the recognition of Muslim holidays for paid leave. The tract was disseminated in Arabic text, though the police reporting on it noted that the majority of North Africans in the Rhône could not actually read classical Arabic. Memo, April 1, 1954, "Le syndicat CGT des métaux de Lyon diffuse un tract à l'intention des travailleurs nord-africains" (ADR, 437 W 79).

123. Saint-Priest was also a traditionally leftist town, but not PCF. Charles Ottina, mayor from 1949 to 1972, belonged to the Parti Radicale.

124. *Le Progrès*, "Le Premier pavillon du Centre nord-africain des usines Berliet a été inauguré, hier, à Vénissieux," October 29, 1954 (ADR, 248 W 284). For more on Berliet and other employers' roles in supporting their North African workers, see chapter 5.

125. See the regular brochure published by the city, *Bulletin Municipal*, as well as the deliberations of the Conseil municipal (AMVén). Among all the news about renovations and construction in the city, for example, the North African foyers are not mentioned at all.

126. See, for example, Deputé Maire de Vénissieux to Préfet du Rhône, March 2, 1965, and Note a l'intention de Monsieur le Préfet, October 8, 1965, "Logement des travailleurs étrangers" (ADR, 248 W 263).

127. Houël to Préfet du Rhône, December 6, 1967 (ADR, 248 W 263).

128. Moulins to Houël, January 15, 1968 (ADR, 248 W 263).

129. Schwartz, *Olivier de Serres*, 37.

130. Grillo, *Ideologies and Institutions in Urban France*, 121–23.

131. Grillo, *Ideologies and Institutions in Urban France*, 138.

132. Préfet du Rhône to Ministre de l'Intérieur, March 10, 1965, "Recherche de terrains pour constructions destinées aux travailleurs étrangers" (ADR, 248 W 263).

133. Houël to Brachet, January 15, 1966 (ADR, 248 W 307). Houël had apparently also sent a critical letter to the previous director in 1964. Le Page to SLPM, "Foyer-Hôtel rue Bonnet-Pernet à Vénissieux Intervention du Député-Maire," February 23, 1966 (ADR, 248 W 307).

134. Brachet to Houël, January 18, 1966, and Houël to Martin, February 7, 1966 (ADR, 248 W 307).

135. Houël to Martin, February 7, 1966 (ADR, 248 W 307).

136. Gat to Houël, March 17, 1966 (ADR, 248 W 307).

137. Notes from meeting between CLORATE and Préfet du Rhône, December 4, 1970 (ADR, 99 J 31).

138. This is compared to 10 percent for the region overall. *L'Humanité*, "Les immigrés dans le Rhône: Un dixième de la population mais un tiers à Vénissieux," December 23, 1970 (ADR, 759 W 262). This number is likely just for the ZUP Minguettes; Municipal Councillor Jean Vilanova claimed only 20 percent of the overall population of the city as foreign in 1972, with the 30 percent figure applying only to certain neighborhoods. Vilanova, "Point de vue," *Bulletin d'informations municipales*, May 1972 (AMVén).

139. *L'Humanité*, "Les immigrés dans le Rhône."

140. *Journal officiel de l'Assemblée Nationale*, April 27, 1971, Question écrite 15049 (ADR, 759 W 262).

141. Houël to Moulins, September 3, 1970 (ADR, 759 W 262). Houël insisted that he had been "scrupulously following" the prefect's directives from 1969 to no longer allow foreign families into the ZUP Minguettes but was worried that other organizations who controlled access to some units might not be as strict. Moulins assured the mayor that while there could be a few foreign families admitted under the current quotas, there would be an attempt to keep them spread out among the different sections of the ZUP. Moulins to Houël, September 22, 1970 (ADR, 759 W 262). On Houël's later policy of keeping Minguettes units empty instead of allowing migrants to move in, see Hajjat, *La marche pour l'égalité et contre le racisme*.

142. RG, "Participation de la fédération du Rhône du PCF à la campagne menée pour la défense des immigrés," October 16, 1970 (ADR, 759 W 262). As chapter 6 explains, the driving force behind this opposition to the prefecture came from far-left and religious groups.

143. Gat to Houël, October 23, 1970, and "Commentaire de la circulaire no 2762 CAB/SLPM en date du 15 juin 1970" (ADR, 759 W 262).

144. Houël to Assistante Sociale, September 8, 1973 (ADR, 759 W 261). The stated concern, reinforced by the prefecture, was the man's desire to bring over his wife and three children—the fact that the family was in Algeria meant they could not be appropriately "evaluated" by French social services. Mangeot to Directeur de la Sociéte Lyonnaise d'HLM, September 28, 1973, and Mangeot to Chardiny, September 28, 1973 (ADR, 759 W 261).

145. *Le Progrès*, "SOS ZUP," December 18, 1975, in Grillo, *Ideologies and Institutions in Urban France*, 127.

146. Meniri, "Les immigrés dans la commune de Vénissieux."

147. Glaes, *African Political Activism in Postcolonial France*, 65. Glaes offers a close examination of local leftists of varying stripes and their support for striking Black Africans in Ivry.

148. Bulletin Municipal de Saint-Denis, "Pour construire des logements et des écoles," June 1951 (AMSD, 6 AC 2).

149. Sections Communistes de Saint-Denis, January 2, 1961 (AMSD, 37 AC 11).

150. "Aux mal-logés et sans-logés de Saint-Denis."

151. Conseil municipal, "Voeu concernant les libertés en Algérie."

152. Gillot, "Schéma de discours aux travailleurs algériens en France," undated.

153. "Interventions des députés communistes français" (1948–50) and PCF pamphlet, "Travailleurs algériens" (AMSD, 37 AC 16). This second source, which included the details of Thorez's prison sentence, was printed in French on one side and Arabic on the other.

154. Gillot, "Schéma de discours aux travailleurs algériens en France."

155. PCF, "Travailleurs algériens," for January 2, 1956, elections (AMSD, 18 ACW 25).

3. In Defense of Empire

1. Massenet to Ministre de l'Intérieur, May 20, 1953 (ADR, 248 W 152).

2. Cerdan (Director of the MAN) to local newspapers, June 1, 1953 (ADR, 248 W 152).

3. Napoleon Bonaparte was one of the first to insist that the French were "true friends of the Muslims" as part of his Egyptian campaign. Bonaparte, "Déclaration au people égyptien," Wikisource, 1798, https://fr.wikisource.org/wiki/Déclaration _du_général_Bonaparte_au_peuple_égyptien. French imperial officials looked for ways to shore up their pro-Muslim credentials in Africa and the Near East throughout the nineteenth and early twentieth centuries—and quickly adapted this approach to the growing population of colonial migrants from the First World War onward. For French West Africa, see Robinson, *Paths of Accommodation*. For Muslims in the metropole, see Coller, *Arab France*; and Davidson, *Only Muslim*. For a more developed version of the argument that secular French officials were willing to support Islamic practices as a means of shoring up the empire, see Byrnes, "Ramadan in the Republic."

4. Maurice Viollette, interview in *Le populaire*, January 7, 1937, cited in Lewis, *Boundaries of the Republic*, 213. Viollette was Léon Blum's Socialist minister of state and a former governor-general of Algeria. The Blum-Viollette act was never brought to a vote.

5. "Statuts du 'Comité d'Assistance aux Indigènes Algériens,' sous le haut patronage de Monsieur le Gouverneur Général de l'Algérie" (Algiers, 1920), in Lewis, *Boundaries of the Republic*, 195. Clifford Rosenberg also relates French legislators' desire to reform Algerians' legal status in the interwar years to their concerns over "the legitimacy of the French Empire." Rosenberg, *Policing Paris*, 138–39.

6. Report by Ministre Délegué en Afrique du Nord, October 24, 1944 (CHAN, F60 192).

7. Gouvernement général de l'Algérie, Service des liaisons nord-africaines, "Bulletin Mensuel des Questions Islamiques," April 1951 (CHAN, F1a 5046).

8. Directeur de l'Office Administrative du Gouvernement général de l'Algérie to Ministère de l'Intérieur, Services de l'Algérie et des départements d'Outre-mer, March 7, 1951 (CHAN, F1a 5114).

9. On the long-standing connections between Paris policing practices and French imperial policy, see Prakash, "Colonial Techniques in the Imperial Capital."

10. Moris, "Instruction sur les Sections Administratives Techniques en Métropole," August 11, 1960; attached draft memo, undated (AHPP, HA 60).

11. In some ways, the policy of engaging Algerians in the bidonvilles and attempting to rehouse them in foyers echoed the colonial practice of sending Algerians into resettlement camps to prevent nationalist mobilizations. By 1959, these camps had been inscribed within the Constantine Plan as a means of curbing peasant flight to the cities. Cornaton, *Les regroupements de la décolonisation en Algérie*, 70–71.

12. Bernardot, "Une politique de logement," 37–38.

13. Stora, *Ils venaient d'Algérie*. On the FLN's work in France, see pp. 159–69 and numerous annexes; on the broader intra-Algerian conflict, see chapters 9, 10, and 12.

14. Sayad and Dupuy, *Un Nanterre algérien*, 108–9.

15. Lyons, *Civilizing Mission in the Metropole*, 143.

16. SAT-FMA, Rapports (AHPP, HA 58).

17. Papon to Ministre de l'Intérieur and Ministre d'Etat chargé des Affaires Algéri-ennes, "Au sujet du rôle du Service d'Assistance Technique aux Français Musulmans d'Algérie," May 7, 1962 (AHPP, HA 60). On the development and role of the North African Brigade, see Beaujon, "Policing Colonial Migrants"; Prakash, "Colonial Tech-niques in the Imperial Capital"; and Rosenberg, *Policing Paris*.

18. Brigade de voie publique, Synthèse de l'activité, 1955 and 1956 (ADR, 437 W 134). Special thanks to my undergraduate research assistant, Sarah Woods, for her acute insights on this set of police documents (as well as the SAT files discussed later in this chapter).

19. Marc Bernardot argues most forcefully on the links between social services for and surveillance of North Africans. See also Abdelfettah, "'Science coloniale' et modalités d'encadrement de l'immigration algérienne à Paris (1917–1952)"; Hmed, "'Tenir ses hommes'"; House, "Contrôle, encadrement, surveillance et répression"; Peter Jones, "Race, Discourse and Power in Institutional Housing," in Silverman, *Race, Dis-course and Power in France*; Lyons, *Civilizing Mission in the Metropole*, chap. 5; Mac-Master, *Colonial Migrants and Racism*, 194–95; Rosenberg, *Policing Paris*, part 2 (for the history of the interwar years); and Viet, *La France immigrée*, 185–213.

20. Bernardot, "Une politique de logement," 11–12. Hmed cautions that this "logic of control" should not be too strictly interpreted and suggests that the establish-ment of SONACOTRAL within the Ministère de l'Intérieur (as opposed to the Labor Ministry) should not be viewed as a victory of surveillance over assimilation. Hmed, "'Tenir ses hommes,'" 15.

21. See SAT-FMA reports in AHPP, HA 60 and 61.

22. Lyons, *Civilizing Mission in the Metropole*, 143 and 156.

23. Lyons, *Civilizing Mission in the Metropole*, 160–62.

24. Viet, *La France immigrée*, 213.

25. House, "Contrôle, encadrement, surveillance et répression," 152–56. The expan-sion of police-managed Algerian social services to all North and sub-Saharan migrants indicated a desire to maintain influence over populations French authorities did not believe to be as socially and culturally evolved as Europeans. The SAT-FMA became simply the SAT in 1963, with expanded jurisdiction over all North and sub-Saharan Africans. House asserts that police were particularly concerned with the "Black problem" in 1963–64; as the number of workers coming from Mali, Mauritania, and Senegal jumped after the decolonization of these states, "these migrations saw the (re)birth of the methods of control elaborated in the colonies during the colonial era—or even those already practiced on other groups in the metropole." House, "Contrôle, encadrement, surveillance et répression," 153.

26. In 1965, 91 percent of families living in cités de transit north and west of Paris were Algerian. Lyons, *Civilizing Mission in the Metropole*, 204–5.

27. House notes that the Interior Ministry ran its SLPM services parallel to the FAS projects in the new Direction des populations et migrations until 1969. Though no

longer solely applicable to Algerians, their mission included careful monitoring of migrant political activities with a view to limiting the impact of leftist propaganda. House, "Contrôle, encadrement, surveillance et répression," 154–55.

28. Ministère de l'Intérieur, Circular 430, November 10, 1953. This requirement was revised by Circulaire no. 313 du 22 juillet 1957 to be trimesterly. These reports were meant to capture the general state of the population: broad currents of public opinion, political activity, and social and economic trends.

29. See Rapports du Préfet du Rhône, CHAN, F1CIII 1315, 1316, 1361, and 1367.

30. See Rapport périodique d'information, November 13, 1957 (CHAN, F1CIII 1361).

31. Rapport mensuel, September 21, 1954 (CHAN, F1CIII 1315).

32. Just like Gillot, he cowrote a memoire with his wife, Marthe, on their shared experiences of the war: *Journal d'une longue nuit: Carnet de route de deux Français moyens, 1939–1944.*

33. It is hard to gauge Massenet's involvement with the North African population of Marseille in this short tenure; existing scholarship on Marseille mostly picks up in 1950, though Massenet would have been the prefect in charge of the early response to—and repression of—the broader squatters' movement in the city. See Nasiali, *Native to the Republic*, 23–32.

34. Lyons, *Civilizing Mission in the Metropole*, 62–63 and 168.

35. Pierre's great-grandfather Alexis Massenet (1788–1863) was also Michel's great-great-grandfather. Michel Massenet's work as Délégué à l'action sociale pour les Français musulmans d'Algérie en métropole is mentioned later in this chapter and in chapter 1. The two men's work on Algerian issues in the same time period has led to some confusion over their respective identities.

36. Rapport mensuel, November 19, 1954 (CHAN, F1CIII 1315).

37. Rapport mensuel, May 14, 1954, and August 12, 1954 (CHAN, F1CIII 1315).

38. Rapport mensuel, December 14, 1954 (CHAN, F1CIII 1315).

39. Rapport mensuel, February 21, 1956 (CHAN, F1CIII 1316).

40. Rapport mensuel, January 15, 1957 (CHAN, F1CIII 1316).

41. Rapport mensuel, March 21, 1956 (CHAN, F1CIII 1316).

42. Massenet to Ministre de l'Intérieur, May 20, 1953. For the continuation of the tradition, see further documentation in ADR, 248 W 152.

43. "Une heureuse initiative en faveur de nos amis musulmans" (ADR, 248 W 152).

44. *Le Progrès*, "Le canon sera tiré à Lyon pour le Ramadan," May 14, 1953 (ADR, 248 W 152).

45. As part of his endorsement for Zitouni as a possible Contrôleur social de la main-d'oeuvre nord-africaine in 1955, the prefect called Zitouni a "competent and gifted agent, who has already rendered valuable [*précieux*] services in the domain of social action on behalf of Muslim workers." "Note au sujet des émigrés citoyens Français Musulmans originaires de l'Algérie," June 20, 1955 (ADR, 248 W 90). By 1960, Zitouni was secretary general for the Association lyonnaise pour l'hébergement des Nord-Africains. ALHNA, Réunion du 15 mars 1960, March 15, 1960 (ADR, 248

W 303). In 1961, Zitouni also served as the Lyon delegate for the Société coopérative algérienne d'habitation (ADR, 248 W 251).

46. Zitouni, "Aid-Sehir [sic] 1953," June 13, 1953 (ADR, 248 W 152).

47. Massenet to ben Gharit (Director of the Institut Musulman and the Paris Mosque), March 11, 1955, and Council to David, February 1, 1962 (248 W 152).

48. Rapport mensuel, December 14, 1954.

49. Rapport mensuel, October 15, 1955 (CHAN, F1C111 1316).

50. Rapport mensuel, February 21, 1956 (CHAN, F1C111 1316).

51. Rapport mensuel, April 19, 1957 (CHAN, F1C111 1361).

52. Rapport mensuel, May 28, 1957 (CHAN, F1C111 1361).

53. Rapport mensuel, June 19, 1957 (CHAN, F1C111 1361).

54. Rapport mensuel, October 15, 1955.

55. Massenet to Direction des Renseignements généraux, January 18, 1955, "Recensement des opérations de police contre les nationalistes algériens (MTLD)" (ADR, 437 W 83).

56. Brigade de voie publique, Synthèse de l'activité, 1953 (ADR, 437 W 133) and 1956 (ADR, 437 W 134).

57. Brigade de voie publique, Synthèse de l'activité, 1956 (ADR, 437 W 134).

58. Massenet to Ministère de l'Intérieur, March 13, 1956, "Mesures préventives de contrôle sur les milieux nord-africains" (ADR, 437 W 78).

59. Massenet to Ministère de l'Intérieur, March 13, 1956.

60. In the first report he signed, he saw two main components to public opinion: "1—Concern over the length of the conflict [and] 2—Support for the principle of French sovereignty in Algeria, adapted to local conditions." Rapport périodique d'information, August 10, 1957 (CHAN, F1C111 1361).

61. Rapport périodique d'information, February 14, 1958 (CHAN, F1C111 1367).

62. Rapport périodique d'information, November 13, 1957.

63. Rapport périodique d'information, February 14, 1958.

64. Rapport périodique d'information, February 14, 1958.

65. Counil to Préfet, April 9, 1962, "Diffusion de la brochure 'l'Algérie de demain'" (ADR, 437 W 91). For a discussion of Algerian women in prison in the region, see André, *Femmes dévoilées*, chap. 5. For more on the camp at Thol, see Grosjean, "L'action des conseillers techniques aux Affaires musulmanes."

66. For notes on the creation of the Rhône's SAT forces, see ADR, 248 W 67 and 68.

67. The teams comprised representatives from the prefecture, Lyon's Municipal Hygiene Office, the Association d'entre-aide aux travailleurs nord-africains de la région lyonnaise, the MAN, and the Police des garnis. "Note de l'information relative à l'action psychologique et sociale entreprise dans les milieux musulmans du département du Rhône," August 4, 1958 (ADR, 437 W 91).

68. See reports in ADR, 248 W 74.

69. Brigade de voie publique, Synthèse de l'activité, 1956.

70. See reports in ADR, 248 W 74.

71. On a similarly dismissive attitude toward Algerian nationalism by the Marseille police, see Beaujon, "Controlling the Casbah," 324–26.

72. Beaujon, "Controlling the Casbah," 18 and 76.

73. Bertrand, Rapport trimestriel, July 5, 1961 (ADR, 248 W 74).

74. Bertrand, Rapport trimestriel, October 6, 1961 (ADR, 248 W 74).

75. Bertrand, Rapport trimestriel, July 7, 1962 (ADR, 248 W 74).

76. Bertrand, Rapport trimestriel, January 9, 1962 (ADR, 248 W 74).

77. Bertrand, Rapport mensuel, January 6, 1961 (ADR, 248 W 74). This FLN dominance also meant that the Lyon-Nord office got very few visits from MNA supporters. See Bertrand, Rapport mensuel, February 9, 1961, and Rapport trimestriel, July 5, 1961 (ADR, 248 W 74).

78. Bertrand, Rapport trimestriel, January 9, 1962.

79. Bertrand, Rapport trimestriel, July 1, 1963 (ADR, 248 W 74).

80. Bertrand, Rapport trimestriel, July 1, 1963, and October 1, 1963 (ADR, 248 W 74).

81. Massenet to Ministre de l'Intérieur, October 27, 1955, "Emissions radiophoniques en langue arabe" (ADR, 437 W 78). The Interior Ministry had initiated a survey of North Africans' radio-listening habits in the fall of 1955.

82. "Surveillance des milieux musulmans à Lyon," July 1958 (ADR, 437 W 91).

83. "Note de l'information relative à l'action psychologique et sociale entreprises dans les milieux musulmans du département du Rhône."

84. Préfet to Président de la MAN, et al., June 8, 1960, "Allocution de Monsieur le Président de la République sur l'Algérie" (437 W 91).

85. Counil to Prefect, April 9, 1962, "Diffusion de la brochure 'l'Algérie de demain.'"

86. Président d'Anciens de la 1ère Division Française Libre to Ricard, June 23, 1959 (ADR, 437 W 92).

87. Montaldo to Ricard, June 26, 1959 (ADR, 437 W 92).

88. Busson to Ricard, June 25, 1959 (ADR, 437 W 92).

89. Bonsirven to Ricard, June 28, 1959 (ADR, 437 W 92).

90. Ricard to David, July 4, 1959 (ADR, 437 W 92). Ironically, the prefect here was defending himself against an attack from the left. Camille Vallin, a PCF senator, had lodged a complaint against Ricard on the Senate floor on July 1, accusing him of using overbearing police force to suppress the meeting. Ricard countered that the police were present at the meeting given the threats of a counterdemonstration; the commissioner dissolved the meeting once the two sides started to exchange blows and no police violence ensued. See also Redon, "Réunion publique sur 'le problème algérien et la Paix en Algérie,'" June 26, 1959, and follow-up questioning by Vallin in the Senate, *Journal official* du July 7, 1959 (ADR, 437 W 92).

91. Le Diraison to Ricard, February 8, 1965, "Documentation sur les départements français" (ADR, 759 W 83).

92. Ricard to Le Diraison, March 18, 1965 (ADR, 759 W 83).

93. Synthèse des rapports mensuels des préfets, January 1957 (CHAN, F1CIII 1368).

94. Ministère de l'Intérieur, Circular 54, February 1, 1952, "Affectation dans la Métropole de fonctionnaires spécialisés dans les questions musulmanes" (ADR, 248 W 1). By the end of the program, there were thirty-four CTAMs assigned throughout metropolitan France. Martin's jurisdiction shifted over his years of service to include, at various times, the additional departments of Ain, Drôme, Ardèche, Loire, Haute-Loire, Puy-de-Dôme, Allier, Cantal, Savoie, Haute-Savoie, and Hautes-Alpes. De Barros, "Contours d'un réseau administratif 'algérien.'"

95. On the creation of the communes mixtes, see Christine Mussard, "Réinventer la commune?"

96. For a thorough examination of the creation, practices, and lingering influence of the CTAM, see de Barros, "Contours d'un réseau administratif 'algérien'" and "Des 'Français musulmans d'Algérie' aux 'immigrés.'"

97. CTAM Alfred Martin played the same role in Marseille. Naylor, "'Un âne dans l'ascenseur.'"

98. Belmessous, "Georges Martin," 46–55; and De Barros, "Contours d'un réseau administratif 'algérien,'" 103.

99. De Barros, "Contours d'un réseau administratif 'algérien.'"

100. Belmessous, "Georges Martin."

101. Georges Martin, CV, 1961 (ADR, 248 W 4).

102. De Barros, "Contours d'un réseau administratif 'algérien,'" 109.

103. Martin to Rogues, May 3, 1953 (ADR, 437 W 107). Martin kept in close contact with the Gouvernement général de l'Algérie; he attended meetings in Algiers and sent reports to the secretary general there. The paragraph on migrant surveillance was crossed out in this draft report, suggesting that Martin was not keen on advertising this part of his duties.

104. Belmessous, "Georges Martin," 42.

105. Martin, "Note relative aux affaires sociales Musulmanes du Département du Rhône," October 20, 1957 (ADR, 248 W 2).

106. CTAM Bonfils, "Note d'information sur le service des affaires musulmanes du cabinet du Préfet du Rhône," September 27, 1963 (ADR, 248 W 1).

107. Martin to Lacoste, January 16, 1957 (ADR, 248 W 4).

108. The full Comité de Haut Parrainage included Edouard Herriot (mayor of Lyon), Laurent Bonnevay (President of the Conseil Général du Rhône), Pierre Montel (a national deputy and former minister), Jacques Soustelle (deputy, former minister, and former governor-general of Algeria), Gagnaire (deputy and mayor of Villeurbanne), Voyant (a senator), and Pierre Massenet (Préfet du Rhône and IGAME for the 8e Région). Martin was one of the main administrateurs. Listed as "participation consultative" were representatives from the Maison de l'Afrique du Nord (Mme Massenet), Amitiés africaines, the Association d'Entraide aux travailleurs nord-africains, and the Comité Lyon-Oran. Comité France-Afrique du Nord, Flyer, February 1957 (ADR, 248 W 4).

109. De Barros, "Contours d'un réseau administratif 'algérien,'" 107–8 and 114.

110. De Barros, "Contours d'un réseau administratif 'algérien,'" 114n70.

111. Belmessous, "Georges Martin," 43. Emphasis in original.

112. Martin to Soustelle, July 26, 1957 (ADR, 248 W 4).

113. Conference at Rotary-Club de Lyon Ouest, March 19, 1959, "La population musulmane dans le département du Rhône" (ADR, 248 W 4).

114. De Barros, "Contours d'un réseau administratif 'algérien,'" 113.

115. In an official memo, Martin had explained that this was one of the reasons that private associations played such a central role in migrant welfare issues; association could act as an interface between the state and the migrants (or between migrants and metropolitans) in ways that the state itself could not, given that "Algerians being French citizens, there is no question of creating for them any special administrative services, which would be by nature discriminatory." Martin, "Note relative aux affaires sociales Musulmanes du Département du Rhône."

116. For more on Martin's role in overseeing the SAT services, see Belmessous, "Georges Martin," 43–45.

117. Belmessous, "Georges Martin," 53–55.

118. This was the case to the extent that Martin actively sought to ensure that a contract for a Lyon foyer was granted to MAN and not ALHNA in 1960. De Barros, "Contours d'un réseau administratif 'algérien,'" 102–4.

119. Lombard to Fouconnet, July 29, 1958 (ADR, 437 W 114). Le Page replaced Emile Grand, himself a retired lieutenant-colonel. As the prefect explained, many local associations dealing with North African welfare "have been obliged, for the proper functioning of their social services and for want of competent candidates, to call upon retired civil and military officers who know the Arab language, and Muslim morals and psychology." Préfet to Ministère de l'Intérieur (Direction des Affaires d'Algérie), January 20, 1956 (ADR, 437 W 114).

120. Le Page, CV (ADR, 437 W 114).

121. MAN, Rapport d'activité pour l'année 1953 (ADR, 437 W 107). For additional background on the MAN and its functioning, see André, *Femmes dévoilées*, chap. 3, paras. 12–21.

122. Lyautey to Préfet, June 24, 1955 (ADR, 248 W 170).

123. The Comité Lyautey was founded in Paris to commemorate the work of Marshall Hubert Lyautey, who played a vital role in the French colonization of Morocco.

124. See ADR, 248 W 320.

125. Lombard to Truchot, November 29, 1955 (ADR, 248 W 320).

126. Speaking from his position within Amitiés africaines, Le Page insisted that Lyon faced a housing crisis, that offering more beds to North Africans would support the "bringing together of the two French and Muslim Communities," and that engaging North African veterans would be "particularly fruitful." Le Page to Serieyx, October 11, 1959 (ADR, 248 W 306).

127. Part-Dieu's lengthy deconstruction is discussed at length in chapter 1; the MAN ran a number of the SONACOTRA/L-built foyers to which Part-Dieu residents were sent.

128. See the dossier on the bidonville des Poilus in ADR, 248 W 361. The MTE (as the MAN was renamed in 1965) was similarly involved in the closing of the bidonvilles at 286 Cours Emile Zola in Villeurbanne in 1965–66. See the dossier in ADR, 248 W 362.

129. "Action contre les bidonvilles," April 1967 (ADR, 248 W 358). The MTE shared this honor with the Association Notre Dame des Sans Abri, which is discussed at length in chapter 6.

130. MTE to Gat, December 20, 1967, "Résumé des interventions du Colonel Le Page au Colloque 'France-Algérie" (248 W 89).

131. Le Page to La Gaillarde, March 17, 1959 (ADR, 437 W 114). The Comité des amitiés africaines was founded in 1935; for more on their functioning in the interwar years, see Hassat, "Catering for and Controlling Subject Veterans." Georges Martin also belonged to the local committee.

132. Amitiés africaines Comité de Lyon, Procès verbal de réunion, June 1959 (ADR, 248 W 306).

133. Le Page to Martin, August 4, 1959, "Recrutement de Musulmans ou de Métropolitains pour le 3ème Régiment de Tirailleurs Algériens" (ADR, 437 W 91).

134. Contil to Le Page, April 11, 1962 (ADR, 248 W 84).

135. MAN, Rapport mensuel, July 1965 (ADR, 248 W 12).

136. Bertrand, Rapport mensuel, January 6, 1961. SAT leaders were also present at meetings hosted by Amitiés africaines. Amitiés africaines Comité de Lyon, Procès verbal de réunion, June 12, 1962 (ADR, 248 W 306).

137. This was originally in response to noise complaints, which the MAN actually pushed back on, asserting that their residents were not the loudest in the neighborhood. Le Page, Note de Service, August 12, 1959 (ADR, 248 W 320).

138. Le Page to Martin, October 9, 1961 (ADR, 248 W 320).

139. Rapports de gestion, Année 1960 and 1961 (ADR, 248 W 321).

140. LePage to Martin, May 9, 1962 (ADR, 248 W 306).

141. Le Page to Préfet, June 4, 1962 (ADR, 248 W 320). Monthly reports on entrants to Inkermann had been tracking "dangerous" and "very dangerous" individuals known to the police since March.

142. He also suggested that TV nights could draw local metropolitans into the foyer and cultivate further contact between French and Muslim communities. Le Page to IGAME, February 18, 1960 (ADR, 248 W 320).

143. Le Page, Note de renseignements, "Discours télévisé du Général de Gaulle," undated (ADR, 437 W 91).

144. See Le Page reports for September 16, 1959, November 10, 1959, and June 14, 1960 (ADR, 437 W 91).

145. Le Page, Note de renseignements, September 28, 1959 (ADR, 437 W 91).

146. Le Page, Note de renseignements, undated.

147. MAN memo, April 12, 1961 (ADR, 248 W 243).

148. MAN memo, February 7, 1962 (ADR, 248 W 243).

149. MAN memo, "a/s des inscriptions sur les listes électorales pour le scrutin d'autodétermination," June 12, 1962 (ADR, 248 W 243 and 437 W 95). Days before,

Le Page also passed along information about a planned FLN strike. MAN memo, "a/s interdiction d'aller au travail donnée par le FLN," June 9, 1962 (ADR, 248 W 243).

150. MAN memo, "a/s des manifestations organisées dans les Foyers d'hébergement, à l'occasion de la Fête de l'indépendance algérienne," July 5, 1962 (ADR, 248 W 243).

151. See, for example, Le Page to Martin, October 12, 1962 (ADR, 248 W 243); and MTE, Rapport d'activité, September 1965 (248 W 12).

152. See monthly MTE reports, July–November 1965 (ADR, 248 W 12). Given the expanded migrant population, these reports also include sections for Spanish, Portuguese, and Yugoslav residents, though these are much briefer than the sections on Algerians, Tunisians, and Moroccans.

153. Rapport de gestion (Pressensé), Années 1963 and 1964 (ADR, 248 W 321).

154. Rapport de gestion (Pressensé), Année 1962 (ADR, 248 W 321).

155. MTE, Rapport d'activité, August 1965 (ADR, 248 W 12). Later that fall, North Africans were said to be paying little to no attention to the disappearance of Moroccan anticolonial activist Mehdi Ben Barka; and few eligible Algerians were registered to vote in the upcoming French presidential election. MTE, Rapport d'activité, November 1965 (ADR, 248 W 12).

156. MTE, Rapport d'activité, July 1965 (ADR, 248 W 12).

157. Le Page claimed that Massenet assured him of his confidence and support in a personal meeting. He further emphasized that though the MAN had been part of the "pacification" campaign for Algeria under French rule, they had now "reconverted from a psychological standpoint" and had been saying so in all reports since the summer of 1962. MTE, Rapport d'activité, October 1965 (ADR, 248 W 12).

158. MTE, Rapport d'activité, October 1965.

159. MTE to Gat, December 20, 1967. An earlier version of this discussion can be found in Le Page to SONACOTRA, May 5, 1966 (ADR, 248 W 263).

160. Le Page specified that the prohibition against visitors to the foyers was not a problem, since there was no "right" to have visitors, and residents signed a contract including this rule when they agreed to accept a place. MTE to Gat, December 20, 1967.

161. See chapter 2.

162. Le Page to SLPM, February 23, 1966 (ADR, 248 W 307). For Le Page's response to an earlier iteration of Houël's confrontation with the foyer, see correspondence in ADR, 248 W 306.

163. Gastaut, L'immigration et l'opinion publique en France sous la Ve République, 286.

164. Lewis, Boundaries of the Republic.

165. See chapters 1, 5, and 6.

4. Anti-imperialism

1. 16ème Congrès du Parti communiste français, Saint-Denis, 11–14 mai 1961, Cahiers du Communisme, juin 1961, in Joly, French Communist Party, 51.

2. Joly, French Communist Party, 112. In 1957, all PCF deputies voted against continuing the Special Powers, following a strong public condemnation of the vote by

Jacques Duclos. Duclos, "Réquisitoire contre les pouvoirs spéciaux," Assemblée Nationale, July 16–17, 1957 (AMSD, 18 ACW 24).

3. Evans, *Memory of Resistance*, 15, 137–38.

4. Wall, *French Communism*, 189; and Joly, *French Communist Party*, 115–17.

5. Joly, *French Communist Party*, 50. On the role of anticommunist former members of the Resistance who also opposed French conduct in Algeria on the basis of parallels with Nazi crimes, see Kuby, "From Auschwitz to Algeria," in *Political Survivors*, 193–222.

6. Joly, *French Communist Party*, 128.

7. Wall, *French Communism*, 191.

8. Wall, *French Communism*, 193. Bell and Criddle maintain that "the Soviets scented anti-American possibilities in de Gaulle's foreign policies which the French Communist Party did not." Bell and Criddle, *French Communist Party*, 85.

9. A striking number of those who involved themselves directly with the Algerian independence movement began their activist careers in the PCF, which seems to affirm the level of dissent that existed within the party. See Evans, *Memory of Resistance*. On the *oppositionnels*, who opposed the war more or less openly but did not leave the PCF altogether, see Joly, *French Communist Party*.

10. Pitti, "Renault, la 'forteresse ouvrière' à l'épreuve de la guerre d'Algérie," 137–39.

11. Joly, *French Communist Party*, 132; and Evans, *Memory of Resistance*, 138.

12. In November 1956, Mayor Auguste Gillot spoke to a meeting of local party members on the pressing need "to fight against the fascist fire-bombers"; "denounce the massacres of the Hungarian counter-revolution, directed by those who allied themselves with Hitler, Mussolini and Franco in the great war"; and "affirm our solidarity with the Hungarian workers." Yet Gillot followed this unquestionably pro-Soviet version of the rebellion in Hungary with a firm denunciation of the "dirty war in Algeria"—invoking the phrase the PCF had reserved for the Vietnamese conflict. Discours de Gillot, November 16, 1956, Théâtre municipal (AMSD, 37 AC 2). Gillot had developed a special relationship with his Hungarian colleagues; when he fell ill in 1953, he left Saint-Denis in order to be "cared for in one of the great democratic republics, . . . surrounded by the attention, both medical and affectionate, of this population which moves everyday further and further towards progress." Compterendu de la séance du conseil municipal, May 10, 1953 (AMSD, 17 ACW 38).

13. The only evidence of disagreement conserved by the city (though it is unlikely that the municipality would have kept many records of tangles with the party) came in correspondence over an article printed by *Saint-Denis Républicain* in 1950, under the name Ben-Younès. Gillot soon received a letter from André Marty, one of the PCF's leaders and a deputy to the National Assembly, declaring that the article was "very dangerous" and demanding that a follow-up article right the mistakes. "Les ouvriers nord-africains et la lutte pour la paix." See *Saint-Denis Républicain*, May 26, 1950; and Marty to Gillot, June 13, 1950 (AMSD, 37 AC 16). For a lengthier discussion of this incident, see Byrnes, "French like Us?," 98–100. On similar cases of Dionysien opposition to PCF policies before World War II, see Brunet, *Saint-Denis*, 442–43.

14. See Conseil municipal, "Voeu concernant les libertés en Algérie et le logement des Nord-Africains venant travailler en France," October 4, 1946 (AMSD, 10 S 89), also discussed in chapter 2.

15. See various leaflets, including "Travailleurs algériens: Pour qui nous prend-on à Moscou?" (AMSD, 37 AC 16).

16. In his history of Saint-Denis, Jean-Paul Brunet records numerous attempts by local officials to intervene in global politics, beginning with vehement turn-of-the-century pacifism and devotion to an internationalist platform. Brunet, *Saint-Denis*, 68–71.

17. Abdelkrim El Khattabi led a rebellion against Spanish colonial occupation in northern Morocco; the French intervened, fearful that the unrest would spread into their Moroccan territories. In May 1924, Jacques Doriot—then representing Saint-Denis in the National Assembly—wrote to Abdelkrim on behalf of the party and the Jeunesses communistes (JC), congratulating him on his successes against the Spanish army and calling on him to further "the fight against all imperialists, including the French, until the complete liberation of Moroccan soil." Brunet, *Saint-Denis*, 268–72. For a more general view of Doriot's anti-imperialism in the mid-1920s, see Brunet, *Jacques Doriot*, 53–70. Doriot, of course, is now remembered far less for his anticolonialism than for his rupture with the PCF and founding of the fascist Parti Populaire Français (PPF); he became a convinced collaborator with Nazi occupation forces after 1940, bound in part through his own virulent antisemitism.

18. Besides opposing the war in Morocco, the PCF focused on official recognition of the Soviet Union and the evacuation of the Ruhr Valley. Brunet, *Saint-Denis*, 272. Doriot was a pivotal figure in realigning the PCF toward a Bolshevized and explicitly anticolonial party. Drew, *We Are No Longer in France*, 37.

19. During this period, the Spanish neighborhood in the southern outskirts of Saint-Denis gained the name "Little Spain." See Lillo, *La petite Espagne*.

20. Lillo, *La petite Espagne*, 89–92. Lillo notes that Doriot used this program to garner public support in his fight to oppose Maurice Thorez within the PCF. This strategy met with some success; once Doriot split openly with the central committee (in the summer of 1934), many Spanish Communists remained loyal to him. Later, as the PCF became the champion for Spanish Republicanism during the Civil War, Doriot's PPF threatened opponents with the suspension of unemployment payments. Lillo, *La petite Espagne*, 94 and 99.

21. Lillo, *La petite Espagne*, 136.

22. 1,665 Dionysiens signed the municipality's petition calling for an "end to the crimes of Francoism" and demanding that the French government "suspend all diplomatic relations with Spain so long as anti-Francoist patriots are threatened with death, so long as the regime does not respect the elemental liberties of Man and Citizen contained in the international Helsinki Agreement." Petition, "Halte aux crimes du Franquisme" (AMSD, 37 AC 10). This petition mirrored the format of earlier petitions and ballots used by the Movement for Peace during the Algerian Conflict. "Vote," Mouvement de la Paix (AMSD, 37 AC 18).

23. Lillo, *La petite Espagne*, 137. Bacqué and Fol likewise cite the Spanish [Civil] War as a "significant influence on the political history of the city." Bacqué and Fol, *Le devenir*, 35.

24. One might further expand this argument to the Dionysien inclusion of their Portuguese residents and the resulting activism against Salazar's regime; the municipality advocated amnesty for all Portuguese political prisoners and exiles and actively participated in the campaign against the use of torture by the Portuguese government (see AMSD, 18 ACW 23). For an excellent examination of Portuguese migration to the Parisian suburbs, see Volovitch-Tavares, *Portugais à Champigny*.

25. In the Rhône, Prefect Massenet's willingness to forsake French Indochina (see chapter 3)—in such contrast with his insistence that Algeria remain French—might likewise be grounded in a lack of experience with Vietnamese migrants to the Lyon region (relative to North Africans).

26. Auguste Gillot, "Schéma de discours aux travailleurs algériens en France" (AMSD, 37 AC 16).

27. On May 8, 1945, in the Algerian town of Sétif, a parade celebrating the Nazi surrender brought North African marchers into conflict with local law enforcement. The next five days witnessed attacks on European settlers in the region. The French attempt to reassert control was disproportionately violent, but the number killed in their pacification campaign has been hotly debated. Gillot's figure of forty thousand is at the high end of the spectrum, aligning him with anticolonialist forces.

28. Gillot termed Charles de Gaulle a "fascist adventurer" and "frenzied colonialist," with his "friend" Phillippe Pétain. Pétain was hailed after World War I as the "savior of Verdun" but was convicted of treason following his collaboration with the Nazis as head of the Vichy government (de Gaulle commuted his sentence to life in prison). Gillot made a point of including Pétain's role as commander during the Rif War, leaving no variable out of his equation of fascism and colonialism.

29. See chapter 2.

30. Martin Evans identifies "war" as one of the five major "keywords" of the resistance to the Algerian War. Evans, *Memory of Resistance*, 11–23.

31. Evans, *Memory of Resistance*, 181. Evans provides an excerpt of his interview with Mourad Oussedik, one of the defense lawyers in the 1960 trial of members of the Jeanson network (a group of French militants who worked closely with the FLN), who described an alternative resistance vocabulary: "'War' rather than 'pacification' and 'police operations,' 'kidnappings,' 'disappearances,' 'prisoners of war,' 'solidarity,' . . . these were the keywords." Evans, *Memory of Resistance*, 182.

32. Evans, *Memory of Resistance*, 189.

33. AHPP, GA S 12. In 1953 and 1954, reports cited municipal mobilization against the War in Indochina. These actions would have been influential in forming the Dionysien response to events in Algeria, but it is worth noting that the level of activity during the Algerian War was significantly higher and attracted a great deal more energy from the city officials.

34. AMSD, 18 ACW 33.

35. AMSD, 10 S 64.

36. For example, in 1958, one young man wrote to Gillot to complain that soldiers were forced to attend Mass during a funeral for a fellow serviceman in Strasbourg. This was particularly troubling, as "the republican—and therefore: secular—army prevents the soldiers of the Saint-Denis contingent from listening to the—republican and secular—mayor, but obliges these same soldiers to listen to the priest of Strasbourg!" Clearly Gillot and his officers had won some loyalty among the soldiers in their community. Equally clear was the distrust of army officers for the municipality and its possible influence on conscripts. Letter to Gillot, March 10, 1958 (AMSD, 50 ACW 32).

37. L'Aurore, "Appels à la désobéissance," March 6, 1956 (AMSD, 50 ACW 32). The PCF's position on military service was mixed. Georges Lavau calls the party "outspoken" in its opposition to desertion and insubordination. Lavau, "PCF, the State and Revolution," 95. However, the PCF strongly supported a group of airmen who locked themselves in their barracks to protest the war in 1955 (three days of fighting with riot police ensued). See Fysh and Wolfreys, Politics of Racism in France, 28.

38. As of August 1961, twenty-five Dionysien soldiers had been killed in Algeria (AMSD, 50 ACW 32). In an intriguing parallel, the municipality kept a similar list of victims of internecine Algerian violence. Memo, "Algériens décédés par attentat," December 16, 1957 (AMSD, 37 AC 17).

39. Police memo, "Obsèques à Saint-Denis," April 6, 1956 (AHPP, GA S 12).

40. Police memo, "Obsèques du soldat," May 26, 1956 (AHPP, GA S 12). Gillot was not the only local official to turn funeral orations into appeals for action. Fernand Grenier, PCF deputy for Saint-Denis (and member of the PCF's central committee), joined Gillot at a May 1957 funeral, where both demanded an end to the war. Police memo, "Obsèques du soldat," May 24, 1957 (AHPP, GA S 12). In May 1958, yet another member of the municipal council asserted the need to bring peace to Algeria, expressing the fear that the war could seep into both Morocco and Tunisia. Police memo, "Obsèques à Saint-Denis," May 23, 1958 (AHPP, GA S 12).

41. Conseil municipal, "Séance extraordinaire du 30 mai 1961" (AMSD, 17 ACW 94).

42. Conseil municipal, "Séance extraordinaire du 30 mai 1961."

43. Miscellaneous notes on Conseil municipal, "Séance extraordinaire du 30 mai 1961."

44. Conseil municipal, "Séance extraordinaire du 30 mai 1961."

45. Letter from E. Pelletier to Maire, July 30, 1956, "Annulation de délibération" (AMSD, 17 ACW 94).

46. La voix des communaux, March 1957 (AHPP, GA S 12).

47. La voix des communaux, March 1957.

48. AMSD, 18 ACW 24.

49. The forty-six delegations that presented signatures for petitions included twenty-eight companies (Aster, EDF, SIFA_SAF, Wagons-Lits, Paris-Outreau, Hotchkiss, Roser, Francolor, Aubagnac, Usine A Gaz Nord, Usine A Gaz Cornillon, Ateliers Modernes de Cartonnage, Jeumont, RATP, Centre d'Apprentissage rue E. Renan, Chantiers de

l'Atalntique, Sulzer, Renault, Bardin, BDR, Hôpital, Verrerie de la Plaine, Christofle, PTT, Comité de Paix des Enseignants, Comité de Paix Spiros, Comité de Paix SAMAS, Comité de Paix des Communaux); eleven neighborhood committees (Comité de Paix de la Cité Fabien, Comité de Paix de la Cité Langevin, Comité de Paix de la Cité P. Eluard, Comité de Paix du Quartier Parmentier, Comité de Paix du Quartier République, Comité de Paix du Quartier Champ de Courses, Comité de Paix du Quartier Francs-Moisins, Comité de Paix du Quartier Pleyel, Quartier Vieux Saint-Denis, Quartier de l'Avenue de Stalingrad, Quartier Plaine Saint-Denis); and seven local organizations (Les Bretons de Saint-Denis, Les Prisonniers de Guerre de Saint-Denis, Section de Saint-Denis de la FNDIRP, Foyer UJFF de la Cité Barbusse [which sent six sisters and fiancées of soldiers as their delegates], UJCF Langevin-Jaurès, UFF Parmentier, UFF Pleyel). Four more neighborhood committees and fifteen businesses sent petitions, without delegations. "Liste des résolutions et pétitions déposées à l'Hôtel de Ville de SD le vendredi 25 Janvier 1957 dans le cadre de la semaine d'action pour la paix en Algérie" (AMSD, 18 ACW 25).

50. Guenne, "Compte rendu relatif à la physionomie de la circonscription," November 5, 1957 (AHPP, GA S 12).

51. Jean Bellanger, "Saint-Denis se souvient du 17 octobre 1961," Mairie de Saint-Denis, October 17, 1997. *Bicot* is a racial slur used to describe an individual of Arab or North African origin.

52. For a glimpse at how Gillot and the Dionysien municipality were perceived by the Far Right—especially by pro-French-Algeria soldiers—see *Djebel*, "Soirée scandaleuse à Saint-Denis," July–August 1958 (AHPP, HA 106).

53. Extracts from letter by Gillot to soldiers, May 8, 1961 (AMSD, 10 S 64).

54. "Appel aux anciens résistants" (AMSD, 10 S 64).

55. *Saint-Denis Républicain*, front page photograph, April 28, 1961 (AMSD, 10 S 64).

56. Gillot to Mères des soldats, March 29, 1962 (AMSD, 17 AC 3).

57. Letter to President de Gaulle, March 31, 1962 (AMSD, 17 AC 3).

58. Conseil municipal, "Voeu concernant les libertés en Algérie et le logement des Nord-Africains venant travailler en France," October 4, 1946 (AMSD, 10 S 89). The official vote described Messali Hadj as a "resistant of the first hour, who was deported by the Vichyists." Special thanks to my former student Meili Criezis for her help with the research on this question of city officials' engagement with specific nationalist groups.

59. Gillot, "Schéma de discours aux travailleurs algériens en France."

60. "Appel de Messali Hadj au peuple français," December 13, 1955 (AMSD, 18 ACW 24). That same year, the municipality held onto an MNA statement asserting their innocence in a well-publicized attack on a café-hotel owner in the city. Fontenis, "Communiqué du MNA," *Le libertaire*, Xe, June 9, 1955 (AMSD, 37 AC 17). Fontenis accused the victim of the attacks of being a police informant and asserted the incident was orchestrated by the police. The French press, presumably following police reports, described the attack as part of the "guerre des cafés" between the MNA and FLN, though some mentioned the victim's "Francophile sentiments" as a source of tension with his

"coreligionists." See *Le Monde*, June 1, 1955, "Un hôtelier nord-africain est attaqué"; and *France-Soir*, June 1, 1955, "Le café-hôtel assailli par les Nord-Africains gardé par la police" (AMSD, 37 AC 17), among others.

61. *L'Humanité*, "Le parti communiste algérien," June 13, 1956 (AMSD, 18 ACW 25). The following year, the PCA published a defense of the FLN to counter a "propaganda campaign" against FLN violence in Melouza. Bachir Hadj Ali, "Lettre d'Algérie," June 12, 1957 (AMSD, 18 ACW 24). As the war came to an end, the PCA asserted in their paper *L'avenir* that "during the entire war, the PCA, which has maintained its position as an independent organization, has resolutely supported the anti-imperial platform of the FLN and the Gouvernement provisoire de la République algérienne (GPRA), both within Algeria and abroad." *L'avenir*, no. 35, June–July 1962 (AMSD, 18 ACW 25). For a detailed examination of the PCA's role in the Algerian nationalist struggle, see Drew, *We Are No Longer in France*.

62. *L'Humanité*, "Ferhat Abbas au peuple algérien," December 17, 1960 (AMSD, 18 ACW 25). Gillot also circled the rallying cry at the end: "Vive le peuple algérien! Vive la République algérienne! Vive l'Algérie indépendante!"

63. *L'Humanité*, "Que représente Messali Hadj?," April 9, 1961 (AMSD, 18 ACW 25); and Fédération de France du Parti Communiste Algérien, "Aux pressions et aux agressions les communistes Algériens répondront en redoublant d'efforts pour l'union du peuple algérien et la démocratie réelle," June 20, 1962 (AMSD, 18 ACW 24).

64. "Conférence des officiers du SAT: Conclusions," October 4, 1962 (AHPP, HA 61).

65. In 1956, police maps of FLN and MNA perceptions of territory they controlled showed both groups claiming the center of Saint-Denis as their own and the outskirts of the city as their rival's (AHPP, HA 29). This suggests that their competition was intense and strength nearly equal in the city. By 1957, police maps show the MNA with control of the center and the FLN with most of the rest of the city (AHPP, HA 24).

66. See dossier, "Physionomie," AHPP, GA S 12.

67. Guenne, "Compte rendu relatif à la physionomie de la circonscription," October 3, 1959 (AHPP, GA S 12).

68. See, in particular, Guenne, "Compte rendu relatif à la physionomie de la circonscription," April 4, 1959, and May 4, 1959 (AHPP, GA S 12).

69. For example, a 1957 police report mentions "numerous attacks" and "numerous investigations" linked to extortion letters from "the MNA, the FLN, or the 'Armée de Libération Algérienne,'" lumping all the groups together. Guenne, "Rapport mensuel d'activité," June 2, 1957 (AHPP, GA S 12). Emmanuel Blanchard explains, "Caught between reciprocal and contradictory solicitations from the FLN and MNA, the Algerians of Paris were in fact the target for police who did not hesitate to pursue even simple contributors to the nationalist movements." Blanchard, "Police judiciaire et pratiques d'exception pendant la guerre d'Algérie." On the press side, a set of articles about an attack on a café in Saint-Denis mentions only "North Africans"—and occasionally "terrorists" (see AMSD, 37 AC 17).

70. Gillot to Taleb, October 30, 1964 (AMSD, 18 ACW 24).

71. The socialists who came to power in 1892 saw the police as a force for work-ers' oppression (they were often called to break up strikes and demonstrations) and repeatedly accused them of causing more violent incidents than they prevented. The municipality used what little budgetary power they had to reduce available funds and even attempted to evict the police from their offices in municipal buildings. In June 1893, the municipal council ran a poster campaign calling upon responsi-ble citizens "to arm themselves with revolvers to oppose the continual aggressions by the police." Brunet, *Saint-Denis*, 64–68. For a broader look at socialist munici-palities' confrontations with local police, see Scott, "Mayors versus Police Chiefs."

72. One hundred twenty-three Algerian workers were taken from their beds in a Gennevilliers foyer and kept overnight in an Asnières garage with armed guards. Gillot and his colleagues denounced this "operation of a racist character" and voiced their concern that these violent incidents might spread. Conseil général de la Seine, Bulletin municipal official, February 5, 1952 (AMSD, 37 AC 17). Oddly, Waldeck de l'Huillier, the PCF mayor of Gennevilliers, was not one of the authors of this par-ticular question.

73. Conseil général de la Seine, Bulletin municipal official, April 28, 1952; and *L'Humanité*, "Les policiers de Baylot arrêtent et menacent les Algériens de Saint-Denis," April 25, 1952 (AMSD, 37 AC 16).

74. The summer had seen an upswing in violence in the Algerian neighborhoods of Saint-Denis, including a nationally reported attack by a crowd of two hundred on a café whose owner refused to bow to nationalist racketeering. See press clippings, May 31 and June 1, 1955 (AMSD, 37 AC 17).

75. *L'Humanité*, "Extension des opérations policières contre les travailleurs algéri-ens de la Région Parisienne," August 8, 1955; and *La patriote de Nice et du Sud-Est*, "Des CRS à Saint-Denis," August 9, 1955 (AMSD, 37 AC 17).

76. SDR, "Nous dira-t-on comment a été tué Guy Prestot?," July 23, 1959, in "A.S. d'un tract édité par les sections de Saint-Denis, de Stains, de Villeneuve et de Pier-refitte du Parti Communiste" (AHPP, GA S 12).

77. PCF tract, "Des tués dans nos rues: Pourquoi?," July 1959 (AHPP, GA S 12).

78. SDR, "La cité Danièle-Casanova investie," September 22, 1961 (AMSD, 10 S 121). This article discussed popular indignation after police raids on three households, made specific note of the targeted men's work and family situations (in one case, the wife was also detained, leaving the children alone), then denounced the war in Algeria and the conduct of OAS bombers and characterized such police actions as a worrying descent into fascism.

79. The decree instructed FMAS to stay out of the streets from 8:30 p.m. to 5:30 a.m. (unless they received documents exempting them for purposes of their work) and to travel alone and avoid small groups; cafés frequented by Algerians were to close at 7:00 p.m. *L'Humanité*, "Couvre-feu pour les Algériens à Paris et en banlieue," Octo-ber 6, 1961 (AMSD, 10 S 121).

80. Allegations of a police cover-up date from the event itself. Attention to this event was renewed in 1997 when Papon was placed on trial for crimes against humanity—he

was found guilty of organizing the deportation of 1,700 Jews from Bordeaux dur-ing the Vichy period—and his role in the repression of Algerians in Paris and in orchestrating the violence of October 17 came to light. See Gildea, *France since 1945*.

81. Initial police reports mentioned only a couple of deaths; critics have charged more than three hundred. Careful research by Jim House and Neil MacMaster set-tles around 120. House and MacMaster, *Paris 1961*, 167.

82. CMSD, "Voeu demandant le règlement pacifique du problème algérien et des mesures énergiques contre les plastiqueurs," November 3, 1961 (AMSD, 37 AC 17).

83. Conseil général de la Seine, Bulletin municipal official, November 7, 1961 (AMSD, 10 S 121). Much of the municipal language echoed an FLN declaration they had received and kept, including the conclusion that current police policies were reminiscent of those used by collaborators under the Nazi regime. "Déclaration du FLN sur la répression et les mesures policières dans la région parisienne," Octo-ber 17, 1961 (AMSD, 10 S 235).

84. "Un groupe de policiers républicains déclarent," October 31, 1961 (AMSD, 10 S 121). Michel Massenet (Délégué aux affaires sociales des FMAS en métropole) likewise alerted Louis Joxe (Secrétaire d'Etat aux affaires algériennes) to his con-cerns that "events in the Paris region"—that is, the violent repression following the October 17, 1961, demonstration—might impact the future treatment of European Algerians in a new Algerian state unless significant progress was made "to improve migrants' social condition." Viet, *La France immigrée*, 212–13.

85. SDR, "Déclaration du Bureau Politique du Parti Communiste Français après la journée sanglante du 17 octobre," October 20, 1961 (AMSD, 10 S 121).

86. Sections PCF de Saint-Denis, "Travailleurs et habitants de Saint-Denis: Les Communistes vous appellent à l'union et à l'action," October 3, 1961 (AMSD, 10 S 121).

87. Evans, *Memory of Resistance*, 176.

88. Hazemann, note to Persancier, October 25, 1961 (AMSD, 37 AC 17). That the two men had not actually been part of the demonstration but had been arrested before-hand did not dampen the effort to locate them. The request emphasized that one of the men was a father of five with a sixth to arrive soon; city officials were assured that "fathers of large families were kept in France" and not deported to Algeria. Her-fuy to Vialla, October 1961 (AMSD, 37 AC 17).

89. Gillot to Vialla, November 15, 1961 (AMSD, 37 AC 17).

90. As a nod to growing public pressure, Guy Mollet created the commission in 1957 to investigate French military policies in Algeria. For a discussion of their lack-luster accomplishments, see Branche, "La commission de sauvegarde pendant la guerre d'Algérie." The SPF, a social welfare NGO with close ties to the PCF, followed the campaign of Algerian detainment closely, contacting authorities on behalf of individuals and running publicity campaigns that listed detained men and provided instructions on what citizens should do if "in your city, in your neighborhood, your factory, an Algerian is arrested and taken to Vincennes or an internment camp." The SPF sought to create an information network linking the Interior Ministry, the Commission de sauvegarde des libertés, municipal and departmental authorities,

deputies and senators, the International Red Cross, and above all, the population. SPF, "Le Secours Populaire vous dit toute la vérité sous le martyre des travailleurs algériens résidents en France," *La défense*, no. 446, December 1961 (AMSD, 10 S 121).

91. Didier et al. to Gillot, November 14, 1961 (AMSD, 37 AC 17).

92. Maire to Ministère de l'Intérieur, December 1, 1961 (AMSD, 37 AC 17).

93. Registre des délibérations, Bureau d'aide sociale de Saint-Denis, October 31, 1961 (AMSD, 37 AC 17).

94. Conseil général de la Seine, Bulletin municipal official, March 9, 1962, (AMSD, 37 AC 17). The police prefect responded that all "Français Musulmans d'Algérie" detained more than twenty-four hours did in fact receive certificates for social security benefits and that the police themselves often appealed directly to employers to take back those workers detained only for verification purposes.

95. Conseil général de la Seine, Bulletin municipal official, August 25, 1962 (AMSD, 37 AC 17). Here the prefect for the Seine denied that any orders were given to the detriment of Algerians, maintaining that many of those without work had sought new positions instead of returning to their previous employment, that nearly all were eligible for unemployment benefits, and that considerable attention was given to those few who found neither work nor aid.

96. Conseil général de la Seine, Bulletin municipal official, May 15, 1962 (AMSD, 37 AC 17).

97. Séance du Conseil municipal, November 3, 1961 (AMSD, 37 AC 17).

98. Séance du Conseil municipal, May 28, 1962 (AMSD, 37 AC 17).

99. Séance du Conseil municipal, June 28, 1963 (AMSD, 37 AC 17).

100. *L'Humanité*, "Au dossier de 'l'affaire des harkis' deux Algériens témoignent," August 7, 1961 (AMSD, 10 S 121). The police prefect had warned the Interior Minister in March of an impending PCF campaign against the FPA: "In order to permit Muslim workers, newly recruited by the FLN, to one day brandish the *fellagh* flag in Paris. Thus [the PCF] will have thereafter a monopoly of influence over this popular force." Préfet de police to Ministre de l'Intérieur, "Au sujet de la campagne menée contre la Force de Police Auxiliaire," March 16, 1961 (AHPP, HA 88). *Fellagh* (or *fellah*) is Arabic for "laborer" or "peasant."

101. Séance du Conseil municipal, September 15, 1961 (AMSD, 10 S 121). For biographies of the senators, see Le Sénat, March 15, 2023, https://www.senat.fr/anciens-senateurs-5eme-republique/senatl.html.

102. Gillot to Préfet de police, August 17, 1961 (AHPP, HA 88 and AMSD, 10 S 121).

103. While the prefect deemed no response to be necessary, he instructed his office to follow the municipal council's actions in order to annul any further resolutions.

104. Séance du Conseil municipal, September 15, 1961 (AMSD, 10 S 121 and 37 AC 17).

105. Conseil général de la Seine, Bulletin municipal official, September 18, 1961 (AHPP, HA 68). Papon rejected Gillot's version of these events, claiming that no Algerian with the initials Gillot provided had been taken that evening. His office assumed the appeal to the General Council was a mere publicity stunt, noting that a direct letter to the prefect would have been more efficient, though less visible to the public.

106. Séance du Conseil municipal, September 15, 1961 (AMSD, 10 S 121 and 37 AC 17).

107. Conseil général de la Seine, Bulletin municipal official, October 9, 1961 (AMSD, 37 AC 17).

108. Gillot to Benedetti, October 10, 1961 (AMSD, 10 S 121). For the police version of events, see Préfecture de police, "Manifestation organisée en signe de protestation contre la présence de F.P.A. à Saint-Denis," October 2, 1961 (AP, PEROTIN 101/78/1).

109. Benedetti to Gillot, October 7, 1961 (AMSD, 10 S 121).

110. Papon to Benedetti, "Comportement de la Municipalité de Saint-Denis," October 5, 1961 (AP, PEROTIN 101/78/1, "Events of 2 Oct").

111. "La terreur ne règnera pas à St-Denis," October 3, 1961 (AMSD, 10 S 121).

112. *Saint-Denis Républicain*, "Pour la défense de nos libertés," October 6, 1961 (AMSD, 10 S 121).

113. See chapter 2 for a discussion of Benhamou's background.

114. Correspondence between Papon and Benedetti, October 5, 1961, "Comportement de la Municipalité de Saint-Denis"; and Benedetti's response, October 7, 1961 (AP, PEROTIN 101/78/1). Papon solicited the Seine prefect, Jean Benedetti, for one-month suspensions for Gillot, Benhamou, and Persancier as well as for support for his request to the Interior Ministry to extend these to three months. Benedetti initially sided with Papon, demanding that Gillot and his deputies account for their actions. Following their responses, Papon protested, "The elected officials from Saint-Denis are trying to foist responsibility for the incidents of 2 October 1961 onto the police, who are implicitly accused of being at the origin of all the disorder. Far from excusing these magistrates, such affirmations only condemn them further."

115. Letters from Gillot, Benahamou, and Persancier to Benedetti, October 10, 1961 (AP, PEROTIN 101/78/1). Gillot's letter also appears in AMSD, 10 S 121.

116. Gillot to Bernedetti, October 10, 1961 (AP, PEROTIN 101/78/1).

117. Ministère de l'Intérieur to Benedetti, November 16, 1961 (AP, PEROTIN 101/78/1). Ironically, the Dionysiens' savior proved to be none other than Charles de Gaulle: in view of the president's upcoming visit to the banlieues, the Seine prefect alerted the interior minister that although he believed a suspension to be "wholly justified," he thought it unwise to alienate—or infuriate—further a man of Gillot's standing as "mayor of the largest Communist city in the Department, a General Councillor besides, who enjoys preponderant influence among his Communist colleagues in the communes of the Seine." Letter from Benedetti to the Ministre de l'Intérieur, November 20, 1961 (AP, PEROTIN 101/78/1).

118. Conseil général de la Seine, Bulletin municipal official, February 15, 1962 (AMSD, 37 AC 17 and 10 S 121).

119. Desmedt, Géhel, and Bourgeois to Maire, April 30, 1957, cc. Préfet de la Seine (AP, PEROTIN 101/78/1–19).

120. Municipal council records show hardly any attention paid to questions of war or imperialism. Two votes called for a general amnesty for antiwar activists (1962) and for releasing young soldiers condemned for their refusal to fight in Algeria

(1960). See Conseil municipal, July 12, 1960, and June 14, 1962 (AMVén, Délibérations du Conseil municipal).

121. Massenet to Ministre de l'Intérieur, May 7, 1956, "Incidents . . . à l'occasion d'une conférence sur l'Algérie" (ADR, 437 W 78). The Comité d'action de défense de l'Algérie française had planned an event at the city hall of Lyon's sixth district, for which a number of Left and Far Left groups had organized a counterprotest. The event was canceled at the last moment; while a number of protestors stayed to continue their demonstration, Dupic left as soon as the cancelation was announced. See also Commissaire Central, "Interventions du Service d'ordre," May 4, 1956 (ADR, 437 W 78).

122. Cot and Cagne wrote to the Interior Minister in 1951, for example, to complain about the mistreatment of Algerians in Lyon at the hands of the police and demand immediate measures to provide better housing for North African migrants. Cot and Cagne to Ministre de l'Intérieur, September 22, 1951 (ADR, 437 W 78). Cot, who was a member of the Union progressiste and a former minister of the Popular Front government, spoke at a protest in 1956 in terms that sounded more like Gillot's, calling Algerians "brothers" and "equals" deserving of their own 1789. Renseignements généraux, May 28, 1956, "Rassemblement lyonnais du Mouvement de la Paix" (ADR, 437 W 78).

123. For a look at the Mouvement de la Paix elsewhere in France, see Boëldieu, "Le Mouvement de la Paix dans la Sarthe."

124. Renseignements généraux, "Conférence fédérale du Rhône du PCF—Villeurbanne—2 & 3 Juin 1956" (ADR, 668 W 88). Mayor Louis Dupic was part of the Bureau Fédéral at this time, as was future mayor Marcel Houël (who was then a member of Villeurbanne's municipal council). Only one speaker made overt reference to Algerian nationalism and the idea that "Algeria is not France"; the consensus for this meeting was simply for a ceasefire and negotiations.

125. Drogue cited, in particular, Vénissieux municipal councillor Sylvestre as a socialist who was also a member of the Comité pour la Paix en Algérie.

126. Ministre de l'Intérieur to Préfet, October 24, 1960, "A l'appel du Mouvement de la Paix" (ADR, 437 W 92). CGT activists at the Berliet factory in Vénissieux figured prominently in the planning and execution of a work stoppage on October 27 (about 970 workers there took part). Nineteen thousand workers stopped work across the region, but only about 1,200 joined the protest in Lyon that evening. Renseignements généraux, October 28, 1960, "Journée pour la Paix en Algérie du 27 Octobre 1960" (ADR, 437 W 92).

127. This is not to discount the harm that was also done to migrants in this period: massive internment, violence, torture, and even death, as in the harsh repression of the October 1961 demonstration in Paris. Indeed, I intend not to weigh the benefits of state activism against the injuries perpetrated against Algerians but rather to raise the troubling links that exist between these two state agendas and emphasize that this tension lies at the foundation of French migrant policy.

128. The relationship between local communists and "gauchistes" is detailed in chapter 6.

5. Profit

1. "Rapport de MM. Laroque et Ollive, auditeurs au Conseil d'État sur la main-d'oeuvre nord-africaine," March 1938 (AHC, JU 11), 273.

2. "Rapport de MM. Laroque et Ollive," March 1938, 55–56, 165.

3. Simoneau to Ministère de la Reconstruction et de l'Urbanisme, April 3, 1952, "Construction d'une société immobilière en vue de la construction de centres d'hébergement pour les travailleurs musulmans nord-africains" (CHAN, F1a 5122).

4. "Enquête sociale sur les conditions d'emploi et de logement offertes aux travailleurs Musulmans originaires d'Algérie: Dans l'agglomération lyonnaise et le département du Rhône," January 1, 1960 (ADR, 248 W 91).

5. "Situation générale des travailleurs nord-africains dans le département du Rhône," October 30, 1947 (ADR, 437 W 83).

6. Martin to Ministre de l'Intérieur, March 26, 1953, "Recensement des travailleurs musulmans dans la 8e Région" (CHAN, F1a 5046).

7. Commission consultative nationale pour l'étude des questions nord-africaines, Compte rendu de la réunion, April 5, 1955 (CHAN, F1a 5043).

8. Service des renseignements généraux du Rhône, March 15, 1949, "AS de l'immigration nord-africaine" (ADR, 437 W 82).

9. Many worked in schools and hospitals; others worked as prostitutes. Wives often took up work, at least temporarily, when their husbands were imprisoned for political activity. See André, *Femmes dévoilées*, chaps. 2 and 4. Postindependence, North African girls who grew up in the cités de transit seemed more likely to develop technical expertise and use education as a means for gaining higher salaries. See Pétonnet, *Ces gens-là*, 179.

10. Service des renseignements généraux du Rhône, March 15, 1949, "AS de l'immigration nord-africaine."

11. Commission consultative nationale pour l'étude des questions nord-africaines, April 5, 1955. Note that in the original, *propreté* could signal both physical hygiene and moral rectitude. This comment was made in the context of discussing renovations to the Part-Dieu center that overcame the facility's original problems of "gigantism."

12. Centre d'hébergement nord-africain, "Rapport sur la situation des travailleurs nord-africains au centre de la Part-Dieu," 1949 (ADR, 437 W 78). Part-Dieu's history is addressed at greater length in chapter 1.

13. Centre d'hébergement nord-africain, "Subventions," undated (ADR, 437 W 83).

14. AFNA, "Foyer de Saint-Denis: Règlement Intérieur," May 31, 1954 (CHAN, F1a 5105).

15. "Enquête sociale sur les conditions d'emploi et de logement offertes aux travailleurs Musulmans originaires d'Algérie," January 1, 1960. For a detailed look at Berliet's employment of North Africans in 1974, see Grillo, *Ideologies and Institutions in Urban France*, 39–41.

16. "Ouvrier spécialisé" and not "manœuvre." Rotary Club Lyon-Est, "Le problème des Nord-Africains," March 16, 1955 (ADR, 437 W 107).

17. Massenet to Ministre de l'Intérieur, February 5, 1952, "Projet de création d'un centre d'hébergement pour les Nord-Africains aux usines Berliet" (ADR, 437 W 78). In 1954, Berliet employed a total of 711 North Africans: 344 unskilled workers, 336 specialized workers, and 31 skilled workers. Établissements Berliet, "Répartition qualitative de la main-d'oeuvre nord-africaine," October 29, 1954 (ADR, 248 W 284).

18. Massenet to Ministre de l'Intérieur, February 5, 1952; and Ministre de l'Intérieur to Massenet, December 21, 1951 (ADR, 437 W 78).

19. In 1952, the mayor's office cited a petition from the neighborhood worrying about the difficulties in proper police surveillance for the area and the proximity of the proposed buildings to local schoolchildren's regular route. Moreover, the mayor asserted, "The suspicion surrounding North Africans is entirely justified. It is enough to read the Lyon newspapers to discover their subversive activity in the Lyon region—thefts, rapes, armed assaults, etc." The political situation in North Africa itself only heightened his resistance. Maire to Bornarel, December 13, 1952, "Construction d'un cantonnement de Nord-Africains à St-Priest" (ADR, 248 W 284). By 1954, the city was no longer "systematically opposed" to the project but still concerned about the location—now emphasizing the lack of shops and services for residents but repeating the concerns of the existing neighborhood for their safety. Ottina to Préfet du Rhône, February 6, 1954 (ADR, 248 W 284).

20. Martin to Ministre de l'Intérieur, March 30, 1954, "Construction d'un centre d'hébergement pour travailleurs Français Musulmans à Saint-Priest" (ADR, 248 W 284).

21. *Le Progrès*, October 29, 1954, "Le premier pavillon du centre nord-africain des usines Berliet a été inauguré, hier, à Vénissieux" (ADR, 248 W 284). As mentioned in chapter 2, Vénissieux's mayor, Louis Dupic, was notably absent from this ceremony, again highlighting the larger role of local businesses than municipal officials in the region. Rhône-Poulenc, a textile factory also in Vénissieux, opened a housing complex for seventy North Africans on rue Gabriel Péri that December. *Le Progrès*, "Soixante-dix ouvriers nord-africains emménagent aujourd'hui," December 21, 1954 (ADR, 248 W 252).

22. Berliet to Préfet du Rhône, October 4, 1955 (ADR, 248 W 284).

23. Conseil municipal de Vénissieux, December 16, 1960 (AMVén, Délibérations du Conseil municipal). The other major business partner was the Société nouvelle des Ateliers de Vénissieux.

24. MTE to Ministère du Travail, de l'Emploi, et de la Population, August 27, 1969 (ADR, 759 W 111).

25. For Ricard's role in enforcing imperial ideology in the region, see chapter 3.

26. SLPM, "Note sur l'immigration étrangère dans le Rhône," August 15, 1971 (ADR, 759 W 40).

27. "Liste nominative d'entreprises et établissements," 1953 (ADR, 248 W 284).

28. Département du Rhône, "Enquête sociale sur la situation des musulmans originaires d'Algerie résidant en métropole," 1953 (ADR, 248 W 90).

29. Laurent, *Le service médico-social du centre d'hébergement nord-africain de la Part-Dieu (Lyon)* (Lyon: Imprimerie BOSC Frères, 1959) ADR, 248 W 303; and Truchot to Préfet du Rhône, May 7, 1952 (ADR, 248 W 253).

30. Commission consultative nationale pour l'étude des questions nord-africaines, April 5, 1955.

31. Cabinet du Préfet, "Note relative au problème du logement des Musulmans (célibataires et familles) originaires de l'Algérie," July 29, 1960 (ADR, 248 W 172).

32. Préfet du Rhône to Directeur départemental du Travail et de la Main-d'œuvre, June 26, 1961 (ADR, 248 W 284). At the same time, the head of SAT forces was recommending that Berliet send its North African workers to a new foyer in Villefranche-sur-Saône. Lopez to Automobiles Berliet, March 13, 1961 (ADR, 248 W 80).

33. Commission consultative nationale pour l'étude des questions nord-africaines, April 5, 1955.

34. De Meaux, "L'immigration familiale Nord-Africaine dans l'agglomération lyonnaise: Monographie d'un groupe de 120 familles," 1956 (ADR, 248 W 172).

35. See, among others in this file, President Directeur General STOCA to Préfecture du Rhône (FAS), May 12, 1971 (ADR, 248 W 73). By this point, Gat, as head of the Rhône SLPM, tended to respond in the negative and suggest that appeals go directly to HLM agencies or even private owners known to accept migrant families. For letters from employers (including Berliet) in the late 1950s and early 1960s, see ADR, 248 W 76 and 248 W 251. One Villeurbanne employer also reached out to the prefecture on behalf of two North African factory workers during the closing of the Centre Part-Dieu. Bertrand to Kramer, February 21, 1962 (ADR, 248 W 77).

36. A 1971 Rotary Sud-Est report from the Rhône showed unanimous employer support for the presence of workers' families. "Note sur l'immigration étrangère dans le Rhône," August 15, 1971. The prefecture's report suggests that many employers voiced their opposition on moral grounds, invoking individual rights, as well as on the economic effects.

37. Chardiny to Directeur SLPM (Rhône), September 16, 1973 (ADR, 759 W 261). For more on Houël's role, see chapter 2.

38. Borrel to Préfet du Rhône, September 9, 1974 (ADR, 759 W 290). Delle-Alsthom's factory was composed of 15.38 percent foreign workers and convened an internal commission on housing to aid them. The company had unfilled requests from fifteen Algerian families already in France and fourteen more workers hoping to bring their families over. By this time in 1974, family reunification was the only means of migrating from Algeria to France.

39. De Mauroy to Préfet du Rhône, July 26, 1974 (ADR, 759 W 40).

40. This dynamic was equally visible in the Paris region, whose prefect explicitly blamed the guaranteed reservation for migrant workers from employers' 1 percent contribution for the breaching of HLM quotas. Doublet to Premier Ministre, April 11, 1972, "Résorption des bidonvilles et les problèmes des migrants" (ADSSD, 1801 W 227). Family resettlement into HLMs was also an important factor in the decision by Saint-Denis and nearby cities to make their 1974 request to halt new migration—see chapter 2. Note, July 3, 1974, "Introduction en France des Familles de Travailleurs migrants relogés par leurs employeurs" (ADSSD, 1801 W 230).

41. "Conférence des officiers du SAT: Conclusions," April 3, 1963 (AHPP, HA 61).

42. One Rhône boss summed up his impression of Algerian workers as *"main-d'oeuvre à former."* "Enquête sociale sur les conditions d'emploi et de logement offertes aux travailleurs Musulmans originaires d'Algérie," January 1, 1960. In 1963, the Paris SAT forces observed that "business bosses want Algerians to undergo professional training programs"; the following year, employers lamented "the absence of all professional qualification on the part of Algerians." "Conférence des officiers du SAT: Conclusions," April 3, 1963; and "Conférence mensuelle des officiers du SAT: Affaires Nord-Africaines et Africaines," October 6, 1964 (AHPP, HA 61).

43. Grellier, Piettre, and Piettre, "Note à l'intention du CLORATE," February 5, 1972 (ADR, 99 J 15).

44. Commission consultative nationale pour l'étude des questions nord-africaines, April 5, 1955.

45. "Inquiétude dans les milieux patronaux au sujet de l'afflux de la main-d'œuvre italienne et nord-africaine," November 19, 1946 (ADR, 437 W 78).

46. "Conférence des officiers du SAT: Conclusions," October 4, 1962 (AHPP, HA 61). This anxiety was heightened by the increasing preference for hiring "Moroccans, Tunisians, and especially Spanish or Portuguese."

47. See, among many others, Directeur des renseignements généraux, "Les mouvements 'gauchistes' tentent de sensibiliser les ouvriers immigrés sur les problèmes de l'emploi," December 6, 1971 (ADHS, 1346 W 19). Chapter 6 has further discussion of leftist involvement with North African migrants.

48. For an excellent analysis of the often-downplayed role of immigrants in the constellation of workers' efforts culminating in May–June 1968, see Gordon, *Immigrants & Intellectuals.* On the relationship between French unions and Black African migrants, as well as the role of African workers in 1968, see Germain, *Decolonizing the Republic,* 119–24, 144–47.

49. Chabout, "Rapport de synthèse concernant les Nord-Africains et les débits de boissons suspects," 1951 (ADR, 437 W 133).

50. Bertrand, Rapport mensuel, April 7, 1961; Rapport trimestriel, July 1, 1963; and Rapport trimestriel, October 1, 1963 (ADR, 248 W 74). Notably, CGT membership was very high among Part-Dieu residents. For an examination of the relations between North African migrants and the CGT in the Rhône, see Grillo, *Ideologies and Institutions in Urban France,* 66–70.

51. Bertrand, Rapport trimestriel, July 6, 1961 (ADR, 248 W 74).

52. Pitti, "La main-d'œuvre algérienne dans l'industrie automobile" and "Les 'Nord-Africains' à Renault."

53. Truchot to Inspector General, September 12, 1957 (ADR, 437 W 78).

54. Martin, "Note," September 14, 1957 (ADR, 437 W 78).

55. Martin, "Note," September 14, 1957.

56. Truchot to Inspector General, September 12, 1957.

57. Truchot to Inspector General, September 12, 1957; Martin, September 14, 1957; and Préfecture du Rhône to Truchot, undated response (ADR, 437 W 78).

58. Pillot, "Eléments pour le rapport trimestriel du 5 octobre 1960," October 7, 1960 (AHPP, HA 61).

59. SAT, "Rapport trimestriel sur l'action psychologique et sociale exercée auprès de la Population Musulmane dans le cadre de la Préfecture de Police," 4ème Trimestre 1960 (AHPP, HA 61).

60. "La direction des Ets. Berliet a décidé de mettre fin à la période d'essai d'un ouvrier Nord-Africain," June 10, 1955 (ADR, 437 W 88).

61. SAT, "Rapport trimestriel sur l'action psychologique et sociale exercée auprès de la Population Musulmane dans le cadre de la Préfecture de Police," 3ème Trimestre 1961 (AHPP, HA 61). Businesses could be a useful arm of police surveillance; see Etablissements Picot & Fils to Préfet du Rhône, August 1, 1958 (ADR, 248 W 303) for an example of an employer forwarding FLN propaganda to the attention of the local police.

62. Herriot to Préfet du Rhône, November 27, 1946 (ADR, 437 W 78). The prefect was less concerned than Herriot about this apparent discrimination, assuring the mayor that local services were successfully placing North African workers and that Italians were simply taking the jobs for which their skills were better suited. Grégoire to Herriot, December 7, 1946 (ADR, 437 W 78).

63. "Rapport de MM. Laroque et Ollive," March 1938, 33.

64. "Rapport de MM. Laroque et Ollive," March 1938, 40–41. The authors asserted that the equal salary requirement was often ignored in practice.

65. Laborie to Ministre de l'Intérieur, April 2, 1963, "Problèmes posés par l'afflux des travailleurs algériens" (CHAN, F1a 5048).

66. Mouchnino, "Problèmes posés par l'immigration nord-africaine dans le département du Rhône," November 17, 1951 (ADR, 248 W 90).

67. Non-Kabyle Algerians "make up large contingents destined for difficult or unhealthy work; chemical products, metal alloys, public works, ballast, etc." Commission consultative nationale pour l'étude des questions nord-africaines, April 5, 1955 (CHAN, F1a 5043).

68. See "Situation générale des travailleurs nord-africains dans le département du Rhône," October 30, 1947; and Mouchnino, "Problèmes posés par l'immigration nord-africaine," November 17, 1951; and others. Laure Pitti has found, to the contrary, that many North African workers at Renault stayed with their employer for lengthy careers. Pitti, "Les 'Nord-Africains' à Renault," 52–53.

69. SAT, Rapport mensuel, September 1959 (AHPP, HA 8). The report also noted that employers were increasingly likely to request support and information from SAT forces. Renault was a notable outlier in this, uninterested in cooperating with SAT. Rapport mensuel, November 1959 (AHPP, HA 8). For more details on Renault-Billaincourt during the Algerian War, see Laure Pitti, "Renault, la 'forteresse ouvrière' à l'épreuve de la guerre d'Algérie," Vingtième siècle 83 (July–September 2004), 131–34.

70. SAT, Rapport mensuel, November 1959 (AHPP, HA 8). Moroccans and Tunisians were also considered to be "cleaner, more resourceful, speaking in general a

more correct French, and not being subject to the same preoccupations as Algerian laborers." SAT, "Rapport mensuel, mois de février 1960," March 3, 1960 (AHPP, HA 61).

71. "Enquête sociale sur les conditions d'emploi et de logement offertes aux travailleurs Musulmans originaires d'Algérie," January 1, 1960.

72. Service des affaires musulmanes et de l'action sociale (SAMAS), "Synthèse des rapports trimestriels établis par les conseillers techniques pour les affaires musulmanes," 1er trimestre 1958 (AHPP, HA 59).

73. "Le problème de l'emploi," undated, likely late 1958 (CHAN, F1a 5056).

74. SAT, "Rapport trimestriel sur l'action psychologique et sociale exercée auprès de la Population Musulmane dans le cadre de la Préfecture de Police," 2ème Trimestre 1960 (AHPP, HA 61).

75. Bertrand, Rapport trimestriel, July 5, 1961 (ADR, 248 W 74).

76. SAMAS, "Compte rendu d'une réunion qui s'est tenue le 26 Mai," June 1, 1959 (CHAN, F1a 5045).

77. Bertrand, Rapport mensuel, January 6, 1961 (ADR, 248 W 74).

78. SAMAS, "Synthèse des rapports trimestriels établis par les conseillers techniques pour les affaires musulmanes," 1ère trimestre 1961.

79. "Conférence des officiers du SAT: Conclusions," November 13, 1962 (AHPP, HA 61).

80. SAT, Rapport mensuel, July 1964 (AHPP, HA 60).

81. SAT, Rapport mensuel, December 1964 (AHPP, HA 61). Most evidence goes against the overly optimistic SAT report in February 1963, which asserted that Algerians were given priority over all other African workers, "notably Blacks," for housing as well as for employment. The same report worried much more about the ostracism facing harkis (especially from their compatriots). SAT, "Conférence mensuelle des Officiers des Affaires Algériennes, Chefs des Secteurs d'Assistance Technique aux Musulmans Algériens," February 5, 1963 (AHPP, HA 61). A year later, the exact opposite was affirmed: SAT officers "run into the reticence of employers" who want less and less to do with Algerians "and who often only make exceptions for former harkis." "Conférence mensuelle du Service d'Assistance technique," May 14, 1964 (AHPP, HA 61).

82. Préfecture de police, "Des divers aspects du problème posé par le mouvement migratoire des Nord-Africains et des Africains vers la France," undated (1964 or later), (CHAN, F1a 5120).

83. "Conférence des officiers du SAT," January 9, 1964, and October 6, 1964 (AHPP, HA 61).

84. "Conférence mensuelle des Officiers du SAT," October 6, 1964; and SAT, "Compte rendu hebdomadaire, période du 8 au 14 Juin 1964," 19 Jun 64 (AHPP, HA 61). The one group over which Algerians still had a clear advantage were sub-Saharan Africans. The Paris police noted, "For a long time favorable towards Africans, our compatriots, sympathetic to the image of the *tirailleur sénégalais* from 1914 or 1939, easily took them for large, inoffensive children. But, through contact with the realities, many now express their irritation with the attitude of these [Africans] in contemporary life.

Without speaking of overt racism, it is certain that the French maintain a growing reserve towards our previous migrants from Black Africa." Préfecture de police, "Des divers aspects du problème posé par le mouvement migratoire des Nord-Africains et des Africains vers la France."

85. SAT, Rapport mensuel, March 1966 (CAC, 19990260–23).

86. "Les industriels de Saint-Ouen et de Saint-Denis remplacent de plus en plus leur personnel algérien par les travailleurs portugais, espagnols et italiens," October 22, 1966 (AHPP, GA S 12).

87. "Les étrangers dans le département des Hauts-de-Seine," June 9, 1967 (ADHS, 1346 W 36).

88. "Conférence mensuelle des Officiers du SAT," October 6, 1964.

89. Préfecture de police, "Des divers aspects du problème posé par le mouvement migratoire des Nord-Africains et des Africains vers la France."

90. Préfecture de police, "Des divers aspects du problème posé par le mouvement migratoire des Nord-Africains et des Africains vers la France."

91. Grillo, *Ideologies and Institutions in Urban France*, 224–26.

92. Grillo, *Ideologies and Institutions in Urban France*, 233.

93. Grillo, *Ideologies and Institutions in Urban France*, 241–55.

94. Bancel, Bencharif, and Blanchard, *Lyon, capitale des outre-mers*, 174.

95. Sayad and Dupuy, *Un Nanterre algérien*, 76–80.

96. "Situation générale des travailleurs nord-africains dans le département du Rhône," October 30, 1947 (ADR, 437 W 83). For an overview of Algerian business owners in the interwar Lyon—and the central communal functions they played—see Massard-Guilbaud, *Des Algériens à Lyon*, 271–89.

97. "Situation générale des travailleurs nord-africains dans le département du Rhône," October 30, 1947.

98. Out of an estimated 330,000 Algerians. "Le problème de l'emploi" (CHAN, F1a 5056).

99. "Note au sujet de l'implantation de la population musulmane dans la ville de Lyon," undated but with "Liste des cafés-restaurateurs musulmanes de Lyon," October 30, 1951 (CHAN, F1a 5114). Between 1945 and 1954, thirteen Algerian women were business proprietors in the Rhône. André, *Femmes dévoilées*, chap. 4, para. 48.

100. "Liste des hôtels, restaurants, débits de boissons tenus par des Nord-Africains—Paris, banlieue," September 1951 (CHAN, F1a 5114).

101. "Considérations au sujet des distributions de denrées alimentaires dont bénéficient les Nord-Africains et particulièrement les restaurateurs Nord-Africains à l'occasion des fêtes religieuses musulmanes," November 26, 1946 (ADR, 437 W 78). The report also criticized café owners for spiking prices on couscous and other holiday foods distributed to them tax-free with the intention of supplementing workers' food.

102. Damelon, "Recensement des hôtels, garnis, restaurants et débits de boissons tenus dans le Département de la Seine par des Musulmans originaires d'Afrique du Nord," March 15, 1951 (CHAN, F1a 5114).

103. Ministre de l'Intérieur to Préfet du Rhône, "Action sur les milieux NA," September 5, 1955 (ADR, 437 W 78). The ministry sought to dampen nationalist activity in the cafés by requiring the owners to be police informants.

104. Ministre de l'Intérieur to Préfet du Rhône, "Achat de débits de boissons," September 20, 1957 (ADR, 437 W 78). The high prices paid for many of these businesses heightened suspicion that they were nationalist fronts.

105. Chaboud, Rapport de synthèse, February 14, 1955 (ADR, 437 W 134).

106. Sayad and Dupuy focus particularly on the tendency of these landlords to become "shack entrepreneurs." Sayad and Dupuy, *Un Nanterre algérien*, 23–24.

107. Sayad and Dupuy, *Un Nanterre algérien*, 34.

108. Devaux to Directeur de la Police judiciaire, February 21, 1961, and April 19, 1951 (CHAN, F1a 5114).

109. Directeur des services de police to Préfet du Rhône, October 19, 1946 (ADR, 437 W 78). The prefect explained that the plans for Part-Dieu were launched to deal with this situation. Grégoire to Directeur des services de police, October 28, 1946 (ADR, 437 W 78).

110. Préfet de police to Ministre de l'Intérieur, "Logement des Nord-Africains dans le Département de la Seine—Rapports avec les Européens," August 7, 1951 (CHAN, F1a 5114).

111. Devaux to Directeur de la Police judiciaire, February 21, 1961 (CHAN, F1a 5114).

112. Montaclair to Préfet de police, January 14, 1949 (AHPP, DA 768).

113. Montaclair to Préfet de police, January 14, 1949, and November 12, 1948 (AHPP, DA 768).

114. Commissaire de police, Saint-Denis, to Préfet de police, December 6, 1948 (AHPP, DA 768). The report did note that "if North Africans can attract women of loose morals, immoral acts cannot take place in public view." Mayor Gillot weighed in on the controversy, emphasizing the insalubrity of the buildings and focusing his ire on the landlord, whom he accused of being a police informant. Gillot to Préfet de police, February 28, 1949; and Conseil général de la Seine, Bulletin municipal officiel, November 30, 1948 (AHPP, DA 768). The police denied this relationship. Préfet de police to Gillot, March 30, 1949 (AHPP, DA 768).

115. Préfet de police to Gillot, March 30, 1949; and Directeur de l'Hygiène et de la sécurité publique (Police) to Directeur du Cabinet, March 9, 1949 (AHPP, DA 768). The lack of hygiene was compounded by renters who allowed "indigents" to spend the night in them, raising occupancy to five or six in rooms made for two.

116. Directeur de police économique to Préfet de police, January 20, 1949 (AHPP, DA 768).

117. Charvolin to Préfet du Rhône, April 2, 1962, "Utilisation transit-bungalows ALGECO" (ADR, 248 W 284).

118. Préfet du Rhône to Inspecteur divisionnaire du travail de la main-d'œuvre, April 5, 1962 (ADR, 248 W 284).

119. Roberrini, "Rapport à M. le Préfet de la Région Parisienne sur la résorption des bidonvilles et les problèmes des migrants," 1972, 68 (BAVP). Starting the following year, Roberrini's report titles replaced "bidonville" with "insalubrious habitats."

120. Roberrini, "Rapport à M. le Préfet de la Région Parisienne sur la résorption des bidonvilles et les problèmes des migrants," 1972, 80.

121. Roberrini, "Rapport à M. le Préfet de la Région Parisienne sur la résorption des bidonvilles et les problèmes des migrants," 1972, 68.

122. Roberrini, "Rapport à M. le Préfet de la Région Parisienne sur la résorption des bidonvilles et les problèmes des migrants," 1972, 70. Roberrini's 1973 report reemphasized migrants' agency in these situations, both in knowing their rights and how to assert them and in choosing freely to live in slums instead of new, state-planned housing projects. Roberrini, "Rapport à M. le Préfet de la Région Parisienne sur la résorption de l'Habitat Insalubre et les problèmes des migrants," 1973, 71, 76 (BAVP).

123. Berthet, *Mémoire du renouvellement urbain*, 11. In total, there were 64 three-room apartments, 168 four-room apartments, and 104 five-room apartments.

124. Schwartz, *Olivier de Serres*, 28.

125. Berthet, *Mémoire du renouvellement urbain*, 11. A 1969 renters' strike opposed this deposit policy but failed because the private company was not subject to the laws that would have regulated this practice. Intriguingly, Marcel Houël, in his role as deputy, broached this issue in the National Assembly in 1968, though without explicit mention of the residents as North African. Houël, Question écrit no. 698, *Journal official*, August 3, 1968 (ADR, 759 W 318).

126. A report to the mayor of Villeurbanne in 1968 claimed that there did not seem to be too many families heading from Olivier de Serres into the bidonvilles or other undesirable housing, but the prefecture later changed tunes to claim this as the standard practice in 1971. Prefect to Gagnaire, "Logements dépendants de la Compagnie Victor Simon," undated; and Moulins to Simon, November 4, 1971 (ADR, 759 W 318). Certainly, it appears that most families by the early 1970s were requesting places on the local HLM housing registries.

127. Gagnaire to Préfet, "Enquête sur les logements de la Régie Simon," February 28, 1968 (ADR, 759 W 318).

128. *Le Progrès*, "Racistes ou pas racistes?," October 15, 1966 (AMvill, 2 D 100). Gagnaire was responding to a lengthy critique of his attitude toward North Africans launched by local groups, including the Cercle Tocqueville, CFDT, and socialists.

129. Gagnaire to Benabid, August 25, 1966 (AMvill, 2 D 100).

130. Simon to Préfet, Direction du Cabinet, July 6, 1970 (ADR, 759 W 318). Emphasis in original.

131. Simon to Préfet, July 6, 1970.

132. Simon to Préfet, September 30, 1971 (ADR, 759 W 318).

133. Simon to Préfet, July 6, 1970. Emphasis in original.

134. Simon to Chebbah, June 12, 1970 (ADR, 759 W 318).

135. Simon to Chebbah, June 12, 1970. Further on, Simon again invokes the notion of "foreign agitators" Simon had not always spoken so highly of his residents. In response

to protests against fee hikes in 1970, he declared that "if the renters wish to bring down their fees in the coming years, they need only reduce the damage that they themselves, and especially their children, inflict on the buildings" and demanded to know of the youth, "What do they have in their brains to commit such stupid acts [as destroying the sports area in the complex]?" Simon goes on to compare his residents to the "*casseurs*" of Nanterre during May–June 1968. Simon to Gat et al., April 9, 1970 (ADR, 759 W 318).

136. Simon, July 6, 1970.

137. Lamy to Simon, June 26, 1970 (ADR, 759 W 318).

138. Préfet to Ministère du Travail, Emploi et Population, draft memo, undated but near May 1970 (ADR, 759 W 318).

139. Simon to Dijoud, July 26, 1974 (ADR, 759 W 318). He continued to decry the local administration as "prisoners of their previous errors, who push on in their aberrant behavior."

140. Arger (for Dijoud) to Préfet, "Demande de renseignements pour une réponse à une lettre de la compagnie Victor Simon," August 26, 1974 (ADR, 759 W 318).

141. Simon to Préfet, September 30, 1971. The prefecture seized on these empty units as proof that Simon's rents and fees were unsustainably high, but Simon countered that he had never had empty units before the new regulations.

142. Mangeot to Secrétaire Général Groupement d'intérêt public (GIP) pour la résorption de l'habitat insalubre, "Groupe d'immeubles constituant la cité Simon," June 11, 1974 (ADR, 759 W 318).

143. Schwartz, *Olivier de Serres*, 6.

144. Schwartz, *Olivier de Serres*, 33.

145. Silber, "Villeurbanne-les-deux-écoles," *Le Point* 169, December 15, 1975 (ADR, 759 W 318).

146. For example, once the first nine apartments were left open in November 1970. Simon to Gat, November 19, 1970 (ADR, 759 W 318); and Simon to Préfet, March 17, 1971 (ADR, 759 W 318).

147. Doueil (SLPM) to Dijoud, 1975 (ADR, 759 W 318).

148. Doueil to Dijoud, 1975.

149. OPAC (Office public d'aménagement et de construction) du Rhône, LOGIREL, la Villeurbannaise d'HLM, and the Villeurbanne municipality. Berthet, *Mémoire du renouvellement urbain*, 12.

150. Schwartz, *Olivier de Serres*, 7.

151. Mangeot to Secrétaire général GIP, June 11, 1974.

152. Even the Villeurbanne HLM offices only offered a few options for Olivier de Serres families. Préfet to Hernu, "Logement des familles sur Villeurbanne," July 20, 1978 (ADR, 759 W 321). See also Berthet, *Mémoire du renouvellement urbain*, 12.

153. Mangeot to Borrel, December 9, 1974 (ADR, 759 W 290).

154. See press coverage, including *Le Progrès*, "M. Roland Simon a retrouvé sa famille," September 10, 1977 (ADR, 759 W 320). The perpetrators and motive for the kidnapping were never discovered. One former resident remembered Roland Simon

as "a good man, not a crook as they often said." He recalled in particular the time that Roland had told off a racist concierge. Schwartz, *Olivier de Serres*, 28.

155. Schwartz, *Olivier de Serres*, 31.

156. Conseil municipal de Villeurbanne, séance du 12 juin 78, "Quartier Olivier de Serres" (ADR, 759 W 320).

157. See correspondence from Hernu for "Étrangers," 1978–79 (AMVill, 142 W 8).

158. Conseil municipal de Villeurbanne, séance du 12 juin 78, "Quartier Olivier de Serres."

159. Hernu to Cavalier, December 1, 1978 (AMVill, 142 W 8); and *Le Progrès*, "Olivier-de-Serres: Le commencement de la fin d'un ghetto," October 21, 1978 (ADR, 759 W 320).

160. Ville de Villeurbanne, "Le commencement de la fin d'un ghetto," November 6, 1978 (ADR, 759 W 320). See also Schwartz, *Olivier de Serres*, 10.

161. Hernu, "Compte rendu de la réunion rue Olivier de Serres le 16 novembre 1979" (AMVill, 142 W 8).

162. *Le Progrès*, "La démolition commence!," November 7, 1978 (ADR, 759 W 320). By this time, one member of the Villeurbanne municipal council was a former rapatrié who had lived at Olivier de Serres when it first opened. Berthet, *Mémoire du renouvellement urbain*, 27–29. One former Algerian resident claimed that the pieds-noirs who lived in the complex had been open and friendly: "They weren't settlers, large land owners, but modest families, and in addition, they spoke Arabic." Schwartz, *Olivier de Serres*, 15.

163. *Le Progrès*, "Jour J du commencement de la fin du ghetto Olivier de Serres," November 6, 1978 (ADR, 759 W 320).

164. Though seven of these families were still within Olivier de Serres. *Le Progrès*, "Démolition de la deuxième barre," March 22, 1979 (ADR, 759 W 320).

165. Berthet, *Mémoire du renouvellement urbain*, 13. This had been one of the concerns raised by residents in their meeting with Hernu—Hernu had insisted that renaming could take place as soon as new construction had begun. Hernu, "Compte rendu de la réunion rue Olivier de Serres."

166. *Le Progrès*, "Olivier-de-Serres: Un ghetto rayé de la carte, 2," August 4, 1984 (ADR, 759 W 320). On the practice of shifting migrant populations out of a given city, see chapter 1.

167. *Le Progrès*, "Le relogment des familles d'Olivier-de-Serres," September 19, 1980 (ADR, 759 W 320).

168. Gastaut, *L'immigration et l'opinion en France sous la Ve République*, 286. The burgeoning economic crisis, with both unemployment and oil prices on the rise, stoked anti-immigrant feelings across the country. Hernu himself bemoaned the way that "nationalist sentiments" are "always exacerbated" in moments of crisis. Hernu to Chaumard, March 15, 1979 (AMVill, 142 W 8).

169. Rouvièle to Préfet, June 19, 1969 (ADR, 759 W 318).

6. Solidarity

1. For a close look at a different cross-confessional relationship, see Ethan Katz on the complex, multifaceted, and situational interactions of Jews and Muslims in France and North Africa. Katz, *Burdens of Brotherhood*.

2. Communists and Christians had recently collaborated to protest the Algerian War (see chapter 4) and to support the post–World War II squatters' movement (see Nasiali, *Native to the Republic*, 24–36).

3. The PCF municipality in Vénissieux again stands in stark contrast to city officials in Saint-Denis.

4. Corneloup, "ROSSET Gabriel." Notably, this entry makes no mention of migrants, even in discussing Rosset and NDSA's work in the bidonvilles.

5. Jewish Telegraphic Agency, "Cardinal Gerlier, Archbishop of Lyon, Denounces Racialism; Urges Fight against It," November 9, 1944, https://www.jta.org/archive/cardinal-gerlier-archbishop-of-lyon-denounces-racialism-urges-fight-against-it. Gerlier worked closely with both the rabbi and the head of the Protestant church in Lyon. Benoit, "GERLIER Pierre-Marie." In rhetoric that foreshadowed much of what Christian leaders would later say in defense of North African migrants, Gerlier's 1942 missive, which was read aloud in all churches in the diocese, protested Vichy's deportation measures and affirmed "the inalienable [*imprescriptible*] rights of the human person, the sacred character of family bonds, the inviolability of the right to asylum and the urgent [*impérieux*] demands of that fraternal charity that Christ made the distinctive sign of his disciples." "Communiqué de son éminence le Cardinal Gerlier, Archevêque de Lyon," September 6, 1942 (Beinecke Rare Book and Manuscript Library, Yale University), https://collections.library.yale.edu/catalog/10267815.

6. Gerlier, "Aide aux Nord-Africains," *La France Catholique*, October 26, 1951, 3, as quoted in Lyons, *Civilizing Mission in the Metropole*, 59. Amelia Lyons further discusses how other French Catholic welfare services followed in this spirit, particularly the Études sociales nord-africaines (ESNA), under the direction of Father Jacques Ghys. Lyons, *Civilizing Mission in the Metropole*, 56–60.

7. NDSA, "C'est un problème vraiment angoissant" (ADR, 759 W 317).

8. The shelter (providing a bed and soup) was free for the first night of any stay, and lodgers could stay on at a small fee; a second shelter was soon built for women and children. NDSA, "Le saviez-vous?" (ADR, 248 W 12).

9. Corneloup, "ROSSET Gabriel."

10. NDSA, "Le saviez-vous?"

11. Priest, member of the Resistance, and former deputy to the National Assembly, Abbé Pierre delivered an address on *Radio-Luxembourg* on February 1, 1954, alerting the nation to the death of a homeless woman on the sidewalk of the boulevard Sebastopol and launching a charity drive to provide emergency housing and food for the least fortunate. Pierre, "L'appel de 1954."

12. NDSA, "Le saviez-vous?" Some of the young people were likely Rosset's students, as he was known to involve them in his charitable work. Berthod and Comby, *Histoire de l'église de Lyon*.

13. *Le Progrès*, "Les compagnons bâtisseurs de Notre-Dame des Sans-Abris reçus hier à l'hôtel de ville," September 2, 1965 (ADR, 248 W 12).

14. NDSA, "Suppression des Bidons-Villes—Cité de Transit," Sep 23, 1959 (ADR, 248 W 339). See chapter 1 for a lengthier discussion of education and integration policies within the cités de transit.

15. "Note justificative d'une demande adressée à Monsieur le Directeur du Ministère de l'Equipement," undated; and Préfecture du Rhône, Arrêté no. 525, October 16, 1972 (759 W 160).

16. Corneloup, "ROSSET Gabriel."

17. In 1965, "French" families constituted 47 percent of those housed in the cités, while Algerians were 32 percent. By the early 1970s, two-thirds of the residents in the cités were "foreign families in distress." NDSA, report to SLPM, November 18, 1965 (CHAN, F1a 5112); and "Note justificative d'une demande adressée à Monsieur le Directeur du Ministère de l'Equipement."

18. Cabinet du Préfet to Secrétaire de l'Etat a l'Intérieur chargé des questions nord-africaines, "Note," December 21, 1956 (ADR, 437 W 78).

19. The prefect's cabinet asserted that Rosset's letter was a publicity stunt aimed at garnering funding for the association, "as inelegant as it is regrettable." Cabinet du Préfet to Secrétaire de l'Etat a l'Intérieur chargé des questions nord-africaines, December 21, 1956.

20. Martin to Rosset, August 18, 1957 (ADR, 248 W 253). For more on Martin's own positions and motivations, see chapter 3.

21. NDSA, report to SLPM, November 18, 1965. With the end of French Algeria, NDSA also worked closely with Algerian repatriates (both pieds-noirs and harkis). NDSA, "L'arche sous l'arc en ciel," February 1965 (ADR, 248 W 12).

22. NDSA, report to SLPM, November 18, 1965.

23. Indeed, some of the Rhône prefects refused to deal with certain issues affecting North African migrants (burial rites, in particular) on the grounds that the separation of church and state had to be maintained. See correspondence in ADR, 248 W 152 and discussion in chapter 3.

24. The last Sunday of every month. NDSA, "Le saviez-vous?"

25. Rosset, "Le mot du responsable" and "Dieu le veut," *L'arche sous l'arc en ciel*, February 28, 1965. *L'arche* was a trimesterly bulletin put out by NDSA (for 1F).

26. NDSA, "C'est un problème vraiment angoissant qu'avec vous nous devons résoudre," undated but in a dossier for 1965 (ADR, 248 W 12).

27. NDSA, "Le saviez-vous?"; and Claude Roffat, "Saint-Joseph," *L'arche sous l'arc en ciel*, February 28, 1965.

28. Rosset, "Le Cardinal Gerlier et les Sans-Abris," *L'arche sous l'arc en ciel*, February 28, 1965. Rosset's essay in the cardinal's memory listed many masses Gerlier held both within the foyer and on its behalf—even requiring all

churches in Lyon to mention the organization during Christmas mass in 1954.

29. Rosset, "Aborder un pauvre," undated—likely early 1970s (ADR, 759 W 160).

30. See dossier, "Polémique sur les cités gérées par NDSA" (759 W 160). For reactions of North African residents in a cité de transit run by NDSA in Vaulx-en-Vélin, see Grillo, *Ideologies and Institutions in Urban France*, 118–22, 139.

31. Rosset, "Dieu le veut," *L'arche sous l'arc en ciel*, February 28, 1965.

32. Rosset, "Aborder un pauvre."

33. Vatican, *Ad Gentes*, 12, http://www.vatican.va/archive/hist_councils/ii_vatican _council/documents/vat-ii_decree_19651207_ad-gentes_en.html. For a close examination of the church's navigation of decolonization, see Fontaine, *Decolonizing Christianity*, 135–39.

34. Fontaine, *Decolonizing Christianity*, 139.

35. Rosset, "Aborder un pauvre."

36. Letter from "des Chrétiens appartenant à des milieux variés et de tendances politiques différentes" to Préfet, May 7, 1957 (ADR, 437 W 78). This was actually the ACA's second antiwar declaration; a 1955 statement that was widely published in the Catholic press had already caused consternation for French imperial authorities. See Fontaine, *Decolonizing Christianity*, 110–12.

37. Fontaine, *Decolonizing Christianity*, 110. For a closer look at French and European Christian groups who did support Algerian nationalism, see Fontaine, *Decolonizing Christianity*, chap. 2.

38. André, *Femmes dévoilées*, chap. 3, 38–45. André notes that nearly all parish bulletins in the region encouraged outreach to local North Africans.

39. On Delorme's support for the youth activists of les Minguettes, particularly the 1983 hunger strike and subsequent organization of the national movement for migrant rights, see Hajjat, *La marche pour l'égalité et contre le racisme*.

40. Préfet to Ministre de l'Intérieur, August 6, 1970 (ADR, 759 W 262). For more on the role of these social assistants in France, see Lyons, *Civilizing Mission in the Metropole*. For the parallel case of Christians who staffed the Centres Sociaux in French Algeria, see Fontaine, *Decolonizing Christianity*, 79–82. The CFDT broke off from the original CFTC (Confédération française des travailleurs chrétiens) in 1964, in part to pursue a more secular syndicalism, but retained the idea of Christian humanism as a means of holding on to a majority of its more devout members. For an in-depth look at the founding and evolution of the CFDT, see Georgi, *CFDT: L'identité en questions*.

41. Renard to Préfet, July 11, 1970 (ADR, 759 W 262).

42. United Press International, "Cardinal Alexandre Renard, 77, retired Roman Catholic archbishop," October 8, 1983, https://www.upi.com/Archives/1983/10/ 08/Cardinal-Alexandre-Renard-77-retired-Roman-Catholic-archbishop-of/ 3747434433600/. Renard had also been active in Lyon during May–June 1968, supporting a resolution by mostly young priests to "participate more closely in the common life of men of our time (professional life, housing, sociocultural activities, political life, etc.)." Berthod and Comby, *Histoire de l'église de Lyon*.

43. "Biographie, Jean-Pierre Monsarrat," Who's Who in France, accessed July 23, 2022, https://www.whoswho.fr/decede/biographie-jean-pierre-monsarrat_12288.

44. Monsarrat to Préfet, July 7, 1970 (ADR, 759 W 262). Monsarrat also did not hesitate to pull some political weight, opening his letter by recounting a meeting between his predecessor (Daniel Atger, president of CIMADE) and the prime minister where they discussed the importance of helping "these workers needed by the French economy."

45. In 1988, he denounced the Front national as "racist, anti-Semitic, and xenophobic," insisting that "it is not enough to denounce the demons. We must mobilize Protestants in the affirmation of a fraternity of men and women of all races, all nations, all cultures." Henri Tincq, "Le Pasteur Jean-Pierre Monsarrat," *Le Monde*, April 11, 2000, https://www.lemonde.fr/archives/article/2000/04/11/le-pasteur-jean-pierre-monsarrat_3613583_1819218.html.

46. Moulins to Renard, August 31, 1970 (ADR, 759 W 262). An earlier draft was even more defensive: "My decision had no xenophobic or racist motivation, it resulted simply from my conviction that it is unhealthy [*malsain*] for all involved to live in separate communities." Moulins to Renard, undated draft (ADR, 759 W 262). For more on Moulins's connections to the French Empire, see chapter 3.

47. Moulins to Monsarrat, August 31, 1970 (ADR, 759 W 262). Moulins's first draft of the letter admitted he was "shocked" by Monsarrat's "severe judgment." Moulins also had both Lamy (his directeur du cabinet) and Gat (chef du SLPM) meet with organizations most involved with students and with migrants: "I believe I have convinced all of them that there was nothing discriminatory in these measures and that our concern was not to discourage family migration, but rather to make sure that the conditions of admission for these families are the least bad possible on both the material level and that of their welcome by the French population." Préfet to Ministre de l'Intérieur, August 6, 1970.

48. Moulins to Renard, August 31, 1970, and Moulins to Monsarrat, August 31, 1970.

49. Moulins's approach to this issue was considerably more nuanced than the Villeurbanne resident who wrote to Mayor Gagnaire in 1966 to complain that the CFDT had no business supporting local "Arabs" because Charles Martel had fought and won against the "Saracens" to save Christianity in 732. Balmont to Gagnaire, October 16, 1966 (AMvill, 2 D 100).

50. *Essor*, "Etranges mesures pour les étrangers," September 25, 1970 (ADR, 759 W 262).

51. CFDT to Préfet, July 28, 1970 (ADR, 759 W 262). Signed by UDCFDT, AGEL, APF, ASF, PS, Conventions des Institutions Républicaines, Cercle Tocqueville, PSU, CIMADE, ACFAL, Mouvement International pour la Réconciliation, UFCS, Vies Nouvelles, Amis de Témoignage Chrétien, Groupe de Préparation à la non-violence.

52. CFDT to Préfet, July 28, 1970.

53. Victor Simon, owner of the Cité Olivier de Serres, featured heavily in these critiques.

54. CFDT to Préfet, July 28, 1970.

55. The PCF's 1936 eighth congress—in Villeurbanne—emphasized both the need for a broader political coalition and for cooperation between French and Algerian workers. In response, the Algerian-based *Lutte sociale* expressed a desire for a "union of the colonial oppressed and the metropolitan exploited" in place of "narrow nationalism." See Drew, *We Are No Longer in France*, 91.

56. Lillo, *La petite Espagne*, 113. Lillo also admits that local officials may have been looking for electoral support—though the Spanish did not have the right to vote enjoyed by Algerians (from 1945 to 1962), they often did become naturalized, enfranchised French citizens.

57. Conseil municipal, "Séance extraordinaire du 30 mai 1961" (AMSD, 17 ACW 94).

58. "Rapport à M. le Maire sur l'activité de la Municipalité et du Conseil municipal en faveur des Nord-Africains," May 26, 1950 (AMSD, 37 AC 16).

59. Report to Maire, January 20, 1953 (AMSD, 37 AC 17).

60. Manoel, Rapport au Bureau municipal, May 5, 1972 (AMSD, 261 W 37). Maurice Manoel was the deputy-mayor in charge of social affairs. For more on this comparison, see Byrnes, "Liberating the Land or Absorbing a Community."

61. Dionysiens also employed modern urbanization theories along the lines of Le Corbusier. For an analysis of the plans drawn up by the municipality's chief architect, André Lurçat, see Bacqué and Fol, *Le devenir*, 58–66. On Lurçat's promotion of democratic planning principles for construction (and failure to employ these in Saint-Denis), see Newsome, *French Urban Planning*.

62. *Saint-Denis: Hier, aujourd'hui, demain*, November 1967 (AMSD, 38 C 4).

63. Gillot's wife, Simone, had trained as a nurse in 1950 and was a major proponent of easing childbirth for women, working closely with Dr. Fernand Lamaze (whose techniques originated in Soviet methods). Maude Le Fichant and Fonds Simone Gillot, "Introduction de l'inventaire," AMSD, https://archives.ville-saint-denis.fr/archive/fonds/fram93066_000000151/vta9e61fb5a4f701577.

64. This vision for the future did not give up entirely on whiteness as its center: the portraits were accompanied by the image of a small white girl playing in a dress, while the opposite page featured a white mother and her newborn.

65. "Saint-Denis, demain," September 1970 (AMSD, 37 AC 57). Unfortunately, city records did not keep the actual images from the exhibit.

66. One visitor had an opposite reaction, concerned that local communists were not doing enough to support migrants, while a set of migrant visitors worried that urban renovation would push rents too high. "Réflexions générales," October 22, 1970 (AMSD, 37 AC 57).

67. See, for example, the joint communist-socialist program that was part of the "Saint-Denis, demain" exhibit. "Saint-Denis, demain: Programme d'action municipale proposé par la liste d'Union pour une gestion sociale, moderne, et démocratique, présentée par le Parti communiste avec la participation du Parti socialiste," November 1970 (AMSD, 38 C 4).

68. Manoel, Report to Bureau municipal de Saint-Denis, May 5, 1972 (AMSD, 261 W 37).

69. Manoel, "Projet de mémoire à adresser à M. Edgar Faure, relatif aux problèmes posés par l'immigration à Saint-Denis," September 5, 1972 (AMSD, 261 W 37).

70. Stovall terms this the "phase hypothesis of community development," whereby community solidarity is often created when new groups of people begin to live together but gradually dissipates. Stovall, *Rise of the Paris Red Belt*, 160.

71. "Préparations de la quinzaine de l'immigration à Saint-Denis," October 10, 1972 (AHPP, GA S 12).

72. "La municipalité de Saint-Denis organise une réunion préparatoire d'une 'Quinzaine de l'immigration,'" March 25, 1972 (AHPP, GA S 12).

73. "Quinzaine de l'immigration à Saint-Denis," 1972 (AHPP, GA S 12).

74. These visits were less popular than the other activities; police cited a lack of logistical coordination on the part of the municipality as well as a lack of interest among the general population. "Opération portes ouvertes au foyer de la Courtille à Saint-Denis," October 25, 1972; and "Bilan de la Quinzaine de l'immigration qui s'est déroulée à Saint-Denis," November 13, 1972 (AHPP, GA S 12).

75. A double feature at the city theater brought in over three hundred attendees—most were young; thirty were North African. On screen were "Remparts d'argile" (1968), Jean-Louis Bertucelli's award-winning film about a mine strike and female liberation in a Tunisian village (based on a book by Jean Duvignaud), and "Le vent des Aurès" (1966), Mohammed Lakhdar-Hamina's story of an Algerian mother searching for her son after his imprisonment in a French army camp. "Une soirée-cinéma a eu lieu le samedi 28 octobre 1972 au Théâtre Municipal Gérard Phillipe à Saint-Denis," October 30, 1972 (AHPP, GA S 12).

76. Yves Courrière and Phillippe Mounier's 1972 documentary on the Algerian War attracted 250 city residents, mostly "Muslims," Portuguese, and local students. "Environ 250 personnes ont assisté le samedi 28 octobre à 16 heures à la projection du film 'La guerre d'Algérie' qui a eu lieu au théâtre Gérard Philippe à Saint-Denis," November 2, 1972 (AHPP, GA S 12).

77. "Une projection de film suivie d'un débat," October 26, 1972 (AHPP, GA S 12).

78. "Quinzaine de l'immigration," November 7, 1972 (AHPP, GA S 12).

79. The local press claimed that the campaign was a great success; police records wrote it off as a "fiasco" that did not "result in fruitful action on behalf of the immigrant populations." "Bilan de la Quinzaine," November 13, 1972.

80. Tony Judt traces the development of French Maoism out of Marxist disaffection with French communism as well as the belief that "the West had broken down" and so ideologues should look to the Far East. Judt, *Marxism and the French Left*, 195–96. Danièle Joly maintains that youth disaffection with the PCF's delayed and weak opposition to the Algerian War in particular created an "embryo of an alternative left" and launched the *gauchisme* of the late 1960s. Joly, *French Communist Party*, 146–48. Kristin Ross likewise invokes "the proximity of the Algerian War to the '68 events" and the formative experience provided to students whose childhood was played out before the backdrop of the Algerian War. Ross, *May '68 and Its Afterlives*, 33–57. Daniel Gordon similarly includes French responses to Algerian protests

and French police violence (especially October 17, 1961) as the foundation for the New Left's engagement with migrants. Gordon, *Immigrants & Intellectuals*, 25–28.

81. For examinations of transnationalism, third-worldism, and anticolonialism among French radicals, see Mark, Townson, and Voglis, "Inspirations," 88–103; and Mohandesi, "Bringing Vietnam Home."

82. Gordon, *Immigrants & Intellectuals*, 76, 80. Félix Germain speaks to the contrasting experiences of sub-Saharan migrants, who mostly avoided participation, and Caribbean migrants, many of whom were actively involved. Germain, *Decolonizing the Republic*, 144–55.

83. Gordon, *Immigrants & Intellectuals*, 5.

84. Gordon, "A Nanterre, ça bouge."

85. Senegalese militant Sally N'Dongo went so far as to accuse the gauchistes of using African migrants similarly to the French army, who sent African units into battle first during the two World Wars. Gordon, "A Nanterre, ça bouge," 78–79, 82–86.

86. Note from G. Brottes (Paris prefecture) to Bonnaud-Delamare (chef, SLPM), June 19, 1968, "Répercussions dans les bidonvilles et dans les établissements sociaux des événements de mai-juin 1968" (CAC, 19770317/1).

87. Many New Left groups explicitly targeted PCF-run cities to call attention to what they believed was communist "collusion with capitalism and state power." "Mode d'intervention et d'action des mouvements gauchistes dans les foyers de travailleurs immigrés de la région parisienne," February 13, 1970 (AHPP, GA A7).

88. Gordon, *Immigrants & Intellectuals*, 60.

89. "Mode d'intervention," February 13, 1970; and police report, December 6, 1971, "Les mouvements 'gauchistes' tentent de sensibiliser les ouvriers immigrés sur les problèmes de l'emploi" (ADHS, 1346 W 19).

90. "Mode d'intervention," February 13, 1970.

91. The police insisted that these classes had "no other goal but to bring the Africans to political consciousness through an intense political propaganda program." "Mode d'intervention," February 13, 1970.

92. Roberrini to Préfet de Seine-Saint-Denis, May 19, 1971, "Agitation maoïste et comportement des Africains dans un foyer de la SONACOTRA à SD" (CAC, 19770317/1).

93. Gordon, "A Nanterre, ça bouge," 81; and Gordon, *Immigrants & Intellectuals*, 105.

94. Glaes, *African Political Activism in Postcolonial France*, 66–69.

95. "Des militants gauchistes font échouer l'expulsion de locataires nord-africains d'un foyer que la municipalité PCF de St-Denis voulait faire évacuer," February 18, 1970 (AHPP, GA A7).

96. "Des militants gauchistes de SD ont procédé à une distribution de tracts, pour protester contre les mesures d'expulsion de 96 locataires d'un foyer Nord-Africain envisagé par la municipalité de Saint-Denis (SSD)," February 20, 1970 (AHPP, GA A7).

97. "Physionomie de l'après-midi du 17 février au Centre Universitaire Expérimental de Vincennes," February 18, 1970 (AHPP, GA S 12).

98. "La Gauche Prolétarienne diffuse à SD un tract . . . ," April 17, 1970 (AHPP, GA S 12).

99. Schwartz, *Olivier de Serres*, 28.

100. Gat, "Synthèse de l'action concernant les immigrées," October 24, 1970 (ADR, 759 W 100). This is part of a series of reports requested by the Interior Ministry in August to track and counter Maoist influence on migrant populations.

101. Tract, "A Olivier de Serres, cité de la honte et de la misère, c'est l'heure de révolte" (ADR, 759 W 100). In contrast, one former resident mused that since Simon had built the apartments, he had a right to make money off them. Schwartz, *La médina bruemeuse*, 28.

102. District de Police de l'agglomération lyonnaise to Préfet du Rhône, July 7, 1970, "Distribution de publications maoistes dans les immeubles de la rue Olivier de Serres à Villeurbanne" (ADR, 759 W 100).

103. "Oser lutter, oser vaincre," *Journal inter-foyers la cause du peuple* 1 (ADR, 759 W 100).

104. Gat, "Action maoistes en direction des travailleurs immigrés," reports for October 1–11, October 12–18, and October 19–25, 1970 (9ADR, 759 W 100).

105. Glaes, *African Political Activism in Postcolonial France*, 70.

106. This followed African activists' own trajectories in the wake of successful independence movements. Glaes, *African Political Activism in Postcolonial France*, 2, 56.

107. Left-leaning communities have generally demonstrated less of a tendency to rely solely upon national definitions of identity. Linguist Simone Bonnafous's analysis of French political press found that newspapers to the left, particularly the communist *L'Humanité*, employed a "we" centered on party membership, while other newspapers routinely used a more nationalist "we" to designate traditional (white) French nationals and citizens (against foreigners). By the 1980s, *L'Humanité Dimanche* was the only major paper in her sample to denounce racism consistently, discuss the difficulties of migrant integration, and criticize other papers for their less sympathetic approach to migrant issues. Bonnafous, "Immigrés et immigration dans la presse politique française," 507, 615.

108. Robert Hue, "Auguste Gillot: Un responsable éminent," *L'Humanité*, September 1, 1998.

109. *Le Progrès*, December 31, 1974, "Un dernier homage . . ."; and "M. Gabriel Rosset n'est plus" (ADR, 759 W 160).

110. The WCC was particularly focused on worldwide action on issues of social justice, racism, and decolonization—they also spoke openly against apartheid in South Africa and racial discrimination in the United States. Fontaine, *Decolonizing Christianity*, 115, 139–41.

111. Rosset, "Aborder un pauvre."

112. See brochures and bulletins, ADR, 248 W 12.

113. This last café cited by Gillot had twice been the object of municipal intervention to prevent the mistreatment of Algerian lodgers, though each time the owner had been released from prison (the municipality charged that he was a police informant and so given immunity). Bulletin municipal officiel de la Ville de Paris, Conseil Général de la Seine, November 24, 1948, no. 18, 617–23 (AMSD, 37 AC 16).

114. Gillot to Préfecture de Seine, February 27, 1958 (AP, PEROTIN 101/78/1–19).

115. "Oser lutter, oser vaincre."

116. The same pattern can be seen in French activism on other causes. See Hendrickson, "March 1968"; and Byrnes, "Anti-Salazarism and Transnational Solidarity."

Conclusion

1. Hollande, "C'est un acte de guerre," France 24, November 14, 2015, https://www.france24.com/fr/20151114-attentats-paris-hollande-bataclan-stade-france-armee-daech-syrie; Décret no. 2015–1475 du 14 novembre 2015, Légifrance, accessed September 5, 2021, https://www.legifrance.gouv.fr/jorf/id/JORFTEXT000031473404. France previously declared a state of emergency during the Algerian War (three times), in New Caledonia in 1984 (amid independence protests) and for the 2005 unrest—all notably connected to imperial and postcolonial issues.

2. Paillard, speech, LeJSD, November 13, 2015 (page no longer extant).

3. Paillard, declaration, Ville de Saint-Denis, November 15, 2015 (page no longer extant).

4. Paillard, declaration, Ville & banlieue, November 18, 2015, https://www.ville-et-banlieue.org/saint-denis-appel-a-un-rassemblement-en-hommage-aux-victimes-des-attentats-14452.html; and *L'Humanité*, "Didier Paillard," November 14, 2015.

5. Epstein, *Collective Terms*, 141.

6. *L'Humanité*, "Didier Paillard," November 19, 2015.

7. Paillard, declaration, November 18, 2015.

8. *L'Humanité*, "Didier Paillard," November 14, 2015.

9. *L'Humanité*, "Didier Paillard," November 19, 2015.

10. Paillard, declaration, November 18, 2015.

11. *L'Humanité*, "Didier Paillard," November 14, 2015.

12. Mgr. Pascal Delannoy, "Plus que jamais servons la fraternité et la paix!," Diocèse de Saint-Denis en France, November 18, 2015, https://saint-denis.catholique.fr/actualites/plus-que-jamais-servons-la-fraternite-et-la-paix; and Jean Bellorini, "Vite au théâtre!," November 18, 2015, Communistes unitaires (page no longer extant).

13. Paillard, speech at Rassemblement en hommage aux victimes, November 19, 2015 (page no longer extant).

14. *L'Humanité*, "Crapuleux!," November 19, 2015.

15. "Le FN demande 'la mise sous tutelle immédiate de Saint-Denis,'" LeJSD, accessed September 5, 2021 (page no longer extant).

16. "Le Parti de gauche va porter plainte contre le FN," LeJSD, accessed September 5, 2021 (page no longer extant).

17. "Pierre Laurent répond au FN," LeJSD, accessed September 5, 2021 (page no longer extant).

18. Paillard, "Saint-Denis représente tout ce que le FN déteste," LeJSD, accessed September 5, 2021 (page no longer extant).

19. *L'Humanité*, "A Saint-Denis, les oubliés de la République veulent se faire entendre," November 23, 2015.

20. *L'Humanité*, "Didier Paillard," November 19, 2015.

21. Michel Kokoreff, Pierre Barron, and Odile Steinauer, "Enquêtes sur les violences urbaines: Comprendre les émeutes de novembre 2005, L'exemple de Saint-Denis," Centre d'analyse stratégique (Premier Ministre), November 2006, http://www.loldf.org/ressources/pdf/Comprendre_les_%e9meutes.pdf.

22. *Le Parisien*, "Saint-Denis: Trois jours de débats autour des émeutes de 2005," October 21, 2015.

23. *L'Humanité*, "Didier Paillard," November 19, 2015.

24. Beaman, *Citizen Outsider*; Epstein, *Collective Terms*; Newman, *Landscape of Discontent*; and Silverstein, *Postcolonial France*.

25. Hajjat, *La marche pour l'égalité et contre le racisme*; Germain, *Decolonizing the Republic*; Glaes, *African Political Activism in Postcolonial France*; and Nasiali, *Native to the Republic*.

26. Annie Fourcaut cites the "taste for individual habitats" as one of the major stumbling blocks in the city of Bobigny's interwar urban development projects. Fourcaut, *Bobigny*, 178. The "irrepressible" desire for a "single-family home [*pavillon*], alone on its plot of land" carried through the Second World War; in 1946 an Institut national d'études démographiques (*INED*) poll found that the vast majority of the French wanted to live in their own houses and gardens. Fourcaut, "Qu'elle était belle," 6.

27. Fysh and Wolfreys, *Politics of Racism in France*, 159.

28. Fourcaut, "Qu'elle était belle," 10.

29. See Fourcaut, "Qu'elle était belle," 9. For an account of Sarcelles's construction, settlement, and especially the participation of its inhabitants, see Cupers, *Social Project*, 137–66. On the development of the idea of *sarcellite*, see Mulvey, "Problem That Had a Name."

30. Blanc-Chaléard, "Les immigrés et le logement," 10.

31. For example, Yves Lequin cites the experience around the Porte de Clichy (in Paris's seventeenth arrondissement): "The folks [*petits gens*] who lived in this working-class neighborhood resisted accepting, and finally refused, the classic ensemble of towers and blocks [*barres*], without soul or imagination. Into these disdained residences rushed those who had come from Asia." Lequin, "Immigrés en ville," 417.

32. Bacqué and Fol, *Le devenir*, 135, 161.

33. Fourcaut, "Qu'elle était belle," 11; and Blanc-Chaléard, "Les immigrés et le logement," 9. See Silverstein, *Algeria in France*, 98–102, on the stark differences in the two halves of the city of Pantin.

34. This pattern should not be mistaken, of course, as uniquely French. Anne Power concludes her study of social housing in France, Germany, Britain, Denmark, and Ireland with the observation that "the strong development of owner-occupation cut demand for 'mass' estates and encouraged access by vulnerable groups (often immigrants) to the most unpopular housing areas." Power, *Hovels to High Rise*, 369.

Across the Atlantic, Emily Rosenbaum and Samantha Friedman describe how Black and Puerto Rican migrants to New York City confronted a different housing situation than white migrants. Friedman and Rosenbaum, *Housing Divide*, 49. Arnold Hirsch likewise demonstrates the segregationist tendencies in Chicago's urban development in the mid-twentieth century. Hirsch, *Making the Second Ghetto*.

35. After some initial disagreement with the Hauts-de-Seine prefecture over the proper location, ground was broken in 1975. Correspondence, plans, and reports, February 1974–March 1975 (ADHS, 1103 W 17). City officials did ensure that most of the spaces would be given to workers still living in poor conditions in the city's northern zone to prevent them from having to accept many migrants from other towns. Préfet des Hauts-de-Seine to Maire, September 16, 1974 (ADHS, 1103 W 17, "Construction d'un foyer pour travailleurs immigrés"). Though the original contract was with "Le Logement Français," the foyer still operates today, under the auspices of Adoma (the successor to SONACOTRA).

36. The mosque was run by an Algerian man out of an abandoned church (ADHS, 1308 W 3). The bank offices were opened by Banque Chaabi du Maroc and Banque Centrale Populaire du Maroc; the Moroccan population in the region was large enough in 1974 to merit a new travel office in Asnières dealing solely with Moroccan destinations. "La colonie marocaine dans les Hauts-de-Seine," April 8, 1974 (ADHS, 1346 W 36).

37. For a thorough analysis of the reconstruction of Saint-Denis's city center and its effects on class dynamics in the city, see Bacqué and Fol, *Le devenir*. For further consideration of the Basilica neighborhood project's displacement of specifically North African migrants, see Byrnes, "French like Us?," 303–9.

38. Epstein, *Collective Terms*, 140, 161.

39. On the development of a lens of "institutional racism" in French scholarship on migration, see Vulbeau, "Roubaix," 18–20.

40. Jacques Mayard, deputy to the National Assembly from President Nicolas Sarkozy's UMP party, declared, "The problem is not economic . . . but is feeding on basic anti-French racism even if the rioters have French nationality." Ben Hall, "Elysée to Get Tough on Rioting Youths," *Financial Times*, November 28, 2007. See Beaman, *Citizen Outsider*, 48, for a discussion of the academic version of this argument.

BIBLIOGRAPHY

Archives and Collections

Archives de Paris (AP)

Archives Départementales de Seine-Saint-Denis, Bobigny (ADSSD)

Archives Départementales des Hauts-de-Seine, Nanterre (ADHS)

Archives Départementales du Rhône, Lyon—Section Ancien and Section Moderne (ADR)

Archives d'Histoire Contemporaine, Institut d'études politiques de Paris (AHC)

Archives Historiques de la Préfecture de Police, Paris (AHPP)

Archives Municipales d'Asnières-sur-Seine (AMASS)

Archives Municipales de Saint-Denis (AMSD)

Archives Municipales de Vénissieux (AMVén)

Archives Municipales de Villeurbanne (AMVill)

Bibliothèque Administrative de la Ville de Paris (BAVP)

Centre des Archives Contemporaines, Fontainebleau (CAC)

Centre Historique des Archives Nationales, Paris (CHAN)

Published Works

Abdelfettah, Nedjma. "'Science coloniale' et modalités d'encadrement de l'immigration algérienne à Paris (1917–1952)." *Bulletin de l'Institut d'histoire du temps présent*, no. 83 (June 2004): 108–27.

André, Marc. *Femmes dévoilées: Des Algériennes en France à l'heure de la décolonisation*. Lyon: ENS Éditions, 2017. https://doi.org/10.4000/books.enseditions.7265.

———. "Les groupes de choc du FLN: Particularités de la guerre d'indépendance algérienne en métropole." *Revue historique* 669, no. 1 (2014): 143–78. https://doi.org/10.3917/rhis.141.0143.

Applegate, Celia. "A Europe of Regions: Reflections on the Historiography of Subnational Places in Modern Times." *American Historical Review* 104, no. 4 (October 1999): 1157–82.

Bacqué, Marie-Hélène. "Le Stade de France à Saint-Denis: Grands équipements et développement urbain." *Les annales de la recherche urbaine*, no. 79 (1998): 26–133.

Bacqué, Marie-Hélène, and Sylvie Fol. *Le devenir des banlieues rouges*. Paris: Éditions Privat, 1997.

Bancel, Nicolas, Léla Bencahrif, and Pascal Blanchard. *Lyon, capitale des outre-mers: Immigration des suds & culture coloniale en Rhône-Alpes et Auvergne*. Paris: Découverte, 2007.

Beaman, Jean. "Are French People White? Towards an Understanding of Whiteness in Republican France." *Identities* 26, no. 5 (November 2018). https://doi.org/10 .1080/1070289x.2018.1543831.

———. *Citizen Outsider: Children of North African Immigrants in France*. Oakland: University of California Press, 2017.

Beaujon, Danielle. "Controlling the Casbah: Policing North Africans in Marseille and Algiers, 1920–1950." PhD diss., New York University, 2021.

———. "Policing Colonial Migrants: The Brigade Nord-Africaine in Paris, 1923–1944." *French Historical Studies* 42, no. 4 (October 2019): 655–80.

Beaune, Colette. "Saint-Denis: Apôtre ou imposteur?" In Bourderon, *Histoire de Saint-Denis*, 26–55.

Begag, Azouz. *Le gone du Chaâba*. Paris: Éditions du Seuil, 1986.

Béghain, Patrice, Bruno Benoit, Gérard Corneloup, and Bruno Thévenon. *Dictionnaire historique de Lyon*. Lyon: Editions Stéphane Bachès, 2009.

Bell, David S., and Byron Criddle. *The French Communist Party in the Fifth Republic*. New York: Oxford University Press, 1994.

Bellanger, Emmanuel. "Administrer la 'banlieue municipale': Activité municipale, intercommunalité, pouvoir mayoral, personnel communal et tutelle préfectorale en Seine banlieue des années 1880 aux années 1950." PhD diss., Université de Paris 8-Vincennes-Saint-Denis, 2004.

Belmessous, Fatiha. "Du 'seuil de tolérance' à la 'mixité sociale': Répartition et mise à l'écart des immigrés dans l'agglomération lyonnaise (1970–2000)." *Belgeo*, no. 3 (2013): 1–19. https://doi.org/10.3917/tt.039.0031.

———. "Georges Martin, un fonctionnaire ordinaire de l'administration coloniale française à Lyon (1940–1960)." *Terrains & travaux*, no. 39 (2021): 31–59.

———. "L'émergence du problème des quartiers d'habitat social: Une 'fenêtre d'opportunité' pour l'Agence d'urbanisme de Lyon? (1978–1984)." *Territoire en mouvement*, no. 2 (2007): 44–56.

Benoit, Bruno. "GERLIER Pierre-Marie." In Béghain, Benoit, Corneloup, and Thévenon, *Dictionnaire historique de Lyon*, 598–99.

Bernardot, Marc. *Loger les immigrés*. Paris: Croquant, 2008.

———. "Une politique de logement: La SONACOTRA (1956–1992)." PhD diss., Université de Paris I Panthéon-Sorbonne, 1997.

Berthet, Jean-Marc. *Mémoire du renouvellement urbain ou renouvellement des mémoires urbaines? L'exemple de la cité Olivier de Serres à Villeurbanne et du*

quartier de Parilly à Bron. Report to Ministère de l'Equipement, 20. https://prtra
.hypotheses.org/files/2010/01/rapport-de-recherche-JM-Berthet.pdf.

Berthod, Bernard, and Jean Comby. *Histoire de l'église de Lyon*. Châtillon-sur-Chalaronne: Editions la Taillanderie, 2007.

Blackmer, Donald L. M., and Sidney Tarrow. *Communism in Italy and France*. Princeton NJ: Princeton University Press, 1975.

Blanc-Chaléard, Marie-Claude. "Des baraques aux bidonvilles." In *Baraques: L'album photographique du dispensaire la Mouche-Gerland, 1929–1936*, edited by Vincent Lemire and Stéphanie Samson, 89–92. Lyon: ENS Éditions, 2003.

———. *En finir avec les bidonvilles*. Paris: Publications de la Sorbonne, 2016.

———. *Histoire de l'immigration*. Paris: Éditions La Découverte & Syros, 2001.

———. "Les immigrés et le logement en France depuis le XIXe siècle: Une histoire paradoxale." *Hommes & migrations*, no. 1264 (November–December 2006): 20–34.

———. *Les Italiens dans l'Est parisien (années 1880–1960): Une histoire d'intégration*. Rome: École français de Rome, 2000.

Blanchard, Emmanuel. "La dissolution des Brigades nord-africaines de la préfecture de police: La fin d'une police d'exception pour les Algériens de Paris (1944–1953)?" *Bulletin de l'Institut d'histoire du temps présent*, no. 83 (June 2004): 94–107.

———. *La police parisienne et les Algériens (1944–1962)*. Paris: Nouveau Monde, 2011.

———. "Police judiciaire et pratiques d'exception pendant la guerre d'Algérie." *Vingtième siècle*, no. 90 (February 2006): 61–72.

Blévis, Laure. "La citoyenneté française au miroir de la colonisation: Étude des demandes de naturalization des 'sujets français' en Algérie coloniale." *Genèses*, no. 53 (December 2003): 25–47.

Boëldieu, Gérard. "Le Mouvement de la Paix dans la Sarthe: Une dynamique contrariée." In Branche and Thénault, *La France en guerre 1954–1962*, 228–40.

Bonnafous, Simone. "Immigrés et immigration dans la presse politique française de 1974 à 1984: Analyse de discours." PhD diss., Université Paris IV Paris-Sorbonne, 1990.

Bonneville, Marc. "La désindustrialisation urbaine, le cas de Villeurbanne (1963–1974)." *Revue de géographie de Lyon* 50, no. 1 (1975): 97–105.

———. *Naissance et métamorphose d'une banlieue ouvrière: Villeurbanne; Processus et formes d'urbansiation*. Lyon: Presses Universitaires de Lyon, 1978.

Bouhet, Bernard, and Philippe Videlier. *Vénissieux de A à V, 1921–1931*. Lyon: Presses Universitaires, 1983.

Bourderon, Roger, ed. *Histoire de Saint-Denis*. Paris: Éditions Privat, 1997.

Branche, Raphaëlle. "La commission de sauvegarde pendant la guerre d'Algérie: Chronique d'un échec annoncé." *Vingtième siècle*, no. 61 (January 1999): 14–29.

———. *La guerre d'Algérie: Une histoire apaisée?* Paris: Éditions dc Seuil, 2005.

Branche, Raphaëlle, and Sylvie Thénault, eds. *La France en guerre 1954–1962*. Paris: Autrement, 2008.

Bresson, Sabrina, Sylvette Denèfle, Annie Dussuet, and Nicole Roux. *Habiter Le Corbusier: Pratiques sociales et théorie architectural*. Rennes: Presses Universitaires de Rennes, 2006.

Brunet, Jean-Paul. *Immigration, vie politique et populisme en banlieue parisienne (fin XIXe–XXe siècles)*. Paris: Harmattan, 1995.

———. *Jacques Doriot: Du communisme au fascisme*. Paris: Balland, 1986.

———. *Saint-Denis la ville rouge, 1890–1939*. Paris: Hachette, 1980.

Byrnes, Melissa. "Anti-Salazarism and Transnational Solidarity: Franco-Portuguese Student Activism in the 1960s." *French History and Civilization*, no. 10 (August 2021): 4–18.

———. "Criminal Fertility: Policing North African Families after Decolonization." In *Fertility, Family, and Social Welfare between France and Empire: The Colonial Politics of Population*, edited by Margaret Andersen and Melissa Byrnes. Palgrave Macmillan, 2023.

———. "French like Us? Municipal Policies and North African Migrants in the Parisian Banlieues, 1945–75." PhD diss., Georgetown University (2008).

———. "Liberating the Land or Absorbing a Community: Managing North African Migration and the *Bidonvilles* in Paris's *Banlieues*." *French Politics, Culture & Society* 31, no. 3 (Winter 2013): 1–20.

———. "Ramadan in the Republic: Imperial Necessity and Religious Assistance in the Rhône Department." *French Cultural Studies* 28, no. 1 (February 2017): 5–16.

Charbit, Tom. "Un petit monde colonial en metropole." *Politix*, no. 76 (2006): 31–52.

Choi, Sung. *Decolonization and the French of Algeria: Bringing the Settler Colony Home*. Basingstoke UK: Palgrave Macmillan, 2016.

Cohen, Mathilde, and Sarah Mazouz. "A White Republic? Whites and Whiteness in France." *French Politics, Culture & Society* 39, no. 2 (June 2021): 1–25.

Cohen, Muriel. *Des familles invisibles: Les Algériens de France entre intégrations et discriminations (1945–1985)*. Paris: Editions de la Sorbonne, 2020.

Cohen, Muriel, and Cédric David. "Les cités de transit: Le traitement urbain de la pauvreté à l'heure de la décolonisation." *Métropolitiques*, February 29, 2012. http://www.metropolitiques.eu/Les-cites-de-transit-le-traitement.html.

Coller, Ian. *Arab France: Islam and the Making of Modern Europe*. Berkeley: University of California Press, 2010.

Confino, Alon. *Germany as a Culture of Remembrance: Promises and Limits of Writing History*. Chapel Hill: University of North Carolina Press, 2006.

Conklin, Alice. *A Mission to Civilize: The Republican Idea of Empire in France and West Africa, 1895–1930*. Stanford CA: Stanford University Press, 1997.

Connelly, Matthew. *A Diplomatic Revolution: Algeria's Fight for Independence and the Origins of the Post–Cold War Era*. New York: Oxford University Press, 2003.

Cooper, Frederick, *Colonialism in Question: Theory, Knowledge, History*. Berkeley: University of California Press, 2005.

———. "Modernizing Bureaucrats, Backward Africans, and the Development Concept." In *International Development and the Social Sciences: Essays on the History and Politics of Knowledge*, edited by Frederick Cooper and Randall Packard, 64–92. Berkeley: University of California Press, 1998.

Corbel, Maurice. *Vénissieux: Du village à la cité industrielle*. Paris: Temps Actuels, 1983.

——. *Vénissieux la rebelle*. Paris: Editions Cercle d'Art, 1997.

Cornaton, Michel. *Les regroupements de la décolonisation en Algérie*. Paris: Éditions Ouvrières, 1967.

Corneloup, Gérard. "ROSSET Gabriel." In Béghain, Benoit, Corneloup, and Thévenon, *Dictionnaire historique de Lyon*, 1346.

Cross, Gary. *Immigrant Workers in Industrial France: The Making of a New Laboring Class*. Philadelphia: Temple University Press, 1983.

Cupers, Kenny. *The Social Project: Housing Postwar France*. Minneapolis: University of Minnesota Press, 2014.

David, Cédric. "La résorption des bidonvilles de Saint-Denis: Politique urbaine et redéfinition de la place des immigrants dans la ville (années 1960–1970)." *Histoire urbaine*, no. 27 (2010/1): 121–42.

——. "La résorption des bidonvilles de Saint-Denis: Un noeud dans l'histoire d'une ville et 'ses' immigrés (de la fin des années 1950 à la fin des années 1970)." Master's thesis, Université de Paris I Panthéon-Sorbonne, 2002.

——. "Logement social des immigrants et politique municipale en banlieue ouvrière (Saint-Denis, 1944–1995): Histoire d'une improbable citoyenneté urbaine." PhD diss., Paris 10-Nanterre, 2016.

Davidson, Naomi. *Only Muslim: Embodying Islam in Twentieth-Century France*. Ithaca NY: Cornell University Press, 2012.

de Barros, Françoise. "Contours d'un réseau administratif 'algérien' et construction d'une compétence en 'affaires musulmanes': Les conseillers techniques pour les affaires musulmanes en metropole (1952–1965)." *Politix*, no. 76 (2006): 97–120.

——. "Des 'Français musulmans d'Algérie' aux 'immigrés': L'importation de classifications coloniales dans les politiques du logement en France (1950–1970)." *Actes de recherche en sciences sociales*, no. 159 (2005/4): 26–53.

——. "Les municipalités face aux Algériens: Méconnaissances et usages des catégories coloniales en métropole avant et après la Seconde Guerre mondiale." *Genèses*, no. 53 (December 2003): 69–92.

——. "L'État au prisme des municipalités: Une comparaison historique des catégorisations des étrangers en France (1919–984)." PhD diss., Paris I Panthéon-Sorbonne, 2004.

Drew, Allison. *We Are No Longer in France: Communists in Colonial Algeria*. Manchester: Manchester University Press, 2014.

Dubois, Laurent. *Soccer Empire: The World Cup and the Future of France*. Berkeley: University of California Press, 2010.

Eldridge, Claire. *From Empire to Exile: History and Memory within the Pied-Noir and Harki Communities*. Manchester: Manchester University Press, 2016.

Epstein, Beth S. *Collective Terms: Race, Culture, and Community in a State-Planned City in France*. New York: Berghahn Books, 2011.

Evans, Martin. *The Memory of Resistance: French Opposition to the Algerian War (1954–1962)*. New York: Berg, 1997.

Ewane, Émilie Elongbil. "La guerre d'Algérie à Lyon: La bataille pour le contrôle de l'habitat." *Métropolitiques*, February 22, 2012. https://metropolitiques.eu/La -guerre-d-Algerie-a-Lyon-la.html.

Fernando, Mayanthi L. *The Republic Unsettled: Muslim French and the Contradictions of Secularism*. Durham NC: Duke University Press, 2014.

Ferrand, Nathalie. *Créateurs de roses: A la conquête des marchés*. Grenoble: Presses Universitaires de Grenoble, 2015.

Fishman, Robert. *L'utopie urbaine au XXe siècle: Ebenezer Howard, Frank Lloyd Wright, Le Corbusier*. Translated by P. Guillette. Brussels: Architecture + Recherche, 1979.

Fontaine, Darcie. *Decolonizing Christianity: Religion and the End of Empire in France and Algeria*. New York: Cambridge University Press, 2016.

Fourcaut, Annie. *Bobigny, banlieue rouge*. Paris: Les Éditions Ouvrières et Presses de la Fondation Nationale des Sciences Politiques, 1986.

———. "Qu'elle était belle la banlieue." *L'histoire*, no. 315 (December 2006): 1–11.

Friedman, Samantha, and Emily Rosenbaum. *The Housing Divide: How Generations of Immigrants Fare in New York's Housing Market*. New York: New York University Press, 2007.

Fysh, Peter, and Jim Wolfreys. *The Politics of Racism in France*. New York: Palgrave Macmillan, 2003.

Gastaut, Yves. *L'immigration et l'opinion publique en France sous la Ve République*. Paris: Éditions de Seuil, 2000.

Georgi, Frank. CFDT: *L'identité en questions; Regards sur un demi-siècle (1964–2014)*. Nancy: L'Arbre bleu, 2014.

Germain, Félix F. *Decolonizing the Republic: African and Caribbean Migrants in Postwar Paris, 1946–1974*. East Lansing MI: Michigan State University Press: 2016.

Gildea, Robert. *France since 1945*. New York: Oxford University Press, 2002.

Gildea, Robert, James Mark, and Anette Warring, eds. *Europe's 1968: Voices of Revolt*. Oxford: Oxford University Press, 2013.

Gillot, Auguste. *Un forgeron dans la cité des rois*. Paris: Éditions des Halles de Paris, 1986.

Gillot, Auguste, and Simone Gillot. *Un couple dans la Résistance*. Paris: Éditions sociales, 1987.

Glaes, Gillian. *African Political Activism in Postcolonial France: State Surveillance and Social Welfare*. New York: Routledge, 2019.

Gordon, Daniel A. "'A Nanterre, ça bouge': Immigrés et gauchistes en banlieue, 1968 à 1971." *Historiens et géographes*, no. 385 (January 2004): 75–86.

———. *Immigrants & Intellectuals: May '68 and the Rise of Anti-racism in France*. Pontypool UK: Merlin, 2012.

Gordon, David G. *The Passing of French Algeria*. New York: Oxford University Press, 1966.

Green, Nancy L. *Repenser les migrations*. Paris: Presses Universitaires de France, 2002.

Grillo, Ralph D. *Ideologies and Institutions in Urban France*. Cambridge: Cambridge University Press, 1985.

Grosjean, Arthur. "L'action des conseillers techniques aux Affaires musulmanes: L'exemple du camp du Thol." *Matériaux pour l'histoire de notre temps*, no. 92 (2008/4): 15–23.

Hajjat, Abdellali. *La marche pour l'égalité et contre le racisme*. Paris: Éditions Amsterdam, 2016.

Hacquemand, Bruno, and Pierre de Peretti. "Franciade (1789–An VIII)." In Bourderon, *Histoire de Saint-Denis*, 194–205.

Harouel, Jean-Louis. *Histoire de l'urbanisme*. Paris: Presses Universitaires de France, 1993.

Hassat, Dónal. "Catering for and Controlling Subject Veterans: The *Comité des Amitiés africaines* and North African Ex-servicemen in the Interwar Period." *First World War Studies* 10, no. 1 (2019). https://doi.org/10.1080/19475020.2019.1701516.

Hendrickson, Burleigh. "March 1968: Practicing Transnational Activism from Tunis to Paris." *International Journal of Middle East Studies* 44, no. 4 (November 2012): 755–74.

Hirsch, Arnold R. *Making the Second Ghetto: Race and Housing in Chicago, 1940–1960.* New York: Cambridge University Press, 1983.

Hmed, Choukri. "Loger les étrangers 'isolés' en France: Socio-histoire d'une institution d'État: la Sonacotra." PhD diss., Université de Paris 1, 2008.

———. "'Tenir ses hommes': La gestion des étrangers 'isolés' dans les foyers Sonacotra après la guerre d'Algérie." *Politix* 19, no. 76 (December 2006): 11–30.

House, Jim. "Colonial Contaminant? Repression of Pro-independence Street Demonstrations in Algiers, Casablanca, and Paris, 1945–1962." *War in History* 25, no. 2 (2018): 172–201.

———. "Contrôle, encadrement, surveillance et répression des migrations coloniales: Une décolonisation difficile (1956–1970)." *Bulletin de l'Institut d'histoire du temps présent*, no. 83 (2004): 144–56.

House, Jim, and Neil MacMaster. *Paris 1961: Algerians, State Terror, and Memory*. New York: Oxford University Press, 2006.

House, Jim, and Andrew Thompson. "Decolonisation, Space, and Power: Immigration, Welfare and Housing in Britain and France, 1945–1974." In *Writing Imperial Histories*, edited by Andrew Thompson, 240–67. Manchester: Manchester University Press, 2013.

Joly, Danièle. *The French Communist Party and the Algerian War*. New York: St. Martin's, 1991.

Jouan, Lucienne. *Asnières-sur-Seine au cours des siècles*. Asnières: L. Unal, 1976.

———. *Asnières-sur-Seine et son histoire*. Paris: Industries Graphiques de Paris, 2000.

Judt, Tony. *Marxism and the French Left: Studies in Labor and Politics in France, 1830–1981*. New York: Oxford University Press, 1986.

Katz, Ethan. *The Burdens of Brotherhood: Jews and Muslims from North Africa to France*. Cambridge MA: Harvard University Press, 2015.

Kelfaoui, Schérazade. "Le comportement électoral des Français d'origine maghrébine à Saint-Denis." In *Immigration, vie politique et populisme en banlieue parisienne (fin XIXe–XXe siècles)*, edited by Jean-Paul Brunet, 363–80. Paris: Harmattan, 1995.

Kuby, Emma. *Political Survivors: The Resistance, the Cold War, and the Fight against Concentration Camps after 1945*. Ithaca NY: Cornell University Press, 2019.

Lamri, Sophia. "'Algériennes' et mères françaises exemplaires (1945–1962)." *Le mouvement social*, no. 199 (April–June 2002): 65.

———. "L'histoire de la création de l'hôpital franco-musulman à Bobigny." Paper, Colloque international de la Cité national de l'histoire de l'immigration, Paris, September 29, 2006.

Laurens, Sylvain. "La noblesse d'État à l'épreuve de 'l'Algérie' et de l'après 1962: Contribution à l'histoire d'une 'cohorte algérien' sans communauté de destins." *Politix*, no. 76 (2006): 75–96.

Lavau, Georges. "The PCF, the State and Revolution." In Blackmer and Tarrow, *Communism in Italy and France*, 87–140.

Lecroart, Paul. "Regenerating the Plaine Saint-Denis, 1985–2020: Integrated Planning in a Large 'Urban Project.'" Institut d'aménagement et d'urbanisme, September 2008. https://en.institutparisregion.fr/resources/publications/the-plaine-saint-denis-regeneration-in-the-paris-ile-de-france-region/.

Lequin, Yves, ed. *Histoire des étrangers et de l'immigration en France*. Paris: Larousse, 2006.

———. "Immigrés en ville." In Lequin, *Histoire des étrangers*, 408–29.

———. "Les vagues d'immigration successives." In Lequin, *Histoire des étrangers*, 385–406.

Le Rize. "Olivier de Serres: Radiographie d'une 'cité ghetto.'" Le Rize: Villeurbanne, 2009.

Le Sueur, James D. *Uncivil War: Intellectuals and Identity Politics during the Decolonization of Algeria*. Philadelphia: University of Pennsylvania Press, 2001.

Lewis, Mary D. *The Boundaries of the Republic: Migrant Rights and the Limits of Universalism*. Stanford CA: Stanford University Press, 2007.

Lillo, Natacha. *La petite Espagne de la Plaine-Saint-Denis, 1900–1980*. Paris: Autrement, 2004.

Lyons, Amelia. *The Civilizing Mission in the Metropole: Algerian Families and the French Welfare State during Decolonization*. Stanford CA: Stanford University Press, 2013.

———. "The Civilizing Mission in the Metropole: Algerian Immigrants in France and the Politics of Adaptation during Decolonization." *Geschichte und Gesellschaft*, no. 32 (October–December 2006): 489–516.

———. "Invisible Immigrants: Algerian Families and the French Welfare State in the Era of Decolonization (1947–1974)." PhD diss., University of California at Irvine, 2004.

MacMaster, Neil. *Colonial Migrants and Racism: Algerians in France, 1900–62*. New York: St. Martin's, 1997.

———. "The 'seuil de tolérance': The Uses of a 'Scientific' Racist Concept." In Silverman, *Race, Discourse and Power in France*, 14–28.

Mark, James, Nigel Townson, and Polymeris Voglis. "Inspirations." In Gildea, Mark, and Warring, *Europe's 1968*, 72–103.

Masclet, Olivier. *La gauche et les cités: Enquête sur un rendez-vous manqué*. Paris: La Dispute, 2006.

———. "Une municipalité communiste face à l'immigration algérienne et marocaine: Gennevilliers 1950–1972." *Genèses*, no. 45 (June 2001): 150–63.

Massard-Guilbaud, Geneviève. *Des Algériens à Lyon: De la Grande Guerre au Front Populaire*. Paris: Harmattan, 1995.

Massenet, Marthe, and Pierre Massenet. *Journal d'une longue nuit: Carnet de route de deux Français moyens, 1939–1944*. Paris: Arthème Fayard, 1971.

Mazouz, Sarah. "A White Race Blindness? Abstract Universalism and the Unspeakable Making of Race." *French Politics, Culture & Society* 39, no. 2 (June 2021): 116–35.

McDonnell, Hugh. *Europeanising Spaces in Paris, c. 1947–1962*. Liverpool: Liverpool University Press, 2016.

Meniri, Hocine. "Les immigrés dans la commune de Vénissieux." Master's thesis, Université Lyon II, 1979.

Merriman, John. *The Margins of City Life: Explorations on the French Urban Frontier, 1815–1851*. New York: Oxford University Press, 1991.

Meuret, Bernard. *Le socialisme municipal: Villeurbanne, 1880–1982*. Lyon: Presses Universitaires, 1982.

Miller, Jeannette E. "Algerian, French, Refugees, Repatriates, Immigrants? Harki Citizens in Post-imperial France (1962–2005)." PhD diss., Pennsylvania State University, 2011.

Moch, Leslie Page. *Pariahs of Yesterday: Breton Migrants in Paris*. Durham NC: Duke University Press, 2012.

Mohandesi, Salar. "Bringing Vietnam Home: The Vietnam War, Internationalism, and May '68." *French Historical Studies* 41, no. 2 (April 2018): 219–51.

Mulvey, Michael. "The Problem That Had a Name: French High-Rise Developments and the Fantasy of a Suburban Homemaker Pathology, 1954–73." *Gender & History* 28, no. 1 (April 2016): 177–98.

Mussard, Christine. "Réinventer la commune? Genèse de la commune mixte, une structure administrative inédite dans l'Algérie coloniale." *Histoire@Politique* 27, no. 3 (2015): 93–108. https://doi.org/10.3917/hp.027.0093.

Nasiali, Minayo. *Native to the Republic: Empire, Social Citizenship, and Everyday Life in Marseille since 1945*. Ithaca NY: Cornell University Press, 2016.

Naylor, Ed, ed. *France's Modernising Mission: Citizenship, Welfare and the Ends of Empire*. London: Palgrave Macmillan, 2018.

———. "'Solidarisme ou Barbarie': Welfare and the 'Social Question' in France." Review of *Variations of the Welfare State*, by Franz-Xaver Kaufmann; *Léopold Bellan*, by Benoît Charenton; *Laroque and the Welfare State in Post-war France*, by Eric Jabbari; and *Au Secours Maréchal!*, by Jean-Pierre Le Crom. *Contemporary European History* 24, no. 3 (August 2015): 461–72.

———. "'Un âne dans l'ascenseur': Late Colonial Welfare Services and Social Housing in Marseille after Decolonization." *French History* 27, no. 3 (2013): 422–47.

Naylor, Phillip C. *France and Algeria: A History of Decolonization and Transformation*. Gainesville: University Press of Florida, 2000.

Newman, Andrew. *Landscape of Discontent: Urban Sustainability in Immigrant Paris*. Minneapolis: University of Minnesota Press, 2015.

Newsome, W. Brian. *French Urban Planning, 1940–1968*. New York: Peter Lang, 2009.

Noiriel, Gérard. *The French Melting Pot: Immigration, Citizenship, and National Identity*. Translated by Geoffroy de Laforcade. Minneapolis: University of Minnesota Press, 1996. Originally published as *Le Creuset français: Histoire de l'immigration, XIXe–XXe siècles* (Paris: Éditions de Seuil, 1988).

Pervillé, Guy. "Combien de morts?" *Les collections de l'histoire*, no. 15 (2002): 94–95.

Pétonnet, Colette. *Ces gens-là*. Paris: CNRS Éditions, Collection Biblis, 2017.

Pierre, Abbé. "L'appel de 1954." Fondation Abbé Pierre. Accessed June 14, 2023. https://www.fondation-abbe-pierre.fr/la-fondation-abbe-pierre/la-vie-de-labbe-pierre/appel-abbe-pierre-1er-fevrier-1954.

Pitti, Laure. "La main-d'œuvre algérienne dans l'industrie automobile (1945–1962), ou les oubliés de l'histoire." *Hommes & migrations*, no. 1263 (September–October 2006): 47–57.

———. "Les 'Nord-Africains' à Renault: Un cas d'école de gestion coloniale de la main-d'œuvre en métropole." *Bulletin de l'Institut d'histoire du temps présent*, no. 83 (June 2004): 128–43.

———. "Renault, la 'forteresse ouvrière' à l'épreuve de la guerre d'Algérie." *Vingtième siècle*, no. 83 (July–September 2004): 131–43.

Power, Anne. *Hovels to High Rise: State Housing in Europe since 1850*. New York: Routledge, 1993.

Prakash, Amit. "Colonial Techniques in the Imperial Capital: The Prefecture of Police and the Surveillance of North Africans in Paris, 1925–circa 1970." *French Historical Studies* 36, no. 3 (Summer 2013): 479–510.

Quandt, William B. *Revolution and Political Leadership: Algeria, 1954–1968*. Cambridge MA: MIT Press, 1969.

Robinson, David. *Paths of Accommodation: Muslim Societies and French Colonial Authorities in Senegal and Mauritania, 1880–1920*. Athens: Ohio University Press, 2000.

Rosenberg, Clifford. *Policing Paris: The Origins of Immigration Control between the Wars*. Ithaca NY: Cornell University Press, 2006.

Ross, Kristin. *May '68 and Its Afterlives*. Chicago: University of Chicago Press, 2002.

Rudolph, Nicole. *At Home in Postwar France: Modern Mass Housing and the Right to Comfort*. New York: Berghahn Books, 2015.

Saada, Emmanuelle. *Empire's Children: Race, Filiation, and Citizenship in the French Colonies*. Translated by Arthur Goldhammer. Chicago: University of Chicago Press, 2012.

Sahlins, Peter. *Boundaries: The Making of France and Spain in the Pyrenees*. Berkeley: University of California Press, 1989.

Sayad, Abdelmalek, and Éliane Dupuy. *Un Nanterre algérien: Terre de bidonvilles.* Paris: Autrement, 1995.

Sayad, Abdelmalek (as Malek Ath-Messaoud), and Alain Gillette. *L'immigration algérienne en France.* Paris: Éditions Entente, 1976.

Schain, Martin A. *French Communism and Local Power: Urban Politics and Political Change.* New York: St. Martin's, 1985.

Schor, Ralph. *L'opinion française et les étrangers en France, 1919–1939.* Paris: Presse de la Sorbonne, 1985.

Schwartz, Annie. *Olivier de Serres ou "la médina brumeuse."* Villeurbanne: Centre Social de Cusset, 1997.

Scioldo-Zürcher, Yann. *Devenir métropolitain: Politique d'intégration et parcours de rapatriés d'Algérie en métropole, 1954–2005.* Paris: Ecole des Hautes Etudes en Sciences Sociale, 2010.

Scott, Joan Wallach. "Mayors versus Police Chiefs: Socialist Municipalities Confront the French State." In *French Cities in the Nineteenth Century,* edited by John M. Merriman, 230–45. New York: Homes & Meier, 1981.

———. *The Politics of the Veil.* Princeton NJ: Princeton University Press, 2010.

Sessions, Jennifer. *By Sword and Plow: France and the Conquest of Algeria.* Ithaca NY: Cornell University Press, 2011.

Shepard, Todd. "Comment et porquoi éviter le racisme: Causes et effets, culture, 'seuils de tolérance' ou résistances? Le débat français entre 1954 et 1976." *Arts & sociétés: Lettre du séminaire,* no. 51 (March 2013). https://www.sciencespo.fr/artsetsocietes/fr/archives/1410.

———. *The Invention of Decolonization: The Algerian War and the Remaking of France.* Ithaca NY: Cornell University Press, 2006.

———. *Sex, France, and Arab Men.* Chicago: University of Chicago Press, 2017.

Silverman, Maxim, ed. *Race, Discourse and Power in France.* Brookfield VT: Avebury, 1991.

Silverstein, Paul A. *Algeria in France: Transpolitics, Race and Nation.* Bloomington: University of Indiana Press, 2004.

———. *Postcolonial France: Race, Islam, and the Future of the Republic.* London: Pluto, 2018.

Spire, Alexis. *Étrangers à la carte: L'administration de l'immigration en France (1945–1975).* Paris: Grasset, 2005.

Stora, Benjamin. *Ils venaient d'Algérie: L'immigration algérienne en France (1912–1992).* Paris: Fayard, 1992.

Stovall, Tyler. "The Color-Line behind the Lines." *American Historical Review* 103, no. 3 (June 1998): 737–69.

———. *The Rise of the Paris Red Belt.* Berkeley: University of California Press, 1990.

Topolav, Christian. "The Naming Process." In *What's in a Name? Talking about Urban Peripheries,* edited by Richard Harris and Charles Vorms, 36–67. Toronto: University of Toronto Press, 2014.

Viet, Vincent. *Histoires des Français venus d'ailleurs.* Paris: Éditions Perrin, 2004.

———. *La France immigrée, construction d'une politique, 1914–1997.* Paris: Fayard, 1998.

Volovitch-Tavares, Marie-Christine. *Portugais à Champigny: Le temps des baraques.* Paris: Autrement, 1995.

Vulbeau, Janoé. "Reloger les familles populaires dans les années 1960, entre gestion des familles 'inadaptées' et ethnicisation de la question sociale." *Droit et ville* 1, no. 89 (2020): 147–63.

———. "Roubaix: La construction d'une ville face aux Algériens; Politiques urbaines et racialisation (1950–1990)." PhD diss., Université de Rennes, November 1, 2021.

Wall, Irwin M. *French Communism in the Era of Stalin: The Quest for Unity and Integration, 1945–1962.* Westport CT: Greenwood, 1983.

Weber, Eugen. *Peasants into Frenchmen.* Stanford CA Stanford University Press: 1976.

Weil, Patrick. *La France et ses étrangers: L'aventure d'une politique de l'immigration de 1938 à nos jours.* Paris: Gallimard, 1995.

———. *Qu'est-ce qu'un Français? Histoire de la nationalité française depuis la Révolution.* Paris: Grasset, 2002.

Wihtol de Wenden, Catherine. *Les immigrés et la politique: Cent cinquante ans d'évolution.* Paris: Fondation Nationale des Sciences Politiques, 1988.

———. "Une logique de fermeture, doublée de la question de l'intégration." In Lequin, *Histoire des étrangers,* 461–500.

Wilder, Gary. *The French Imperial Nation-State: Negritude and Colonial Humanism between the Two World Wars.* Chicago: University of Chicago Press, 2005.

Zancarini-Fournel, Michelle. "Généalogie des rébellions urbaines en temps de crise (1971–1981)." *Vingtième siècle,* no. 84 (October–December 2004): 119–27.

Zeller, Olivier. *Arriver et se loger à Lyon aux XIXe et XXe siècles: Relégation et sélection communales.* Paris: Éditions de la maison des sciences de l'homme, 2004.

INDEX

Page numbers followed by *f* and *t* refer to figures and tables, respectively.

In the France Overseas series

Regeneration through Empire: French Pronatalists and Colonial Settlement in the Third Republic
Margaret Cook Andersen

To Hell and Back: The Life of Samira Bellil
Samira Bellil
Translated by Lucy R. McNair
Introduction by Alec G. Hargreaves

Colonial Metropolis: The Urban Grounds of Anti-Imperialism and Feminism in Interwar Paris
Jennifer Anne Boittin

Making Space: Neighbors, Officials, and North African Migrants in the Suburbs of Paris and Lyon
Melissa K. Byrnes

Paradise Destroyed: Catastrophe and Citizenship in the French Caribbean
Christopher M. Church

Ecologies of Imperialism in Algeria
Brock Cutler

Bad Subjects: Libertine Lives in the French Atlantic, 1619–1814
Jennifer J. Davis

Nomad's Land: Pastoralism and French Environmental Policy in the Nineteenth-Century Mediterranean World
Andrea E. Duffy

The French Navy and the Seven Years' War
Jonathan R. Dull

Hostages of Empire: Colonial Prisoners of War in Vichy France
Sarah Ann Frank

I, Nadia, Wife of a Terrorist
Baya Gacemi

Transnational Spaces and Identities in the Francophone World
Edited by Hafid Gafaïti, Patricia M. E. Lorcin, and David G. Troyansky

Contesting French West Africa: Battles over Schools and the Colonial Order, 1900–1950
Harry Gamble

Black French Women and the Struggle for Equality, 1848–2016
Edited and with an introduction by Félix Germain and Silyane Larcher

The French Army and Its African Soldiers: The Years of Decolonization
Ruth Ginio

French Colonialism Unmasked: The Vichy Years in French West Africa
Ruth Ginio

French St. Louis: Landscape, Contexts, and Legacy
Edited by Jay Gitlin, Robert Michael Morrissey, and Peter J. Kastor